ISBN 978-0-282-56779-8
PIBN 10082755

Forgotten Books is a registered trademark of FB &c Ltd.
Copyright © 2018 FB &c Ltd.
FB &c Ltd, Dalton House, 60 Windsor Avenue, London, SW19 2RR.
Company number 08720141. Registered in England and Wales.

For support please visit www.forgottenbooks.com

1 MONTH OF
FREE
READING

at

www.ForgottenBooks.com

By purchasing this book you are eligible for one month membership to ForgottenBooks.com, giving you unlimited access to our entire collection of over 1,000,000 titles via our web site and mobile apps.

To claim your free month visit:

www.forgottenbooks.com/free82755

English
Français
Deutsche
Italiano
Español
Português

www.forgottenbooks.com

Mythology Photography **Fiction**
Fishing Christianity **Art** Cooking
Essays Buddhism Freemasonry
Medicine **Biology** Music **Ancient
Egypt** Evolution Carpentry Physics
Dance Geology **Mathematics** Fitness
Shakespeare **Folklore** Yoga Marketing
Confidence Immortality Biographies
Poetry **Psychology** Witchcraft
Electronics Chemistry History **Law**
Accounting **Philosophy** Anthropology
Alchemy Drama Quantum Mechanics
Atheism Sexual Health **Ancient History**
Entrepreneurship Languages Sport
Paleontology Needlework Islam
Metaphysics Investment Archaeology
Parenting Statistics Criminology
Motivational

THE

JOURNAL

OF THE

ANTHROPOLOGICAL SOCIETY

OF

BOMBAY.

Bombay:
PRINTED AT THE
EDUCATION SOCIETY'S PRESS, BYCULLA.
LONDON: LUZAC & Co., 46, GREAT RUSSELL STREET.

1894

CONTENTS.—Vol. III., No. 1.

PAGE

A short Note on Burial-Customs among the Bhuinhâr Brâhmans in the Sâran Distrct, Behar. By Mr. Sarat Chandra Mitra of Behar .. 2

On the Services Rendered to the Society by the late Dr. Dymock. By Mr. Jivanji Jamshedji Modi, B. A. 5

The Treatment of Cattle Diseases. Translated from the Tamil. By Veterinary-Captain James Mills, Principal, Bombay Veterinary College 9

On some Ceremonies for Producing Rain. By Mr. Sarat Chandra Mitra, M.A., B.L. Pleader, Judge's Court, Chupra, District Saran, Behar 22

Two Idiots. By James Mills 33

The Persian Mâr-nâmeh; or, The Book for taking Omens from Snakes. By Mr. Jivanji Jamshedji Modi, B.A. 35

Indian Folk-beliefs about the Tiger. By Mr. Sarat Chandra Mitra. M.A., B.L., Pleader, Judge's Court, Chupra, Behar 45

Caste Measurement Tables... 61

An Interesting Vedic Ceremony... 75

CONTENTS.—Vol. III., No. 2.

PAGE

SEVENTH ANNUAL GENERAL MEETING 77

HONORARY TREASURER'S REPORT 81

PRESIDENTIAL ADDRESS—PROGRESS OF ANTHROPOLOGY IN
INDIA. BY MR. H. H. RISLEY, B. C. S. ... 88

NOTES ON TWO BEHARI PASTIMES. BY MR. SARAT CHAN-
DRA MITRA, M.A., B. L., PLEADER, JUDGE'S
COURT, CHUPRA, DISTRICT SARAN, BEHAR ... 94

NAME-GIVING CEREMONY ON A NEW-BORN CHILD. BY MR.
TRIBOWANDAS MANGALDAS NATHUBHAI ... 98

SOME CURIOUS CUSTOMS AMONG THE KOCHS. BY MR. KEDAR-
NATH BASU 102

DAKKHINA RAYA, A MODERN DEITY. BY MR. KEDARNATH
BASU 104

A WILD BOY AND A WILD GIRL. BY SARAT CHANDRA
MITRA, M.A., B.L., OF BEHAR 107

CASTE MEASUREMENT TABLES 113

CONTENTS.—Vol. III., No. 3.

PAGE

ON HINDU CEREMONIES OBSERVED IN THE MADRAS PRE-
SIDENCY. By Mr. MAHOMED SUFTHER HUSAIN
OF MADRAS 139

THE FIRST YEAR FUNERAL EXPENSES OF A PARSEE OF
THE LAST CENTURY (1763). By Mr. BOMANJI
BYRAMJI PATELL 144

ON SOME ADDITIONAL FOLK BELIEFS ABOUT THE TIGER.
By Mr. SARAT CHANDRA MITRA, M.A., B.L.,
DISTRICT PLEADER, CHAPRA, BEHAR... ... 158

ON THE JEWS. By Surgeon-Lieut-Colonel WATERS ... 164

NOTE ON THE USE OF THE LOCUST AS AN ARTICLE OF
DIET AMONG THE ANCIENT PERSIANS. By Mr.
SURUT CHANDRA MITRA, M.A., B.L., DIS-
TRICT PLEADER, CHAPRA, BEHAR 178

ANTHROPOLOGICAL SCRAPS. 183

CONTENTS.—Vol. III., No. 4.

PAGE

ON SOME RUDE STONE IMPLEMENTS FROM BACK BAY, MIDDLE COLABA, BOMBAY. By Mr. FRED SWYNNERTON, BOMBAY 189

ON AGHORIS AND AGHORAPANTHIS. By Mr. H. W. BARROW, BOMBAY 197

CONTENTS.—Vol. III., No. 5.

PAGE

ON SOME SUPERSTITIONS REGARDING DROWNING AND DROWNED PERSONS. BY MR. SARAT CHANDRA MITRA, M.A., B.L., Pleader, Judge's Court, Chapra, Behar 253

ON THE CEREMONIES PERFORMED BY THE KABIRPANTHI MAHANTS OF THE SARAN DISTRICTS, ON THEIR INITIATION AS CHELAS AND ON THEIR SUCCESSION TO THE MAHANTSHIP. BY MR. SARAT CHANDRA MITRA, M.A., B.L., Pleader, Judge's Court, Chapra, Behar 266

FURTHER NOTES ON THE CHOWK CHÂNDÂ, AND THE PANCHAMÎ VRATA. BY MR. SARAT CHANDRA MITRA, M.A., B.L., Pleader, Judge's Court, Chapra, Behar 270

ON THE RITE OF HUMAN SACRIFICE IN ANCIENT, MEDIÆVAL, AND MODERN INDIA AND OTHER COUNTRIES. BY MR. PURUSHOTTAM BALKRISHNA JOSHI... 275

ANTHROPOLOGICAL SCRAPS 390

CONTENTS.—Vol. III., No. 6.

PAGE

PRESIDENTIAL ADDRESS. BY DR. P. PETERSON 318

CHARMS OR AMULETS FOR SOME DISEASES OF THE
EYE. BY MR. JIVANJI JAMSHEDJI MODI,
B.A. 338

A FEW ANCIENT BELIEFS ABOUT THE ECLIPSE AND A
FEW SUPERSTITIONS BASED ON THOSE
BELIEFS. BY MR. JIWANJI JAMSHEDJI MODI,
B.A. 346

ANTHROPOLOGICAL SCRAPS 360

CONTENTS.—Vol. III., No. 7.

PAGE

ON SOME BEHARI CUSTOMS AND PRACTICES. BY MR.
SARAT CHANDRA MITRA 364

ON MARRIAGE CEREMONIES AMONG THE KAPOLA BANIAS.
BY MR. TRIBHOWUNDAS MANGALDAS
NATHUBHAI 372

ON THE ORIGIN AND ACCOUNT OF THE KAPOLA BANIA
CASTE. BY MR. TRIBHOWUNDAS MANGAL—
DAS NATHUBHAI... 418

CONTENTS.—Vol. III., No. 8.

—————————

	PAGE
ON NORTH INDIAN FOLK-LORE ABOUT THIEVES AND ROBBERS. BY MR. SARAT CHANDRA MITRA, CORRESPONDING MEMBER OF THE ANTHROPOLOGICAL SOCIETY OF BOMBAY	454
NOTES ON THE RECENT OPENING OF SOME PRE-HISTORIC GRAVES IN THE COIMBATORE DISTRICT, MADRAS PRESIDENCY. BY MR. J. R. SANDFORD, MADRAS RAILWAY, ARKONAM... ...	461
ON THE DHANGURS AND THE DHÁVÁRS OF MÁHÁBLESHWAR. BY SHAMS-UL OLMA JIVANJI JAMSHEDJI MODI, B.A.	471
. DEATH CEREMONIES AMONG THE KAPOLA BANIAS. BY MR. TRIBHOWANDAS MANGULDAS NATHUBHAI	483

CONTENTS.—Vol. III., No. 4.

PAGE

ON SOME RUDE STONE IMPLEMENTS FROM BACK BAY, MIDDLE COLABA, BOMBAY. By Mr. FRED SWYNNERTON, BOMBAY   189

ON AGHORIS AND AGHORAPANTHIS. By Mr. H. W. BARROW, BOMBAY   197

CONTENTS.—Vol. III., No. 8.

PAGE

On North Indian Folk-Lore about Thieves and
Robbers. By Mr. Sarat Chandra Mitra,
Corresponding Member of the Anthro-
pological Society of Bombay 454

Notes on the Recent Opening of some Pre-Historic
Graves in the Coimbatore District,
Madras Presidency. By Mr. J. R. Sand-
ford, Madras Railway, Arkonam 461

On the Dhangars and the Dhávárs of Máhábleshwar.
By Shams-ul Olma Jivanji Jamshedji Modi,
B A. 471

On the Death Ceremonies among the Kapola Banias.
By Mr Tribhowandas Mangaldas
Nathubhai 483

THE JOURNAL

OF THE

ANTHROPOLOGICAL SOCIETY

OF

BOMBAY.

ORDINARY GENERAL MEETING, held on Wednesday, the 29th June 1892.

DR. J. GERSON DA CUNHA, *President*, in the Chair.

The Minutes of the previous Meeting were read and confirmed.

Captain Walshe, the Honorary Treasurer, then announced to the Meeting the sad news of the death of the Honorary Secretary, Dr. Dymock, and said that, on learning the news of the sad event, he, as the Honorary Treasurer of the Society, had sent round a circular among the members of the Council proposing to request Mr. Basil Scott to take up once more the duties of the Honorary Secretary which he had from the commencement of the Society discharged with so great ability, and that with the unanimous consent of the Council, he had communicated the request to Mr. Scott who at first kindly gave his consent, but subsequently withdrew it on account of press of other business.

The Members present at the meeting then requested Dr. Gerson Da Cunha to take up the duties of the vacant post. Dr. Da Cunha said that he was sufficiently occupied, and had little time at his disposal for the new work, but that, if it be the unanimous wish of the Meeting and of the Council, he would undertake, as a matter of duty, the post for the good of the Society in whose work he took great interest.

The President then requested Mr. Jivanji Jamshedji Modi to prepare a short paper, enumerating the valuable services rendered to the Society by the late Honorary Secretary, Dr. Dymock.

The following paper was then read :—

A SHORT NOTE ON BURIAL-CUSTOMS AMONG THE BHUINHÂR BRÂHMANS IN THE SÂRAN DISTRICT, BEHAR.
BY MR. SARAT CHANDRA MITRA OF BEHAR.

ONE of the most essential differences between the Hindu religion on the one hand and the Mahomedan and the Christian religions on the other, is that persons following the former persuasion burn their dead whilst those professing the latter creeds dispose of their dead by interring them underneath the ground. This is the popularly-accepted criterion of difference between the two peoples. But, on a careful observation of the practices and customs of the various sects of the Hindus in different parts of the country, it would appear that this criterion does not hold good universally. There are certain circumstances under which certain sects of Hindus dispose of their dead by burying them. In Bengal, there is a certain caste of Hindus, who go by the name of *Jugis*, which differs from all other castes of Hindus in the fact of its disposing of the dead in the following manner : first of all, they perform the मुखमग्नि ceremony, that is, they set fire to the faces of their corpses, and, then, instead of burning them, they bury them under the ground. Similarly, certain classes of वैरागी (*Byragees*) or religious mendicants belonging to the Vaishnava sects are buried in a sitting posture. Thus much for Bengal.

In other parts of India, especially Madras, certain classes of Hindus also practise the custom of burying their dead. The chief sect which practises this custom of burial (*uttara-kriyá*) is the *Lingadháris*—a class of *Sivaites*, as their name indicates,—who mostly bury their dead in sitting posture. The grave is partially filled up with earth to the waist of the deceased when the friends who are present there, throw in handfuls of earth over the grave till a small mound is erected over it. This they do after the usual reading of the *mantras* and the performance of the other ceremonies. Like the *Byragees* of Bengal, *Sanyásis*, or those mendicants who have given up the world and live by begging, are always buried. In their case the performance of the necessary funeral rites is dispensed with, as they are considered to be too holy for these. Some castes of Hindus, like the *Jugis* of Bengal, bury all unmarried girls. The *Sudras* bury those who are below the age of ten and those who die of small-pox. Hindu soldiers who die in battle are all buried. Also boys, who have not had the *upanayanam* cere-mony performed with respect to them, *i.e.*, those who have not been invested with the sacred thread, are buried.

A burial-custom, similar to this last-mentioned one, exists among the *Bhuinhâr* Brâhmans of this district of Behar (Sâran). I have heard on good authority that this practice also obtains among other classes of Hindus in this district, who wear the *upabíta* or the sacred thread. In the March-April Criminal Sessions of this district, which are still going on, a case, *viz.*, *Empress vs. Rampat Rai*, was lately tried, during the trial of which the existence of this curious custom among the *Bhuinhâr* Brahmâns, to which class the accused belonged, came to light. The prosecution, alleged, in this case, that the accused had falsely charged three other persons with murdering his nephew for the sake of his ornaments and had, in order to create evidence against them, disinterred the corpse of his nephew who had died of natural causes, and who had been buried according to the custom of his caste, and had, sub-sequently, thrown it into a well. During the course of the trial it transpired that the *Bhuinhâr* Brahmâns and other sacred-thread wearing castes of this district bury their boys aged up to twelve years. There are two exceptions to this rule, *viz.*:—

(1) Those boys, who are aged twelve years or below that

age, are not buried when they have undergone the *janao* (Sanskrit *upanayanam*) ceremony, *i. e.*, when they have been invested with the sacred thread. The undergoing of this *janao* or sacred-thread-investiture ceremony is considered tantamount to being half-married.

(2) Those boys, aged 12 or below that age, who have been married, are not buried. A boy cannot get married unless he has undergone the *janao* ceremony, *i. e.*, has been invested with the sacred thread.

In the cases of these two classes of boys, who have been either invested with the sacred thread or have been married, they are burned in the usual way, and the *káraj* or *srádh* ceremonies are performed on the expiration of the usual period of mourning. But boys, aged 12 or below that age, who have not undergone either of the aforesaid two ceremonies, are buried underneath the ground. The corpses are taken to the neighbourhood of some tank which is usually used as a burying place for them. Then a grave suited to the dimensions of the corpse is dug, and the body is interred therein. Sometimes a *peepul* tree (*Ficus religiosa*) is planted over it. In cases of boys who are buried no *káraj* or *srádh* ceremony or any other funeral obsequy is performed.

Ordinary General Meeting, held on Wednesday, the 27th July 1892.

Dr. E. Waters, *Vice-President,* in the Chair.

The Minutes of the previous Meeting were read and confirmed.

The election of the following new members was announced :— Veterinary-Captain James Mills, Principal, Bombay Veterinary College ; Eugene Pernon, Esq., Agent to Messrs. Arbuthnot & Co., Coconada.

Mr. Jivanji Jamshedji Modi then read the following paper on the services rendered to the Society by the late Dr. Dymock :—

It is with melancholy pleasure that I undertake the duty imposed upon me by our honorary secretary, at our last monthly meeting, to write in the form of a paper for our Journal, a memo of all the services rendered to our Society by our late lamented colleague, Dr. Dymock, who died on the 30th of April 1892. I wish the duty had been imposed upon one who knew Dr. Dymock more intimately and for a longer period of time than myself. But the short period of my acquaintance with the deceased gentleman, begun in the rooms of the Society, was sufficient at least to impress me with his learning and extensive reading, and with his kindness of disposition and goodness of heart.

Dr. Dymock had joined our Society from its very commencement, when it was started on the 7th of April 1886, at a general meeting of its original members, presided over by the late lamented Mr. Tyrrell Leith, its first president and founder. At the next meeting of the Society, held on the 19th of April 1886, he was elected a member of its Council, an office which he held up to the time of his death. Many of us, who had the honour of serving with him on the Council, know fully well what interest he took in the affairs of the Society. This interest and the learning discovered in the valuable papers that he read before the Society, soon pointed him out for the post of the President for the year 1888. He was elected to the post at the second annual meeting of the Society, held on the 22nd of February 1888. During the period of his presidentship and subsequent vice-presidentships, he was always regular in the chair, and generally enlivened the proceedings of the meetings by his learned and interesting remarks, which generally threw a good deal of side-light on the subjects of the papers read before the Society. His presidential address, delivered on the 27th of February, 1889, the day of his retirement from the chair of the president, very clearly shows what aim he had in view for enlarging the sphere of the usefulness of the Society. It was a practical address, aiming at practical ends. Speaking on his general theme, " India as a field for Anthropological Research, " he suggested several practical problems, economical, social, and religious, the solution of which may tend to the further amelioration of the teeming millions of India. In suggesting those problems for further consideration by the members of the Society, his sole object was to enhance the usefulness of the Society, both for the good of the Government and for the good of the governed. As an instance, I may mention the question of the " Alimentation of the Human Race," with which he began his excellent address. He said : " In a tropical climate like India, man is still to a great extent frugivorous, and only makes use of such animal products as milk and butter, which he obtains from his domesticated animals : that such a diet is sufficient for the development of the highest intellectual capacities we have ample proof in this country. Although man has become an omnivorous animal, still his chief course of alimentation in all great centres of population is derived from the cultivation of certain useful plants, and it is of the utmost importance, in view to an increasing population, to enlarge our resources of this kind to the greatest possible extent. No one can deny that India is very backward in this respect; although we have a number of valuable plants under cultivation, there are probably as many more to be found in our forests which would amply repay attention." In illustration of this, Dr. Dymock mentioned two plants. Out of the many questions suggested for consideration in his learned address I have pointed out this one to illustrate my remarks about the practical usefulness of his address, because it affects millions of the poor of our country.

To proceed further in the enumeration of the several offices held by Dr. Dymock in our Society. At the end of his period of presidentship, he was elected to the post of a vice-president

for the year 1889. The president of the year, Mr. Ibbetson,
not being a resident of Bombay, Dr. Dymock generally occupied the chair at the monthly meetings, and took the same
active and intelligent part in the proceedings that he took as
the president in the previous year.

At the fifth annual meeting, held on the 28th of February
1891, he was elected a vice-president for the second time for
the year 1891, and also the literary secretary, in which capacity
he had already commenced to work from the time of the un-
timely death of Mr. Vaidya. As literary secretary he had to
look to the printing of our Journal, to correct proof sheets, and
to add notes. Then at the last annual meeting he was also
appointed general secretary.

So far I have only spoken of Dr. Dymock's services to the
Society as an office bearer. His literary services as a contributor of papers were not less valuable. It appears from the
Journals of our Society that no member has contributed so
many learned papers as Dr. Dymock. He stands first in the
rank of our contributors. We know that the highest rank in
quantity is not always compatible with the highest rank in
quality. But in the case of Dr. Dymock we find that all his
papers displayed his great learning and extensive reading.
Dr. Dymock was a very good Persian and Arabic scholar, and
many of his papers show to what a great extent he gave us the
advantage of his Oriental knowledge. His oriental learning
and his well-known deep and extensive botanical knowledge
showed themselves to advantage in some of his learned papers,
such as " Anthropogonic trees of the Hindu Castes, " " Narcotics and Spices of the East, " " Flowers of the Hindu Poets"
and in the Notes added to Dr. Peterson's paper on " Vatsyayana on the duties of a Hindu Wife." Besides contributing
papers, he always took an active and intelligent part in the
discussion which followed the reading of papers by members.
The following list of his papers shows the great versatility of
his mind :—

1. Note on Indian Necromancy.
2. The Mumiyai.
3. Anthropogonic trees of the Hindu Castes.
4. On the Narcotics and Spices of the East.
5. 'The Flowers of the Hindu Poets.
6. On the Salamander or Biskhopra.
7. A Note on the Pithora Worship among the Hindus.
8. Note on a form of Fire-worship among the ancient Arabs.
9. A note on a woman who, through dedication to a deity, assumed masculine privileges.
10. On the use of Turmeric in Hindu Ceremonial.
11. On the use of Ganja and Bhang in the East as Narcotics.
12. Presidential Address: India as a Field for Anthropological Research.

In Dr. Dymock the Committee have lost an able, courteous, and useful colleague, and the Society an excellent literary secretary and a learned contributor. We shall miss his intelligent familiar face so regular at all the monthly meetings, whose proceedings were generally enlivened by his interesting remarks.

The following resolutions were then unanimously passed:—

" The Anthropological Society of Bombay record, with deep regret, the loss it has sustained by the death of Brigade-Surgeon Lieutenant-Colonel W. Dymock, who since its formation was one of the most able and zealous of its members. He contributed largely to the Journal of the Society, his papers being characterised by profound learning, deep research and masterly acquaintance with the varied points with which he dealt. He filled with great acceptance the offices of secretary, vice-president and president, and was chiefly responsible for the editing of the Society's Transactions, and always enjoyed the respectful esteem of his colleagues. A copy of this resolution should be sent to Dr. Dymock's family, with an expression of the sympathy of the Society."

" The Anthropological Society of Bombay records with regret
the loss it has sustained by the death of Mr. J. R. Duxbury,
who had rendered valuable services as a councillor and as
an auditor. A copy of this resolution should be sent to Mr.
Duxbury's family with au expression of the Society's
sympathy."

The following paper, by Captain James Mills, Principal,
Bombay Veterinary College, was then read :—

THE TREATMENT OF CATTLE DISEASES.

Translated from the Tamil.

Having had facilities for many years, during my various
tours while Veterinary-Surgeon to the Government of Madras,
for collecting Indian Veterinary literature, I give to those
interested in the subject a translation from the Tamil language
on the treatment of cattle diseases.

The original work, which I have happily secured, is written,
or rather scratched, or punctured, with a sharp instrument on
the leaf of the Palmyra (*Borassus flabelliformis*). The author
is said to be a Rishi.[1] If such be the case it is evidence to
show that the Veterinary Art was practised, although in rather
an empirical and, in some instances, cruel manner by the Hindus
at a very remote era. It will be observed, too, from a perusal
of the work, that their knowledge of the use of drugs,
especially those derived from the vegetable kingdom, was by
no means inconsiderable. Within its brief pages will be found
the names of no less than 48 different plants. Little trust has,
however, evidently been placed in the curative value of minerals,
for only three of this class are employed. The other agents
are the human skull, quails' feathers, urine, blood-suckers,
butter-milk, the fæces of the cow and sheep, &c. many of
which are typical of the wily empiric.

Nothing that will advance our present knowledge can, as

---

[1] A Hindu sage.

far as I am aware, be gathered from the translation, nor have
I forwarded it for publication with this view, but simply to
show the fallacies which exist, and the cruelties inflicted, under
the native methods of treatment, in the hope that, with the
advancement of veterinary education, they may gradually wear
away and give place to a system which is rational and humane.

To enable the plants named in the work to be recognised,
I have given the botanical synonym opposite each.

The translation from the original was carried out by a well-
educated Tamilian, C. Viswanath Iyer, a Cattle Disease Inspector
in the Madras Presidency.

TREATMENT OF CATTLE DISEASES.

Translated from the Tamil.

Divine Honours.

May the God Vishnu[1] prosper well,
May my instructor live long;
I invoke my instructor's assistance.

PRAYER.

My sufferings, my sinful actions, the troubles that I shall
have to undergo as a mortal being, the distresses that cannot be
removed from me, all these will disappear, if I worship the god
Ganapathi[2] who resides in the tower of the temple at the Mount
of Aroouachalam.[3]

Four deadly forms of disease.

Mannadappan (Malignant Sore Throat).

Pinnadappan (Splenic Apoplexy).

Tharian (Malignant Catarrh).

Kolli (a form of Anthrax in which the jaws are affected).

Treatment, common, for all the four forms.

Give a measure of the juice of the plant called Adootunda

---

[1] The second Hindoo divinity whose function is to protect or preserve.

[2] Son of Máheswará or Sivá who is the third divinity. He is the second
deity presiding over learning. To him are ascribed the powers of giving
success or otherwise in any undertaking.

[3] Name of a mountain in the South Aroot District in the Madras Presidency.

palai (*Aristolochia indica*), to the animal suffering from any of the abovementioned four forms. The juice should be obtained by maceration of the whole plant, roots, branches, &c.

Special treatment for each of them.

First.—Mannadappan (Malignant Sore Throat).

Symptoms.

The throat will be choked; the animal will make a peculiar grunting sound; the mouth will be kept open; saliva will be flowing from the mouth, and water from the eyes and nose.

Treatment.

Melahoo (*Piper nigrum*).
Omum (*Ptychotis ajowan*).
Poondoo (*Allium sativum*).
Vasamboo (*Acorus calamus*).
Sitharathâi (*Alpinia chinensis*).
Tippili (*Chavica roxburghii*).

Take ¼ pollem[1] weight of each of the above drugs, powder well, mix with the juice of Kandangatri (*Solanum jacquini*), and give as a drench.

Nassium (medicine per nostrils), take —
Melahoo (*Piper nigrum*), 20 in number.
Poondoo (*Allium sativum*), 1   do.
Ooppoo (*Common salt*), ⅛ pollem.[1]
Moollee (*Premna integrifolia*), one fruit.

Grind well with urine, hold the pulp in a thin cloth and allow drops of the juice to fall into the nostrils, 6 to 8 drops in each nostril.

Second.—Pinnadappan (Splenic Apoplexy).

Symptoms.

The chest will be seen as if there were some pressure from inside; the animal will cough with great pain; breathing will

---

[1] A pollem is equivalent to 9 drachms.

be very difficult ; the animal will not pass fæces, and urine will be passed little by little.

Treatment.

Sitharathai (*Alpinia chinensis*).

Melahoo (*Piper nigrum*).

Tippili (*Chavica roxburghii*).

Vasamboo (*Acorus calamus*).

Poondoo (*Allium sativum*).

Induppoo (*Rock salt*).

Take half a pollem of each of the above drugs, grind well and make into balls with the juice of the Kandangatri (*Solanum jacquini*). Give these balls in the juice of the leaves of the following plants, one in the morning and one in the evening, and continue for three days.

Toolasi elai (*Ocimum sanctum*).

Manatackali elai (*Solanum insertum*).

Murunga elai (*Moringa pterygosperma*).

If the above methods of treatment fail to have effect, try the following :—

Take—Marukaria (*Gardenia dumitorum*) fruit of Adootanda-palai (*Aristolochia indica*), leaves of Adapampattai (*Ipomœa pescapræ*), bark of ; macerate well the above three drugs in warm water and give about half a measure of the infusion ; and when the fore-leg is swollen apply the actual cautery (firing-iron). Internally give—

Coliavarai (*Dolichos gladiatus*).

Omum (*Ptychotis ajowan*).

Third.—Tharian (Malignant Catarrh).

Symptoms.

Breathing will be quick ; the animal will pass soft dung water will be flowing from the eyes and nose.

Treatment.

Melahoo (*Piper nigrum*).

Omum (*Ptychotis ajowan*).

Poondoo (*Allium sativum*).

Vasamboo (*Acorus calamus*).

Take about ¼ of a pollem of each of the above drugs, pound well and give in gingelly oil for three days.

Fourth.—Kolli (a form of Anthrax in which

the jaws are affected.

Treatment.

Tie a bundle of straw, light it up and with it burn the jaw of the animal. Internally give the following medicine:—

Bring a blood-sucker and remove its head. After all the blood has passed out of the body, boil it well with varagoo rice (*Panicum miliaceum*), squeeze well by the hand and give a piece about the size of a wood-apple. Keep the animal in a shed, well covered.

Vackey (*Rinderpest*).

Karai elai (*Canthium parviflorum*), leaves of.

Sooray elai (*Zizyphus glabratai*),   do.

Marudam elai (*Myrica sapida*),   do.

Ahattipoo (*Agati grandiflora*), flowers of.

Seeragham (*Cuminum cyminum*).

Melahoo (*Piper nigrum*).

Take a certain quantity of each of the above six drugs and grind them well.

Take a piece about the size of a lime, mix in the following substances, and give internally:—

2 measures of butter-milk.

2 measures of the water of tender cocoanut.

A small quantity of the juice of cocoanut bark.

A small quantity of rice well roasted and ground.

Or we may give the medicine so prepared from the six drugs in the following mixture:—

1 measure of the juice of plantain flower.

2 measures of the water of tender cocoanut.

½ measure of the juice of cocoanut bark.

2 measures of butter-milk.

Especially when the animal passes dung mixed with blood, give the following medicine :—

Pound well the leaves and bark of Marudam (*Myrica sapida*), mix four measures of water, evaporate it over a fire down to two measures and give.

In addition to the above, grind the leaves of Vidathari (*Mimosa cineria*), mix with rice flour and give.

Padoovan (any inflammation attended with swelling).

Treatment.

Pound well the whole plant called Nanjoomurican poondoo (*Tylophora asthmatica*), and give the animal daily, for two days, a piece about the size of a cocoanut.

Then apply to the swollen part the undermentioned medicine :—

Avoori elai (*Indigofera tinctoria*), leaves of.
Oomathai elai (*Datura stramonium*), do.
Coliavarui elai (*Dolichos gladiatus*), do.
Kottaikeranthi elai (*Sphœranthus hirtus*), leaves of.

Take equal quantities of each of the above four drugs, macerate well and extract the juice; to this add a little Vasamboo (*Acorus calamus*). Heat the whole for some time and apply to the affected part.

Alaripadoovan (inflammation attended with a burning sensation).

Treatment.

Bring the leaves of the plant called Mavalingum (*Cratæva nurvala*), macerate well in warm water and give a measure of the infusion. Keep the animal in a shed, and towards evening wash it well with warm water.

Gunni novoo (Tympanitis).

Symptoms.

The abdomen will be swollen ; there will be a spasm of the bowel ; sometimes the back will be arched ; the animal will not pass fæces, but will urinate.

Treatment.

Omum (*Ptychotis ajowan*).
Tippili (*Chavica roxburghii*).

Fry these a little over a fire, powder and give with ripe leaves of Yerbokay (*Caloptris gigantea*).

Tie round the neck of the animal a string of Koonthumani kodi (*Abrus precatorius*). Apply ashes from head to tail, and fan with a murum (native winnow).

Vakuti novoo, (Phrenitis).

Symptoms.

The animal will be turning round and round, and there will be spasm of all the muscles of the body.

Treatment.

Take the following drugs:—

Kuppamani elai (*Acalypha indica*), leaves of.
Valooparooti elai (*Dœmea extensa*), do.
Ven Nachie elai (*Vitex negundo*), do.

Extract about one measure of juice from the abovementioned drugs; to this add the following ingredients and give internally:—

Tippili (*Chavica roxburghii*).
Poondoo (*Allium sativum*).

External Application.

Perunday (*Vitis quadrangularis*).
Nochie (*Vitex negundo*).
Alingee (*Alangium decapetalum*).

Extract a measure of juice from the leaves of these plants; to this add cow-dung ash and sheep's dung, each as much as the size of a cocoanut, and also a little piece of Vasamboo (*Acorus calamus*). Boil the whole well, and apply all over the body for three days.

Nassium (medicine per nostril).

.Tumba elai (*Leucas indica*).

Ooppoo (Salt, common).

Grind them well with urine and let fall a few drops in each nostril.

Serumbal (Cold and cough).

Treatment.

Kozgikaram (Red sulphur).

Navacharam (*Sal ammoniac*).

Munnipalam (*Premna integrifolia*), fruit of.

Toolasi elai (*Ocimum sanctum*), leaves of.

Moongal elai (*Bambusa arundinacea*), leaves of.

Kodai cragoo (Quails' feathers).

Take one pollem of each of the first two drugs, ¼ pollem of the last one, and sufficient quantity of the remaining ones. Grind them well and give in hot water.

Nassium (medicine per nostril).

Mannipalam (*Premna integrifolia*, fruit of.

Melahoo (*Piper nigrum*).

Ooppoo (Salt, common).

Tumba elai (*Leucas indica*), leaves of.

Tulasi elai (*Ocimum sanctum*), do.

Take equal quantities of the above drugs, grind them a little with water and let fall drops of the juice into the nostrils, by placing the pulp in a piece of thin cloth.

When the eyes of an animal are attacked with flies or injured by blows, &c., try the following three methods of treatment:—

1. Apply the milky juice of the plant called Kattoo amanakoo (*Jatropha curcas*) to the eye.

2. Take a little of Geeragam (*Cuminum cyminum*), and onion (*Allium cepa*), grind them a little in a mortar by adding human milk and let drops fall into the eye.

3. Take a few leaves of Lotus (*Nelumbium speciosum*), and a few of pepper. Grind them a little in a mortar with human milk and apply to the affected eye.

Pannikoravan (Malignant Sore Throat).

Symptoms.

The throat will be choked ; there will be a grunting sound, dribbling of saliva from the mouth, and water will be flowing from the eyes and nose.

Treatment.

Thotheevalai vair (*Solanum trilobatum*), roots of.

Kandangatheri (*Solanum jacquini*).

Grind the two together, and take a quantity about the size of a lime fruit. Take the following other ingredients :—

Sitharathai (*Alpinia chinensis*).

Tippili (*Chavica roxburghii*).

Vasamboo (*Acorus calamus*).

Poondoo (*Allium sativum*).

Take a certain quantity of each of them, powder well, mix with the foregoing preparation, and give in the juice of the leaves of Muruckay elai (*Moringa pterygosperma*).

Yeri poochie (Disease of the Omasum).

The animal will appear exhausted. It will not graze nor take any food, and will keep its back arched.

Treatment.

Omum (*Ptychotis ajowan*).

Vasamboo (*Acorus calamus*).

Yerookay (*Caloptropis gigantea*).

Grind these well in a mortar and give internally. If no cure is effected, give the flowers and flowering tops of *Caloptropis gigantea* with one or two tender leaves.

Musalkanda Vally (Gid or Turnsick).

Symptoms.

The animal will be shivering. It will fall down often; 'here will be great trembling and kicking with the limbs; the eyes will be in a rotatory motion, and the dung will be dry and compressed.

Treatment.

Give pig's ghee with cotton internally.

Kudalpaduvan (Hæmaturia).

Symptoms.

Purging with excess blood. The urine also will be mixed with blood.

Treatment.

Take two measures of the juice of the plant Kovathandoo (*Coccinia indica*), mix with two measures of butter-milk and give internally for two days.

Mar novoo (Chest pain).

Treatment.

Varagoo rice (*Panicum miliaceum*).

Panny kodel (Pig's bowels).

Take one measure of Varagoo rice and a pig's bowels and boil well at night. Early in the morning give the animal a ball about the size of a wood-apple. Continue this for three or four days.

Every day after giving the ball, let the animal graze a little. After an hour or so the animal should be watered. From the fourth day, the animal must be forced to swim in water for three days, two hours a day.

Vadam (Paralysis).

Perundai (*Vitis quadrangularis*).

Nochu (*Vitex negundo*).

Yeroockai (*Calotropis gigantea*).

Kuppamani (*Acalypha indica*).

Velooparuti (*Dæmea extensa*).

Take equal proportions of the juice of the above plants, mix well with a cocoanut size of each of cow-dung ash and sheep's dung, and with five pollems of Vasamboo (*Acorus calamus*). Boil the whole and apply the mixture so prepared to all the affected parts for three days, both morning and evening.

Vayarookalichal (Diarrhœa).

Extract juice from the leaves of Eloopay (*Bassia longifolia*), mix with water used for washing rice and give.

Rattakadoopoo (Dysentery).

Thennagurumbai (young cocoanut).
Pana vellum (Palm sugar).
Vengayam (*Allium cepa*).

Make a ball of these substances and give to the animal. Water must be given after the medicine. It is better to give water after the patient has had a little straw.

Dead Calf, treatment for the removal of, from the mother's womb.

Keela nelli (*Phyllanthus niruri*).
Yelumichay (*Citrus limonum*).

Grind well the roots of these two plants, mix with gingelly oil, and give to the cow. The calf will at once come out.

Medicine for animals weakened by poisons.

Take a quantity of castor beans in the green state, dry them gently by sun's heat, macerate well and extract a measure of juice. Add this to two measures of butter-milk and give. Continue this for three days.

Punnoo (Sores).

Take a small quantity of the root of Pononu sattai (*Sida acuta*), grind well, mix about a lime-size of this with goat's milk and give internally.

External Application.

Mavalingam elai (*Cratæva nurvala*), leaves of.
Perangurandai elai (*Cookia punctata*), do.

Grind the two together and apply to the parts effected.

Besides the above, tie around the neck of the animal a "Kottan kodi."

A cow that does not allow her calf to suck, treatment for.

A man should go about 4 o'clock in the morning, (when the

morning cock crows), to the place where the washerman washes his clothes, and get a little soil from under the washing-stone. It should be mixed with milk and applied all over the body of the cow. The soil should then be wiped away with a cloth of a woman who menstruates. Continue this for three days.

A cow that does not allow her calf to come near, treatment for.

Kundoomani (*Abrus precatorius*).

Kuppamani (*Acalypha indica*).

Othamani (*Dœmea extensa*).

Take about an ollock of juice from each of the three drugs, mix with either butter-milk or toddy and give.

Nassium (medicine for nostrils).

Poondoo (*Allium sativum*).

Vasamboo (*Acorus calamus*).

Grind these a little and put drops in each nostril.

Cracked hoofs, treatment for.

Kazhichi elai (*Cœapenia bondualla*).

Nalla yennai (Gingelly oil).

Take a quantity of the juice of the abovementioned plant, add an equal quantity of gingelly oil and give internally.

In addition to this, pluck five leaves of Adundum elai (*Capparis horrida*) with the mouth and give them to the animal. Continue this for three days.

Maggots in the foot, treatment for.

1. Pull out the plant Jhondoo (*Bryoni grandis*), keep it on another plant in such a way that its roots may face upwards.

2. Pull out the plant Seppoo nevungu(*Indigofera enneaphylla*), and after praying to the sun throw it on another plant in the manner above described. The plants should be so removed from the ground that none of their rootlets may be broken.

To increase the flow of milk.

Take a piece of human skull, powder it well and mix with

the juice of Sonnancani (*Illesebrum sessile*), and give it to the cow.

How to tame a vicious animal.

Take the following ingredients:—

> Ooppoo (Salt, common).
> Manjal (*Curcuma longa*).
> Musalai elai (*Sida acula*), leaves of.

Grind the three together in warm water and give.
Do not give water for five days.

How to strengthen a weak animal.

Take gingelly oil, 10 pollems.

> Eggs, 8 in number.
> Pepper, 2 pollems.

Allow the animal to swim in water for two or three hours and while standing in the water, give the above medicine as a drench. Continue this for three days.

PRAYER.

Success, wisdom, wealth and faith, will be the reward of those who worship the god Ganapathi, the son of Hroonasor.[1]

---

[1] Is another name for Mâheswara.

ORDINARY GENERAL MEETING, held on Wednesday, the 28th September 1892.

DR. G. WATERS, *Vice-President*, in the Chair.

The minutes of the previous meeting were read and confirmed.

The following donation was announced, and thanks voted to the donor:—

To the Library.

From MR. DARAB DASTUR PESHOTAN SANJANA, B.A.

The position of Zoroastrian women in remote antiquity as illustrated in the *Aresta*.

The following note was then read:—

ON SOME CEREMONIES FOR PRODUCING RAIN.

BY MR. SARAT CHANDRA MITRA, M.A., B.L.,

Pleader, Judge's Court, Chupra, District Saran, Behar.

IN these days of advanced civilization and scientific progress when many natural objects and even phenomena are being produced artificially, no surprise need be expressed at the attempts that are being made, throughout the civilized world, at producing rain artificially by exploding dynamite-laden fire-balloons high up in the air. But in the primitive state of mankind, when dynamite and balloons were unknown, and when the rude uncultured folks attributed the failure of their crops or of rain, and the outbreak of disease and the consequent occurrence of deaths among them, to the wrath of some divine being who, they believed, presided over their welfare, or regarded these phenomena as visitations upon them from the same deity for sins committed, primitive men believed that these scourges, which periodically visited them, viz., famine, drought and pestilence, would be averted and their progress stopped should they only appease the wrath of the offended deity. To this end they set their heads together and began to devise means, and as, among savage races—the representatives of primitive men—the conception of the deity was formed from a conception of their own forms and attributes, and the same supernatural entity was supposed to possess in common with human beings, the same penchant for meat and drink and music and mirth, the seers or the wise folk among the tribes hit upon the idea of holding sacrifices, *pujahs*, and religious feasts. Hence, whenever primitive man suffered from the all-withering influences of the drought, he performed sacrifices wherein buffaloes and kine were slaughtered in order to appease the deity's cravings for meat, oblations of spirituous liquors were offered in order to quench his thirst for drink, and songs were sung and dances and processions were held in order to satisfy his tastes for music and mirth. All these he did under the impression that their performance would turn away his wrath, and thus induce his offended deityship to withdraw the scourge visiting them, whether it was drought, famine, or pestilence.

Travellers in all parts of the globe have, from personal observation, recorded the existence and periodical performance of these religious "functions" for producing rain or averting famine, not only among peoples who are still grovelling in the lowermost depths of savagery, but also among those who have emerged therefrom and have adopted the amenities of civilization. Hence we find that some of these ceremonies still survive among such enlightened nations as the modern Europeans, and among such civilized races as the Hindus, the Mahomedans, and the Chinese.

Whenever there is failure of rains, or the country is suffering from the visitation of a long-standing drought, the Hindus of Bengal perform a ceremony known as *pirer gán* (पीरेर गान). This ceremony consists in gathering together a number of Mahomedan *faqirs*, and telling them off to sing songs (in Mussulmani Bengali, a dialect of the Bengali language which is spoken and written by the Bengali Mahomedans) in honour of the *Pirs* or Mahomedan saints. It may be observed here *ne passant* that the Hindus of Bengal worship the Mahomedan *Pirs* or saints, especially the saint Satyapîr (सत्यपीर), to whom *pujahs* and *shirnis* or sweetmeats are offered whenever there is success in some difficult family undertaking, or a recovery in the family from some serious illness. The performance of the aforesaid ceremony, it is said, immediately brings down showers of rain. Holding *sankirtans* (संकीर्तन) or religious processions in honour of the god Hari (हरि) also averts drought. Whenever there is a severe drought in Bengal, the village folks perform these last-mentioned ceremonies. First of all, *pujah* is offered to Hari, who is but another incarnation of the god Vishnu. Then the worshippers form themselves into a company and parade the streets of their native village, singing religious hymns in honor of the god to the accompaniment of the *dhole* or drum, the *singd* or horn and metal castanets. I have observed that in Calcutta, these *sankirtans* are also held whenever there is an outbreak of cholera or any other epidemic in a particular quarter of that city. It is said that these *sankirtans* result in bringing down rain or averting the epidemic. In June or July last, when there was severe drought all over Northern India, a correspondent from Jhansi (N.W.P.) wrote to the *Amrita Basar Patrika* to say that a *Hari-sankirtan* (हरि संकीर्तन) ceremony had been held in that town for the purpose of removing the drought. The correspondent further added that copious showers of rain had fallen shortly after the performance of the ceremony. The *shashtras* also prescribe the performance of certain *yagnas* (यज्ञ) and *homs* (होम) as infallible means for averting drought. The law-givers say that these *homs* should be performed with all the strictness prescribed by the *shashtras*, and large quantities of ghee or clarified butter should be offered as oblations to the sacrificial fire. It is only the other day (as we read in the *Amrita Bazar Patrika*) that that eminent *zemindar*—the Maharajah of Burdwan—performed such a *hom* wherein immense quantities of ghee were burnt, and large numbers of Brâhmans fed. The paper added for our information that that very evening very copious showers rained in Burdwan. The causation of rain by such a ceremony can only be explained on the ground that the smoke generated by the burning ghee and the sacrificial fires forms into rain-clouds which ultimately melt down to the earth in the shape of refreshing showers. It has been uniformly experienced that the heavy cannonading in battles is also followed by copious rain. My Persian teacher, who is a resident of Dubrájpur, in the district of Birbhum, in Bengal, informs me that a curious custom is observed in his native village, whenever there is a failure of rain there. The people of that place throw dirt or filth on to the houses of other people, who abuse the former for doing so. Sometimes they drench the lame, the halt, the blind and other persons who are otherwise physically disabled, by pouring water on them, and so get abused by the latter. The people of Dubrájpur superstitiously believe that this abuse, in times of drought, is sure to bring down rain.

In times of drought, the Hindus of Behar observe the curious ceremony of having their fields and other arable lands ploughed by Bráhman women. In Hindudom, throughout Bengal and Behar, Bráhmans and women never perform agricultural operations like ploughing and harrowing with their own hands, but have their lands tilled by servants and labourers who mostly belong to such low castes as the *Kandus* (कान्दु), the *Dosadhs* (दोसाध), the *Noniyas* (नोनिया) and others. Hence, it is popularly believed that, should the female member of such a high caste as the Bráhmans, to whom such undignified manual labour is forbidden, plough the *khet*, rain would surely pour down in torrents immediately after. Sometimes, when there is hesitation about subjecting such high-caste women to the indignity of actually ploughing in broad daylight, the women are made only to touch the plough early in the morning, before people are astir, for the purpose of complying with the requirements of the custom, and the ploughing operations are subsequently conducted by the male ploughmen. The other

4

day I came across another curious custom, peculiar to this part of the country, the observance whereof is supposed to bring down rain. It was about 10 o'clock in the night of Saturday, the 25th June last, as I was about to retire to bed, I heard a great noise made by the singing in high-pitched tones of some women in front of our house. I thought that the women were singing some songs, as they usually do parading the streets, before some marriage takes place in a family. But on making enquiries next morning, I came to learn that the previous' night's singing formed part and parcel of a rain-bringing ceremony known, at least in this district (Sâran) as the इरकिरिनी, and that some women of the locality had formed themselves into a little band and paraded the neighbouring streets, singing songs—a practice which they superstitiously believed would surely bring down showers. Curiously enough, a tolerably good shower of rain fell during the afternoon of the following day.

In Behar it is believed that the water of the rain which falls during the period wherein the star Âdrâ (आद्रा नक्षत्र) is in the ascendant, is very beneficial to the *bhadoi*, or rainy season crop which usually consists of maize and paddy. Hence agriculturists in this part of the country look forward with great expectation to the falling of the very welcome showers during that period. With a view to ensure the happening of this event, the god Indra is worshipped, and Brahmans are fed, in this district, as if, by feeding them, the rain-god would be so far propitiated as to open the flood-gates of heaven during the period of the ascendancy of the star Âdrâ. This year the aforesaid star had been in the ascendant only very recently, and as the rains were holding off in this district during its period of influence, *pujah* was made to Indra, the lord of the skies, and a number of Brâhmans, I am informed by Râi Bâbu Tara Prasâd Mukerji, Bahadur, Chairman of the Municipality of Revilgunge, a town 4 miles due west of Chupra, were only the other day fed at the Gautama Muni's *Asram* in that town for the purpose of bringing down rain during Âdrâ's ascendancy. The Babu further informs me that the performance of this ceremony was, curiously enough, followed up by tolerably good showers of rain which fell on the day following. Another curious rain-producing custom is observed in this district whenever there is a severe drought threatening it. Troops of children of all ages come to people's houses, and the goodmen thereof have their courtyards turned into immense puddles by pouring large quantities of water thereon. The children then throw themselves into it, and roll and tumble themselves in the temporarily improvised puddle to their heart's content. Doing so, it is believed, surely brings down rain.

In the North-Western Provinces and Oude, another custom is observed for the purpose of averting drought. It is as follows: children of all ages form themselves into little companies and parade the streets of their respective towns and villages, singing Hindi songs having reference to rain and the god who presides over it. It is believed that these children's demonstrations have the effect of drawing forth rain from the skies.

In order to avert drought and produce rain, the Mahomedans utter two words رکعت (rekat) of the نماز اسنسقا (namaz-i-istaska), which is nothing but a prayer for rain, because اسنسقا is defined to mean پاني طلب کرنا or demanding rain. The whole ceremony of the نماز اسنسقا is described thus in Urdu :

جب مينہ نہ برسي تب مسلمان جمع ہووين اور ميدان ميں جاوين
اور دعا کريں اور اسنسقا رکھيں قبلي کيطرف منہہ کرکے اور اکيلے
اکيلے نماز ادا کريں بغير خطبي اور جماعت کي • اسيطرح تين روز باہر
جاوين اور ان تينون روز اسنفغار بہت کہيں اسواسطے کے اسنفغار کو
مينہ کے طلب کرنے ميں بڑا اثر ہي جيساکے الله تعالٰي ظاہر فرماتاہي *

فَقُلْتُ اسْتَغْفِرُوْ رَبَّکُمْ اِنَّہ کَانُ غَفَّارًا یُرْسِلِ السَّمَاءَ عَلَیْکُمْ مِدْرَارًا

یه آیت سورة نوح مین هي• یه بات نوح علیه السلام ني اپني قوم
سے کهي تهي • خلاصه اسکا یه هي ے گناه بخشواؤ اپني رب سے بیشک
وه هي بخشنے والا اور جب نم توبه کرو اور گناه بخشواو تو الله تعالیٰ
تم پر بدلي بهیجي جو خوب دهتاٹ کا پاني برساوي • اور استسقا
کي نماز مین ذمي کو حاضر نکرین بلکِ خاق اپنے گناه سے نلّي سرے
توبه کرین ے الله تعالیٰ اوسکی برکت سے عینه برساوي *

The above description may be thus translated:—When it does not rain, then Mussulmans should assemble and go to a *maidan* and offer up prayers and observe *istaska*, i. e., demand rain with their faces turned towards the *kabarh* at Mecca, and everyone should by himself read *namaz* without a sermon and the assembly. In this way they should go outside on three days and pray for the pardon of their sins on each of those days, because *istaghfár* is very effectual in bringing rain-water as the Almighty God has said :

" Well, say thou, 'I crave pardon from God.' In fact, He is the Pardoner. So that He may send rain-showering clouds upon thee."

This *áyet* (آیت) is contained in the *Surah Nooh* of the *Koran*. These words had been spoken by Noah (upon whom be peace) to the members of his tribe. The purport of all this is that you should crave pardon for your sins from your God (for He certainly can pardon), and when you will seek pardon and wash yourself of sin, then the Almighty God will send you clouds which would shower rain in torrents. And in the *namaz* named *istaska*, no unbelievers ذمي should be allowed to remain in that assembly. On the other hand, people should, with heads bowed down, wash themselves of sin, so that Almighty God may, on account of the good influence exerted by this humbling oneself before one's Creator, cause showers of rain to fall.

The Kolarian tribes living in the rocky fastnesses of Central India, worship a god named Marang Buru or Great Mountain,

who, they suppose, sends down rain. His worship is said to
have originated in the fact that remarkable peaks, bluffs, or
rocks, very naturally suggested the idea of Divinity to their
unsophisticated minds. They reasoned within themselves that
as in such high eminences lie the sources of the streams and
rivers which irrigate their fields and nourish their crops, they
must be the abode of some Divine Beings, and that Marang
Buru must, therefore, be invoked for rain in times of drought.
Offerings are usually presented to him on the summits of hills,
or other conspicuous objects over which his deityship is believed by them to preside.[1]

The Chinese are a very superstitious people. When severe
drought stares the " Flowery Land " in the face, the Celestials
perform various ceremonies, such as offering up prayers for
rain, observing fasts, the closing of the south gates of cities,
performing rain-bringing operas, &c., for the purpose of averting the serious consequences of the drought and producing
rain. Mr. A. J. Little, in his interesting work,[2] entitled
Through the Yang-tse Gorges, has described some of the
aforesaid interesting ceremonies. The custom of closing the
south gates of cities in China is thus alluded to by him at
page 152 of the aforesaid work, in these words:

" *Sunday, March 25th* (Easter Sunday).—Moored all day at
Kwei-chow-fu, waiting for a clearance. The south gate, below
which we lay moored, was closed on account of the drought,
no rain having fallen for the past six months. This shutting
the south gate of a city would seem to be a kind of silent
protest—made in accordance with the Nature-worship which
appears to be the only real, indigenous and universal religion
of the Chinese—against the South, which is the fire quarter,
and the presiding influence over heat and drought. Thus,

[1] *Vide Indian Antiquary*, Vol XIV. (1885), page 125.

[2] *Through the Yang-tse Gorges*; or, *Trade and Travel in Western China*,
by Archibald John Little, F.R.G.S. London: Sampson, Low and Co., 1888

when Auster blows against the south gate and finds it shut, a hint is supposed to be given to him that his presence is *de trop*." As regards prayers for rain, he says (page 154): "The destitution of the Kwei-chow-fu people has been caused throughout the prefecture by the total failure of the winter crops, and we can sympathize with the unfortunate Mandarins, whose sins are responsible for the misery sent by heaven upon the people, and *who are now engaged in humbling themselves and praying for rain.*" *Anent* holding fasts, the author observes (page 156): "Owing to the drought, *a strict fast had been proclaimed throughout the district,* and the beef I had been expecting to buy here, let alone pork or fowls, was unobtainable." Under date Thursday, May 3rd, Mr. Little writes to say : "The fine weather, which had been continuous for the past two months, now at last began to break up; *the prayers for rain, the fasts, and the closing of the south gates of the cities,* which we had observed on our upward voyage, having been at length successful" (page 341).

The Chinese also perform the curious ceremony known as "*The Rain-bringing Opera*" for the purpose of producing refreshing showers in times of drought. Writing under date Sunday, April 1st, the author says : "After supper it was proposed we should adjourn to the opera—a celebrated company having come up from the city of Wau *to aid the villagers in propitiating the rain-god.* The performance was then proceeding in a temple on the bank. Lighting a length of worn-out bamboo tow-line, which our *tai-kung* or pilot (the bowsman) furnished us with, and which made a most efficient torch, we threaded our way up the steep sand-bank, and among the dirty temporary huts, largely composed of opium dens, which in winter cover the low ground adjoining the junks' halting-places; we at length entered a handsome and solidly constructed temple, and there upon the fine stage, in the first court-yard, was the usual gay scene of a Chinese historical play. The stage was lit by two staring oil-lamps, suspended from the proscenium, and reminding me of those of the London coster-monger, and by about a dozen red wax dips. The *auditorium* was in darkness. My intrusion was quickly detected by the crowd of turbaned coolies, but I was not in the least disturbed, and I stood looking on at some very good acting until ten o'clock. *These performances and processions, if they do not always produce rain, at least serve to amuse the people, and to divert their thoughts from their troubles*" (page 184). Curiously enough, the author says that there was heavy rain that night.

In the environs of Ichang are some conical hills on one of which there is a rock-temple. Near it is a deep wide cave, which the trickling water has slowly excavated out of the mountain behind the wood. This cave, called "Lung Wang Tung" or Dragon King Cavern, is about 100 yards across the opening, and extends inwards almost the same distance. The Chinese have a superstitious belief regarding this cave, to the effect that, in times of drought, the dragon inhabiting it, if beseeched by the priests, produces rain. Mr. Little says with regard to this cave: "At the back of it (the Cavern) is a lake, which the priests say extends inwards an unknown distance; only one man has ever tried to explore it, and he never came back again. They objected to my launching their boat upon it, as this is never done but in times of drought, when they go upon the lake to *solicit the dragon to turn himself round and produce rain.* Were the dragon to come out at this opening and escape out of the country, according to Chinese superstition, there would be perpetual drought. Hence the three temples to shut him in safely" (page 93).

The Kakhyens of Burma, who live mainly by following the pursuits of agriculture, worship a *nat* named Sinlah or the Sky-Spirit, who is supposed by them to give rain and good crops.[1]

---

[1] *Mandalay to Momien:* A Narrative of the two Expeditions to Western China of 1868 and 1875, by John Anderson, M.D. London: 1876, page 146.

The Shans, a tribe living north of Burma, celebrate three festivals every year, in which the *nats* or *spirits* presiding over rain, wind, and cold, are worshipped in order that they may send down rain or protect them from the rigours of wind and cold.[1]

At Momien, a town in Yunnan in Western China, a curious rain-ceremony is observed by the Chinese and the Panthays (Chinese Mahomedans) as is testified to by Dr. J. Anderson, who went there in 1868. He says : " In consequence of a long period of drought preceding our arrival, the slaughter of animals had been forbidden, as it was feared that the rain would be withheld as a punishment, a curious instance of Buddhist superstition affecting the Panthays and Chinese ; but in two days the rains set in, and the prohibition was removed. The markets were thenceforward well supplied with bullocks, buffaloes, sheep, goats, and pigs."[2]

A relic of these superstitious ceremonies and beliefs still survives among the enlightened Christian nations of Europe. In these Christian countries, in times of drought, when the country is threatened with famine brought about thereby, people congregate in Churches and offer up prayers to God, beseeching Him to send down rain. Even in India this practice is also resorted to in times of drought and failure of crops. I remember having read in the Indian newspapers, some years ago, when this land was suffering from the consequences of a long-standing severe drought, that prayers for rain were, by the orders of the presiding chaplains, offered in some of the principal Christian Churches throughout this country.

---

[1] *Op cit.*, p. 308.   [2] *Op cit.*, p. 205.

ORDINARY GENERAL MEETING, held on Wednesday, the
26th October 1892.

MR. KHARSHEDJI RASTAMJI CAMA, *Vice-President*, in the
Chair.

The minutes of the previous meeting were read and confirmed.

The election of the following new members was announced :—
Brigade-Surgeon Lieutenant-Colonel J. H. Newman, I.M.D.;
Veterinary-Captain J. W. A. Morgan and Veterinary-Lieutenant
A. C. Newsom, A.V.D.

The Honorary Secretary then read the following Note on
two Idiots, by Veterinary-Captain J. Mills, Principal, Veterinary
College, Bombay.

To

THE HONORARY SECRETARY,

BOMBAY ANTHROPOLOGICAL SOCIETY.

SIR,

It gives me much pleasure to forward, herewith, photographs
of two idiots who were found wandering about Parel, in charge
of the old man standing between them, who said he was their
uncle, but, after enquiry, it was found he was only a distant
relative. I am sure the pictures, poor as they are, will be of
interest to the members of the Society, more especially in regard
to the appearances the heads of the idiots present. Cranial
development seemed to me to have been arrested, and on asking
the so-called " Uncle " the cause, he told me a most wonderful
tale, the text of which was, that the parents of the idiots, having
lost all their children except these two, they decided to dedicate
them to a Hindu temple, in the hope that any future progeny,
which they might be blessed with, would not be snatched
prematurely from them by the merciless hand of death. The
story went on to relate that the priests of this particular temple
placed iron skull-caps upon their heads, with the result that

5

the growth was arrested. Of course, this statement might be a myth, but to me it carries a deal of truth in it, because (a) there were two of them, (b) the heads bore distinct circular marks of pressure having been applied, (c) they presented no symptoms or appearances of being cretins, (d) abnormalities of the skull, the result of external pressure, are produced by many races.

There was nothing about these two men to lead me to conclude that they were congenital idiots, in fact, the very opposite, their bodies were well formed. They had the appearance of men who were not by any means supplied with a liberal diet ; but it seemed to me that, if well fed, they would have been physically very powerful. They were far above the average native in height, or what one would call tall and erect. There was a general want of muscular co-ordination, especially in regard to the muscles involved in speech, in fact, the power of speech was practically absent, and when they tried to answer questions, they did so with a sort of incoherent unintelligible gutteral grunt. The man on the left in the photos was slightly paralytic on the right side, and moved with a shuffling gait. The faculty of observation was extremely limited, and when allowed away from the side of the man in charge of them, they wandered aimlessly about, without knowing where they were going.

They looked upon everything in a most jocular manner, and when being photographed, they laughed incessantly, and had to be held firmly before anything like a picture could be got of them.

JAMES MILLS, *Veterinary-Captain,*

Principal, Veterinary College.

Bombay, 12th September 1892.

THE ORDINARY GENERAL MEETING held on Wednesday, the 30th November 1892.

Surgeon-Major G. WATERS, *Vice-President*, in the chair.

The Minutes of the previous meeting were read and confirmed.

The following present was announced, and thanks voted to the donor:—

To the Library.

From Mr. H. M. PHIPSON, "A Journey of Exploration through the South China Border Lands," by Archibald R. Colquhoun, Vols. I. and II.

The following paper was then read by Mr. Jivanj; Jamshedji Modi, B.A.

The PERSIAN MÂR-NÂMEH; *or, The* BOOK *for*

taking OMENS *from* SNAKES.

THE custom of taking omens from snakes seems to be very ancient. The people of antiquity associated with the snake various peculiar ideas. Some held it in great veneration and made it a symbol of Divine wisdom; others considered it to be a symbol of deceit and cruelty. Those who held it in veneration considered it to be "the most spirit-like of all the reptiles." Others who did not so hold it in veneration, considered it to be the symbol of the power of evil. Again, some held it to be an emblem of eternity; others to be that of fickleness and treachery. For example, the Sesha Nâga of the ancient Hindus, under its name of "Ananta," *i.e.*, the endless, was a symbol of eternity. Those who considered it to be "the most spirit-like of all the reptiles" compared the earth with it, saying that, as the serpent cast off its old skin and appeared in a youthful state, so the earth, after the resurrection, is expected to appear in a rejuvinated state. [1] The ancient Assyrians had made the serpent an emblem over their military flags from

---

[1] *Isis Unveiled*, II., p. 490.

a similar view of veneration, and it is said that the Persian king Cyrus had imitated that emblem over his flag from the Assyrians. [1]

From Herodotus we learn that the sudden appearance of a large number of snakes in a district was considered to be full of omens. In the reign of the Lydian king Croesus, " all the suburbs of Sardis were found to swarm with snakes, on the appearance of which the horses left feeding in the pasture grounds, and flocked to the suburbs to eat them. The king, who witnessed the unusual sight, regarded it very rightly as a prodigy. He, therefore, instantly sent messengers to the sooth-sayers of Telmessus to consult them upon the matter. His messengers reached the city, and obtained from the Telmessians an explanation of what the prodigy portended, but fate did not allow them to inform their lord ; for ere they entered Sardis on their return, Croesus was a prisoner. What the Telmessians had declared was, that Croesus must look for the entry of an army of foreign invaders into his country, and that, when they came, they would subdue the native inhabitants, since the snake, said they, is a child of earth, and the horse a warrior and a foreigner." [2]

According to the same authority, in ancient Thebes some serpents were regarded as sacred. When they died, they were buried in the temple of Jupiter, the god to whom they were sacred. [3]

The idea of attaching sacredness to snakes as to other animals, seems to have originated from the fact that, though injurious to mankind to a certain extent. they did a good service to those who believed in their sacredness in some way. For example, we learn from Herodotus [4] that the ancient Egyptians held the bird Ibis sacred, because it destroyed

---

[1] *Isis Unveiled*, II., p. 490.
[2] Rawlinson's *Herodotus*, Book I., Chap. 78.
[3] Book II., Chap. 74.
[4] Book II., Chap. 75.

the wingèd snakes which made their entrance from Arabia
into Egypt regularly with the commencement of the spring.
Then the asp, a species of venomous snake, was in its
turn held sacred at some places, because it destroyed rats and
other vermin that worked havoc in the fields. Sir George
Rawlinson says that the asp or Naia was the emblem of the
goddess Ranno, and was chosen to preside over gardens from
its destroying rats and other vermins. Altars and offerings
were placed before it as before dragons in Etruria and Rome
. . . . In hieroglyphics it signified " goddess ; " it was attached
to the head-dresses of gods and kings, and a circle of these
snakes composed the " asp-formed crowns " mentioned in the
Rosetta stone. Being the sign of royalty, it was called
βασιλισκος (basilisk) " royal." [1]

Considerations like these would lead us to the large question
of snake or serpent worship which I do not wish to enter into
here. Suffice it to say that, as pointed out above, some nations
held snakes in veneration, on account of the services they were
believed to do directly or indirectly to their country, while
others held them in contempt.

The ancient Persians or Zoroastrians were one of those
nations that held the snake in no veneration. The snake was
one of those " Kharfastars" whom it was always considered meritorious to kill. A believer of the good Mâzdayasnân religion
was recommended to keep with him a (١١٢ ٹدچ) snake-killer,
which was a stick to kill the snakes with. [2] This stick was
also used to punish the criminals who were considered to be as
poisonous spiritually as the snakes were physically. A priest
had always with him such an instrument (Zend [3]
ڊٹدچ-ٴچۑۅۅٴ Pehelvi ١١٢ٹدچ چۑۅۅٴ). Mairya (Mâr) i.e., the
snake, was a synonym for Ahriman, the evil spirit. [4]

---

[1]   Rawlinson's *Herodotus*, Vol. II., p. 123

[2]   *S. B. E.*, Vol. V., West's *Bundehesh*, ch. XXVIII. 22.

[3]   *Vendidad*, XVIII., 4.

[4]   *Vend.*, XXII., 2, 9, 16.

The Persian Mâr-nâmeh or The Book of Snakes—the text
and translation of which I beg to submit before our Society this
evening—is a small metrical composition in modern Persian of
32 couplets, which can lay no claim to elegance of style
or beauty of language. It enumerates the thirty days of a
Parsee month and describes the omens which the sight of a snake
presents on those days. That it is written by a Zoroastrian
Persian appears from two facts: firstly, the names of the
thirty days of the month are Parsee or Zoroastrian names.
This alone will not be sufficient to enable us to say that the
book is a Parsee book, because we know that after the Arab
conquest even the Mahomedan writers had, for some time and
for several reasons, continued the use of the ancient Parsee
names for days and months. But the second reason which
determines that the book is the work of a Parsee is this: that
the Mâr-nâmeh forms a part of the Parsee Revâyats, which are
to a great extent, a collection of various writings both in prose
and verse, on Zoroastrian subjects.

From what we have said about the view of the ancient Persians, it clearly appears that the contents of this Mâr-nâmeh
are not in the spirit of the belief of the ancient Persians who,
not only took no omens from snakes, but were enjoined to kill
them whenever and wherever they saw them. It is true that the
idea of holding the different days of the month auspicious for
particular kinds of work, was not foreign to the ancient Persians
of at least the Sassanian times. This we find from a small Pehelvi
book, the Mâdigân-i-Si-roz, supposed to be written by that great
Zoroastrian divine, Âderbâd Mârespand, who lived at the end
of the third century after Christ. This Pehelvi book enumerates
the thirty days of a Parsee month, just as our Mâr-nâmeh does,
and describes for what particular kinds of work these days are
specially auspicious. But the idea of taking omens from the
sight of snakes on these days is foreign to the views of the
ancient Persians about snakes. It is possible that foreign
views have influenced the Parsee writer of the Mâr-nâmeh.

A foreign belief in the sacredness of the serpents and in the omens presented by their movements, as that which prevailed in Egypt, has possibly influenced the Parsee writer of the Mâr-nâmeh, which, together with the rest of the Revâyats, of which it forms a part, seems to have been written about four hundred years ago.

With these few observations, I beg to submit before the Society the short text of the Mâr-nâmeh, which is not hitherto published, for publication in its Journal. I will add my own translation of the text. I am indebted to my learned friend, Mr. Edalji Kersaspji Antia, Zend Teacher in Sir Jamshedjee Jeejeebhoy Zarthoshti Madressa, for the text which I have copied from his fine manuscript of the Revâyat-i-Dârâb Hormazdiâr.[1] I have collated the text with that of the Revâyat of Burzo-Kâmdin in the Mulla Feeroze Library in Bombay, and have given the variations in footnotes :—

مار نامه

اگر مار بيني بروز هرمزد

زيادت شود حرمت و مال و مزد

اگر روز بهمن به بيني بومار

غمي سخت بيني در آنروزگار

اگر مار بيني باردى بهشت

شود خويش تويك بسوي بهشت [2]

بشهرور اندر به بيني تومار

يكي غايبي را بگيري كنار

سفندارمد روز ببيني تومار

ترا نزد خلقان بود خوربكار

بخورداد گرمار بيني نگر

كه ناگاه پيش توآيد سفر

---

[1] Vol. III., p. 582.

[2] B. K. (Burzo Kamdin's Revayet in the Moola Feeroze Library, p. 355)

يكي خويشي تو ميشود سوى بهشت له

بکام دل خویش گشتن بزود

که غمگین نگردی توخود باوجود ¹

بمرداد گرمار بینی ببین

که ناگاه پش توآید غمین ²

بدپادر اندر ببینی لومار

برآید مراد نواز هرکنار

اگر روز آدر بینی نومار

بیابی بسی خوبی از روزگار

بآبان اگر ببینش در زمان

برآید مراد نواندر زمان ³

اگرمار بینی تودر روز خور

بنزدیک شادان شوی یاز دور

اگر مار بینی تودر روز ماه

زدیدار اوکار گردد تباه

اگر مار بینی در روز تیر

بیابی تومالی قلیل و کثیر

اگر مار بینی تودر روز گوش

سفر پیشت آید تودبری مکوش

اگرمار بینی تودر دپمهر

برآید مرادت زگردان سپهر ⁴

اگرمار بینی تودر روز مهر ⁵

سفر پیشت آبد بزودی نه دیر

اگر مار بینی برزز سروش

بغانه رو وجامه نوبپوش

---

¹ B. K.   بتو اندرون کرد بسیار سود

² B. K.   بگردی زچیزی تو ناگه غمین

³ B. K.   بیابی مرادی هم اندر زمان

⁴ B. K.   بر آید مواد نوای خوبچهر

⁵ B. K.   اگر مهر باشد که بینی نگر

            که ناگاه پیش تو آید سفر

اگر رشته بيني سرشوا بكوب

اگر سنگ باشد وگر خشک چوب

که علت فزايد ز ديدار اوي

بود ناتواني هم از كار اوي

اگر مار بيني بفرور دين

فزايد ترا شادي و نازنين ١

اگر روز بهرام بيني تو مار

از آنروز رخسار خود دور دار

اگر مار بيني تو در روز رام

تو در جنگ و پرخاش ماني مدام

اگر مار بيني تو در روز باد

ز ديدار او مال گردد بباد

اگر مار بيني تو در دپدين

بود رنج و علت دليلست اين

بدين روز گر مار بيني از ان ٢

برايد مرادت شوي شادمان

اگر ارد باشد که بيني همين

که ناگاه گردي ز چيزي غمين

اگر روز آستاد بيني تو مار ٣

هم روز و شب شادماني شمار

اگر مار بيني ٤ بروز آسمان

(٥) تو شنوي ز بهقا نهاي گران

اگر روز زميان بيني تو مار ٥

بيابي تو داد از جهان كردگار

---

١ B. K.   فزايد ترا شادماني دين

٢ B. K.   { اگر مار بيني تو در روز دين

          { برآيد مراد تو اي پاكدين

٣ B. K.   { چو آستاد باشد که بيني بدان

          { تو باشي هم روز و شب شادمان

٤ B. K.   بسي بشنوي ٭ تو در

٥ B. K.   { اگر مار بيني تو در زميان

          { ز دادار گيتي بيابي تو داد

اگر مار بيني بهار سپند
سرش را ¹ جدا کن که رسغي زبند
چون روز انيران بيني تو مار
فم و فکر زان روز چندی شمار ²

TRANSLATION.

1. If you see a snake on the day of Hormazd,³ your honour, property and income will increase.

2. If you see a snake on the day of Bahman, you will meet with great grief at the time.

3. If you see a snake on the day of Ardibehesht, a relation of yours will go to heaven.⁴

4. If you see a snake on the day of Sheherivar, you will (soon) find an absent friend in your arms.⁵

5. If you see a snake on the day of Safendârmad, your affairs with the people of the world will end happily.

6. If you see a snake on the day of Khordâd, expect that you will shortly have a long journey before you, that you will

---

¹ B. K. نروکوب

² B. K. ازان روز رخسار خود دور وار

³ Hormazd is the first day of a Parsee month, Bahman the second day, Ardibehesht the third day, and so on.

⁴ Ardibehesht, the name of the third day of the month for which the omen is described, is also the name of an archangel who is said to have the key of the Gate of Heaven in his charge. Ardibehesht is the later form of the Avesta word "Asha Vahishta," which means "the best purity." When Ardibehesht is said to be in charge of the Gate of Heaven, it means that a man can go to paradise by observing in his life "the best purity." "To go to paradise," has come to mean colloquially 'to die' Therefore, what the Mârnâmeh seems to mean is that, if a man were to see a snake on the third day of the month, it is a bad omen, predicting the death of a near relation.

⁵ In India a peculiar noise made by a crow is supposed to indicate the arrival of a dear relation or at least of a letter from him. Vide my paper before the Society on "A few Superstitions Common to Europe and India," Vol. 11., No. 3. p. 187.

soon return (from it) with the desire of your heart fulfilled, and that you will not be disgusted with your life.[1]

7.   If you see a snake on the day of Merdâd (Amerdâd) do not look at it, (or otherwise) you will soon have a cause to be sorry.

8.   If you see a snake on the day of Depâdar, your desires will be satisfied from all directions.

9.   If you see a snake on the day of Âdar, you will receive a great good from the hand of Time.

10.   If you see it (the snake) on the day of Âbân, your desires will be immediately fulfilled.

11.   If you see a snake on the day of Khur (Khursheed), you will be happy shortly or after some time.

12.   If you see a snake on the day of Mâh, your affairs will be all ruined by seeing him.

13.   If you see a snake on the day of Tir, you will come in possession of some property, whether large or small.

14.   If you see a snake on the day of Gosh, a journey will be soon before you ; you need not wait long.

15.   If you see a snake on the day of Depmeher, the revolving heavens will satisfy your wishes.

16.   If you see a snake on the day of Meher, it will not be long before you will go out on a journey.

17.   If you see a snake on the day of Sarosh, go home and put on a new suit of clothes.

18.   If you see a snake on the day of Rashnê, strike on its head either with a stone or with a dry stick, because a look at it (on that day) increases your defects, and because helplessness results from its works.

19.   If you see a snake on the day of Farvardeen, that will increase your joy and merriment.

20.   If you see a snake on the day of Behcrâm, keep away your face from that day.[2]

---

[1] B. K. R. (Burzo-Kamdin's Revâyat), you will get great profit from it.

[2] The meaning is not clear ; perhaps, it means ' Do not go out on that day.'

21. If you see a snake on the day of Râm, you will always remain in a state of warfare and quarrel.

22. If you see a snake on the day of Bâd (Goâd,) a look at it will destroy all your property.

23. If you see a snake on the day of Depdin, trouble and loss will be the result of that.

24. If you see a snake on the day of Din, your desire will be fulfilled and you will be glad.

25. If you see it on the day of Ard (Ashishang), you will unawares have cause to be sorry for something.

26. If you see a snake on the day of Âstâd, count upon all joy for that day and night.

27. If you see a snake on the day of Âsmân, you will hear of grave charges against you.

28. If you see a snake on the day of Zamyâd, you will obtain justice from the Creator of the world.

29. If you see a snake on the day of Mârespand, sever its head from its body, so that you may be free from difficulties.

30. If you see a snake on the day of Anirân, count upon some grief and anxiety from that day.

ORDINARY GENERAL MEETING, held on Wednesday, the 25th January 1893.

DR. G WATERS, *Vice-President*, in the Chair.

The Minutes of the previous Meeting were read and confirmed.

The election of the following new members was announced :—
Pandit S. E. Gopalacharlu, 8, South Madu Street, Mylapore, Madras.

The following paper was then read :—

On the INDIAN FOLK-BELIEFS ABOUT THE TIGER.
BY SARAT CHANDRA MITRA, M. A., B. L., Pleader,
Judge's Court, Chupra Behar.

RECENT discoveries in prehistoric caves have brought to light the important fact that primitive man was coeval with those terrible monsters—the mammoths, the cave-bear, the cave-lion and many others which are now known to us only from their fossilized bones. The presence of flint spear-heads, hatchets, hammers and other weapons among these relics attest that men in those remote times not only hunted, slew and fed upon these animals but also *held them in great awe, because they were of much larger proportions and far stronger than their own selves.* In this awe, based upon the magnitude of size and the excess of strength of some members of the brute-creation, animal-worship has its origin. Primitive man thought that these brutes resembled himself in so many respects and yet was so much stronger that he believed, in his ignorance, that the latter must have souls much greater than his own soul. Thus he was led to the next step in the process by which animal-worship came to be evolved, namely, that these brutes must be some · beings who possessed some power for either good or evil to themselves and must, therefore, be propitiated for bestowal of favours or for appeasing their wrath. Forms of this animal-worship still survive among races of men all the wide world over, who have as yet hardly emerged from the state of savagery and whose conditions of life very nearly resemble those of man in the palæolithic, the neolithic, and the bronze ages.

The kind of animal worshipped depended very much upon the country in which primitive man lived. Man, in all parts of the world, fears and worships that particular sort of animal which infests in great numbers a particular tract of country, or commits depredations therein. Thus in the farthest regions of North America where the terrible Grizzly Bears roam at large and commits sad havoc on animal-life, the aboriginal Indians

of those parts hold that ferocious beast in great superstitious
awe. In Canada—the home of the ravening wolves, the legend
of the Wehr-Wolf—a goblin brute always thirsting for human
blood, is believed by all classes of the people, thus shewing how
much that animal is feared by all Canadians, both high and low.
To come nearer home, the tiger, the snake, and the shark afford
familiar examples of animal-worship in this country. One of
the much dreaded animals peculiar to the Indian Fauna is the
tiger, which is held in great superstitious awe, not only on
account of its larger size but also of its ferocity and fearful
depredations. Such are its ravening propensities that it annually destroys large numbers of human beings and cattle, thereby depopulating large tracts of country and causing much loss
to the agricultural classes. The snake and the shark also come
under the category of the destructive animals peculiar to this
country ; so many human lives are annually lost from snake-
bites and attacks of sharks. Hence the Bengalis worship
Maushá Deri, the great Snake-Goddess on the Mausha-Pujâ Day
in the month of Srâvana, in order to propitiate the serpent class.
On the Ganga-Pujah Day, the Goddess Gangâ, or the River
Ganges, who is represented as riding on a shark in native
drawings, is worshipped in Bengal, and thus the shark is
propitiated in an indirect way.

In the same way, the tiger is worshipped by many aboriginal tribes of India, and is, in other parts of this country,
held
in much superstitious awe, though not actually worshipped.
Thus a tiger-demon is one of recognized deities in the pantheon
of some of the aboriginal tribes of India. The Kisans,[1]
a partially Hinduised tribe living about Palamow, Sirgujâ, and
Jashpur in the Province of Chota Nagpur, worship the tiger-
demon. They think that by doing so their own lives and
their domesticated animals would be safe from the ravages of
these animals. Among the Santâls living in Râmgarh, only

---

[1] *Vide Indian Antiquary*, Vol. XIX., page 128.

those persons whose relatives have been killed by the tiger, consider it indispensably necessary to propitiate the tiger-demon who had wrought death to his kinsmen. The Gonds also pay devoirs to the tiger-demon out of the same motives which actuate the Kisans and the Santals. In the Santal Pergunnahs, the Santals consider death by a tiger a far greater calamity than anything else, so much so that whenever Santáli witnesses have to be examined in the Courts of that province, the form of oath in Santali, which is administered to them, means that should they tell falsehoods, they would be eaten by tigers. Among the Gonds, the Kúsrú, Súrí, Markám, Netiá and Sársún clans hold Bághesar or the Tiger-lord—a local deified spirit— in great reverence. There is a legend[1] current among them, which has been narrated by Captain W. L. Samuells in the pages of the Journal of the Asiatic Society of Bengal, and is as follows :—

Once upon a time, in a family of the Gond tribe, there were five brothers, named respectively Kúsrú, Súrí, Markám, Netia, and Sarsún. At her second childbirth, Kúsrú's wife gave birth to a tiger's whelp, which was treated by its parents with as much affection and regard as their first-born male-child. From childhood he was the constant companion of Kúsrú. While Kúsrú used to watch his crops, the tiger-child used to remain near him. Now nilgais and sambars used to destroy Kúsrú's crops, but Kúsrú could do nothing to prevent it. On one occasion, seeing a large sambar destroying his young and tender úrid plants, Kúsrú wept and tore his hair, bemoaning his bad lot ; whereupon the tiger-child killed the sambar and tore it to pieces, and went on doing so till Kúsrú's crop was gathered. Hence Kúsrú began to love the young cub all the more. In course of time, the young tiger died and became a bhut.

On the occasion of the marriage of Kúsrú's daughter, one of the party became possessed with a demon. The Baigá or

---

village-priest and necromancer questioned it and found that it
was the spirit of the tiger-child, and demanded worship with
offerings and sacrifices. Fowls, kid, arrack and *ghi* were
offered to him and the spirit thereupon went out of the man.
So from that day forth, the spirit of the Kúsrú's tiger-son was
deified and was worshipped under the name of Bâghesar or the
Tiger-god, by the five Gond clans descended from, and respectively named after the brothers Kúsrú, Súrí, Markám, Netiñ,
and Sársún.

It is only at the marriages of the members of the five clans
named above, that Bâghesar manifests his presence in the above
manner. With them he is held in reverence as a *deified* spirit ;
but with other Gonds, Bâghesar is simply one of the many spirits
who are yearly propitiated with offerings. According to
the latter, he has no such origin as that ascribed to him
by the five clans above-named, but is simply regarded as
' the concentrated essence of spirits,' which have issued
from those Gonds who have met their deaths by tigers ;
for, according to local belief, the spirits of all Gonds thus killed,
are said to unite and form the one great spirit Bâghesar.
It is simply for saving their flocks and herds, and their own
lives also, from the ravages of the tigers, that the inhabitants
of every Gond village yearly make offerings to propitiate this
demon. Another account is given as to how tiger-worship
originated among the Gonds. The latter say that one of their
chiefs was, in early life, devoured by a tiger, and that he afterwards appeared to his friends, telling them that, if worship
were paid to him, he would protect them and their domesticated
animals from the depredations of that animal. They acted up
to his advice, and he was accordingly duly installed as a member of their already-crowded Pantheon.[1]

Some other aboriginal tribes believe that the form of the
tiger can be assumed by certain maliciously disposed persons

---

[1] *Vide Indian Antiquary*, Vol. XIV. (1885), p. 183.

among them, who thereby become possessed of a good deal
of power for evil to living human beings. The Khonds[1] of
Orissa believe that some women can transform themselves into
tigers; and sometimes wicked persons try to spread this impression concerning themselves in order to extort presents from
their neighbours as the price of refraining from injuring them
by their ravages. This belief is also, to a certant extent,
shared in by the Oràons[2] who live in the adjoining districts,
included within the Central Provinces of India. They say
that those persons who have met their death by the tiger are
metamorphosed into that terrible animal.

The Kakhyens, a savage people living in the hills to the east
of Burma, believe in two deities, named Chitong and Muron, who
are two of ten brothers, said to take an especial interest in
Kakhyen affairs. The Kakhyens believe that if hunters do not
present offerings to the former deity, named Chitong, *some one
among them will be killed by tiger*[3] or stag. There is another
Nat or deity worshipped by them under the name of *Ndong* Nat,
who is supposed to preside over the Outside of Home. He is
generally believed to reside in the house, but is *worshipped
outside if one of the family is killed by the bite of a tiger*[4] or snake.

The Burmese worship the Kakhyen Nat, named *Ndong*,
under the name of *Aing-peen Nat, in case if any of the family be
killed by a tiger.*[5] The Burmese believe that this Nat also
sometimes assumes the form of a tiger, for Dr. Anderson says:
" At a place called Thembaw-eng, the headman came down and
compelled us to leave our moorings. We were not assailed by
Kakhyens, but had a nocturnal alarm of a tiger, which the
boatmen declared to be *not a real tiger, but the Nat of the locality*,
who was enraged at their having cut down some branches of a

---

[1] *Op. cit.*, p. 131.
[2] *Op. cit.*, p. 132.
[3] *Mandalay to Momien*, by John Anderson, M. D. London, 1876, p. 147.
[4] *Op. cit.*, p. 459.
[5] *Op. cit*, p. 459.

7

tree." [1]   So great is the superstitious dread of the tiger, entertained by the Burmese that, whenever a person among them is
killed by that animal, they take steps to bury the corpse as
soon as possible.   Dr. John Anderson saw an instance of this
superstition while he was at Bhamô.   He says: "At Bhamô,
a woman was killed by a tiger.   The woman was buried the
same night in accordance with the Burmese custom, followed in
all cases of persons killed by tigers." [2]

The Shans of the Sanda Valley in Yunnan also believe in
the existence of a Nat, which assumes the form of a tiger and
carries off children.   This belief is testified to by Dr. Anderson,
who visited them during the course of the first expedition to
Yunnan, undertaken in 1868.   He says : " A thick grove of
fir trees, marking the burial place of the Tsawbwa's family, was
the only covert, but firing there was looked upon as certain to
bring disease and death upon the chief and his household.   A
formal request was made that we would not shoot on the hills
behind the town.   *A Nat is said to dwell in a cutting*, which
marks the entrenchments made by the Chinese army in 1767,
*and the Shans believe that if a gun was fired, the insulted demon
would come down as a tiger and carry off the children.*" [3]

In the Central Provinces of India prevail a certain number
of superstitions connected with the tiger.   One of them is that
when a man had been killed by a tiger, his spirit possessed
that beast and led him away from all danger.   Lieut.-Colonel
W. H. Sleeman, who sojourned for a long time in these wild
tracts, met with several instances of this and other superstitious
beliefs prevailing there.   He says : [4] "Ram Chund Roo,
commonly called the Sureemunt, chief of Deoree, came to call

---

[1] *Op. cit.*, p 452.
[2] *Vide Report on the Expedition to Western Yunan vii Bhamô*, by
J. Anderson, M. D Calcutta, 1871, pages 235.36.
[3] *Op. cit.*, p. 260.
[4] *Rambles and Recollections of an Indian Official*, by Lieut.-Colonel W.
H. Sleeman. London. Hatchard & Son, Vol I., pages 162.63.

upon me after breakfast, and the conversation turned upon the
number of people that had of late been killed by tigers between
Saugor and Deoree, his ancient capital, which lies about mid-
way between Saugor and the Nerbudda river. One of his followers, who stood behind his chair, said, "that when a tiger
had killed one man he was safe, for the spirit of the man rode
upon his head, and guided him from all danger. The spirit
knew very well that the tiger would be watched for many days
at the place where he had committed the homicide, and always
guided him off to some other more secure place, where he killed
other men without any risk to himself. He did not exactly
know why the spirit of the man should thus befriend the beast
that had killed him; but," added he, "there is a mischief inher-
ent in spirits ; and the better the man the more mischievous is
his ghost, if means are not taken to put him to rest." This is
the popular and general belief throughout India ; and it is supposed, that the only sure mode of destroying a tiger, who has
killed many people, is to begin by making offerings to the
spirits of his victims, and thereby depriving him of their
valuable services."

Another tiger-superstition widely current throughout India
is that human beings are metamorphosed into tigers by eating
the root of a particular kind of plant and that, if in this state, he
can eat the root of another he will instantly be retransformed
into a human being. Lieut.-Colonel Sleeman gives in his
aforesaid work[1] the following instances of the abovementioned
belief : "The Sureemunt was himself of opinion, that the
tigers which now infest the wood from Saugor to Deoree were
of a different kind—in fact, that they were neither more nor
less than men turned into tigers—a thing which took place
in the woods of Central India much more often than people were
aware of. The only visible difference between the two," added
the Sureemunt, "is that the metamorphosed tiger has *no tail*, while

---

[1] *Op cit.*, Vol. I., pp. 163.64.

the *bora*, or ordinary tiger, has a very long one.   In the jungle
about Dooree," continued he, "there is a root which, if a man eat
of, he is converted into a tiger on the spot; and if in this state
he can eat of another, he becomes a man again—a melancholy
instance of the former of which," said he, "occurred, I am told,
in my own father's family when I was an infant.   His washerman,
Rughoo, was, like all washermen, a great drunkard; and being
seized with a violent desire to ascertain what a man felt in the
state of a tiger, he went one day to the jungle and brought
home two of these roots, and desired his wife to stand by with
one of them, and the instant she saw him assume the tiger's
shape, to thrust it into his mouth.   She consented: the washerman ate his root, and became instantly a tiger; but his wife
was so terrified at the sight of her old husband in this shape
that she ran off with the antidote in her hand.   Poor old
Rughoo took to the woods, and there ate a good many of his
old friends from the neighbouring villages; but he was at last
shot and recognized from the circumstance of his *having no tail*.
You may be quite sure," concluded Sureemunt, "when you
hear of a tiger without a tail, that it is some unfortunate man
who has eaten of that root—and of all the tigers he will be
found the most mischievous."

A third superstitious belief connected with the tiger, prevalent in Central India, is that there is a particular kind of
science which endows the men who master its secrets, with the
power of transforming themselves into tigers whenever they
wish to do so.   This is testified to by the same author from
whom I have made extensive quotations above, and who was
thoroughly conversant with the customs and beliefs of the
people inhabiting the Central Provinces of India.   He relates:[1]
" I was one day talking with my friend, the Rajah of Myhere,
on the road between Jubbulpore and Mirzapore, on the subject
of the number of men who had been lately killed by tigers at

---

[1] *Op. cit.*, Vol. 1   pp. 165 167.

the Kutra Pass on that road, and the best means of removing
the danger. " Nothing, " said the Rajah, " could be more
easy or more cheap than the destruction of these tigers, if they
were of the ordinary sort ; but the tigers that kill men by
wholesale, as these do, are, you may be sure, men themselves
converted into tigers by the force of their *science* ; and such
animals are of all the most unmanageable." On being questioned as to how those men converted themselves into tigers,
the Rajah replied : " Nothing is more easy than this to persons
who have once acquired the science ; but how they learn it, or
what it is, we unlettered men know not. There was once a high
priest, of a large temple, in this very valley of Myhere, who was
in the habit of getting himself converted into a tiger by the
force of this science, which he had thoroughly acquired. He
had a necklace, which one of his disciples used to throw over his
neck the moment the tiger's form became fully developed. He
had, however, long given up the practice, and all his old disciples had gone off on their pilgrimages to distant shrines,
when he was one day seized with a violent desire to take his
old form of the tiger. He expressed the wish to one of his
new disciples, and demanded whether he thought he might
rely upon his courage to stand by and put on the necklace.
'Assuredly you may,' said the disciple ; 'such is my faith in you
and in the God we serve, that I fear nothing ! ' The high
priest upon this put the necklace into his hand with the
requisite instructions, and forthwith began to change his form.
The disciple stood trembling in every limb, till he heard him
give a roar that shook the whole edifice, when he fell flat upon
his face, and dropped the necklace on the floor. The tiger
bounded over him, and out at the door ; and infested all the
roads leading to the temple for many years afterwards." On
being questioned whether the old high priest was one of the
tigers at the Kutra Pass, the Rajah replied in the negative, but
further added that they might have been all men who had become imbued with a little too much of the high priest's *science*,

and, when men once acquired this science, they couldn't help exercising it, though it was to their own ruin and that of others. On being asked as to what was the simple plan for stopping their depredations, supposing them to be ordinary tigers, the Rajah said : "I propose to have the spirits that guide them propitiated by proper prayers and offerings ; for the spirit of every man or woman who has been killed by a tiger rides upon his head, or runs before him, and tells him where to go to get prey, and to avoid danger. Get some of the Gonds, or wild people from the jungles, who are well skilled in these mat-ters ; give them 10 or 20 rupees, and bid them go and raise a small shrine, and there sacrifice to these spirits. The Gonds will tell them that they shall, on this shrine, have regular worship, and good sacrifices of fowls, goats, and pigs, every year at least, if they will but relinquish their offices with the tigers and be quiet. If this is done, I pledge myself," said the Rajah, "that the tigers will soon get killed themselves, or cease from killing men. If they do not, you may be quite sure that they are not ordinary tigers, but men turned into tigers, or that the Gonds have appropriated all you gave them to their own use, instead of applying it to conciliate the spirits of the unfortu-nate people ! "

In Bengal, though the tiger is not actually worshipped, there have gathered round him a number of superstitions or semi-mythical beliefs. In the Sundarbans, where Stripes can be seen in his greatest beauty, the tiger is regarded with much super-stitious awe. So infested are the Sundarbans with tigers that men, who have occasion to reside there, such as agents of per-sons who have taken leases of the forest lands for purposes of reclamation and cultivation, and wood-cutters, construct struc-tures of bamboo raised far above the ground, whereon seated they pass the nights. It sometimes happens that tigers, in the course of their peregrinations, find their way to the bases of these structures and do not move away readily. The residents of these structures cannot descend and go to their respective businesses. In order to drive them away, they resort to the expedient of appealing to the *jogis* or ascetics who perform their penances in these forest tracts. It is said that the tigers neither molest these persons nor are the latter at all afraid of the former. On being appealed to, the *jogi* goes to the tiger, pats it on the back, and tells it to go away ; whereupon, it is said, the tiger goes away as if it was a domestic cat. This story may be a myth, pure and simple, and I have narrated it here, as I heard it and the following story from a friend of mine, resident of the Jessore district, as illustrations of the popular belief about the tiger. There is another popular belief current there to the effect that tigers, for the purpose of preying , on human victims, take advantage of the time when wood-cutters busy themselves in cutting wood with their hatchets, lest the sounds of their (tiger's) footfalls may be heard. As soon as the wood-cutter commences his operations and plies his hatchet, the tiger cautiously advances his foot as each blow of the hatchet falls, so that the sounds of his (tiger's) footfalls are drowned by the noise of the hatchet-blows. It is also said that, in the Sundarbans, the tiger is looked upon with feelings akin to reverence, and sometimes offerings are presented to him, out of the superstitious belief that, being thus treated, he won't molest human beings.

The tiger also plays an important part in Indian folk-lore. In Bengal he figures in, at least, two folk-stories that I know of, and which I distinctly remember having heard in my childhood. I can't recollect the whole stories now, but remember the bare outlines of them. In one story, the heroine of it marries a tiger, lives with him peacefully and is ultimately either devoured by him, or the tiger is metamorphosed into a prince. In the second story, a poor man's son took a fancy to become the owner of a horse and a mare's egg. In his ignorance, he thought he had found the mare's egg in a big pumpkin. But he could not get hold of a horse to ride upon. One night as he was easing himself in the outskirts of the village, he saw a huge tiger, which he, mistaking for a horse, rode upon and drove at full speed. The tiger, being frightened, ran at full speed, and ultimately threw him off his back. When the poor boy came to his senses, he thanked his stars that his so-called horse had not made a meal of him.

In Bengal, the tiger also plays a prominent part in the "proverbial philosophy" of its people. In allusion to the snarling disposition of a tigress big with young ones, a termagant woman is called a रायबाघिनी or a " Roy tigress." A dilatory woman is called a बाघेर मासी or the mother's sister of a tiger. The origin of this allusion I do not know. It is said that the wounds inflicted by a tiger are very difficult to heal up and often lead to a variety of other ailments. Hence is the Bengali proverb बत्रूं><भ्रज्विग्रया or, if a tiger wounds one, it will give rise to thirty-six sores. If a mean contemptible person plays himself into the hands of his powerful enemy, then the proverb बाघेर घरे घोघेर बास is quoted in Bengal, meaning "the dwelling of a hyæna in a tiger's den! "

The Bengali expression बाघेर दुध or tiger's milk is used for anything which is difficult of attainment, or any undertaking which is difficult of performance. When a man's enterprising spirit has to be praised, it is said of him that, should any one tell him to bring बाघेर दुध or tiger's milk, he will bring it for him. The allusion is to the fact that no living man can approach a tiger or tigress, let alone the idea of milking a tigress with cubs. There is another vulgar Bengali proverb which runs to the effect that :

बाघार बेये बाघारभय ।

बाघार बेये दिरुदिपेरभय ॥

It means the fear of a tiger is greater than the fear of attending an urgent nature's call in the darkness, and the fear of a mythical animal named Tiptipe is greater than the fear of a tiger.

In Southern India, the tiger also forms the subject of several folk-tales, whereof one is related by Pandit S. M.

Natesa Sastrî in the pages of the *Indian Antiquary*.[1] The story goes on to say how a Bráhman girl was married by a tiger who, for that purpose, assumed the form of a Sâstrî or learned Bráhman; how she lived with him for some time and bore him a tiger-child; how she informed her brothers of her distressed condition through a crow; how they rescued her by showing the tiger a washerman's tub as their belly, the braying of an ass as their voice, a palmyra tree as their leg, and so on; how she ultimately fled with her brothers from the tiger's abode, after having cut up the tiger-child in twain; how the tiger was ultimately killed by being made to sit on a well covered with rushes so as to make it appear as a mat. The same author also relates another folktale of Madras in the pages of the same Journal[2] The tiger-king, along with the rat and snake, plays an important part in this story of "The Soothsayer's Son" and rescues that person from captivity in a dungeon, to which he had been thrown by the order of the king of that country, for having been suspected of murdering the king's father and stealing his crown. Ultimately, through the assistance of the kings of the tigers and the snakes, the Soothsayer's son marries the king's daughter and becomes the heir to the throne.

There are many other folk-tales wherein the tiger figures, which have been collected and edited by Mr. P. V. Ramaswami Raju, of Madras. They at first came out in *The Leisure Hour*, and were subsequently reprinted therefrom in the shape of an elegant complete edition by Messrs. Swan Sonnenschein & Co. of London, with an introduction by Mr. Henry Morley.

In Japan, the tiger forms one of the twelve signs of the zodiac, the others being the rat, ox, rabbit, dragon, serpent, horse, goat, monkey, cock, dog and hog.[3] The tiger's head also forms a subject of carving on the beams of Japanese temples.

---

[1] Vol. XIX. (1885), page 134.
[2] Vol. XIII. (1884), page 256 *ff.*
[3] Bird's *Unbeaten Tracks in Japan*, Vol. I., p. 68.

Among the ancient Greeks, the tiger was known by the name of *Martikhora* (Persian مردخور Mardkhor or man-eater) and was described by Ktesias "as being of the size of the lion, red in colour, with human-like face, ears and eyes, three rows of teeth, and stings on various parts of the body, but especially on the tail, which caused it to be compared with the scorpion." There have gathered a number of superstitious beliefs, prevailing amongst the Indians and other Asiatic races, regarding particular limbs or parts of the tiger's body. Every Indian *shikari* knows that there is a horny claw or nail-like appendage at the end of the tail of the tiger, the lion, and other animals of the cat family. The natives of India believe that this nail-like structure serves the same purpose as the sting of the scorpion. The whiskers of this animal are superstitiously believed by them to be a source of great harm to mankind. Hence, as soon as a tiger is killed, the beaters and the native shikaris pluck out or burn off his whiskers, believing that thereby all accidents likely to arise from their remaining will be averted. Some of the natives of India believe that, if the tiger's whiskers are removed, no human being will be able to assume the form of the tiger for purposes of killing men. Others of them suppose that the possession of the tiger's whiskers conferred on the fortunate possessor of them unlimited influence over the hearts of the fair sex. In former times, a form of oath was administered in Courts of Justice on the skin of a tiger. Its skin is sometimes spread on thrones and judicial seats, as the animal has been, from time immemorial, the accepted insignia of royalty among oriental potentates. Its skin, like that of deer and antelopes, is also considered sacred by the Hindus, and is used by *jogis* and *fakirs* of that creed for performing their devotions upon. The god Siva of Hindu mythology is represented as being draped with a tiger-skin. The front-teeth, the whiskers, the claws, and the rudimentary clavicles (*birnukh*) are preserved as charms, and are often worn on the person as amulets. The Malays believe that eating the flesh of the tiger endows the eater with much bravery and heroism. The Greek idea of the tiger having three rows of teeth, as told by Ktesias, probably arose from the fact that the carnivorous molar teeth of the tiger have three lobes, in which respect they differ from the molars of the *Ruminantia* and the *Equidæ*. The Japanese doctors believe in the highly medicinal properties of the tiger's liver. Miss Isabella Bird, who travelled in Japan[1], bears testimony to this fact. She says : 'Dr. Nosoki (a Japanese practitioner who attended on her during her illness) has great faith in *ginseng* and in rhinoceros horn, and in the *powdered liver of some animal, which, from the description, I understood to be a tiger*—all specifics of the Chinese school of medicines. Dr. Nosoki showed me a small box of unicorn's' horn, which he said was worth more than its weight in gold." The Chinese also labour under the impression that different parts of the tiger's body have different kinds of medicinal properties. The same talented lady, who also stayed at Canton for some time, and from whom I have quoted above, says : [2] " Afterwards in China, at a native hospital, I heard much more of the miraculous virtues of these drugs, and in Salangor, in the Malay Peninsula, I saw a most amusing scene after the death of a tiger. A number of the neighbouring Chinese flew upon the body, cut out the liver, eyes and spleen, and carefully drained every drop of the blood, fighting with each other for the possession of things so precious, while those who were not so fortunate as to secure any of these cut out the cartilage from the joints. The centre of a tiger's eye-ball is supposed to possess nearly miraculous virtues ; the blood, dried at a temperature of 110° is the strongest of all tonics, and gives strength and courage ; and the powdered liver and spleen are good for many diseases. Sultan Abdul Samat claimed the liver, but the other parts were all sold at

---

[1] *Unbeaten Tracks in Japan*, Vol. I., p. 275.
[2] *Op cit.*, Vol. I., p. 275.

high prices to the Chinese doctors. A little later at Qualla, Kangsa in Perak, I saw rhinoceros horns sold at a high price for the Chinese drug market, and Rajah Muda, who was anxious to claim the horns of the district, asserted that a single horn with a particular mark on it, was worth fifty dollars for sale to the Chinese doctors." In Bengal the grease of the tiger is considered as a sovereign remedy for rheumatism and gout.

The Shans, inhabiting north of Burma, entertain similar notions regarding the curative properties of certain parts of the tiger, as is testified to by Dr. J. Anderson. He writes : " We find the Shans placing implicit faith in the curative and strengthening qualities of decoctions of the dried and pregnant wombs of the sambur, *tiger*, and porcupine, and relying on the desiccated stomachs of these animals for relief in the worst forms of disease. The leg-bones of the tiger and the pounded horns of the sambur and serrow are in great repute as medicines that give tone and strength to the frame, exhausted by disease or excess." [1]

---

[1] *A Report on the Expedition to Western Yunan vid Bhamo*, by J. Anderson. Calcutta. 1871, page 114.

TABLES *of* CASTE MEASUREMENTS *compiled by* MR. E. J. KITTS.

(Continued from p. 503, *Vol II.)*

Note.—The tables following give anthropometric measurements for groups of adult males of different caste.

Table I. has been discontinued, as the police anthropometric· system has been taken up by the Local Government of the N.W.P. and Oudh.

Table II. is compiled for ordinary anthropological purposes. All the measurements are in millimetres. The compiler will be glad if information is sent to him of any mistakes which may be discovered in the summary at the end of this table.

E. J. KITTS, C.S.,

Allahabad.

20th January, 1893.

Name of Caste or Tribe—JAT.

No.	Height of Vertex.	Height of Trunk.	Span.	Left Foot.	Left Middle Finger.	Right Bar Height.	Round Head.	Inion to Glabella.	Tragus to Tragus.	Vertex to Chin.	Antero-posterior Diameter.	Maximum Transverse Diameter.	Minimum Frontal Diameter.	Bizygomatic Diameter.	Cephalic Index.	General Index.	Frontal Index.
1	1617	838	1653	254	104	60	536	838	248	213	187	140	114	141	74·7	152	79·2
2	1658	820	1714	257	104	58	538	335	335	214	190	137	116	184	72·1	157	82·3
3	1659	845	1720	247	106	60	548	337	365	214	190	144	106	134	75·8	166	75·2
4	1657	808	1735	248	113	63	537	337	335	210	185	141	109	128	76·2	168	75·7
5	1541	741	1585	23.	103	64	527	322	33.	223	184	141	109	135	76·7	148	79·4
6	1665	800	1727	254	114	67	543	335	335	215	184	144	112	138	78·3	165	75·8
7	1700	874	1780	255	119	63	528	325	340	200	183	141	108	130	78·0	152	73·5
8	1637	787	1730	268	112	61	522	330	343	22)	174	147	107	134	84·5	161	74·8
9	1675	858	1725	247	107	59	538	342	345	198	188	143	109	144	76·1	148	76·2
10	1611	816	1600	250	114	61	533	348	343	216	187	148	109	139	76·5	153	78·8
11	1630	828	1796	243	116	58	535	320	340	213	185	143	115	134	78·8	156	79·5
12	1780	842	1830	279	120	60	550	3·8	357	212	188	146	116	137	77·7	161	82·0
13	1719	839	1812	251	104	65	528	320	333	209	187	153	109		71·1		80·0
14	1689	871	1732	262	101	62	549	390	361	224	189	150	120		79·4		
15	1704		1737	267	104		536	3.5	335		188	136			72·3		
16	1739		1800	259	107		543	525	345		186	151			81·5		
17	1661		1711	244	104		554	343	345		197	147			75·0		
18	1694		1777	274	114		536	320	328		185	140			71·1		
19	1744	871	1880	259	104	64	551	330	328	226	186	138			74·6		
20	1772	861	1770	269	114	66	531	358	353	208	184	138			69·7		
21	1744	922	1866	277	119	71	549	343	353	218	198	144			78·3		
22	1843	815	1904	259	117	58	553	356	343	224	191	141			71·2		
23	1651	813	1711	244	110	61	554	340	345	208	195	187			72·3		
24	1661	841	1785	242	110	46	543	343	356	203	196	141			71·9		
25	1706	842	1894	253	119	59	545	348	348	225	190	141			73·7		
26	1676		1755		108			350				110	163	188		169	73·6

No.																	
27	72·9	161	72·0	136	105	144	200	218	...	...	565	05	112	257	1715	860	1736
28	71·8	160	72·1	141	103	142	197	226	355	853	548	77	110	245	1652	826	1693
29	73·2	179	69·3	128	103	138	198	229	318	853	557	58	113	250	1598	810	1594
30	76·2	161	67·4	135	98	130	193	218	325	345	543	67	187	270	1918	840	1757
31	75·0	159	76·1	186	109	143	198	216	362	342	557	40	112	257	1735	875	1693
32	75·5	140	70·0	134	105	140	200	215	365	803	538	84	121	279	1975	910	1755
33	85·2	150	73·8	188	115	135	183	207	353	825	545	68	118	255	1975	820	1635
34	81·5	148	69·9	185	110	135	193	210	345	840	535	69	100	275	1770	875	1735
35	79·3	148	81·0	142	115	145	179	210	350	345	535	02	113	246	1835	835	1685
36	79·5	112	76·4	137	116	146	191	208	355	355	560	58	108	243	1762	803	1690
37	79·0	140	71·4	142	112	140	196	199	385	330	550	61	108	260	1716	848	1675
38	70·4	162	76·3	130	100	142	181	211	347	331	530	65	116	248	1695	880	1675
39	77·3	162	77·3	125	108	140	188	203	354	375	553	52	133	274	1755	895	1735
40	79·2	152	79·1	138	114	144	198	210	355	350	542	61	110	203	1820	900	1755
41	79·9	144	79·1	140	115	144	198	201	333	810	541	68	107	244	1825	855	1645
42	79·9	161	69·7	185	109	138	198	218	355	370	555	70	104	251	1755	935	1735
43	74·8	148	72·4	139	104	139	201	206	348	340	540	73	112	252	1727	820	1610
44	75·0	140	72·9	137	105	140	195	219	346	352	585	71	112	269	1712	910	1770
45	82·7	164	73·9	133	115	139	196	205	353	373	567	62	103	252	1873	815	1640
46	83·3	163	67·7	189	111	132	190	215	313	354	543	86	122	231	1740	840	1735
47	80·4	150	73·0	135	115	143	172	208	369	355	550	71	110	234	1852	850	1760
48	72·5	156	72·6	129	100	138	181	211	359	845	548	62	100	259	1795	853	1710
49	75·6	149	80·2	133	102	139	181	192	360	334	516	80	117	258	1835	875	1743
50	76·6	157	75·7	125	105	137	181	209	330	332	530	67	119	277	1756	894	1764
51	74·2	164	70·6	130	98	132	187	205	350	362	554	59	116	240	1863	872	1770
52	73·8	135	80·6		104	141	175	176	350	824	542	68		259	1813	850	

SUMMARY.

	70·4	135	67·4	125	98	130	172	175	325	320	516	52	102	238	1535	786	1541
Variation from No. to No.	*38*	*52*	*30*	*39, 51*	*51*	*30*	*40*	*52*	*30.37*	*111, 218*	*40*	*30*	*36*	*5*	*5*	*5*	*5*
	85·2	179	84·5	144	120	154	201	229	369	375	567	73	133	284	1918	935	1843
Mean	*33*	*20*	*8*	*11*	*14*	*16*	*45*	*20*	*47*	*30*	*45*	*43*	*30*	*18*	*30*	*42*	*22*
	77·3	157	74·3	135	109	141	189	211	347	342	543	63	112	258	1755	855	1690
Average.	77·3	157	74·4	135	109	141	187	211	347	342	543	63	112	259	1768	850	1696

Name of Caste or Tribe—BHANGI.

No. (1)	Height of Vertex (2)	Height of Trunk (3)	Span (4)	Left Foot (5)	Left Middle Finger (6)	Right Ear Height (7)	Head Round (8)	Inion to Glabella (9)	Tragus to Tragus (10)	Vertex to Chin (11)	Antero-posterior Diameter (12)	Maximum Transverse Diameter (13)	Minimum Frontal Diameter (14)	Bizygomatic Diameter (15)	Cephalic Index (16)	General Index (17)	Frontal Index (18)
1	1706	841	1841	272	117	63	523	345	340	216	191	134	…	…	70·1	…	…
2	1633	820	1701	241	107	64	513	343	335	221	183	140	…	…	76·5	…	…
3	1579	787	1615	241	110	61	533	343	333	221	190	139	…	…	73·2	…	…
4	1701	884	1711	274	107	69	546	358	371	249	191	142	116	129	74·3	153	88·9
5	1635	843	1738	257	116	64	538	318	315	194	183	140	119	134	74·5	151	86·0
6	1633	843	1610	239	103	64	541	345	335	203	192	110	108	128	73·9	159	82·4
7	1562	797	1600	221	98	58	513	330	315	213	185	131	108	133	70·8	160	81·8
8	1722	838	1838	264	117	58	554	356	330	213	199	133	107	186	66·8	149	90·5
9	1618	815	1752	264	114	64	508	338	335	203	185	113	118	133	71·9	155	83·1
10	1691	845	1790	259	112	63	508	380	318	203	184	112	112	135	77·2	150	83·6
11	1625	846	1737	249	110	58	531	323	323	208	186	134	105	135	77·3	154	77·2
12	1762	853	1765	262	112	61	537	348	361	210	193	136	109	135	70·5	156	77·8
13	1652	785	1733	217	107	56	530	341	333	245	188	131	107	131	69·7	139	84·4
14	1650	830	1740	245	120	63	517	325	385	220	193	138	110	139	75·8	158	77·5
15	1672	833	1785	265	100	58	515	350	360	195	180	140	100	131	72·9	149	78·6
16	1667	797	1608	255	104	59	585	325	317	217	181	134	103	135	74·4	160	74·7
17	1602	812	1789	241	119	70	546	343	340	217	190	133	112	136	72·8	161	77·4
18	1703	828	1696	265	104	63	536	365	359	224	189	144	115	130	75·8	160	77·8
19	1695	854	1774	253	121	61	544	370	370	223	193	141	97	133	74·1	172	82·1
20	1743	890	1733	247	117	66	543	344	343	220	193	138	115	140	68·9	163	72·9
21	1686	890	1769	260	119	60	524	345	356	210	187	140	104	135	72·0	159	68·1
22	1700	892	1735	261	110	63	558	381	350	205	203	134	115	188	71·1	163	77·6
23	1671	846	1745	260	111	59	5·8	360	338	213	184	138	117	186	68·3	158	83·3
24	1685	857	…	280	110	69	5·0	335	345	…	185	142	110	133	77·2	151	88·4
25	1698	876	…	…	…	16	53)	345	…	…	…	140	…	…	75·7	159	78·6

No.																	
26	1648	828	1727	259	120	61	552	849	343	203	200	185	116	142	67·5	143	85·9
27	1663	850	1705	240	118	67	525	336	353	198	180	140	108	134	77·7	144	77·1
28	1675	870	1721	273	110	69	546	370	366	210	183	188	113	139	75·4	151	81·9
29	1637	820	1717	252	114	59	530	332	341	211	177	188	107	134	78·0	157	77·5
30	1693	805	1770	259	110	57	523	339	352	227	179	182	98	126	73·2	162	68·2
31	1690	870	1665	255	102	03	535	343	359	209	189	140	115	129	74·1	176	82·1
32	1720	850	1820	262	112	57	545	840	330	211	200	132	110	129	66·0	163	83·1
33	1730	875	1745	263	111	61	555	852	338	226	197	198	117	186	70·1	155	84·8
34	1748	865	1825	277	113	08	555	852	355	199	200	188	109	181	69·0	173	79·0
35	1640	825	1732	246	111	56	522	835	310	195	186	126	98	130	67·7	153	77·8
36	1490	770	1495	227	103	59	521	839	343	205	183	133	92	124	73·7	157	69·2
37	1619	830	1632	249	110	68	511	825	337	202	177	131	99	126	74·0	163	75·6
38	1621	820	1711	250	112	62	501	810	330	206	178	132	94	126	74·2	140	71·2
39	1630	830	1605	232	104	62	532	863	360	199	186	139	103	134	74·5	154	74·1
40	1623	815	1651	255	109	56	585	852	310	202	183	139	105	129	75·4	154	71·8
41	1614	825	1647	245	107	56	527	852	339	201	187	135	97	129	72·2	157	72·1
42	1622	835	1711	250	111	57	539	945	349	198	186	140	101	132	75·3	152	75·6
43	1663	855	1730	247	107	65	530	859	352	207	183	185	102	131	71·8	151	71·5
44	1649	830	1672	248	103	59	537	847	322	205	190	130	93	121	68·4	165	77·6
45	1615	819	1679	256	110	63	531	837	330	206	178	188	107	131	77·5	156	76·6
46	1650	830	1749	260	112	57	535	840	319	204	180	187	105	133	76·1	155	72·7
47	1690	860	1765	254	105	63	530	852	341	193	185	182	96	127	71·4	161	75·9
48	1595	805	1619	250	104	60	520	340	333	190	177	137	104	130	77·4	148	73·5
49	1609	816	1555	251	103	69	524	350	340	190	180	138	100	120	75·6	147	75·6
50	1649	800	1697	257	108	53	515	333	333	185	176	187	103	131	77·8	141	75·2
Variation From No.	1490 *(36)*	770 *(36)*	1495 *(36)*	221 *(7)*	98 *(7)*	53 *(50)*	501 *(38)*	310 *(38)*	310 *(35)*	190 *(49)*	177 *(29,37,48)*	128 *(35)*	90 *(30)*	121 *(44)*	66·0 *(32)*	139 *(14)*	68·2 *(30)*
to No.	1762 *(12)*	892 *(22)*	1841 *(1)*	277 *(34)*	121 *(20)*	70 *(18)*	558 *(23)*	370 *(19,28)*	371 *(4)*	249 *(4)*	202 *(23)*	144 *(18)*	119 *(6)*	142 *(26)*	78·0 *(29)*	176 *(37)*	95·0 *(6)*
Mean	1650	833	1727	255	110	60	531	343	340	206	186	137	103	125	73·0	156	78·0
Average	1658	836	1716	254	110	61	535	343	340	210	187	136	98	121	73·0	156	78·2

Name of Caste or Tribe—PATHAN.

Frontal Index.	General Index.	Cephalic Index.	Bizygomatic Diameter.	Minimum Frontal Diameter.	Maximum Transverse Diameter.	Antero-posterior Diameter.	Vertex to Chin.	Tragus to Tragus.	Inion to Glabella.	Bound Head.	Right Ear, Height.	Left Middle Finger.	Left Foot.	Span.	Height of Trunk.	Height of Vertex.	No.
18	17	16	15	14	13	12	11	10	9	8	7	6	5	4	3	2	1
79·7	104	72·2	134	114	143	198	220	353	350	569	61	114	259	1752	838	1666	1
78·7	163	78·8	128	111	141	179	208	356	330	523	64	112	267	1635	825	1572	2
79·4	169	75·1	128	108	180	181	210	350	338	518	63	102	251	1686	844	1625	3
80·1	176	74·2	131	113	141	190	240	343	338	538	58	110	234	1691	797	1612	4
85·4	160	72·9	132	117	137	188	211	345	325	520	64	112	239	1711	846	1668	5
86·0	176	71·1	136	123	143	201	240	360	360	561	61	114	272	1777	863	1700	6
77·5	154	73·6	130	110	142	193	209	360	350	545	65	102	247	1647	803	1675	7
81·5	161	72·2	131	114	135	197	211	342	352	538	60	104	251	1695	890	1657	8
84·4	150	72·9	132	110	135	185	198	318	325	525	67	102	240	1560	840	1555	9
79·7	158	73·8	130	116	138	197	208	322	333	535	63	109	250	1662	830	1618	10
80·0	153	75·1	139	99	145	173	213	367	351	543	68	110	257	1705	843	1720	11
70·2	156	75·4	131	97	141	187	209	342	345	550	63	112	259	1705	848	1729	12
68·8	156	73·8	180	106	141	191	203	353	338	539	60	118	204	1812	890	1680	13
75·9	148	74·3	185	99	140	187	2·0	351	344	540	62	127	274	1905	950	1605	14
71·1	161	74·9	128	104	139	187	190	340	340	531	57	105	240	1680	844	1620	15
74·3	160	69·2	135	100	140	195	218	353	316	544	65	111	251	1670	833	1670	16
74·4	161	76·8	134	108	135	190	223	350	360	544	65	120	266	1767	839	1755	17
74·0	178	73·3	137	102	148	191	220	368	365	543	66	113	252	1695	860	1566	18
72·8	15·	70·9	125	100	140	188	223	357	349	553	69	121	270	1760	924	1745	19
77·6	14·	75·7	127	110	129	185	2·0	328	834	538	67	102	238	1583	812	1590	20
78·6	162	73·2	186	100	140	183	202	345	322	534	58	125	276	1732	845	1665	21
74·6	160	80·1	184	110	134	176	217	346	827	518	55	107	238	1627	819	1755	22
78·0	169	75·7	128	98	141	181	205	350	350	529	60	118	249	1742	858	1735	23
71·5	178	74·1	188	110	187	185	2·0	352	859	529	61	120	268	1753	903		24
76·6			130	105	187		225	300		541		121	278	1839	901		25

No.	C1	C2	C3	C4	C5	C6	C7	C8	C9	C10	C11	C12	C13	C14	C15	C16	C17
26	75·0	181	74·8	125	100	132	177	236	350	848	529	61	113	274	1835	840	1739
27	73·0	178	75·4	132	103	141	187	235	365	360	552	59	108	270	1805	885	1710
28	77·2	168	73·9	129	105	136	184	217	350	359	533	60	105	251	1725	880	1700
29	75·0	171	72·9	132	105	140	192	226	360	863	540	67	115	277	1867	905	1775
30	75·4	157	75·5	137	107	142	198	215	340	363	546	63	110	261	1719	845	1650
31	69·9	177	76·5	128	100	143	187	223	361	350	556	64	114	270	1909	865	1810
32	69·3	140	73·3	185	97	140	191	189	359	356	549	59	120	283	1865	895	1770
33	77·9	148	76·1	133	109	140	184	197	350	353	544	63	110	254	1768	890	1725
34	73·9	163	74·5	128	109	138	184	209	360	340	550	60	111	250	1730	840	1635
35	77·7	148	77·2	130	102	139	180	193	352	360	550	60	107	248	1610	815	1593
36	72·7	139	76·3	127	102	135	177	176	350	336	521	54	110	249	1670	780	1610
37	74·8	151	72·3	129	101	130	181	195	310	320	530	52	109	247	1699	820	1635
38	72·3	151	73·3	130	95	137	187	191	347	330	537	59	110	251	1784	870	1715
39	75·2	152	76·5	132	103	140	183	201	330	345	540	63	109	260	1841	880	1721
40	78·6	136	73·1	129	110	139	190	179	360	339	551	61	111	252	1720	840	1665
41	75·6	152	75·1	140	105	133	177	196	350	352	525	59	107	236	1710	885	1715
42	72·2	134	79·0	139	98	147	186	187	350	362	519	61	103	255	1710	845	1640
43	72·8	146	76·2	142	107	147	193	200	370	325	572	66	140	274	1782	860	1700
44	76·9	159	74·3	135	113	138	179	207	313	347	535	56	112	255	1750	865	1695
45	72·7	142	75·5	133	110	139	184	215	340	810	532	59	107	242	1651	823	1665
46	71·2	146	77·6	130	99	137	178	189	345	320	500	61	105	245	1710	325	1600
47	82·7	165	71·5	127	109	133	186	190	321	350	522	60	108	252	1720	820	1615
48	71·2	166	70·4	130	109	133	189	210	350	350	518	59	112	249	1790	834	1720
49	80·0	150	71·7	130	104	137	191	216	360	350	53	30	115	271	1820	865	1765
50	75·2	150	74·9	139	107	140	187	218	350	370	562	61	107	257	1705	820	1660
Variation From	68·8	134	69·2	125	95	129	176	176	318	310	500	52	102	238	1560	780	1555
No.	13	42	17	19,26	37	20	23	36	9	46	46	37	3,7,9	20,22	9	36	9
To	86·0	181	80·1	139	123	147	201	240	370	370	572	68	127	283	1939	950	1830
No.	6	26	23	11,43,50	6	42,43	6	6	43	50	43	29	14	32	31	14	14
Mean	75·2	158	74·4	131	105	139	187	208	350	941	539	61	111	255	1735	859	1680
Aver	75·2	158	74·4	132	106	139	186	208	350	337	539	60	111	254	1736	858	1680

SUMMARY

Name of Custe or Tribe—MURAO.

No.	Height of Vertex.	Height of Trunk.	Span.	Left Foot.	Left Middle Finger.	Right Ear Height.	Round Head.	Inion to Glabella.	Tragus to Tragus.	Vertex to Chin.	Antero-posterior Diameter.	Maximum Transverse Diameter.	Minimum Frontal Diameter.	Bizygomatic Diameter.	Cephalic Index.	General Index.	Ophthalmic Index.	Frontal Index.
	2	3	4	5	6	7	8	9	10	11	12	13	14	15	16	17	19
1	1709	835	1820	249	112	61	549	353	338	203	191	140			73.3			
2	1633	795	1742	267	114	64	543	361	333	198	190	140			73.7			
3	1617	795	1643	241	107	58	536	348	338	190	184	140			76.1			
4	1620	834	1661	259	107	61	531	351	340	198	191	139			76.8			
5	1678	820	1722	251	104	58	521	333	333	198	183	139			76.4			
6	1676	813	1742	259	107	66	538	340	335	190	191	138			72.3			
7	1653	848	1706	241	110	64	533	336	350	211	190	138			72.6			
8	1658	835	1815	269	117	58	554	345	335	203	199	141			72.9			
9	1615	790	1651	236	107	60	526	338	330	200	182	134			73.6			
10	1656	850	1704	251	112	61	528	338	335	201	183	138			75.8			
11	1645	8.0	1717	251	112	64	546	366	350	216	192	139	109	181	72.4	103		80.1
12	1617	792	1625	257	104	66	559	356	356	208	194	142	105	185	73.7	151		76.8
13	1618	833	1625	250	106	63	532	337	356	214	189	136	116	140	72.0	157		83.5
14	1657	820	1755	259	115	63	536	340	355	204	183	138	109	138	71.5	152		76.2
15	1612	800	1727	203	117	67	548	343	335	220	193	139	103	121	72.4	168		75.8
16	1640	845	1670	217	110	60	530	340	350	210	183	143	108	132	68.1	157		77.1
17	1635	837	1727	247	112	60	533	330	350	203	189	132	104	129	74.1	178		75.4
18	1587	810	1665	241	112	65	550	352	358	207	198	140	110	130	69.7	172		77.8
19	1650	833	1783	250	117	60	545	336	348	230	190	138	103	132	77.8	155		76.9
20	1583	820	1578	241	103	59	535	330	337	223	189	140	107	127	70.9	162		75.5
21	1632	835	1655	233	101	65	525	339	336	205	185	184	98	138	71.4	189		73.5
22	1636	827	1770	240	115	66	520	329	345	208	181	132	110	131	73.5	103		73.9
23	1586	850	1635	252	112	66	545	310	335	185	192	133	115	138	74.5	148		76.9
24	1631	845	1725	245	110		555	340		218	197	143						
25	1658	865	1830	262	118	58				204		139			70.6			88.7

No.																	
26	79·5	162	66·8	130	105	132	192	211	338	385	588	55	118	260	1925	850	1705
27	81·2	148	75·4	185	112	138	183	200	332	390	520	58	110	245	1730	845	1680
28	:	165	69·6	121	......	128	184	200	322	388	514	62	114	260	1786	843	1682
29	72·1	147	79·1	186	161	140	177	200	350	340	533	82	111	256	1745	845	1570
30	71·9	154	77·2	127	160	139	180	195	339	383	540	55	108	249	1680	823	1615
31	79·0	141	79·8	140	113	148	181	198	345	335	532	63	108	254	1685	847	1645
32	79·2	100	75·8	137	117	138	189	203	330	393	530	54	108	247	1700	833	1625
33	78·1	166	73·7	181	110	137	186	217	385	390	535	55	104	241	1565	795	1535
34	81·5	151	75·8	183	161	135	178	207	320	823	515	66	107	243	1700	815	1605
35	73·8	160	74·9	125	107	187	183	200	339	824	530	60	107	227	1625	870	1576
36	68·4	165	75·3	121	107	133	178	200	330	849	515	58	105	250	1712	786	1610
37	75·6	159	75·4	127	106	135	179	190	345	345	523	51	106	230	1587	780	1530
38	68·2	153	76·3	180	104	142	186	194	350	340	536	59	104	254	1725	880	1630
39	74·1	157	74·2	181	100	135	182	206	360	851	535	62	117	253	1750	800	1632
40	69·1	165		127	96	139	:	210	345	360	519	53	110	252	1698	880	1600
41	73·9	174	74·3	120	100	130	175	209	331	380	525	56	110	246	1570	805	1555
42	79·0	176	74·5	125	99	137	184	220	360	870	554	66	104	244	1624	835	1644
43	75·4	170	74·3	122	105	130	175	207	350	844	525	56	110	249	1693	830	1670
44	72·3	145	74·1	138	108	137	185	191	324	831	530	62	115	270	1687	833	1653
45	82·1	154	80·1	134	100	140	175	206	344	344	530	54	99	265	1715	89	16.5
46	80·0	148	77·5	130	110	135	177	180	330	830	540	60	115	279	1660	830	1672
47	74·6	:	76·1	128	105	134	176	:	320	835	570	53	120	244	1725	840	1640
48	81·5	:	71·1	125	100	135	190	:	350	350	560	58	115	254	1800	865	1733
49	79·5	144	68·4	130	110	131	193	187	360	870	540	64	115		1655	815	1600
50	84·6	:	71·0	134	105	130	183	:	340	820		53	115	254	1705	820	1620

SUMMARY.

	66·2	139	68·4	120	91	128	175	185	330	324	514	51	101	227	1565	780	1530
Variation from No.	38	23	49	41	36	28	41, 43·45	23	34·47	35	28	37	21	35	3·3	37	37
to No.	83·5	178	80·1	140	116	143	199	230	360	370	570	67	120	279	1825	870	1738
	15	19	45	15, 31	15	16, 24, 31	8	19	39, 42, 49	42, 49	48	15	48	48	26	35	48
Mean Avrge	76·6	157	74·3	130	105	138	185	204	340	340	534	60	110	250	1704	530	1632
	76·6	158	75·3	133	105	137	185	204	341	342	534	63	110	251	1701	688	1633

Name of Caste or Tribe—GUJAR.

No.	Height of Vertex	Height of Trunk	Span	Left Foot	Left Middle Finger	Right Ear Height	Round Head	Glabella to Inion	Tragus to Tragus	Vertex to Chin	Antero-Posterior Diameter	Maximum Transverse Diameter	Minimum Frontal Diameter	Bizygomatic Diameter	Cephalic Index	General Index	Frontal Index
1	1653	841	1750	241	112	76	538	358	348	213	199	134	110	133	67.3	160	82.1
2	1639	783	1696	251	103	66	536	330	345	213	180	141			78.3		
3	1673	820	1691	241	104	64	513	343	359	206	186	143			77.2		
4	1734	881	1767	267	110	69	513	358	395	231	191	137			71.7		
5	1636	818	1728	257	107	69	531	343	386	178	181	130	114	140	71.8	161	78.6
6	1639	922	1930	284	124	71	564	381	370	188	209	140	115	131	68.9	164	82.1
7	1663	823	1711	269	114	68	561	320	350	206	190	145			76.3		
8	1620	818	1671	234	103	63	513	302	399	215	175	140	111	142	80.0	168	75.0
9	1755		1839	207	117		554	348	353		195	147	115	130	74.4	175	81.6
10	1813	890	1927	274	122	62	564	348	345	239	201	148			74.1		
11	1678	818	1837	264	117	62	541	320	340	228	190	141			70.1		
12	1633		1635	249	103		561	350	356	210	201	149	119	139	71.8	155	81.0
13	1722	871	1770	254	113	69	564	301	348	210	205	139	119	145	70.1	152	81.0
14	1741	828	1683	272	114	69	516	838	317	208	181	133	99	127	67.8	166	72.8
15	1653	821	1734	254	114	71	539	381	317	211	192	130	108	139	72.9	153	77.3
16	1539	805	1673	249	107	70	556	345	333	216	194	141	106	140	67.8	162	74.1
17	1770	894	1910	251	112	69	551	350	370	221	194	143	102	135	72.7	167	74.5
18	1673	843	1719	249	99	64	559	856	378	215	193	140	111	141	73.7	157	79.9
19	1833	802	1867	285	122	66	563	343	339	221	204	147	114	135	72.5	167	82.0
20	1674	850	1757	250	113	72	550	337	345	211	186	147			72.1		
21	1678	797	1753	261	113	65	533	348	353	213	191	136			79.0		
22	1774	830	1935	276	127	70	545	333	348	213	196	141			71.2		
23	1613	799	1683	241	105	71	543	852	345	225	184	143			71.9		
24	1553	800	1687	237	103	05	527	830	344	222	192	137			74.5		
25	1617	829	1703	258	100	70	546	840	350	222	192	139			73.4		
26	1613	810	1677	240	106	63	543	850	350	226	191	139	114	135	72.8	167	82.0

No.																	
27	80·7	161	74·9	187	113	140	197	221	340	345	537	62	106	247	1755	870	1687
28	75·0	163	77·8	134	108	144	195	218	348	342	540	62	108	248	1725	833	1661
29	73·1	153	79·2	135	106	143	183	208	360	390	530	63	113	257	1755	820	1646
30	88·7	104	69·3	133	110	133	192	218	350	840	541	70	119	245	1727	875	1662
31	74·3	155	73·7	139	104	140	192	215	345	845	560	60	117	278	1765	865	1715
32	76·2	167	69·6	135	103	185	190	225	335	355	555	65	111	268	1740	842	1685
33	88·7	151	74·0	136	115	139	194	200	335	328	535	61	110	235	1770	827	1662
34	78·5	155	74·6	130	113	144	183	201	336	840	538	69	100	253	1677	850	1625
35	82·2	155	78·5	134	120	146	193	208	315	830	539	69	104	253	1820	850	1715
36	82·7	153	71·3	131	115	189	186	200	350	870	567	61		255	1725	875	1710
37	76·9	158	71·0	130	103	134	196	206	337	358	552	56	108	280	1810	846	1755
38	78·9	141	71·8	132	105	133	189	186	362	330	542	62	118	276	1855	925	1831
39	89·7	160	70·0	181	101	143	189	210	340	867	555	57	115	278	1856	870	1770
40	78·5	167	74·4	131	100	139	195	219	395	860	545	64	110	258	1877	890	1780
41	69·7	165	71·3	130	103	186	186	214	353	868	547	60	109	279	1714	880	1710
42	71·9	147	74·8	183	97	185	191	196	351	338	533	58	114	280	1752	850	1743
43	75·7	140	74·3	131	105	130	181	181	330	323	519	59	128	280	1821	900	1720
44	71·9	150	73·8	127	107	138	175	190	335	343	531	65	123	243	1835	810	1770
45	80·8	163	69·1	28	101	130	187	208	330	320	535	61	115	261	1815	872	1745
46	77·5	177	69·9	30	100	134	186	230	323	850	564	59	120	259	1853	846	1765
47	77·7	143	76·4	40	108	143	194	211	310	850	535	55	114	250	1753	852	1701
48	74·7	168	72·2	133	99	140	187	233	355	875	564	61	110	263	1830	837	1700
49	75·5	105	75·4	130	111	138	194	215	355	830	535	61	105	250	1700	837	1633
50	80·4	165	79·4	123	108	143	183	203	335	825	550	56	140	263	1837	832	1720
Variation from No.	69·7 *39*	140 *43*	67·3 *1*	123 *50*	97 *42*	130 *5,15,43*	175 *8,43*	178 *5*	317 *4,15*	302 *8*	513 *8*	55 *47*	99 *18*	237 *24*	1627 *24*	782 *2*	1560 *24*
to No.	88·7 *30,33*	177 *46*	80·0 *8*	145 *20*	120 *35*	149 *12*	209 *6*	239 *10*	378 *20*	381 *6*	586 *19*	76 *1,16*	124 *6*	285 *19*	1930 *6*	925 *38*	1838 *6*
Mean Average	78·5 / 77·5	160 / 159	73·5 / 73·5	133 / 134	108 / 108	140 / 140	191 / 189	213 / 210	345 / 345	354 / 358	544 / 545	64 / 65	112 / 113	257 / 260	1787 / 1767	833 / 832	1700 / 1688

SUMMARY.

Name of Caste or Tribe—CHAUHAN.

No.	Height of Vertex.	Height of Trunk.	Span.	Left Foot.	Left Middle Finger.	Right Ear Height.	Round Head.	Ilion to Glabella.	Tragus to Tragus.	Vertex to Chin.	Antero-posterior Diameter.	Maximum Transverse Diameter.	Minimum Frontal Diameter.	Bizygomatic Diameter.	Cephalic Index.	General Index.	Frontal Index.
	2	3	4	5	6	7	8	9	10	11	12	13	14	15	16	17	18
1	1517	...	1689	257	107	69	528	305	333	...	180	140	...	...	77.8	...	72.6
2	1663	833	1671	263	102	69	516	315	353	230	190	157	114	139	82.7	165	...
3	1694	...	1747	269	112	64	556	325	343	...	195	145	...	...	73.3	...	...
4	1635	...	1663	240	107	64	513	312	331	...	180	138	...	...	76.7	...	...
5	1671	...	1760	267	112	64	546	338	323	...	191	142	...	...	73.2	...	...
6	1597	...	1658	246	107	69	531	315	333	...	183	146	...	...	79.5	...	...
7	1691	...	1830	262	117	69	556	335	345	...	200	135	...	...	66.8	...	74.5
8	1717	850	1787	269	119	71	549	340	343	221	202	135	105	132	77.5	164	79.7
9	1816	840	1835	270	119	61	530	319	390	217	182	111	114	131	74.1	163	89.3
10	1693	885	1737	247	110	60	551	330	379	218	183	141	117	136	65.9	154	81.9
11	1725	864	1715	255	119	59	537	315	340	210	190	131	117	131	88.4	159	81.0
12	1633	832	1632	244	119	63	533	338	338	208	177	143	111	132	70.3	169	81.7
13	1633	875	1625	249	105	64	517	335	354	224	195	137	116	137	73.1	145	77.5
14	1700	845	1610	252	111	60	545	310	355	209	190	142	100	130	73.0	178	76.3
15	1593	815	1632	246	96	61	500	345	334	205	178	129	102	127	68.6	161	81.8
16	1570	840	1657	247	110	62	525	358	315	208	191	131	106	129	71.6	151	77.3
17	1610	815	1690	247	111	61	552	340	352	217	194	139	112	135	71.0	161	80
18	1638	815	1630	248	103	64	536	332	315	220	193	137	102	130	70.9	164	73.9
19	1605	848	1720	239	103	58	542	345	350	217	186	132	112	127	73.5	163	81.3
20	1620	832	...	240	108	67	533	332	355	215	189	139	102	137	73.6	145	83.2
21	1535	830	1757	250	115	73	523	345	315	199	182	134	98	131	71.3	157	78.1
22	1663	859	1775	269	110	65	585	332	321	200	185	134	109	131	70.0	144	...
23	1703	810	1650	228	106	54	548	339	363	220	194	137	114	126	...	144	...
24	1601	852	1745	239	110	60	510	345	398	199	171	133	96	119	76.4	167	...
25	1657	870	1893	249	120	68	580	334	330	199	170	120	105	126	...	158	...
26	1745	...	...	...	...	...	549	370	331	218	187	139	108	138	74.3	104	74.3

27	1670	839	1756	240	115	52	550	350	359	212	183	140	96	125	76·5	170	68·6
28	1695	835	1749	257	112	64	535	344	351	197	180	132	103	126	73·3	156	78·0
29	1640	818	1722	258	110	64	510	320	340	216	174	136	99	132	78·1	164	72·8
30	1650	845	1749	247	114	55	534	330	350	206	179	140	103	123	78·2	167	73·6
31	1712	855	1816	256	111	63	575	357	362	219	202	148	108	140	73·3	156	73·0
32	1618	820	1692	248	110	62	540	343	365	226	188	140	108	129	74·5	175	77·1
33	1716	855	1845	264	122	63	553	310	358	224	194	148	117	146	76·8	153	79·1
34	1750	845	1785	258	114	68	520	335	357	230	181	143	109	134	79·0	172	76·2
35	1605	793	1695	248	100	65	552	345	337	221	199	139	110	136	69·8	163	79·1
36	1610	820	1690	244	112	60	548	348	355	230	190	147	111	184	77·4	172	75·5
37	1638	833	1748	240	110	69	562	352	355	218	200	145	112	141	72·5	155	77·2
38	1612	812	1698	288	108	64	545	325	338	225	178	138	106	130	77·5	173	76·8
39	1627	825	1650	235	104	63	528	335	355	217	183	143	109	133	78·1	163	76·6
40	1605	790	1630	236	106	59	530	330	335	218	184	140	106	131	76·1	166	75·5
41	1630	870	1700	260	113	71	525	340	345	212	183	130	94	132	71·0	161	72·3
42	1703	880	1760	270	117	63	561	360	316	230	196	139	104	135	70·9	170	74·8
43	1720	810	1821	275	112	64	525	335	338	...	...	...	...	...	...	...	...
44	1586	810	1740	245	113	62	534	334	325	213	185	130	100	120	75·7	178	76·9
45	1735	867	1838	266	116	59	528	305	325	223	178	130	115	124	72·5	180	88·5
46	1603	820	1710	253	111	64	543	331	338	214	190	135	100	131	71·1	163	74·1
47	1532	765	1615	234	111	59	512	324	341	...	...	...	...	...	...	...	...
48	1603	810	1665	240	107	63	550	360	350	224	187	140	109	130	74·9	172	77·9
49	1620	820	1690	251	108	60	509	325	335	220	176	130	106	127	73·9	174	81·5
50	1680	815	1770	250	109	60	518	325	335	223	175	138	97	127	78·9	176	70·2
									SUMMARY								
Variation from	1532	765	1600	234	100	52	500	305	320	197	170	123	94	119	66·8	145	68·6
No.	*47*	*47*	*15*	*47*	*35*	*27*	*15*	*1, 45*	*22*	*28*	*25*	*24*	*41*	*24*	*8*	*14, 20*	*27*
to	1816	890	1885	275	122	73	575	370	380	230	202	157	117	146	86·4	180	88·5
No.	*9*	*9*	*9*	*43*	*33*	*21*	*31*	*26*	*9*	*2, 34, 36, 42*	*8, 31*	*2*	*11, 12, 33*	*33*	*12*	*45*	*45*
Mean	1650	818	1740	252	111	63	535	335	345	211	187	139	107	132	73·4	164	77·4
Average.	1651	818	1743	256	113	63	536	336	345	211	188	139	108	131	74·4	162	77·4

ANTHROPOLOGICAL SCRAPS.

To

THE HONORARY SECRETARY,

ANTHROPOLOGICAL SOCIETY,

BOMBAY.

DEAR SIR,

I beg to take the liberty of drawing the attention of the Society to the following points of difference, bordering on antagonism, among the customs prevailing among the Aryan and Semitic Nations, now settled in India, I mean the Hindus and the Mahomedans :—

(1) The Hindu writes from left to right; the Mahomedan from right to left.

(2) The Hindu scriptures commence from the left ; the Mahomedan books from the right

(3) The Hindu in going round his place of worship goes from left to right ; the Mahomedan the contrary way.

(4) The Hindu (represented by the Brahmin) shaves his face and keeps a tuft of hair on his head ; the orthodox Mahomedan takes a clean shave of his crown, but never allows the razor to touch his beard, which he considers to be "*noor-i-khuda*," i. e., "the light of God." The Hindu can never take a clean shave of his crown, unless he becomes a *sanyasi*.

(5) The Hindu, when he wants to perform his ablutions, begins by washing his feet and hands and lastly his face. In fact, the orthodox Hindu, especially a Brahmin, cannot enter his house without first washing his feet. On the other hand, the Mahomedan begins by washing his face, and then goes on to his lower extremities.

(6) If, for instance, a Hindu and a Mahomedan are walking on the road, and meet an obstacle, it invariably happens that the Hindu moves to his left and the Mahomedan to his right.

(7) Even in such an ordinary matter as grinding corn in a hand-mill the Hindu woman turns it from left to right ; the Mahomedan from right to left.

These diametrically opposed customs are very curious. Other observers may formulate the causes.

Yours faithfully,

R. VASUDEVA RAO,

B. A., A. G. M.,

Principal, Dharmwant College.

AN INTERESTING VEDIC CEREMONY.

A correspondent writes :—An interesting Vedic ceremony, called Atirudra, meaning the Great Offering to god Rudra, is now being performed at his Bhuleshwar residence by Mr. Jagmohandas Vandravandas Bhaisett, one of the Municipal Corporators of that ward. The ceremony, which is believed to be the first of its kind ever performed in Bombay, began on Thursday last, and will be concluded on Monday next. A visit during the performance of the ceremony, especially going round the sacrificial booth, is believed to confer great spiritual merit, especially during the present especially holy Hindoo month of Shrawan, and numbers of Hindoos of all classes attend from morning to eve to earn their quota of merit   Rudra, or the "Howler" as all readers of Max Müller and Barth know, is one of the chief early Vedic gods. He is the god of storm, and father of the Maruts or lightning and tempest gods. Rudra is armed with the thunderbolt, and is author of sudden deaths. He is a near relation of the gods of rain and wind. He and the troops at his command are invoked as protectors of the house, the fields, the herds, and the roads. He is the patron of craftsmen, of cart-wrights, carpenters, smiths, potters, hunters, and watermen, and is himself a crafty merchant ; but he is also the head of armies, the god of the brave, of foot soldiers, and of all those who live by the bow, the sword, and the spear. It is his cry which echoes in the thick of battle, and his voice which resounds in the war drum. He is also a bandit, the patron of thieves, of freebooters and brigands, of all those who go forth by night in troops and live on plunder. He is also the god of beggars and *fakirs*, and by himself, or by the numberless spirits under him, he is omnipresent in houses, fields, rivers, fountains, in the wind and the passing cloud, in the grass as it springs up, in the tree as it grows green, in the leaf ,as it falls. But his dwelling is specially in forests and solitary places, and he reigns over the mountains. The figure which stands out from this piece of rude realism as given in the chief Yajurveda hymn to the hundred Rudras, has very little in it of Brahmanic ritual or sacred custom. The above array of epithets is pretty sufficient to assimilate him with Shiv or Mahadeo, an adoption which savants belive was *un fait accompli* several centuries before our era. The old Vedic god Rudra was not a sovereign deity ; but in later Hindooism he is elevated to the rank of Mahadev or the Great God. With his followers he is the greatest of all ; with everybody he is one of the greatest, who has none equal or superior to him, except Brahma or Vishnu. The Dumar Lena cave at Ellora, and the main cave at Elephanta, shew very clearly in its general weird and fierce outline the face of Rudra in the famous three-headed bust called the *Trimurti*. This *Atirudra* sacrifice, then, is an oblation with prayers to this all-powerful sovereign god. In its grossest sense, a sacrifice is a mere bargain, a giving and receiving between god and man. To the religious sense, sacrifice is an act of affection and gratitude towards the god, through which man renders him thanks for benefits and hopes to obtain others in the future, either in this life or after death. 1,361 prayers have to be recited every day for eleven days, and the total number of offerings, which are of clarified butter and black sesamum, amount to the number of 2,357,201. This heavy work of reciting so many prayers and offering such a large number of oblations is being performed at this sacrifice by sixty Brahmans learned in all the Vedas, who recite prayers and present offerings from eight in the morning to five in the afternoon. A special *mandap* or booth is erected for this sacrifice. It is supported on seventeen pillars of a uniform height regulated by the height of the person performing the sacrifice, and contains in the middle the main altar or *Vedi* on which a gold image of Rudra is installed, while all round it, at prescribed distances, are nine other sacrificial pits or *kunds* of a uniform depth, but shaped in different geometrical patterns in which the offerings of clarified butter and sesamum are cast and burnt. Besides Rudra all the numerous gods of the Hindoo Pantheon, as also the mothers, the planets, and various minor deities have been invoked and installed all round the altar and the *mandap*. The most interesting ceremonies took place on Thursday last which was the opening day, while Monday, being the concluding day, will have an equally interesting array of Vedic prayers, rites, and the final offering.

THE JOURNAL

OF THE

ANTHROPOLOGICAL SOCIETY

OF

BOMBAY.

THE SEVENTH ANNUAL GENERAL MEETING was held on Wednesday, the 22nd February 1893.

MR. KHARSETJI RASTAMJI CAMA, *Vice-President*, in the Chair.

The Minutes of the previous Meeting were read and confirmed.

The election of the following new members was announced :—
P. Beni Madho, Private Secretary to V. B. P. Lall Chandra Guru to H. H. Maharaja Kishore Singji, C.I.E., Jodhpore Marwar.

The following donation was announced, and thanks voted to the donor :—

To the Museum.

From Mr. ISAAC BENJAMIN, Slippers worn by Arab Ladies at Zanzibar.

The following office-bearers were elected for the ensuing year :—

PRESIDENT.

Dr. P. PETERSON.

VICE-PRESIDENTS.

Rev. D. MACKICHAN.

Mr. H. A. ACWORTH.

„ JIVANJI JAMSHEDJI MODI.

„ C. E. G. CRAWFORD.

11

COUNCIL.

Ex-Officio Member.

Mr. H. H. Risley, Past President.

Ordinary Members.

Mr. G. A. T. Bennett.

„ Tribhuvandas Mangaldas Nathubhai.

„ Basil Scott.

„ Yasavant Vasudev Athalye.

„ Nasarwanji Jivanji Readymoney.

„ Kharsetji Rastamji Cama.

Surgeon-Major G. Waters.

Mr. W. F. Sinclair.

Rao Bahadur Ganpatrao Bhaskarji.

Mr. Purrushotam Balkrishna Joshi.

„ E. J. Kitts.

„ Bahmanji Behramji Patel.

„ H. W. Barrow.

Surgeon-Major K. R. Kirtikar.

General and Literary Secretary.

Dr. J. Gerson da Cunha.

Foreign Secretary.

Mr. O. S. Pedraza.

Treasurer.

Captain W. P. Walshe.

Curator of the Museum and Librarian.

Mr. H. M. Phipson.

The Treasurer's report, showing the financial condition of the Society up to the 31st day of December 1892 was read, confirmed, and adopted.

The report of the Council was then read and adopted. It contained the following information :—

Number of Members.—At the commencement of the year there were 197 Life and Ordinary Members, and that 7 new members were elected during the year. The names of 22 members were struck off owing to deaths, resignations, &c., &c., thus leaving 182 members on the roll at the close of the year.

Meetings.—During the same period ten Ordinary Meetings were held.

Communications.—At such Meetings the following papers were read:—

List of Papers read during the year.

On Funeral Rites and Ceremonies, by Mr. Kedarnath Basu.

On some Superstitions prevalent in Bengal, by Mr. Sarat Chandra Mitra, of Chupra, Behar.

On Vestiges of Moon-worship in Behar and Bengal, by Mr. Sarat Chandra Mitra of Chupra, Behar.

Note on Burial-Customs amongst the Bhuinar Bráhmans in the Saran District, Behar, by Mr. Sarat Chandra Mitra, of Chupra, Behar.

Note on the Services rendered to the Society by the late Dr. Dymock, by Mr. Jivanji Jamshedji Modi.

On the Treatment of Cattle Disease, translated from the Tamil, by Captain J. Mills, Principal, Veterinary College Bombay.

On some Ceremonies for producing Rain, by Mr. Sarat Chandra Mitra, of Chupra, Behar.

Note on Two Idiots, by Veterinary-Captain J. Mills, Principal, Veterinary College, Bombay.

On the Persian Mâr-nameh or the Book for taking Omens from the Snakes, by Mr. Jivanji Jamshedji Modi.

On the Indian Folk-beliefs about the Tiger, by Mr. Sarat Chandra Mitra, of Chupra, Behar.

Journals.—The seventh and eighth numbers of Vol. II., and the first number of Vol. III., of the Society's Journal, were published during the year.

Donations.—Numerous donations, books and articles of Anthropological interest were received by the Society during the year.

HONORARY TREASURER'S REPORT

For the Year 1892.

STATEMENT A.

ANTHROPOLOGICAL SOCIETY OF BOMBAY

STATEMENT SHOWING THE NUMBER OF MEMBERS.

Remaining on 31st December 1891 197

Add.

Admitted from 1st January to 31st December 1892 ... 7

—

204

Deduct.

Struck off on account of Deaths 6

Resignations 13

Left India 3

— 22

—

Number of Members remaining on the 31st December

1892 182

(Signed) W. P. WALSHE,

Honorary Treasurer.

ANTHROPOLOGICAL SOCIETY OF BOMBAY,

Bombay, 31st December 1892.

STATEMENT

Statement showing the Receipts and Expenditure of the

Receipts.	Rs. a. p.	Rs. a. p.
Balance with the Bank of Bombay on the 31st December 1891 ...　...　...	....	1,384　8　10
Balance in hand of Treasurer on the 1st January 1892 (remaining from previous year)...　...　...　...　...	10　0　0	
Amount realized by Cash sale of Journals, &c., Rs. 43-2-0 and as Commission on a cheque ans. 4 ...　...	43　6　0	
Amount of Subscriptions received during 1892, as per Statement C　...	1,885　0　0	1,938　6　0*
Advance Account.		
Remaining in hands of the Honorary Curator from year 1891 ...　...　...	....	13　1
Total Rs ..	....	3,336　0　4

* Paid into the Bank of Bombay during the year Rs. 1,928-6-0
In hands of Honorary Treasurer Rs.　10-0-0

Total, Rs. 1,938-6-0

Examined and found Correct.

(Signed)　K. R. CAMA,

(　„　)　W. S. MILLARD,

Auditors.

B.

Anthropological Society of Bombay during the year 1892.

Expenditure.	Rs.	a.	p.	Rs.	a.	p.
Clothing to Peons		0	0			
Establishment	767	2	1			
House Rent (For 11 months)	550	0	0			
Stamps (including Post Cards and Postage on journals and letters, &c.)	63	15	0			
Printing Charges	982	5	0			
Stationery and Binding Charges ... - ...	18	5	6			
Miscellaneous Charges	9	0	0	2,343	11	7
Balance, *viz.* :—						
In hands of the Honorary Treasurer ...	10	0	0			
Do. do. Curator ...	13	1	6			
In the Bank of Bombay	969	3	3	992	4	9
Total Rs...	....			3,336	0	4

(Signed) W. P. WALSHE,

Honorary Treasurer.

Anthropological Society of Bombay,
Bombay, 31st December 1892.

STATEMENT

Statement showing in detail the amount of Subscriptions payable for
balance remaining

	Rs. a. p.	Rs. a. p.
Balance remaining to be recovered from previous year	......	1,025 0
AMOUNT PAYABLE FOR 1892 AS UNDER.		
Members, Life.		
4 Life members remaining on Roll from previous year (by whom no further subscriptions are due)	....	....
Members, Annual.		
Special Subscriptions.		
1 His Highness the Nizam of Hydrabad, (Deccan) (annual subscription, Rs. 100)	100 0 0	
1 His Highness the Nawab of Joonagad ...	15 0 0	
1 Raja Murli Manohur Bahadur	15 0 0	130 0 0
Ordinary Subscriptions.		
190 Old Members continuing from previous year	......	1,900 0 0
Carried over... ...	......	3,055 0 0

C.

the year 1892, and also showing the actual amount received and the
to be recovered.

Amount of Subscriptions actually Received as under.	Rs.	a.	p.	Rs.	a.	p.
Members, Life.						
Life Members remaining on Roll from previous year	......			......		
Members, Annual.						
(Special Subscriptions.)						
1 His Highness the Nizam of Hyderabad (Deccan)	100	0	0			
1 His Highness the Nawab of Junagad .	15	0	0			
1 Raja Murli Manohur Bahadhur ...	15	0	0	130	0	0
Ordinary Subscriptions.						
137 Ordinary Members	......			1,370	0	0
From Outstanding Subscriptions.						
For the year 1888.						
Ordinary Members	10	0	0			
For the year 1889.						
Ordinary Members	30	0	0			
For the year 1890.						
Ordinary Members	70	0	0			
For the year 1891.						
Ordinary Members	275	0	0	385	0	0
Total actual receipts during 1892	......			1,885	0	0
Carried over ...	......			1,885	0	0

	Rs.	a.	p.	Rs.	a.	p.
Brought forward ...	......			3,055	0	0
Elected during the year.						
4 New Members elected up to 31st October 1892...	40	0	0			
3 Ditto from 1st November 1892.	30	0	0			
				70	0	0
Total ...Rupees	......			3,125	0	0

	Rs. a. p.	Rs. a. p.
Brought forward ...	......	1,885 0 0
By amount written off as irrecoverable from members, by reason of death, Rs. 60, by departure from India, Rs. 60, and by resignations, Rs. 210	......	330 0

Balance.

	Rs. a. p.	
Remaining to be recovered from 2 Members for 1888...	20 0 0	
Do. do. 6 do. 1889 ...	60 0 0	
Do. do. 15 do. 1890 ...	150 0 0	
Do. do. 23 do. 1891 ...	230 0 0	
Do. do. 45 do. 1892 ...	450 0 0	*910 0 0
Total ..Rupees	......	3,125 0 0

* Of this amount Rs. 200 have since been recovered.

(Signed) W. P. WALSHE,

Honorary Treasurer.

ANTHROPOLOGICAL SOCIETY OF BOMBAY,
Bombay, 31st December 1892.

After the adoption of the report, thanks were voted to Captain W. P. Walshe, the Honorary Treasurer, for the very clear and lucid way in which the accounts were kept by him, and for his exertions in collecting the arrears of past years.

Thanks were then voted to Mr. Kharsetji Rustomji Cama and Mr. W. S. Millard for their kindness in auditing the accounts of the Society.

The following Presidential Address on the progress of Anthropology in India, by Mr. H. H. Risley, B.C.S., the Retiring President, was then read :—

PROGRESS OF ANTHROPOLOGY IN INDIA.

AFTER much consideration, I have come to the conclusion that the address which it devolves upon me to deliver as President of this Society can most properly be devoted to reviewing the progress that has been made during the last two years in Anthropological work in India and to indicating the lines of research which can most profitably be pursued in the future.

The scientific study of Anthropology is of comparatively recent growth, and has only been introduced into India within the last ten years. Hodgson and Dalton, the earliest labourers in this field, were quite unacquainted with the methods of research followed in Europe, and were to some extent hampered in their own inquiries by their ignorance of the line that European ethnologists were taking. A conspicuous illustration of this is afforded by their treatment of the important subject of exogamy. Hodgson does not refer to it at all, while Dalton only mentions casually that certain groups are "what Mr. McLennan calls exogamous." Had Dalton realised the extreme scientific importance of the subject, it can hardly be doubted that he would have given more attention to the subject and collected more extensive data than the meagre lists of exogamous groups given in the Ethnology of Bengal.

Within the last few years all this has been changed. The necessity of working in concert with European ethnologists has been fully recognised; a special Sub-Committee of the British Association has been appointed to look after Indian Anthropology, and all recent inquiries in India have followed the instructions laid down by the Committee of the Anthropological Institute which sat in 1874 and drew up a set of instructions for inquirers.

Working on these lines, we have now got for Bengal a fairly complete account of the tribes and castes found in the census of 1881. For the N.-W. P., Mr. Nesfield's interesting sketch and Mr. Croode's valuable Ethnography give as much information as can be looked for without special inquiries being instituted. It is to be hoped that the extensions recently undertaken will result in similar works being published for other Provinces. I will state briefly what extensions of Anthropological work I refer to.

The Government of Bengal has sanctioned a grant of Rs. 2,000 a year to the Asiatic Society of Bengal for the encouragement of Anthropology and Ethnography. The Society has started a special branch to deal with these subjects, and proposes shortly to publish a third section of its journal dealing exclusively with Anthropology and Ethnography. Arrangements have also been made for prosecuting systematic inquiries under the supervision of the Anthropological Secretary. Under the head of Anthropology it is proposed to work on the lines approved by Professors Flower, Turner and Topinard, and to measure representative specimens of the chief tribes and castes in India. Mr. Kitts of the Civil Service has undertaken this work in the North-West Provinces; Surgeon-Captain Roberts proposes to measure the very interesting tribes subject to the Gilgit Political Agency; Dr. Saise, of Giridih, is engaged in measuring the tribes of the Hazaribagh district, and it is hoped that no difficulty may be found in getting similar assistance in the Panjab and in other Provinces of India. Our Anthropological data will then be fairly complete, and we shall be in a position to attempt to draw the conclusions which the statistics indicate. Under this branch of the subject I should mention that Dr. D. D. Cunningham, F. R. S., has undertaken to make a microscopic examination of any specimens of hair that may be sent in. The microscopic structure of the hair is regarded by European ethnologists as a very important racial character, and Dr. Cunningham's inquiries will fill a gap in the Anthropological record.

Turning now to Ethnography, I have to report that the Government of the North-West Provinces have adopted certain proposals, put forward by me two years ago in a letter addressed to the Government of Bengal, for the systematic prosecution of Ethnographic inquiries. A Standing Committee, with Mr. W· Crooke as President and Messrs. Nesfield, Kitts and V. Smith as members, has been appointed to deal with the subject in Northern India, and they are understood to have a regular plan under preparation. The Provincial Government gives a grant of Rs. 1,000, and the Committee have agreed to work in concert with the Asiatic Society of Bengal and to follow the same methods of research· In Madras the Government have given the Asiatic Society a grant of Rs. 500 a year, and have told off a Special Officer, Mr. F. C. Mullaly of the Police, the author of an excellent book on Criminal Tribes, to be Provincial Director of Ethnography. During a recent visit to Madras I had an opportunity of conferring with Mr. Mullaly on the subject of Ethnography, and arranged with him the system on which operations should be carried on. The field open in Madras is virtually untouched and promises to yield results of great interest ; the caste system has developed there on peculiar lines, and there seems to be a rich growth of survivals of archaic usage. In Bombay my attempts to secure the co-operation of Government, without which no scientific inquiries can be expected to make much progress in India,have been less successful than in Madras. The Bombay Government has refused either to make a grant to the Asiatic Society, or to appoint a special officer to supervise Ethnographic inquiries locally. They suggest that the work should be done through the agency of the Anthropological Society. No doubt it will be possible to effect something in this manner. I can supply the Society with copies of my Anthropometic Instructions and Manual of Ethnographic Research, and they must then endeavour to induce members of the Society and others resident in the districts to take the subject up on those lines and to send me their replies to the questions. Those replies I should then work up into monographs on the castes concerned. In this way we should by degrees get together a complete account of the chief tribes and castes in the Presidency. The Chief Commissioner of Assam has sanctioned a grant of Rs. 1,000 a year for Ethnographic purposes, and has appointed Mr. Gait, C.S., the officer who had charge of the census, to be Provincial Director of Ethnography.

I am still in communication with the Governments of the Panjab and the Central Provinces on the subject of extending Ethnographic researches to those areas, and am not without hope that favourable replies may be received. The Chief Commissioner of Burma has not yet been addressed; but Major Temple, who is a recognised authority on these subjects, has expressed his willingness to supervise any inquiries that may be started, and in the last resort we could therefore commence operations in that Province without asking for any assistance from Government.

This completes my sketch of the work actually done at present in the way of extending Ethnographic and Anthropological operations throughout India. It remains to indicate lines of inquiry which might with advantage be taken up in addition to those already in operation.

The first is the formation of an Ethnographic Museum, such as exists in a high state of perfection in the Museum fur Völker-Kunde in Berlin, which owes its existence to the exertions of Dr. Adolf Bastian. Here the student may watch the gradual evolution of all the objects which have exercised the ingenuity and taxed the resources of primitive man and can see how steady the progress has been from the simpler to the more complex. It is easy, I may here remark, to over-estimate the value to Ethnographic science of collections of material objects, such as tools, weapons, means of locomotion, and the like. All these things are the products of many forces. The material surroundings of a people, the materials available, the climate, the fauna and flora, and a variety of factors which it would be tedious to enumerate, have played a part in shaping the wants which have eventually found an expression in some instrument or invention : and here one may remark that similarity of circumstances rather than affinity of race seem to have contributed in the most marked degree to the development of these activities. External conditions have in this connexion a stronger influence than inherited tendencies. Nevertheless, after all allowance has been made for these limitations, there remains a large field within which the work of collection might profitably be carried on, and India, containing as it does so many tribes in very various grades of material progress; offers special facilities for forming a representative collection.

Another object which ethnologists would do well to bear in mind is the formation of a good collection of photographs of the different castes and tribes of India. Such a collection was made many years, with brief letter-press notices, by Dr. Forbes Watson and Sir John Kaye, under the title of the People of India. But permanent processes had not then come into vogue, and the book, which is extremely rare and costly, has now lost much of its value by reason of the photographs having faded. There is believed to be no prospect of Government undertaking a new edition, and the only chance of anything of the kind getting done is for private inquirers to lose no opportunity that presents itself of taking characteristic photographs. Such photographs should always include one view directly front face and one exactly in profile. It is of course not suggested that any precise scientific value attaches to photographs of people ; but they serve to illustrate dress and peculiarities and help to render intelligible the verbal description which the Manual of Ethnography provides for.

A more precise value belongs to accurately made casts of typical representatives of particular tribes and castes, especially if they are coloured and made of some durable material like plaster of Paris. Some casts, prepared under my supervision for the Paris Exhibition of 1889, attracted considerable notice there, and were admitted to possess a definite scientific value, as they were made to measure. The difficulty about casts is that they are very expensive, especially when made life-size, and no other agency but Government is ordinarily in a position to undertake them.

Lastly, I wish to invite attention to the desirability of making a representative collection of the skulls and skeletons of the chief castes. This sounds simple enough ; but it is really beset with very special difficulties, which cast the gravest doubt upon the collections of Asiatic skulls which are found in European Museums. Skulls and bones must be cleaned by somebody : in India, work of this kind is done by low class people, and there is no security against their mixing the skulls made over to them to be cleaned. Special care must, therefore, be taken to attach some sort of label to the head before it is given out to be cleaned, and to see that this is securely attached, so that it cannot be removed in the process of cleaning. Neglect of this simple precaution has rendered worthless many of the specimens now preserved in Museums. It should be added that, if it is desired to make a craniological examination of any skulls, they had better be sent to Dr. Paul Topinard of Paris, Professor Flower of the British Museum, or Dr. Gerson of the Anthropological Institute. These gentlemen have the requisite laboratories and instruments at hand, and can work with a degree of accuracy to which hardly any one in India can hope to attain.

13

ORDINARY GENERAL MEETING, held on Wednesday, the 26th April 1893.

DR. G. WATERS, *Presided*.

The Minutes of the previous Meeting were read and con-firmed.

The election of the following new members was announced. Mr. William Crooke, B.C.S., Magistrate and Collector, Mir-zapore, N.-W. P., and P. R. Natesa Aiyar, Vakil, High Court, Tanjore.

The following donation was announced and thanks voted to the donor :—

To the Library.

From Mr. Camillo Tugliabuc, Professor di Lingua Indostana, Nel R. Institute Orientale in Napoli, Grammatica della Lingua Indostana o Urdu.

The following paper was then read :—

NOTES ON TWO BEHARI PASTIMES.

BY Mr. SARAT CHANDRA MITRA, M.A., B.L.,

District Pleader, Chupra, Behar.

IT is said that the customs and usages of the ancient Hindus were promulgated by the reverend sages of that race, in order to meet the exigencies of some physical phenomena of this country. In the same way it is evident that some customs and practices now obtaining among the same race are found to fulfil the conditions of some physical laws. For instance, the practice of early marriage prevalent amongst the Hindus in some parts of India, is said to have had its origin in the well-known physical law that, in a tropical country like India, the physical development of boys and girls takes place at an earlier period than in countries situated in the colder latitudes, and that, therefore, the procreative instinct manifests itself in them at a very early age.

In the same way, the usages observed while sitting at meals while performing ablutions, and the thousand and one practices that go to make up the daily routine of an orthodox Hindu are all based on the necessity of complying with the requirements of the physical laws of this country. Even the games and the pastimes of the Hindus are found to tally exactly with the requirements of those laws.

Recently I have come to know of the existence of two pastimes in Behar which fulfil the conditions of those laws precisely, and which seem to be suited to the physical conditions of the particular seasons during which they are indulged in. The one is हिरोजा or swinging, and the other is निलंगी उड़ाना or kite-flying.

In Behar the rainy season commences, roughly speaking, from the month of June (Jeyt-Asadh months of the Hindus) and lasts till September and October (Asin of the Hindu Calendar). And the cold weather sets in in the month of Kartick and lasts till the month of Falgoon. Now, in accordance with a custom prevailing in Behar, the pastime of हिरोजा or swinging is indulged in only during the rainy season. The pastime is commenced to be indulged in from the Jeyt Dusserah which usually falls on the 25th of the month of Jeyt and lasts till the Asin Dusserah which usually falls on the 25th of the Hindi month of Asin. So strict is this custom that no one would indulge in this sport at any other period of the year except that mentioned above. Now this period almost exactly coincides with the period during which the rainy season lasts in Behar.

The pastime may be described thus: four ropes are firmly tied to a beam or rafter supporting the roof of the house inside the zenana, and they are allowed to dangle in the air to such a length that a woman can easily get on to them. Then a piece of wooden plank is placed on the hands of the ropes which are now firmly secured so as not to give way beneath the weight of the person or persons sitting thereon. Then two girls of the

family take their seat on the plank and two propel them from
behind. Thus the girls seated on the plank are swung to and
fro. While swinging, the girls seated usually sing वर्षानी or
songs which are meant to be sung during the rainy season by
young girls whose husbands are absent from home and are
away in foreign parts. These songs usually describe the
sufferings endured by young girls separated from their husbands
during the rainy season.

This sport, namely, हिंडोला, is indulged in only by women,
especially by young girls, aged up to 25 or 26 years, in order
to revive their own drooping spirits which are rendered duller
by the dull leaden aspect of the cloud-covered sky during the
rainy season. During the rainy season, it sometimes rains so
heavily in Behar that, at times, it becomes well nigh impossible for any person to stir out of the house. It is on occasions
like these that women in Behar, who, by custom, do not appear
in public and keep inside the zenana, have recourse to this pastime in order to while away the tedium of those dull moments.
This sport is seldom, if ever, indulged in by males.

Professor Bain has somewhere observed, in his "*Mental
Science*," that the effect of a dull leaden aspect of the atmosphere, just as of the sky which is overcast with clouds, is to
render the spirits of man dull and drooping. In primitive
times in Behar, the man who first originated the pastime of
हिंडोला must have been aware of this phenomenon. He must
also have been aware of the necessity which primitive women
in Behar must have felt of devising some scheme for relieving
the *ennui* of the dull hours in the rainy season when they were
compelled to keep in-doors. Hence this pastime was invented.

The second pastime which is extensively indulged in in
Behar is विलंगी उड़ाना or kite-flying. Like the हिंडोला, it also
commences and ends at stated periods. It usually commences
during the Asin Dussera which usually falls on the 25th of the
Hindi month of Asin corresponding to September and October
of the English Calendar. It ends on the day of the Sivarâtri

(शिवरात्रि) festival which falls on the fourteenth day (चतुर्दशी) of the waning period of the moon during the month of Falgoon which corresponds with the months of February and March of the English Calendar. On that day, even old men will pawn their brass utensils, should they have no money with them, to buy लाटाई or the wooden roller on which the thread is wound, लख or thread and तिलंगी or kites, and will indulge in the pastime of kite-flying. After the Sivarátri festival, the implements of kite-flying are broken and thrown away; and no one would touch them after that festival is over. There is also a custom of flying kites near the temple of the नजिया महादेव (an incarnation of the god Siva) at Banki-pore, the head-quarters of the Patna District. I have also heard that there is a similar kite-flying festival observed at Lucknow in the North-Western Provinces.

This pastime is only indulged in by males. It is begun, as stated before, after the Dusserah, and continued till the Siva-rátri day. As a matter of fact, I have not observed a single kite flying after the Sivarátri festival.

It will have been observed that the months, namely, October to March, during which the pastime of kite-flying remains in vogue, coincide, roughly speaking, with the duration of the cold season in Behar. Primitive man must have observed that kite-flying during the grilling hot weather of Behar would be attended with serious risks to health. Hence he must have ordained that kites should be flown only during the cold weather, and, in order to make his ordinance binding, must have prescribed the limits above referred to, beyond which no one is per-mitted to indulge in this latter pastime.

Another noteworthy fact is that, just as the time for indulging in the pastime of हिरोला ends, the time for indulging in तिलंगी उड़ाना commences. These two pastimes show the care and foresight displayed by primitive man even in selecting the appropriate time for indulging in his games and pastimes.

A Note on NAME-GIVING CEREMONY *of a* NEW-BORN CHILD. By MR. TRIBHOWANDAS MANGALDAS NATHUBHAI.

OF the ceremonies to be necessarily performed for a new-born child, the one of giving a name to a baby is of no little interest. The ceremony is mentioned in very old works of Indian ritual literature. We find nearly a half of a chapter devoted to the matter in the *Grihya Sutras* of Ashvaláyana. The subject really begins from Aphorism 4 of Chapter 15, in Book 1. The fourth aphorism contains the following:—" Then they give him name." The time when the name should be given is a question left to be treated by later writers like Manu and others. The commentator, Narayen, son of Garga, says that it should be given after the *Jatkarma* (birthday) ceremonies are over. Aphorism 5 discusses the letters of the alphabet to be selected in giving the initial of the child's name. The author then gives an injunction that soft letters should be preferred. The injunction also says that a name should consist either of two or four letters, or finally says that names of males should consist of an even number of letters and those of females must have odd number of letters. It will be of some interest to know that even at present many female names consist of odd number of letters. Only this much we find in these *sutras* which were composed, perhaps, before the time in which the well-known four castes were introduced in India. Passing over the period we come to Manu and authors after him, who give us further instructions, that the names of Brahmins should end in शर्मन् and those of क्षत्रिय, or the warrior race, end in वर्मन्. The above rule is bettert observed in Bengal and Madras than in this Presiden cy. Bu even here, while performing a religious ceremony, the Brahmins add the affix शर्मन् to their names (for example विष्णुशर्मा) ; those of Banias or the mercantile race must signify money (अंक-द वा-मुख), and those of Shudras must signify service (अयरदासा).

Of these four castes, only one, the Brahmins, have kept to the

traditional mode of names, while the others have mostly neglected it. The warrior castes have almost changed into merchants;
for example, the Bhatias and Luwanas, who are now only
merchants, were originally warriors. Their names used to end
in वर्म in the old ages, and सिंह and पाल in the middle ages : for
example, आकारसी is the corruption of आकुरसिंह तेर्पाण. Now
they have changed into Dasas (servants), yet there are princes in
India who still keep to the old form of names, and, no doubt,
corruptions of old names are still seen in Bhatias and Luwanas.
The Banias, excepting those who in the Middle Ages accepted
the Jain religion, the influence of which made them faithful
to the old way of taking names, have almost all become Dasas.
The Bania followers of the Jain faith do not terminate their
names in the word "Das," which means a servant. But the
word "Dasas" here signifies not a servant or slave, but the
servant of God; the Banias thus preferring to be called themselves the devotees of the Almighty, and not lords or lions
among the mortals. Who were the real Shudras is still a
matter of dispute, and, therefore, I need not enter here on the
discussion of their names. Having gone through the nature
of names, I now come to the original point of the ceremony of
giving a name. Therein the first point of consideration is the
day on which the ceremony should be performed. The oldest
authority that we get is Manu. He says that it should be performed on the tenth or the twelfth day after birth, or on an
auspicious day having a favourable astrological conjunction.
Another author, Brihaspati, says that it should be done either
on the tenth, twelfth or thirteenth in the case of a Brahmin,
on the sixteenth in the case of a Kshatriya, on the twentieth
in the case of Banias, and on the twenty-second in the case of a
Shudra. Yajnavalkya improves upon him a little, and says that
the other days should be taken only if the tenth day is not found
convenient. But the authority that speaks very decidedly
on the point is *Sanskar-Bhaskar*, where the author says that the
ceremony in a Brahmin family should be performed either on
the eleventh or twelfth day, in a Kshatriya family on either

the thirteenth or sixteenth, in a Vaishya family on the sixteenth or twentieth day, and in a Shudra family on the twenty-second or at the end of the month. However, convenience has over-ruled these injunctions, and the twelfth or any auspicious day, fixed upon after due consideration by the family astrologer, is taken for the ceremony. Now we come to the very cream of the thing—the ceremony. Pundit Ram Krishna Moreshwar Páthak, the author of *Sanskar-Bhaskar*, says, that, on the eleventh or twelfth day, at least three Brahmins should be invited for dinner. The father of the child takes a bath, puts on two unsewn clothes, and then makes a beautiful *tilak* on the forehead. Having gone through the usual ceremonies of the day, he worships Ganpat (the elephant-headed god), who is reputed for warding off all obstacles. Offerings are also made to several other gods to get blessings for the child. The most important ceremony, though now almost neglected, yet necessarily performed by those who perform the thread-ceremony (Brahmins and Kshatriyas), is one in which a dish of bell-metal is filled with rice, and in the rice with a piece of gold wire are written the words: " Devoted to *particular* god, the month, the initial of the name corresponding to the constellation at the time of birth, and lastly, the name given to the child." The dish is then presented to the family priest. After this the mother says to the child, " Boy be a devotee of Ganpati, be a devotee of the family deity. You are Martand (the sun). By the mouth you are the god Vishnu. By the favourable aspects of the planets you are foremost of all. And you are Moon by your new name." Of course, these are very favourite expressions of the mother fond of her child. Similar expressions are used by his father at the time of distributing money to the Brahmins present. The Brahmins in return repeat *mantras* of blessings. In the performance of the name-giving ceremony the father of the infant performs Ganpati Pujan, Nava Graha Pujan, Swasti Punyaha Vachana, Matrika Pujan, and Nandi Shradha, and then the sister of the father of the infant plays a very important part. She brings from her own place a present of silk shirt (*zabla*), gold embroidered cap, and gold wrist ornaments to the infant, together with one seer and a quarter of wheat, one cocoanut, seven pieces of turmeric, and one rupee in a copper sieve. At the end of the ceremony, the infant's parent compensates her in cash with some addition to the value of the presents she made to the infant. In a selected place in the residence of the parents of the infant a *swastik* of wheat is formed, and a *pimpul* leaf, copper coin, and one betelnut are placed over it. Above this are held by four children the four ends of the *patola* (a particular kind of silk cloth) with four *pimpul* leaves marked with a *kunkoo* (red powder applied by the Hindoos on the forehead) *swastik*.[1] The wheat, the cocoanut, the seven pieces of turmeric, and the one rupee brought by the father's sister of the infant are put into the *patola*. The aunt (father's sister) then holds the infant in this *patola*. The children swing the *patola* and the infant is rocked to and fro over the *patola* by the aunt singing the couplet, " Swing, swing, with the *pimpul* leaves, thy aunt gives thee the name of *Goverdhan*." This couplet, some families sing four times, and some seven times. There is also an additional ceremony performed in some families. The aunt makes a pipe of the *pimpul* leaf [2] and blows with it over a silver coin placed on the navel of the child. The meaning seems to be of giving family strength to the boy. It has its history. Some authors say that the name-giving ceremony should be performed before the navel cord falls off. The blowing with *pimpul* pipe, perhaps, meant that the aunt blows in the navel to its proper position. The letters given in the divisions of the circle over the sign of the Zodiac in which the Moon is placed indicate the initial name to be given to the child. In the present instance the Moon is in the sign of Aquarius, whose corresponding alphabets being " Go, &c.," the name Goverdhandas is given.

---

[1] ॐ

[2] This leaf is considered sacred amongst the Hindoos by the following authority:—

† आप ग्म्बू मधूकाक्ष-ग्रग्रीवोऽ .त्यग्साक्षिनाम् ॥ पक्त्रा: पञ्च पञ्चानामभिषेकार्थमुत्तमा:

11

Note on Some CURIOUS CUSTOMS *among the* KOCHS.

BY KEDARNATH BASU, Cor. Memb., Anthrop. Soc., Bombay.

THE Kochs are an aboriginal race inhabiting the State of Koch-Behar and other parts of North Bengal. The Kochs are allied to the Australoid group. Some scholars, however, think them to belong to the Mongoloid group. This view seems to me to be erroneous, as the dark colour of their skin, the cut of the face, and the formation of the head prove them to belong to the Dravidian stock of the Australoids. The Kochs call themselves *Rájbansis* (literally of the Royal Family), and claim their descent from Aryan stock. They are, however, recognised as a distinct caste of the Hindus in many parts of Bengal.

Hajo, the first of the Kochs, established the Koch Kingdom after the fall of the Hindu Kingdom of Kamrup. During the reign of his grandson, Visú, the Kochs became converts to Hinduism and assumed the title of Rájbansi. This title is reserved only by the cultivators and respectable classes, while that of the Koch is restricted to labourers, and especially to palanquin-bearers. It seems that there is some slight amount of admixture of Mongolic blood in them, as they were used to intermarry among the neighbouring tribes belonging to the Mongoloid group.

Although the Kochs have adopted Hinduism, they have not forgotten their old forms of religion and worship. Every Koch village has its *Thákúrpát*, or the seat of god, where the *deos* or evil spirits reside. Whenever anything goes wrong in a family, the members make offerings to these evil spirits to appease their wrath. A singular relic of their old superstitions is the worship of *Húdúm deo*. The worship consists in a plantain stem or a young bamboo being stuck in the ground in some distant and solitary part, where the women of a village assemble (no male being allowed to be present), and throwing off their garments, thus becoming perfectly nude, they dance round the mystic tree, singing old songs and charms. This rite is observed in order to get rain and a good harvest of crops, when they are either suffering or are likely to suffer from drought Besides, the Hindu god *Kartikeya* is worshipped by the Koch women in a manner peculiar to them. When a woman is without child, she supplicates this god. At the night of the *pújá*, when ceremonies and rites are over and the worship completed, all the male kind are made to retire from the presence of the idol. Then all the young women of the neighbourhood assemble together, and, divesting themselves of their clothes, dance round the idol throughout the night, while the musicians, shut up in a shed, keep up a brisk rataplan of drums and fifes during the whole time. This custom is undoubtedly a relic of phallic worship, which was so common all over the world. The Kochs also worship *Madan* or *Kamadeva*, and erect in the courtyard a tall bamboo covered with red cloth and surmounted by *chámars* (yaks' tails) representing the god, and then great rejoicings take place. Obscene songs are sung on the occasion. The worship continues for three days and the bamboo is thrown away; on the fourth, the red cloths and chámars taken off. They make sacrifices of buffaloes and pigs before their gods and partake of their flesh, but they do not eat beef or fowls.

Note on DAKIKHINÁ RÁYA, A MODERN DEITY.

BY KEDARNATH BASU, Cor. Memb., Anthrop. Soc., Bombay.

IN the latter part of June 1889 I had an occasion to visit a number of villages in the vicinity of the Sunderbans, on the outskirts of the sub-division of Barúipur, in the District of the 24-perganahs. While passing by a village my attention was drawn to several rude images of human heads made of burnt clay, under bamboo clumps and otherwise jungly solitary

places, placed upon raised platforms or mounds of earth. The
manner in which these images were set up bespoke that they
had been placed in those jungly places by the villagers for
some set purpose of theirs. I sketched one of these clay figures,
which were painted in white, black, and red; and then proceeded to a neighbouring village where I had to halt for the
day. During my stay here I made enquiries of the villagers,
who were for the most part agriculturers, about those clay
figures, and learnt that they were representations of Dakikhiná
Ráya or Dakikhiná Thákúr, a local deity of the Sunderbans,
worshipped to get immunity from the depredations caused by
tigers upon men and cattle. The villagers could not give me
further information on the subject, so I had to look for an
intelligent person for more particulars about the deity, which
was quite new to me. I fortunately met with an intelligent
Brahmin, who gave me to understand that the worship of these
clay images is of a recent origin. The date of the origin
of the worship in its present form, according to his
computations, would not go farther back than 50 or
60 years, for he informs
me that he has heard from
his father, who is about 70
years old, that the worship
of the images of Dakikhiná
Ráya were not in vogue in
his father's youthful days.
It was then enough to take
the name of Dakikhiná
Ráya to keep tigers in check
from making depredations
upon cattle and men. The
name had such a charm
that by uttering it men
could keep tigers spell-
bound.

From these facts I am inclined to infer that among the early reclaimers of the Sunderbans, there lived a man named Daki-khiná Ráya who was reputed to have been a great tiger-charmer, and was believed to have immense power over the ferocious beast. The reclaimers and wood-cutters, who frequented the tiger infested Sunderbans on their daily avocation, no doubt, believed that he had such a hold upon the tiger that his name uttered before the wild beast would keep it spell-bound, and thus incapacitate it from inflicting injuries upon themselves or their cattle. This belief gradually became so firm and strong in them, on account of the supposed charm of his name, which they took to be the sole factor in the continual decrease of the frequency of depredations caused by the tiger, as to lead them to consider Dakikhiná Ráya to have been a Superhuman Being. Having arrived at this stage of belief they naturally deified their supposed benefactor and commenced to worship his image. The real factors, in the decrease of depredations by tigers,—the unremitting slaughter of these wild beasts by hunters and sportsmen, and the retreat of the remaining few far into the woods from their old haunts on account of the gradual but steady clearance of the jungle for agricultural purposes— are, however, not taken into account by these simple folk.

This modern deity is chiefly confined among the outskirts of the Sunderbans, and its worship is found nowhere else in Bengal. The sketch of the deity which I furnish herewith was taken from an image which was set upon an inverted earthen bowl and placed upon a raised platform of earth under-neath a clump of bamboos outside of one of the villages visited by me.

On a WILD BOY and a WILD GIRL.

By SARAT CHANDRA MITRA, M.A., B.L.,

Pleader, District Judge's Court, District Saran, Chupra.

FROM the dawn of the remotest antiquity, instances have been known of the children of human beings having been nurtured by wild animals. The student of ancient history will remember that the most notable among those was the case of Romulus and Remus, the traditionally reputed founders of Rome. There is a bronze still preserved in the Museum of the Vatican at Rome which pourtrays those two children as sucking the teats of a large-sized she-wolf, and whereof a photograph, which I have seen, is in the possession of Professor Rowe, of the Presidency College, Calcutta.

In India, such instances frequently turn up in the North-Western Provinces, especially in Oude. Several examples have been recorded by Professor V. Ball, formerly of the Geological Survey of India, in his work entitled " *Jungle Life in India*" [1] and in the "*Proceedings of the Asiatic Society of Bengal.*" [2] Particulars of several cases were collected by Colonel Sleeman, and several have been recorded by Sir Roderick Murchison, Director of the Geological Survey of Great Britain and Ireland, in the pages of the " *Annals and Magazine of Natural History.*" [3] The Rev. Mr. Lewis, author of a short history of the Secundra Church Mission Orphanage, near Agra, gives the following account of a wolf-reared child who has been brought up there and may be still living in that Orphanage : —
" On February 4th, 1867, he was sent to the Superintendent of the Orphanage by the Magistrate of Bulandshahr, with the statement that he had been taken out of a wolf's hole or den. Some natives, it turned out on further enquiry, had been travelling by some unfrequented part of the jungle in the Buland-shahr district and had been surprised to see a small boy, of five

---

[1] Ball's *Jungle Life in India*, pp. 455-466.
[2] *Proc. Asiatic Society of Bengal* for 1873, p. 128.
[3] *Annals and Magazine of Natural History*, 2nd Series, Vol. VIII., p. 153.

or six years of age, walking about on his hands and feet. On drawing near to see this strange sight, they were amazed to see the boy disappear quickly within the interior of a large hole, which, on close inspection, turned out to be the dwelling-place of some wild beast. Finding that all efforts to unearth the boy were fruitless, and fearing to venture in after him, they set off to report the unusual occurrence to the Magistrate of Bulandshahr. This gentleman, on hearing the story, despatched messengers to the spot, with instructions to light a fire at the mouth of the cave, so as to force out the occupant of the hole by means of the smoke. This was done, and on the blinding and choking fumes making their way into the furthest corner of the hole, a fine snarling she-wolf sprang forth with a bound, and after scattering the bystanders in considerable terror, rushed away for safety and dear life. A moment later, the boy too came forth, when he fell an easy prey to those intent on securing him. On conveying him to the Magistrate, the boy was found to be speechless, imbecile, and as near an approach to an animal as a human creature can possibly be. Vegetable food was offered to him, but this he refused. And it was only when meat was placed before him that he would eat. Finding it impossible to ever make the boy rational and useful, the Magistrate forwarded him to Secundra, with the request that he might be allowed an asylum there."

The circumstances under which these children are brought up by wild animals are that the mother of the unfortunate child abandons it, as is frequently the case in India, either for concealing her shame on account of some illicit love whereof the child is the fruit, or for want of means to support it. The child, being thrown away into the jungle or some other out-of-the-way place, is found out by some wild animal. Sometimes the child is carried off from its parents' homestead by some wild animal and taken to its den. Should the animal have no young ones, or, having had them, have lost them, it frequently spares the child and transfers its maternal feelings to it.

The child is suckled by her, and, with the wild animal's milk, it also imbibes the ways and manners of its wild foster-mother. The child learns to imitate all the doings of its foster-mother, and tries to walk on all fours. Seeing her make her meal off the carcases of dead animals, it also learns to eat raw animal food. If the mother was attacked, she tore at and bit her assailants, so the foster-child also scratched and bit all who thwarted its movements. In this way the wild-animal-reared-child learnt the ways and manners of its foster-mother.

Curiously enough, all the wolf-reared children hitherto recorded have been boys, and all of them idiots. But recently two cases have turned up in Bengal and Behar, the former of which is, at least, an exception to the above generalization. The case from Bengal is in the person of a girl.

All of these instances are of great interest to the anthropologist or the student of the evolution of human culture, inasmuch as they afford illustrations of the circumstances under which primitive men imbibed their ferine ways, in those far-off times when they more resembled wild animals than human beings. To the anthropologist, they also set forth the truth of the theory that the faculty of reason is evolved in infants by the imitation of the ways and manners of its adult fellow-beings. These also demonstrate to him how the infants of human beings, conscious only of the cravings of nature, and having all the faculties of its knowledge undeveloped, will, if placed amidst wild brutes, have these faculties developed and trained after the ways of their wild companions of the forest.

When I was in Calcutta in September last, I heard that a wild girl had been brought down to Calcutta and that people had been flocking by hundreds to see her. Owing to pressure of business, I could not pay a visit to the wild girl and have a look at her. The following short history of this strange girl appeared in the *Amrita Bazar Patrika* of Wednesday, the 14th December 1892 :—

" One of the missionaries of the New Dispensation Church (the late Babu Keshub Chunder Sen's Brahmo Somaj), in

15

his recent tour to Jalpaiguri, came across an idiot girl of about eight years of age. The girl roved through the streets, appeasing her appetite with whatever food the people offered her, and at nights slept under trees or under open sky. The history of the girl is wonderful. We sometimes read in books of legendary stories of human beings nursed by lions, wolves and bears, the girl is a living instance of such nursing. The girl has the features of the hill people. She was discovered by some coolies belonging to a tea garden in the den of a bear. It is presumed that she was brought there by some unaccountable circumstances, and when very young was nursed by her bear-mother. When first taken out of the den, she was a strange combination of a bear and a man, she was ferocious like a bear, and attempted to bite and scratch men when she saw them. In her locomotion she used her legs as well as hands, and moved like a bear. She growled at intervals like a bear and ate and drank as a bear; in short, all her habits were like those of a bear, while by her features no one could fail to recognise her as a human being. The police afterwards took her under its custody; this happened when she was about three years of age. Sh.... .... n ....t. to the Jalpaiguri hospital, where she forgot much of her stu. ....e habits. She learnt to walk, eat and drink like a human be.... and showed certain emotions which were peculiar to man. The .... spital authorities retained her about three years, and afterwards thinking her an incur- able discharged her. She was thrown en .... rely upon the mercy of nature. The said missionary, who l.... the manager of an orphanage, took pity on her, and broug.t her down to the office of the *Unity and the Minister* newspaper (the organ of the New Dispensation Church of the late Babu Keshub Chunder Sen) at No. 20, Patuatolla Lane, Calcutta. When we first saw her we were greatly impressed by her .... miable and inno- cent appearance. She is rather bulky a.d has long hair. Even now she has not forsaken bear-like gr.wls, and it is with some difficulty that she can walk like man. Traces of the bear can still be discerned in her movements. The only emotion which she incessantly expresses is by means of smiles, which oftentimes develop into loud laughter. She is more a laughing girl than anything else. She does not seem to understand human language, though her powers of hearing and seeing have been found on examination to be unimpaired. When food was brought to her, she readily stretched forth her hand to grasp it, and when she was in possession of it or when she was engaged in consuming it, she laughed loudly, and her smiles and laughter at times appeared very attractive and sweet. If there is anything about her that commands human sympathy, it is her smile. The Orphanage being considered an unsuitable place for her, she has been removed to the *Das Asram*, a philanthropic institution of Calcutta, founded by some Brahmo gentlemen on the lines of the Salvation Army, to afford an asylum to the poor and homeless waifs and strays of the Calcutta streets, where she is now taken great care of. Hundreds of men and women now go to see her daily, but she shows an aversion to being exhibited as an object of curiosity before a large number of people. By contact with society, she is now gradually acquiring human habits. It has been pronounced by medical men that she will gradually regain her humanity."

Some time ago I wrote to the Editor of the *Unity and the Minister* newspaper, requesting him to let me have further particulars regarding this phenomenal girl, and asking him whether a photograph of her is available for submission to the Anthropological Society of Bombay, but I regret to say that I have not been favoured with any reply as yet, otherwise I could have given a fuller account of this strange girl.

The following account of a boy of strange habits was communicated by a correspondent from Mozufferpore, in Behar, to the issue of the *Indian Mirror* (of Calcutta) of Sunday, the 19th February 1893 :—

"Babu Bhagelu Singh, a Zemindar of the Bhagalpore District, lately came out for hunting in his *diara lands* near a village called Bazitpore, a few miles off Dalsingsarai Station, on the Tirhut and Bengal North-Western Railway. As he was aiming at a wild animal, he found some one like a human being at a distance entering the jungle, as if through fear. This aroused his curiosity, and he ordered his followers to search for the object. After diligent search they found a boy, about fourteen years old, who was stark naked. He has been brought from the jungle and kept in the *Cutcharry-barry* of the Zemindar Babu at Bazitpore. He cannot speak, but can laugh and make a chattering sound. He does not eat any cooked things, but eats everything raw, such as raw fish, frogs, &c. When catching frogs and such other living creatures, he walks on all fours and jumps upon his prey like a cat. If the prey is secured, he at once puts it into his mouth and devours. Daily a large number of people resort to the place to have a look at him. If money or any other metallic things are given to him, he throws them away. He is now being taught to eat cooked food, and has learnt to eat fried rice. Still he wears no clothes, and never enters a place of shelter save that of a tree. Lately he was attacked with cholera, and the Zemindar Babu having attempted to administer some medicines, he fled from his *Cutcharry* to a river bank, and there drank water to his heart's content, and thus escaped out of the clutches of the fell disease. In all respects, he resembles a man, the only difference is that he cannot speak. It is not yet known how he got into the jungle. Some say that either he was lost during his infancy, or thrown away by his parents owing to their extreme poverty, while others say that he was carried away from his cradle by a wild animal, such as jackal, and was left unhurt in the jungle, where he grew up under providential care. But the popular belief is that he is a Yogi. In case, any of your readers be inclined to satisfy his curiosity, he may find the boy at village Bazitpore, near Dalsingsarai Railway Station, on the Tirhut and Bengal North-Western Railway."

TABLES *of* CASTE MEASUREMENTS *compiled by* MR. E. J. KITTS.
(Continued from p. 73, Vol. III.)

Note.—The following tables give anthropometric measurements for groups of adult males of different castes.

Table I. has been discontinued, as the police anthropometric system has been taken up by the Local Government of the N. W. P. and Oudh.

Table II. is compiled for ordinary anthropological purposes. All the measurements are in millimetres. The compiler will be glad if information is sent to him of any mistakes which may be discovered in the summary at the end of this table.

E. J. KITTS, C.S.,

Allahabad.

1893.

Name of Caste or Tribe—SHEKH (KHURESHI).

No.	Height of Vertex	Height of Trunk	Span	Left Foot	Left Middle Finger	Right Ear Height	Round Head	Inion to Glabella	Tragus to Tragus	Vertex to Chin	Antero-posterior Diameter	Maximum Transverse Diameter	Minimum Frontal Diameter	Bizygomatic Diameter	Cephalic Index	General Index	Frontal Index
1	1633	806	1671	244	104	76	541	838	343	211	190	138	...	...	72·6	...	...
2	1668	851	1694	203	107	88	566	866	361	236	206	140	...	...	68·0	...	...
3	1661	...	1738	262	107	58	543	833	333	...	190	144	...	...	75·8	...	...
4	1617	...	1623	264	107	69	543	848	345	...	194	135	...	...	69·6	...	...
5	1656	...	1671	254	110	56	536	840	340	...	198	138	...	...	72·9	...	...
6	1700	913	1818	272	119	61	569	838	353	202	198	150	101	129	75·8	157	73·8
7	1706	870	1735	250	107	80	545	858	380	213	198	137	105	133	71·4	159	77·8
8	1721	871	1794	273	110	64	519	845	350	211	179	135	108	132	75·4	160	77·1
9	1695	840	1710	263	111	62	550	846	349	227	190	140	107	130	73·7	167	75·4
10	1630	800	1715	256	107	59	549	852	344	202	192	142	105	133	74·0	151	76·1
11	1624	845	1700	248	106	61	530	845	343	280	188	188	109	187	73·4	168	73·4
12	1617	877	1675	250	113	67	553	860	357	228	189	144	113	140	75·7	163	80·6
13	1744	895	1807	259	110	66	560	870	377	217	203	154	116	137	75·9	158	76·1
14	1765	895	1781	263	118	61	544	840	355	213	186	144	108	133	77·4	168	76·9
51	1752	860	1808	257	112	64	538	845	353	213	180	142	105	135	78·9	160	77·5
16	1725	873	1840	273	128	65	542	837	353	215	183	138	113	134	71·5	146	77·5
17	1687	840	1730	250	109	66	552	845	380	200	189	147	107	187	77·8	169	76·9
18	1639	867	1636	237	104	66	585	842	349	225	185	188	110	183	74·6	169	80·8
19	1755	915	1860	278	123	64	537	845	347	214	188	142	103	127	75·6	157	74·6
20	1800	855	1862	272	125	53	530	340	342	204	190	134	97	130	74·4	159	68·7
21	1804	906	1621	249	114	80	533	845	353	209	185	189	103	181	75·1	159	72·4
23	1705	840	1746	254	120	58	538	844	349	207	192	138	99	180	71·9	162	68·7
43	1690	867	1734	280	113	63	553	860	350	210	194	144	97	180	74·2	161	...
32	1627	870	1653	247	107	66	595	845	352	199	186	184	90	181	72·0	...	...
53	1755	...	1840	274	125	...	595	885	335	...	175	135	...	181	77·1	...	...

No.																	
26	69·8	163	76·0	115	90	130	171	188	334	317	549	51	103	237	1605	814	1563
27	74·8	166	74·2	131	107	143	194	218	358	378	562	69	103	258	1657	870	1625
28	74·5	160	72·1	134	106	141	195	215	355	344	530	67	104	260	1758	820	1680
29	67·1	154	77·2	136	98	146	189	210	360	350	568	70	109	268	1769	875	1705
30	76·5	159	73·5	125	100	136	185	199	350	365	540	55	105	264	1716	895	1715
31	76·1	172	73·1	127	105	138	189	219	375	369	536	63	104	268	1769	896	1730
32	71·1	155	74·2	130	97	135	179	210	380	335	510	69	114	266	1811	905	1785
33	74·1	169	75·4	128	100	135	179	216	359	370	527	63	110	270	1740	845	1730
34	75·0	159	76·9	129	105	140	182	205	350	340	539	56	103	240	1728	840	1660
35	79·8	150	73·7	130	103	129	176	195	330	332	520	54	110	257	1680	883	1620

Name of Caste or Tribe—SHEKH (SADIKI).

No.	Height of Vertex	Height of Trunk	Span	Left Foot	Left Middle Finger	Right Ear Height	Round Head	Inion to Glabella	Tragus to Tragus	Vertex to Chin	Antero-posterior Diameter	Maximum Transverse Diameter	Minimum Frontal Diameter	Bizygomatic Diameter	Cephalic Index	General Index	Frontal Index
1	2	3	4	5	6	7	8	9	10	11	12	13	14	15	16	17	18
36	1767	881	1823	267	117	69	561	353	350	218	200	140			70·0		
37	1704	830	1790	282	117	60	533	335	348	213	182	140			80·2		
38	1678	841	1729	257	110	56	526	335	323	229	185	132			71·3		
39	1666		1750	244	112	63	554	338	340		197	140			71·3		
40	1656	823	1744	264	110	63	531	333	345	200	188	142			75·5		
41	1638	853	1681	257	112	71	541	348	350	208	190	139	107	135	73·2	158	75·9
42	1668	815	1797	263	112	64	526	335	333	216	194	189	106	128	75·5	161	79·1
43	1683	863	1740	264	114	67	550	345	350	213	192	141	102	135	73·4	154	72·9
44	1630	830	1728	257	111	65	517	323	340	204	181	134	109	145	74·0	152	74·7
45	1670	870	1727	243	113	67	529	330	345	219	182	140	100	128	76·9	155	71·9
46	1645	830	1900	267	120	61	566	369	358	220	196	143	98	128	74·5	156	70·6
47	1754	866	1715	257	107	72	547	345	357	198	197	139	95	127	70·6	157	72·5
48	1780	906	1890	262	110	65	555	303	360	200	192	136	104	135	70·8	146	75·4
49	1600	880	1700	251	114	54	527	329	342	200	183	131	103	132	70·3	151	78·6
50	1725	920	1734	264	112	63	519	336	339	197	174	138	106	132	72·0	155	77·4
51	1728	805	1656	260	110	73	532	336	349	199	185	131	95	127	79·3	153	77·2
52	1637	890	1770	259	120	63	530	337	340	205	190	137	103	132	70·8	155	77·4
53	1635	834	1718	287	105	58	534	336	333	194	194	132	108	137	72·1	150	75·5
54	1635	846	1644	245	109	57	540	327	323	204	187	138	103	138	62·8	145	77·4
55	1764	920	1830	278	123	62	546	358	372	205	186	143	104	131	71·1	156	78·8
56	1668	865	1744	251	114	61	543	345	351	300	187	133	110	141	76·9	143	78·6
57	1615	825	1661	243	110	57	533	328	321	275	186	132	100	130	71·1	150	74·1
58	1656	838	1748	282	118	54	562	320	347	201	178	140	103	133	70·9	144	73·6
59	1575	818	1696	260	109	59	525	350	345	195	177	135	104	130	78·7	156	
60	1679	876	1753	260	110	53	521	330	345	191	177	140	110		78·6		
61	1663	843	1695		113	59	543	330	345	203	183	144	100	130	79·1		70·1

74·1	74·3	74·1	77·8	74·6	73·3	71·4	69·1	71·1
150	152	153	167	164	186	172	174	183
75·5	73·7	78·9	76·3	80·0	72·6	78·2	69·8	80·5
199	128	131	127	132	126	132	127	128
103	104	103	105	108	99	100	95	103
189	140	139	135	148	185	140	136	149
184	190	175	177	177	186	179	182	176
193	194	200	213	217	197	227	221	185
334	353	345	360	353	360	350	330	340
335	358	840	845	840	357	840	850	319
530	540	520	519	510	540	538	530	518
61	57	60	55	61	59	59	60	52
110	107	113	101	103	105	112	107	103
234	254	259	240	263	255	259	245	261
1730	1764	1790	1615	1726	1770	1799	1718	1700
807	832	855	820	866	866	945	820	840
1648	1670	1674	1614	1708	1730	1665	1655	1635
62	63	84	85	86	87	68	69	70

Name of Caste or Tribe—SHEKH.

No.	Height of Vertex	Height of Trunk	Span	Left Foot	Left Middle Finger	Right Ear Height	Round Head	Inion to Glabella	Tragus to Tragus	Vertex to Chin	Antero-posterior Diameter	Maximum Transverse Diameter	Minimum Frontal Diameter	Bizygomatic Diameter	Cephalic Index	General Index	Frontal Index
1	2	3	4	5	6	7	8	9	10	11	12	13	14	15	16	17	18
71	1775	880	1848	274	119	61	551	350	358	218	195	137			70·3		
72	1584	868	1582	249	107	64	559	360	361	221	192	141			73·4		
73	1663	830	1661	241	99	58	526	343	330	216	183	145			79·2		
74	1544	704	1663	259	107	61	516	325	323	193	181	136			75·1		
75	1767	886	1848	269	117	69	546	345	361	226	190	140			73·7		
76	1683	825	1704	254	110	64	566	361	361	221	200	143			71·5		
77	1734	871	1752	269	117	61	564	361	361	221	194	150			77·3		
78	1541	818	1592	231	99	53	518	333	338	211	182	138			75·8		
79	1648	848	1709	254	112	61	546	323	330	213	192	140			72·9		
80	1645	838	1681	262	107	53	538	330	348	213	191	138			77·3		
81	1633	840	1757	259	110	61	546	333	350	200	185	148			75·8		
82	1651	823	1724	257	104	64	538	345	330	216	189	137			72·3		
83	1602	838	1722	257	107	66	536	343	348	231	185	111			80·0		
84	1686	855	1750	269	117	64	531	330	323	203	189	134			72·5		
85	1684	795	1607	241	104	61	516	358	338	218	180	133			76·2		
86	1694	803	1739	259	107	58	538	326	359	200	193	133			70·9		
87	1690	846	1759	260	111	61	529	339	338	203	177	140			73·9		
88	1715	864	1780	261	120	66	519	349	352	195	180	187			68·9		
89	1770	875	1830	262	122	60	518	325	353	193	181	185	103	131	79·1	154	73·6
90	1643	815	1690	263	115	58	539	367	345	200	178	131	102	132	78·1	148	74·5
91	1635	855	1710	245	116	68	519	315	319	205	186	187	94	128	74·6	150	69·6
92	1601	865	1680	298	107	68	546	388	360	180	176	130	100	126	73·7	159	78·3
93	1680	895	1695	267	122	57	544	350	365	215	186	139	97	126	73·9	163	70·9
94	1683	840	1750	249	113	61	544	380	340	194	178	186	100	130	74·8	138	76·9
95	1690	810	1640	256	110	60	516						98	131		164	69·1
96													94	130	76·0	149	69·1

	C1	C2	C3	C4	C5	C6	C7	C8	C9	C10	C11	C12	C13	C14	C15	C16	C17
96	1690	855	1790	264	115	64	538	340	350	198	179	144	109	134	80·8	144	75·7
97	1709	845	1835	270	117	56	528	344	352	216	180	135	98	129	75·0	107	72·6
98	1605	810	1670	243	110	52	540	350	340	218	179	135	105	124	75·4	144	77·8
99	1670	870	1725	281	110	60	540	350	340	214	188	184	110	127	71·3	169	88·1
100	1620	810	1750	238	105	57	520	320	330	197	176	128	100	124	75·8	159	78·1
101	1620	810	1665	250	110	62	550	340	350	210	182	188	107	127	75·5	165	77·5
102	1670	805	1725	253	110	63	530	340	340	206	179	183	105	124	74·3	141	78·9
103	1660	800	1775	253	110	57	540	340	340	...	...	...	...	...	...	...	...
104	1695	850	1750	261	120	61	520	330	334	200	181	182	96	127	72·9	157	72·7
105	1680	830	1765	260	120	54	520	340	340	195	176	133	104	128	75·2	152	78·2
Variation from No. to No.	1541 (78) 1830 (93)	764 (74) 945 (68)	1582 (72) 1900 (46)	231 (78) 293 (37)	99 (73,78) 128 (16)	51 (26) 76 (1)	505 (25) 580 (13)	315 (92) 373 (27)	319 (92) 381 (2)	180 (92) 236 (2)	176 (26) 206 (2)	128 (100) 154 (13)	90 (25,26) 116 (14)	115 (26) 145 (46)	62·8 (53) 80·8 (96)	133 (70) 174 (69)	68·7 (25) 82·1 (99)
Mean Arge.	1670 / 1672	860 / 860	1730 / 1729	258 / 256	110 / 111	62 / 61	538 / 536	341 / 342	348 / 351	208 / 206	184 / 182	138 / 137	103 / 107	130 / 130	74·9 / 72·9	156 / 156	74·7 / 74·7
Do. for Khureshi alone.	1684	862	1736	258	111	63	541	345	350	211	187	140	101	131	75·1	160	74·5
Do. for Sadiki alone.	1670	878	1725	255	111	61	534	342	345	205	176	138	103	132	74·4	154	74·5
Do. for others.	1662	841	1727	256	112	61	534	340	343	204	184	132	102	129	69·3	154	75·1

SUMMARY.

Name of Caste or Tribe—BHANTU.

No.	Height of Vertex	Height of Trunk	Span	Left Foot	Left Middle Finger	Right Ear Height	Round Head	Inion to Glabella	Tragus to Tragus	Vertex to Chin	Antero-posterior Diameter	Maximum Transverse Diameter	Minimum Fronial Diameter	Bizygomatic Diameter	Cephalic Index	General Index	Frontal Index
1	1732	846	1887	269	122	61	546	356	363	211	185	143	116	128	73·0	165	81·1
2	1635	858	1678	264	110	61	538	338	348	193	184	140	114	131	70·7	151	81·4
3	1643	820	1701	269	114	61	531	315	333	211	186	146	123	134	78·5	157	84·2
4	1661	846	1734	264	113	84	528	330	345	196	184	146	124	140	79·3	140	84·9
5	1706	834	1775	267	110	64	521	323	330	206	185	140	115	140	75·7	147	82·1
6	1623	806	1678	239	110	56	528	305	338	208	185	142	121	134	78·0	155	85·2
7	1693	820	1729	251	113	58	533	333	335	224	187	136	113	132	72·7	169	83·1
8	1666	843	1683	241	104	64	495	317	330	216	173	129	112	132	74·6	108	86·8
9	1592	797	1587	224	102	64	531	305	330	208	185	140	113	134	75·7	155	87·1
10	1468	858	1607	263	114	64	546	333	338	216	194	141	122	135	72·7	160	85·1
11	1666	871	1607	260	119	68	528	383	335	216	186	135	120	131	73·4	105	82·2
12	1727	808	1582	260	107	56	531	330	353	198	188	141	111	127	75·8	154	79·6
13	1636	838	1676	299	114	64	528	320	335	188	189	143	108	136	78·6	138	84·6
14	1638	820	1635	249	103	66	530	312	345	180	188	136	121	132	74·7	144	89·9
15	1714	868	1676	241	114	64	536	343	312	208	190	139	115	143	71·3	145	
16	1569	780	1672	263	103	69	521	330	363	198	186	137	126		74·5		
17	1706	886	1732	261	114	61	518	330	330	226	172	132			71·0		
18	1507	825	1581	264	110	61	516	312	323		188	141	188	192	80·0	167	75·0
19	1725	876	1685	246	113	68	503	390	350	220	189	138	100	199	75·6	167	73·5
20	1715	835	1675	297	110	59	539	349	381	215	190	138	97	130	76·8	154	69·8
21	1617	840	1757	294	113	54	531	327	389	200	184	137	93	126	74·1	163	75·2
22	1655	868	1788	240	112	59	535	331	383	204	190	128	100	135	76·1	147	78·3
23	1693	868	1726	250	106	62	535	326	383	199	191	139	103	123	72·7	163	75·5
24	1682	854	1782	258	98	58	544	385	390	207	174	139	100	128	71·6	155	77·5
25	1615	835	1682	267	119	68	508	310	390	199	185	129	100		69·7		

	26	27	28	29	30	Average
	75·5	79·4	77·0	75·7	80·0	73·5
	156	161	156	161	152	140
	77·7	77·4	74·8	75·6	73·8	75·3
	130	127	131	125	128	128
	105	112	104	103	108	97
	139	141	135	136	135	138
	179	188	182	180	183	184
	203	205	205	201	195	199
	340	342	359	339	329	336
	325	330	349	336	328	327
	519	532	536	526	529	527
	62	57	61	62	60	65
	99	106	111	115	109	110
	254	251	250	245	234	252
	1737	1604	1619	1665	1708	1711
	•850	838	808	862	856	841
	1654	1560	1555	1632	1683	1640

Name of Caste or Tribe—BRAHMAN (GAUR).

No.	Height of Vertex	Height of Trunk	Span	Left Foot	Left Middle Finger	Right Ear Height	Round Head	Inion to Glabella	Tragus to Tragus	Vertex to Chin	Antero-posterior Diameter	Maximum Transverse Diameter	Minimum Frontal Diameter	Bizygomatic Diameter	Cephalic Index	General Index	Frontal Index
1	1584	797	1691	246	110	69	533	345	345	213	181	141			77.9		
2	1648	841	1704	267	114	69	546	348	343	244	188	143			72.2		
3	1584	818	1582	246	99	64	541	343	340	231	192	139			72.4		
4	1723	874	1750	257	114	58	564	368	368	224	188	142			71.7		
5	1662	838	1666	244	104	61	561	358	350	211	188	141			71.2		
6	1663	846	1661	264	107	61	538	350	340	213	187	138			73.8		
7	1617	810	1633	262	112	60	538	338	353	229	194	141			78.7		
8	1663		1711	257	110		579	353	356		183	152			78.8		
9	1607		1594	257	110		541	328	345		191	141			73.4		
10	1742		1623	279	119		559	335	353		195	151			77.0		
11	1549		1772	279	99		546	325	343		192	146			76.5		
12	1699		1656	344	110		536	312	325		183	140			72.7		
13	1643		1739	269	104		554	340	325		194	141			76.3		
14	1651		1648	246	110		541	358	350		190	145			76.4		
15	1658		1691	246	107		546	353	343		186	142			74.1		
16	1615		1643	236	114	64	536	350	348		189	142			72.3		
17	1693		1709	267	113	64	541	350	343		195	140			73.5		
18	1694		1744	269	114	64	541	391	366		200	141			75.3		
19	1665		1818	274	117	66	564	347	347		190	147			75.0		
20	1560	892	1745	258	113	69	543	330	363	215	188	143	120	187	69.6	157	83.9
21	1540	867	1752	254		71	548	324	396	209	181	141	102	188	74.6	157	73.3
22	1615	777	1657	242		63	519	335	333	195	181	126	96	122	71.1	160	76.1
23	1590	808	1735	232		59	534	341	339	194	187	135	105	125	74.8	155	77.7
24	1540	818	1660	230	114	60	536	330	342	205	176	133	103	126	71.1	163	77.4
25	1565	783	1680	230	104	63	597			198		131	108	125	74.8	158	82.4

	26	27	28	29	30	31	32	33	34	35	36	37	38	39	Average
	72·5	74·6	75·6	69·6	77·4	74·2	84·6	77·4	72·6	80·0	76·9	74·3	76·7	70·0	75·8
	160	150	157	158	160	155	171	173	166	172	177	170	159	174	163
	69·3	71·7	75·0	79·2	67·8	74·8	68·4	66·2	72·9	68·4	68·1	71·8	72·1	74·1	73·3
	131	135	125	135	124	127	126	132	125	128	130	135	128	130	128
	95	100	102	101	96	96	110	103	98	104	100	104	98	98	102
	131	134	135	145	124	132	130	138	135	130	130	140	129	140	138
	199	157	199	193	193	179	199	193	199	199	188	195	179	189	191
	210	203	209	211	195	197	216	228	208	218	230	239	203	226	213
	348	343	345	350	334	339	345	333	349	330	333	345	330	368	335
	338	350	344	840	825	318	331	334	381	342	840	368	822	345	336
	586	544	534	546	510	528	535	551	537	537	539	564	522	533	528
	68	69	58	60	59	58	62	60	60	71	54	58	60	62	63
	113	111	103	107	117	117	115	116	108	117	112	108	109	110	113
	249	256	234	239	263	351	357	269	235	264	255	256	250	251	253
	1730	1702	1635	1687	1739	1825	1798	1833	1714	1740	1683	1753	1702	1794	1735
	891	835	848	860	870	860	845	849	780	840	825	865	833	853	837
	1705	1615	1635	1647	1720	1715	1692	1801	1519	1661	1635	1710	1635	1645	1669

Name of Caste or Tribe—DHIMAR.

No.	Height of Vertex.	Height of Trunk.	Span.	Left Foot.	Left Middle Finger.	Right Ear Height.	Round Head.	Inion to Glabella.	Tragus to Tragus.	Vertex to Chin.	Antero-posterior Diameter.	Maximum Transverse Diameter.	Minimum Frontal Diameter.	Bizygomatic diameter.	Cephalic Index	General Index.	Frontal Index.
1	1630	828	1665	240	108	59	548	800	350	201	195	138	108	130	70·8	148	78·3
2	1606	865	1616	260	113	68	543	385	347	203	195	138	116	143	70·8	142	84·1
3	1586	845	1585	251	105	69	560	365	355	209	195	139	106	131	70·2	160	76·3
4	1602	816	1700	255	118	62	535	385	338	205	198	133	103	132	68·6	155	77·4
5	1697	825	1685	245	104	58	538	330	330	207	191	134	90	127	72·0	163	67·2
6	1705	852	1845	276	119	59	545	350	356	215	186	138	108	130	70·9	158	73·3
7	1618	833	1705	253	110	67	545	350	355	205	192	140	105	137	73·7	150	75·0
8	1640	842	1700	260	108	57	543	353	350	220	190	142	108	134	72·4	164	76·1
9	1666	865	1775	264	111	60	530	355	345	220	196	143	107	133	74·5	165	74·1
10	1545	813	1565	235	110	62	538	345	340	203	192	138	110	128	70·7	159	82·7
11	1680	830	1675	245	110	63	560	352	338	210	188	141	110	133	72·3	158	82·8
12	1580	800	1645	238	104	63	598	385	340	212	195	133	106	131	68·2	162	81·0
13	1610	885	1690	230	98	69	553	325	355	201	189	143	120	139	76·2	145	83·9
14	1685	576	1675	240	108	65	560	352	345	220	194	138	107	133	71·1	165	77·8
15	1606	855	1700	230	119	60	587	348	375	220	184	184	110	133	75·0	165	79·6
16	1668	861	1805	265	98	60	574	375	350	240	208	142	115	143	68·3	169	79·0
17	1676	866	1765	258	105	62	545	358	345	203	190	139	110	133	73·2	153	81·3
18	1685	830	1650	249	101	60	532	350	354	208	187	136	103	131	72·2	169	79·3
19	1637	885	1715	240	119	59	535	345	347	204	192	134	109	135	69·8	151	76·3
20	1635	816	1700	234	111	62	553	344	339	215	185	135	101	125	73·0	157	81·3
21	1680	815	1750	250	115	60	517	323	345	200	181	135	97	127	74·6	171	74·8
22	1720	884	1689	270	113	60	530	334	340	199	185	133	97	127	71·9	157	71·9
23	1621	810	1708	251	113	57	540	334	350	198	187	136	105	129	72·7	153	72·9
24	1680	800	1795	250	110	56	539	334	340	192	182	181	96	125	72·0	154	77·2
25	1688	847	1785	257	110		539	344	340	198	197	140	98	125	74·9	157	73·3

	26	27	28	29	30	31	32	33	34	35	36	37	38	39	40	41	42	43	44	Average
	78·5	74·6	73·5	77·3	79·1	75·1	77·2	74·6	67·9	77·8	74·1	77·8	72·9	70·3	75·2	83·7	76·6	76·6	79·7	76·6
	149	168	157	170	147	140	151	159	164	165	164	152	170	164	155	157	159	171	161	158
	72·6	72·6	75·4	72·3	78·1	75·5	76·4	69·5	76·1	72·6	73·0	76·3	68·6	78·0	72·7	75·0	70·3	66·7	70·2	73·5
	130	128	125	130	135	128	132	125	120	130	129	130	130	125	130	135	128	129	126	131
	106	103	100	105	110	109	105	97	95	105	100	105	57	97	100	113	100	100	105	106
	135	138	136	138	139	145	136	130	140	135	135	135	133	138	133	135	130	130	132	138
	186	190	179	188	178	192	178	187	184	186	185	177	194	177	183	180	185	195	188	187
	194	208	194	220	198	205	210	199	207	215	21?	198	221	205	202	218	203	221	208	203
	330	330	315	335	324	345	340	310	335	335	324	310	330	330	345	332	325	328	326	332
	320	330	310	327	315	343	338	310	330	335	330	304	320	318	315	329	340	330	330	336
	510	535	503	530	534	543	520	530	528	534	538	510	525	505	526	543	528	531	530	535
	82	60	56	58	61	61	61	65	60	69	64	64	84	59	62	63	66	56	56	61
	106	111	111	101	111	111	105	103	103	105	110	100	110	110	105	111	109	110	110	108
	243	263	254	249	262	254	251	234	253	279	249	252	270	251	245	255	246	255	234	253
	1705	1770	1730	1723	1755	1760	1730	1638	1723	1815	1723	1750	1750	1700	1735	1673	1756	1610		1655
	802	810	822	874	890	850	832	852	820	915	852	820	855	865	850	785	810	755		838
	1623	1658	1675	1720	1671	1665	1692	1580	1610	1725	1660	1655	1670	1665	1655	1685	1565	1630	1560	1814

16

Name of Caste or Tribe—GADARIYA.

№	Height of Vertex	Height of Trunk	Span	Left Foot	Left Middle Finger	Right Ear Height	Round Head	Union to Umbilicus	Trunk to Tarsus	Vertex to Chin	Antero-posterior Diameter	Maximum Transverse Diameter	Minimum Frontal Diameter	Bizygomatic Diameter	Cephalic Index	General Index	Frontal Index
	2	3	4	5	6	7	8	9	10	11	12	13	14	15	16	17	19
1	1606	820	1612	242	101	56	540	345	343	207	187	139	109	137	74.3	151	78.4
2	1526	780	1562	239	105	67	533	355	343	198	188	133	99	125	70.7	158	74.4
3	1595	805	1650	235	102	62	557	310	353	190	193	113	117	138	74.1	138	81.8
4	1648	872	1670	242	103	67	545	300	366	201	198	142	105	127	75.5	158	73.9
5	1632	845	1685	238	108	69	528	338	335	205	181	137	110	131	75.7	156	80.3
6	1705	855	1720	253	112	65	537	335	345	200	187	140	110	131	74.8	143	81.3
7	1647	855	1700	256	106	61	550	348	345	207	191	149	117	140	78.0	146	73.6
8	1694	863	1800	260	116	59	546	370	365	212	199	140	102	142	78.0	154	78.5
9	1626	790	1676	231	118	66	494	350	325	193	176	130	101	138	74.1	147	72.9
10	1615	865	1703	262	121	53	553	350	350	200	185	134	100	131	73.8	153	77.7
11	1810	780	1700	250	109	61	513	320	339	188	173	128	100	131	72.4	145	72.5
12	1622	803	1730	246	114	56	500	310	328	192	171	130	97	130	79.8	119	74.6
13	1594	785	1715	258	121	64	523	391	345	145	180	135	102	129	76.0	141	75.6
14	1590	707	1690	243	105	60	495	329	326	290	176	130	96	124	75.0	169	73.8
15	1709	829	1771	260	107	63	532	353	349	209	190	139	99	123	73.8	163	71.2
16	1770	854	1875	274	120	62	540	310	334	228	185	134	110	124	73.2	182	79.7
17	1615	802	1690	257	110	63	540	333	336	223	183	134	110	125	74.6	172	79.7
18	1685	850	1720	254	110	56	540	330	342	220	190	135	112	130	73.4	166	83.0
19	1610	840	1755	240	110	61	533	330	354	204	185	132	110	125	71.1	163	83.3
20	1670	870	1785	240	108	61	540	341	342	232	185	131	105	125	71.4	186	78.3
21	1685	870	1745	274	120	65	529	324	330	220	180	125	100	129	72.4	171	80.0
22	1603	810	1697	263	112	63	544	344	350	189	182	135	100	127	69.4	149	74.1
23	1535	815	1680	260	110	58	526	336	343	190	179	133	97	135	74.3	152	72.9
Average	1632	826	1713	252	110	61	535	339	343	204	189	136	105	130	74.0	157	81.3

Name of Caste or Tribe—HABURA.

No.	Height of Vertex	Height of Trunk	Span	Left Foot	Left Middle Finger	Right Ear Height	Round Head	Inion to Glabella	Tragus to Tragus	Vertex to Chin	Antero-posterior Diameter	Maximum Transverse Diameter	Minimum Frontal Diameter	Bizygomatic	Cephalic Index	General Index	Frontal Index
1	1727	853	1795	239	114	66	508	330	368	224	178	140	117	137	78·7	164	83·6
2	1666	878	1734	236	114	71	556	343	340	216	198	145	117	140	73·2	154	80·7
3	1656	843	1727	241	114	61	541	530	356	216	191	142	111	132	74·9	164	78·2
4	1744	914	1803	272	123	64	551	361	361	226	191	143	116	139	74·0	163	81·1
5	1742	861	1742	207	110	68	521	317	363	229	188	139	121	184	74·9	171	87·1
6	1632	823	1656	251	110	66	528	338	363	218	186	143	105	191	76·9	166	73·4
7	1671	879	1704	259	110	61	546	356	363	229	186	142	105	132	76·8	173	73·9
8	1747	901	1807	272	119	64	546	361	361	226	188	160	116	140	76·9	161	77·3
9	1493	805	1579	234	107	69	503	315	328	204	188	129	108	131	70·9	157	83·7
10	1567	795	1572	230	107	61	505	328	335	200	180	138	108	122	71·1	164	84·4
11	1742	894	1752	263	119	71	541	340	361	216	190	141	114	144	74·2	150	80·9
12	1590	889	1590	246	104	61	528	330	361	218	183	147	101	130	80·3	166	68·7
13	1607	851	1617	236	99	58	546	313	361	218	182	149	118	135	78·7	161	79·2
14	1714	881	1658	214	110	58	526	335	343	224	187	141	109	125	77·4	179	77·3
15	1711	851	1739	254	107	66	531	335	373	231	192	142	109	133	75·9	166	76·8
16	1699	863	1772	251	117	51	546	340	350	231	189	144	117	132	75·0	175	81·2
17	1681	838	1684	244	102	64	528	356	343	208	194	147	111	125	77·7	170	81·0
18	1595	843	1590	254	107	58	523	338	343	213	185	137	115	133	70·8	164	79·5
19	1663	871	1625	241	107	66	516	330	333	218	198	140	113	130	78·8	151	80·7
20	1625	830	1696	259	114	60	555	341	350	196	180	140	109	134	76·9	166	74·8
21	1635	870	1800	257	115	60	52）	329	332	223	180	147	105	129	73·3	157	79·5
22	1675	830	1740	250	110	55	530	334	346	202	186	132	103	133	74·2	149	76·9
23	1630	840	1665	251	106	54	526	328	339	198	186	134	99	128	69·9	148	76·2
24	1690	820	1770	250	105	57	525	340	340	190	186	130	103	133	74·0	150	74·6
25		860	1760	256	101					199		188					
Average.	1664	853	1704	252	110	62	531	338	350	214	187	141	113	128	75·2	162	78·8

Name of Caste or Tribe—KAYASTH.

No.	Height of Vertex	Height of Trunk	Span	Left Foot	Left Middle Finger	Right Ear Height	Round Head	Inion to Glabella	Tragus to Tragus	Vertex to Chin	Antero-posterior Diameter	Maximum Transverse Diameter	Minimum Frontal Diameter	Bizygomatic Diameter	Cephalic Index	General Index	Frontal Index
	2	3	4	5	6	7	8	9	10	11	12	13	14	15	16	17	19
1	1656	846	1694	254	102	64	546	348	338	234	196	137			69·9		
2	1684	843	1714	244	107	71	549	358	361	203	193	139			72·0		
3	1640	838	1727	254	107	69	551	356	356	200	197	139			70·1	157	
4	1567	791	1556	223	96	55	522	343	337	200	187	137	109	127	73·3	161	79·6
5	1687	824	1678	253	105	60	523	347	337	218	187	136	115	135	72·7	171	84·6
6	1600	779	1637	235	102	57	523	320	322	215	185	135	100	128	73·0	156	74·1
7	1710	816	1780	246	105	58	530	340	320	206	188	135	105	132	71·8	160	77·8
8	1745	829	1777	247	117	60	537	355	320	215	198	137	110	134	69·2	157	87·6
9	1697	825	1763	261	106	53	538	357	338	212	188	138	108	135	73·4	154	78·3
10	1657	842	1700	261	107	61	560	303	345	212	203	139	103	139	68·5	138	73·4
11	1608	802	1710	260	113	70	550	345	360	197	189	143	117	113	76·7	167	81·8
12	1690	865	1840	251	105	57	520	331	345	204	175	136	106	122	77·7	161	77·9
13	1635	857	1677	249	105	57	537	340	340	205	183	140	106	127	76·5	161	75·7
14	1700	895	1685	251	110	61	530	344	347	209	190	131	100	130	68·9	162	76·3
15	1694	860	1766	267	108	58	540	350	344	206	185	134	102	127	72·4	148	76·1
16	1695	855	1715	254	100	57	526	360	361	193	177	131	108	130	74·1	153	82·4
17	1725	820	1801	250	104	56	544	352	359	220	183	113	109	143	78·1	150	76·2
18	1610	845	1695	255	107	61	529	370	350	202	188	143	103	135	76·1	144	72·0
19	1650	840	1750	240	103	58	535	346	331	184	183	141	98	128	77·0	153	69·5
20	1665	825	1705	237	106	51	533	334	364	193	179	135	98	126	75·4	158	71·1
21	1655	853	1760	259	108	59	560	370	334	212	184	140	100	134	76·1	158	71·4
22	1530	825	1616	238	106	64	561	340	370	209	192	135	110	132	70·3	166	81·5
23	1625	815	1742	248	110	60	550	342	340	220	190	140	109	133	73·7	155	77·9
24	1710	825	1796	250	110	56	530	330	330	209	186	139	100	128	74·7		71·9
25	1680	815	1765	251	114	60	530	335	340	200	180	136	102	128	75·6	156	75·0
Average.	1659	839	1722	250	106	59	537	346	344	207	133	138	105	132	73·4	157	76·7

Frontal Index (19)	(17)	(16)	Bizygom. distance (15)	Minimum Frontal Diameter (14)	(13)	(12)	(11)	(10)	(9)	(8)	(7)	(6)	(5)	(4)	(3)	(2)	No. (1)
79·5	104	78·6	141	120	151	192	231	376	876	566	76	117	257	1851	891	1714	1
78·8	160	75·3	135	115	146	194	216	361	363	559	71	114	254	1765	869	1694	2
78·9	143	76·2	140	116	147	193	200	366	358	559	64	114	259	1838	879	1770	3
81·1	131	77·4	140	116	143	185	189	348	349	541	66	112	249	1729	858	1668	4
87·4	148	69·7	135	118	135	178	200	366	328	518	71	119	254	1803	838	1752	5
83·8	147	68·4	136	114	136	185	200	366	358	549	69	114	254	1760	856	1676	6
79·9	159	70·0	138	111	139	203	216	353	361	554	69	124	264	1815	884	1734	7
78·6	156	70·6	132	110	140	200	206	353	348	549	64	110	249	1760	838	1686	8
86·8	149	76·0	142	125	144	204	211	376	358	566	61	119	264	1825	909	1770	9
82·8	158	71·6	135	120	145	191	213	356	350	546	66	117	251	1714	833	1661	10
:	:	:	:	:	139	194	221	353	350	541	64	103	244	1650	828	1630	11
81·9	145	71·8	142	118	140	195	211	356	356	543	58	112	262	1727	853	1671	12
79·1	159	73·8	129	110	144	195	206	354	358	564	67	109	248	1730	895	1658	13
79·8	137	71·6	143	115	139	194	205	364	345	562	60	105	263	1767	865	1658	14
76·6	157	73·1	132	109	144	197	225	373	359	571	63	117	275	1835	925	1783	15
78·6	160	73·2	132	104	143	194	207	370	360	553	59	99	241	1648	876	1665	16
75·7	103	69·6	126	103	133	191	213	329	348	542	70	105	240	1665	863	1610	17
74·3	161	75·6	137	107	136	180	203	328	320	516	61	109	252	1695	878	1665	18
84·3	159	72·0	140	118	144	200	220	350	350	570	65	104	254	1761	872	1708	19
76·9	171	71·0	133	103	140	197	222	347	335	553	63	111	264	1830	890	1785	20
75·0	159	66·0	140	112	134	187	227	355	360	545	68	112	264	1755	945	1740	21
73·0	169	78·1	133	103	146	186	223	370	369	545	67	110	260	1850	880	1720	22
71·2	172	75·1	130	99	141	185	225	354	345	540	64	110	255	1729	895	1680	23
76·9	154	71·0	131	100	139	184	224	349	332	535	61	115	255	1750	870	1690	24
71·9	157	77·0	134	100	131	180	203	335	334	525	62	108	255	1895	815	1780	25
73·9	175	74·5	135	103	139	195	212	348	330	533	65	104	265	1828	855	1765	26
71·4	167		133	100	139	195	236	360	370	562	61	108	265	1749	863	1710	27
					140	188	221	352	353	540	00	108	251	1670	790	1590	28
78·9	158	73·3	136	110	137	192	214	372	351	549	65	111	257	1767	866	1702	Aver-age.

Name of Caste or Tribe—BARGUJAR RAJPUTS.

No.	Height of Vertex	Height of Trunk	Span	Left Foot	Left Middle Finger	Right Ear Height	Round Head	Inion to Labella	Tragus to Tragus	Vertex to Chin	Antero-posterior Diameter	Maximum Transverse Diameter	Minimum Frontal Diameter	Bizygomatic Diameter	Cephalic Index	General Index	Frontal Index
1	2	3	4	5	6	7	8	9	10	11	12	13	14	15	16	17	18
1	1732	884	1815	279	119	66	538	318	356	213	195	137	...	...	70·3	...	...
2	1759	884	1859	259	107	64	571	383	363	241	203	142	...	...	70·0	...	...
3	1731	888	1772	261	119	64	564	371	381	241	201	145	...	...	72·6	...	...
4	1569	792	1635	246	102	58	526	330	353	200	187	141	...	...	75·6	...	...
5	1693	813	1612	262	110	58	511	341	371	239	194	142	...	...	73·2	...	...
6	1655	841	1797	254	107	69	556	318	376	236	201	143	...	...	71·1	...	...
7	1734	849	1869	267	117	68	551	340	376	210	198	145	...	...	73·2	...	...
8	1849	806	1931	282	117	64	539	330	345	206	192	140	...	...	72·9	...	...
9	1709	858	1815	257	110	69	541	340	361	231	195	142	130	130	72·8	145	85·6
10	1656	813	1765	257	110	76	539	313	363	188	191	139	138	138	72·8	153	89·0
11	1734	881	1830	242	117	64	533	333	350	211	186	136	...	...	73·1	...	...
12	1658	...	1797	234	117	61	549	333	330	...	190	130	119	...	68·4	...	...
13	1628	...	1673	251	107	58	533	330	330	204	188	130	122	...	69·1	...	...
14	1755	858	1741	207	112	69	539	358	356	199	193	137	111	128	71·0	158	79·3
15	1633	830	1766	256	112	60	540	335	340	215	182	140	106	131	76·9	150	78·7
16	1695	855	1755	257	112	57	541	347	339	219	187	133	105	142	71·1	154	75·5
17	1739	840	1812	260	120	70	535	335	350	223	185	139	103	133	75·1	168	72·5
18	1770	890	1911	271	120	63	555	360	355	207	193	142	102	135	73·6	153	78·4
19	1718	875	1805	277	121	64	535	335	335	224	190	130	102	137	68·4	161	73·4
20	1709	880	1805	263	110	62	545	329	340	217	187	139	102	...	74·3	...	...
Aver. age.	1701	845	1791	262	113	64	543	345	354	217	192	139	109	134	71·8	156	77·7

Name of Caste or Tribe—BRAHMAN (SANÁDH).

No.	Height of Vertex	Height of Trunk	Span	Left Foot	Left Middle Finger	Right Ear Height	Round Head	Inion to Glabella	Tragus to Tragus	Vertex to Chin	Antero-posterior Diameter	Maximum Transverse Diameter	Minimum Frontal Diameter	Bizygomatic Diameter	Cephalic Index	General Index	Frontal Index
1	1744	881	1836	279	119	60	533	328	345	211	193	138	...	...	71·4	...	...
2	1633	846	1717	254	107	69	541	333	340	216	192	144	...	...	75·0	...	...
3	1700	848	1772	259	107	61	541	333	348	208	184	146	...	...	79·4	...	...
4	1706	856	1828	259	112	64	566	343	353	234	200	148	...	...	74·0	...	...
5	1770	896	1841	264	114	66	551	358	368	221	191	144	...	...	75·3	...	...
6	1709	874	1702	274	110	69	549	366	361	208	199	139	...	...	68·9	...	...
7	1747	843	1815	274	119	64	549	358	361	208	191	146	...	...	76·4	...	...
8	1724	863	1820	269	114	69	566	350	356	208	201	146	...	...	72·6	...	...
9	1612	835	1711	257	167	56	538	348	348	221	190	139	...	...	73·2	...	...
10	1607	823	1700	254	104	64	559	353	348	213	200	144	...	...	72·0	...	...
11	1810	909	1864	282	117	64	546	345	373	200	195	140	...	...	71·8	...	...
12	1765	898	1823	282	117	64	559	356	363	226	194	145	...	...	74·7	...	...
13	1663	850	1694	282	112	66	549	344	343	218	195	135	...	...	74·1	...	...
14	1727	820	1765	267	110	68	536	345	350	208	190	136	...	...	73·1	...	...
15	1660	855	1740	266	105	57	526	340	350	222	186	128	102	131	74·2	169	75·0
16	1583	835	1627	260	114	71	549	345	320	229	188	134	57	136	71·7	168	70·3
17	1590	810	1637	241	110	61	525	315	357	207	187	135	107	130	67·5	160	79·9
18	1672	832	1722	248	111	63	553	361	331	236	200	130	103	130	69·9	182	73·8
19	1630	835	1749	256	117	64	526	325	352	222	186	143	105	130	78·4	171	78·9
20	1594	778	1670	234	104	64	536	343	341	211	185	142	113	130	76·9	162	77·9
21	1660	827	1768	244	107	56	534	330	370	222	182	133	102	128	71·0	173	72·9
22	1732	915	1770	265	114	67	573	378	325	225	200	132	110	130	74·3	173	77·5
23	1673	805	1782	254	117	57	508	320	343	220	179	140	110	126	71·4	175	83·7
24	1685	840	1755	249	116	59	520	336	340	230	185	136	112	135	75·7	163	84·8
25	1604	824	1724	227	107	56	535	322	360	190	185	140	94	130	71·6	146	67·1
26	1605	850	1685	252	114	60	538	360	330	224	190	136	102	126	72·1	178	75·0
27	1625	826	1686	233	105	61	534	349	330	194	179	129	98	129	72·1	150	76·0
Aver. age.	1675	848	1749	260	111	63	542	343	349	191	191	140	104	130	73·7	167	76·6

Name of Caste or Tribe—BHI'RJI.

	Height of Vertex.	Height of Trunk.	Span.	Left Foot.	Left Middle Finger.	Bizib Ear Height.	Roundy Head.	Inion to Cubella.	Tragus to Tragus.	Vertex to Chin.	Antero posterior Diameter.	Maximum Transverse Diameter.	Minimum Frontal Diameter.	Bizygomatic Diameter.	Cephalic Index.	General Index.	Frontal Index.
	2	3	4	5	6	7	8	9	10	11	12	13	14	15	16	17	18
1	1554	805	1549	229	99	60	528	310	330	190	190	139	109	127	73·2	150	78·4
2	1591	845	1567	237	98	58	558	342	362	206	193	145	116	138	76·3	149	80·4
3	1663	820	1765	245	108	59	535	835	338	215	186	139	110	136	74·7	158	79·1
4	1667	857	1740	250	117	60	532	365	353	207	196	134	112	132	63·3	157	83·6
5	1615	825	1705	251	108	66	538	330	335	218	181	134	104	127	74·0	168	77·5
6	1630	843	1690	248	110	62	520	345	344	212	190	139	102	128	73·2	166	77·6
7	1580	839	1621	250	111	63	542	341	350	212	191	138	102	126	72·6	160	73·5
8	1585	823	1650	241	109	63	542	320	323	202	173	130	101	128	75·1	148	72·5
9	1649	820	1684	255	111	65	512	330	341	186	186	129	96	131	69·4	148	77·7
10	1680	830	1725	246	105	57	522	322	335	190	176	138	101	130	78·4	162	74·4
11	1650	850	1775	253	115	59	508	323	325	212	184	132	100	124	71·7	165	73·3
12	1600	804	1718	212	103	63	520	325	333	214	185	130	99	125	70·3	165	75·8
13	1590	808	1759	247	100	58	536	350	336	206	183	134	102	126	73·2	173	76·1
14	1600	820	1695	254	111	63	530	330	335	215	195	142	105	127	72·8	171	73·9
15	1640	825	1695	243	105	66	538	326	388	214	178	134	102	130	75·8	163	76·1
16	1591	780	1695	233	104	58	526	335	327	206	188	134	98	131	71·3	163	73·1
17	1612	810	1718	246	110	61	525	329	330	207	185	131	108	125	72·4	154	73·1
18	1680	845	1718	241	114	68	528	330	332	200	180	138	100	127	76·7	167	80·6
19	1600	810	1666	243	108	61	536	336	330	217	184	134	98	130	72·8	155	71·7
20	1590	805	1709	245	109	60	529	360	360	204	179	180	100	131	72·6	157	73·1
21	1580	825			106	60	523			196	184	143	100	125	77·7	164	76·9
Average.	1618	833	1691	246	108	64	529	335	337	206	185	136	117	189	73·2	160	75·9

19			16	14		13											1
					133	201	229	376	373	546	61	112	284	1807	881	1742	1
					133	194	231	348	358	538	58	103	241	1739	858	1671	2
					140	195	234	350	356	538	49	102	234	1753	836	1669	3
					141	184	193	348	335	526	58	107	259	1783	835	1694	4
					131	190	208	330	343	526	61	112	254	1755	881	1694	5
					139	185	203	335	330	516	58	104	239	1701	833	1643	6
84·8	161	66·2	131	117	138	184	211	340	323	533	61	110	249	1734	900	1651	7
83·8	159	69·6	133	114	136	200	211	340	350	554	69	117	269	1783	853	1724	8
78·0	152	71·8	132	107	137	198	200	330	330	533	61	107	274	1732	830	1668	9
84·7	176	76·6	131	117	138	193	281	350	343	541	64	114	257	1737	838	1658	10
84·7	150	68·9	141	116	137	193	211	361	356	538	66	107	287	1841	808	1737	11
81·0	176	75·1	130	111	137	194	229	330	338	523	64	117	236	1638	742	1549	12
85·2	155	75·0	139	121	143	198	216	361	350	549	64	112	267	1869	828	1714	13
80·0	156	68·0	126	108	135	185	196	343	338	526	61	105	257	1671	841	1648	14
74·2	160	72·9	128	98	132	191	205	320	330	575	63	107	235	1558	815	1546	15
75·0	159	71·5	132	105	140	191	210	350	343	637	65	120	250	1760	825	1656	16
83·0	153	71·0	135	117	141	195	206	358	357	560	64	100	267	1865	890	1703	17
76·9	156	74·5	141	110	143	195	220	350	300	548	54	113	251	1745	865	1669	18
74·4	155	73·9	128	99	133	194	199	335	308	506	71	114	255	1765	900	1725	19
75·7	149	73·0	135	109	144	173	201	340	306	512	58	105	248	1680	865	1645	20
78·4	158	72·9	130	109	139	190	205	360	363	545	61	109	248	1715	820	1610	21
73·9	169	73·3	132	105	142	185	223	380	370	560	54	113	243	1698	835	1650	22
75·8	151	72·8	129	100	132	182	196	330	334	533	57	117	259	1720	800	1656	23
70·6	160	73·3	128	98	136	185	200	313	342	545	66	110	258	1762	825	1659	24
80·3	146	83·2	135	102	127	179	187	318	315	518	57	112	244	1664	803	1600	25
75·0	153	73·8	125	105	140	196	207	358	349	540	58	105	252	1700	830	1635	26
75·6	169	72·5	128	102	135	189	211	335	330	529	53	113	242	1627	794	1577	27
72·3	155	73·5	128	99	137	190	195	329	330	526	57	120	237	1634	825	1590	28
72·5	150	70·9	129	100	138	181	192	334	344	532	61	105	262	1783	815	1694	29
76·9	147	71·4		100	130	182	189	335	340	528	61	105	238	1664	833	1623	30
78·0	157	72·5	127	105	137	188	208	344	341	356	61	110	253	1727	838	1643	Average

Name of Custe of Tribe—SAYAD.

No.	Hei.t of Ver.tex.	Hei.t of Trunk.	Span.	Left Foot	Left Middle Finger	Bigh. Ear Height.	Br. and Head.	Inion to Glabella.	Tragus to Tragus.	Vertex to Chin.	Antero-Posterior Diameter.	Maximum Transverse Diameter.	Minimum Frontal Diameter.	Bizygomatic Diameter.	Cephalic Index.	General Index.	Frontal Index.
	2	3	4	5	6	7	8	9	10	11	12	13	14	15	16	17	19
1	1724	840	1775	263	110	64	520	333	333	216	165	134	108	130	72·4	161	80·6
2	1602	797	1607	246	102	58	520	328	330	200	183	139	114	129	75·9	155	82·0
3	1691	851	1734	254	103	56	530	350	343	218	189	138	125	138	73·0	158	90·6
4	1645	849	1587	241	117	63	523	330	343	221	185	133	117	135	71·8	164	87·9
5	1582	795	1633	249	110	61	513	317	330	188	182	132	105	127	72·5	148	79·5
6	1709	858	1795	292	110	71	538	358	360	218	185	140	109	130	71·8	164	77·9
7	1700	890	1710	252	113	59	537	344	347	203	181	150	105	141	82·8	141	70·0
8	1645	810	1711	250	113	57	545	323	336	210	181	140	101	133	77·3	158	72·1
9	1727	893	1724	250	106	67	555	360	369	228	192	140	103	136	78·8	168	73·6
10	1683	895	1683	240	110	60	539	358	350	204	188	147	99	130	83·8	157	73·8
11	1803	905	1852	266	130	65	530	338	339	191	190	133	104	138	70·0	138	67·4
12	1612	825	1576	234	104	53	520	330	330	193	182	132	93	122	72·5	158	78·1
13	1700	870	1768	256	107	57	515	357	335	205	183	135	104	135	75·4	152	73·5
14	1620	890	1794	241	100	57	534	325	350	210	187	138	107	127	70·6	165	77·5
15	1690	840	1785	246	117	60	553	365	360	210	178	132	108	132	77·5	163	77·3
16	1670	850	1772	262	110	63	540	330	335	185	179	134	107	137	73·7	135	77·5
17	1615	815	1699	260	110	63	538	360	330	204	186	182	97	130	78·0	157	73·5
18	1575	820	1610	251	104	62	540	350	350	193	187	145	110	131	71·7	147	75·9
19	1630	855	1700	253	112	60	545	350	335	214	182	134	105	127	75·3	109	78·4
20	1590	807	1695	250	107	59	534	335	340	194	180	137	102	130	76·1	151	74·5
21	1575	825	1625	251	114	62	537	330	330	193	181	137	95	135	71·8	144	78·1
22	1580	825	1680	236	102	62	524	354	351	200	199	130	103	126	73·5	159	73·1
23	1580	780	1659	251	110	57	540	334	360	212	184	137	105	127	70·7	167	75·2
24	1530	830	1580	240	112	57	537	360	389	206	186	130	105	127	73·5	182	80·8
25	1590	815	1675	250	115	58	550		370	209		130	108	132	69·9	158	88·1

26	27	28	29	30	31	32	33	Average.
71·9	81·5	81·5	76·9	81·5	84·6	79·7	80·6	77·6
148	145	170	148	145	151	158	164	157
73·0	73·0	73·0	72·6	71·1	70·7	73·2	68·0	73·2
125	130	125	127	133	130	125	134	131
97	110	110	100	110	110	110	108	106
135	135	135	130	135	130	138	134	136
185	185	185	170	190	184	190	197	184
185	189	213	182	193	196	197	219	203
360	360	360	330	360	330	350	375	345
360	840	350	857	370	330	875	880	345
530	540	560	530	560	550	550	570	537
56	82	58	56	61	53	63	58	60
115	120	115	105	115	115	115	120	111
252	278	256	225	257	240	238	252	252
1725	1780	1760	1720	1745	1795	1750	1790	1709
890	865	885	820	815	865	850	885	838
1650	1730	1730	1638	1650	1740	1653	1640	1653

Name of Caste or Tribe—NAT.

No.	Height of Vertex	Height of Trunk	Span	Left Foot	Left Middle Finger	Right Ear Height	Round Head	Union to Glabella	Tragus to Tragus	Vertex to Chin	Antero-posterior Diameter	Maximum Transverse Diameter	Minimum Frontal Diameter	Bizygomatic Diameter	Cephalic Index	General Index	Frontal Index
1	1574	782	1668	246	102	64	549	338	330	198	198	143	116	131	72.2	151	81.1
2	1777	886	1823	263	107	66	541	345	353	208	194	144	120	137	74.2	152	83.3
3	1633	859	1678	249	102	61	536	313	348	193	188	146	114	123	77.7	156	78.1
4	1663	870	1719	257	110	51	523	330	348	211	184	138	123	139	75.0	153	89.1
5	1630	841	1633	241	102	58	523	330	318	218	185	135	118	132	73.0	165	87.4
6	1645	858	1739	262	117	61	541	338	356	221	183	139	117	139	72.0	159	84.2
7	1511	772	1546	224	102	53	535	345	335	208	190	137	119	133	72.1	155	86.9
8	1739	876	1793	272	123	64	552	359	361	216	190	151	124	150	79.5	144	82.6
9	1617	843	1691	240	112	61	564	358	353	200	202	146	124	140	72.3	144	84.9
10	1612	770	1698	245	106	62	553	356	355	219	192	142	110	132	73.9	166	77.5
11	1667	830	1745	250	110	65	548	362	365	217	190	137	108	138	75.1	157	78.8
12	1654	810	1712	253	108	64	514	320	336	203	181	136	108	133	75.1	154	79.4
13	1633	830	1688	245	104	65	520	320	320	196	177	133	114	132	74.5	148	85.7
14	1545	818	1490	225	96	51	540	330	340	197	188	140	114	129	70.5	143	81.4
15	1780	895	1795	278	118	58	528	334	342	218	190	134	109	141	74.7	169	81.8
16	1656	849	1700	279	111	61	548	349	364	215	194	145	115	134	73.3	152	79.3
17	1675	855	1750	268	115	65	555	362	360	226	195	143	117	130	72.3	109	81.8
18	1708	874	1743	265	120	57	539	345	354	202	191	138	100	123	75.7	165	72.5
19	1661	820	1685	255	112	57	539	324	335	201	185	130	102	139	77.8	163	69.3
20	1680	865	1757	270	112	60	517	330	334	191	180	140	97	127	73.3	145	68.4
21	1606	785	1665	239	107	61	518	340	339	202	179	133	91	130	74.7	150	76.7
22	1590	814	1653	247	104	51	510	319	333	200	178	133	102	136	78.6	155	74.8
23	1608	815	1696	244	100	57	539	350	349	185	183	143	107	131	76.1	147	73.5
24	1572	800	1620	243	99	60	530	332	335	195	184	140	103	131	75.7	141	74.5
25	1640	845	1650	257	105	59	518	338	340	195	181	137	102	132		148	

	26	27	28	29	30	31	32	33	34	35	36	37	38	39	40	Average
	76·1	79·3	75·0	78·5	78·6	74·6	73·5	79·2	76·9	70·4						78·7
	143	153	158	145	161	145	153	150	148	160						153
	76·2	73·0	71·6	72·2	71·4	71·3	73·5	73·5	73·8	78·9						73·9
	137	128	133	126	136	128	130	129	125	130						133
	105	107	108	102	110	100	100	103	110	100						109
	138	135	136	130	140	134	136	130	130	142						138
	181	185	190	180	196	188	185	179	176	180						187
	196	191	204	183	219	186	199	193	185	208						202
	334	336	330	325	315	338	338	324	320	329						345
	320	835	860	323	851	348	834	342	823	328						342
	534	514	544	521	568	556	558	524	500	532						534
	60	56	59	69	58	61	55	53	54	57						59
	110	98	121	112	113	111	113	107	112	110						109
	232	230	242	256	258	220	240	225	233	228						260
	1710	1585	1765	1650	1694	1584	1626	1636	1674	1623						1681
	835	770	845	800	842	830	840	760	819	811						830
	1620	1520	1684	1580	1620	1562	1642	1540	1594	1552						1627

19

THE JOURNAL

OF THE

ANTHROPOLOGICAL SOCIETY

OF

BOMBAY.

ORDINARY GENERAL MEETING, held on Wednesday, the 28th June 1893.

DR. P. PETERSON, the *President*, in the Chair.

The Minutes of the previous Meeting were read and confirmed.

The election of the following new Member was announced:—

Mr. Sambhunath Sukul, Graduate and Member, Royal Asiatic Society, Benares City.

The following donation was announced, and thanks voted to the donors:—

To the Library.

From Dr. David Hooper, Quinologist to the Government of Madras, "Pharmacographia Indica," Part VI.

From E. Man, "Dictionary of the Central Nicobarese Language."

The following papers were then read:—

ON HINDU CEREMONIES *observed in the* MADRAS PRESIDENCY.

BY MR. MAHOMED SUFTHER HUSAIN of Madras.

AT the present time, when the study of Hindu Sociology is absorbing so much attention, it may be interesting to give a short account of some of the religious and social ceremonies

20

performed by the Hindus in this Presidency. Every family incident in a Hindu household is attended with ceremonies— ceremonies at puberty, ceremonies at birth, ceremonies at marriage, and ceremonies at funerals. In fact, the life of a Hindu is emphatically one of ceremonies. Savings of ages, hoarded by dint of thrift and frugality, are dissipated in a day or in a few days to meet the expenses concomittant to some ceremonial that is proposed to be performed. The Romans revelled in ceremonies, but the Hindus may be fairly said to eclipse them. It has been suggested that the internal resemblance of Roman ceremonies renders it possible that the former nation gathered its customs and rituals on the banks of the Ganges. But as this paper is not concerned with Ethnological researches, nothing shall be attempted in that way. Leaving the suggestion to stand in its primitive simplicity, we will proceed to describe some of the ceremonies that obtain among the Vaishnava Brahmans on the occasion of a girl attaining her puberty.

Puberty is reckoned an important epoch in the calendar of a Brahman-girl's life, and is marked with condign ceremonies. A girl is considered polluted during the menstrual period of puberty, so much so that she can have no part in the matters appertaining to her household, nor can she live, move or have a being among her elders in the house. Her uncleanness forbids her to approach them within a radius of about 10 yards. In truth, she has to keep herself to herself, being relegated to some out-of-the-way corner or possibly being ensconced in the covered extremity of the street or backyard pial of the family residence. The precise time of the occurrence of the menses is attempted to be ascertained with scrupulous exactitude, as it is the foundation upon which a horoscope in respect of her future career has to be calculated. The cloth worn by her at the time, the gaudiness or plainness of her attire, the day and the hour, are all factors in the determination of her destiny and give a forecast of her future. If, at the occurrence, her vesture was either pure-white or white with a border of a gay colour, her hair bedecked with flowers, herself in the genial occupation of chewing betel and in the best humour with all things around, then her future bliss is assured to her, but should the event befall her when she is asleep or when attired in sombre raiment or in clothes innocent of borders, her future would not be as one could wish. These are the many key-holes through which the elders of the family peep into the new maiden's futurity to learn her fate. As age has its privileges, the elderly women are generally asked to note the foregoing circumstances, and this done, the celebration of the event enters next into the programme, for, whether the parents of the girl are rich or poor, whether indigent or destitute, means must be found to commemorate the event with characteristic rejoicing. The maidens of the village where the matured girl lives, receive a *carte-blanche* to come and lend *éclat* to the festivity by their presence. They come, but their commingling with the girl just matured taints them as it were with her pollution, thus restricting them to her company only and forbidding them to mix with others.

The festivities occupy 4 days, during the whole of which period the maidens of the village remain the guests of the new maiden, but instead of confining themselves to her society, they make a tour round the village in a joyous group, singing sweet songs and clapping their hands to the measured beat of their amatory odes. In their tour they, mischievously inclined, attempt to taint the relations of the young maiden and other rich villagers with their polluting touch, and thus compel the latter to purchase immunity from defilement by payment of a liberal subsidy. They also indulge in chants of questionable modesty to draw down better collections. Money now flows copiously from the tight purses of the relations and the villagers into the open hands of the little joyous group. The collections are handed to the young heroine, who is for the nonce constituted treasurer and accountant, and who ultimately

distributes the sum total among her companions, share and share
alike. The little maiden group sit together to mess. The
characteristic meal for the first 3 days is the "Pongal," a
composition of rice, dall, turmeric, and ghee mixed with sugar.
The days are spent in fun, frolic, and frivolities. As all terres-
trial happiness is transitory and fleeting, the 3 days of merry-
making glide imperceptibly by into the shade of eternity, land-
ing the maiden group upon the events of the 4th day. The
programme for the 4th day is not devoid of interest. Comparing small things with great, the first event on the card reminds
one of Diana at the bath, for the new maiden is conducted to
a tank to bathe. This ablution is considered purificatory,
restoring her to her original cleanness. She is now dressed in
her best and bedecked, and often so loaded with jewels as to
render her recognition hardly feasible. In this gorgeous attire
she passes through the village in company with her other
maiden companions. In this procession, she is burdened with
that cumbrous commodity—a child—which is carried on her
waist. She stops at each door, in front of which a piece of oblong
plank has been placed. The heroine mounts this plank, and an
inmate of the house comes out with a tray filled with water—
a mixture of turmeric and chunam—and draws some circles in
the air close to her face with a view to cast off the effects of an
evil eye. If the inmate of the house happen to be a relation,
the young maiden is invited inside and given a piece of plantain
and milk to swallow. The person that performs the above
friendly ceremony is presented by the guardian of the maiden
with betel-nut and sandal, in acknowledgment evidently of the
courtesy shown. The circuit finished, the maiden reaches
her house, where the female members of the village have con-
gregated upon invitation. She now sets down the animated
burden which embarrassed her waist hitherto, with a sigh
probably of relief, but only to form again the central figure of
another interesting ceremony, which is commonly called the
"Achanthe leppu." From the assemblage of female elders

present, three, selected for experience in such matters, are appointed to officiate in the approaching ceremony. The maiden just matured is requested to stand upon a low platform in the main hall of the house, the striking feature in the decoration of which is the drawings with powdered rice. Before her is placed a plantain leaf, and within its foldings are kept a style, kadjan leaves, kowries, &c., and also a narrow-necked vessel filled with water and a burning lamp. One of the three officiating females comes forward and places nine sweet cakes over the heroine's body, one on the head, one on each of her shoulders, one on each of the palms of her hands, one on each side of right and left waist, and one on each of her feet. She repeats this process twice again, and concludes her part of the ceremony by taking up the filled vessels and the burning lamp over it, and describing with them circles in the air in front of the young woman's face. She performs her task in such a way as not to cause the incident to be marred with any untoward event. For instance, if in the process the vessel is upset, or the lamp is upset or extinguished, these circumstances or any of them would cause no small anxiety to the new maiden and her relatives, for such events are regarded as ill-omens. The other two elderly females go through the identical ceremony, each in her turn, with studied care to avoid mishaps. Petals of flowers are now universally employed in the place of cakes, as the unctuosity in their composition not unfrequently soils and stains the costly robes worn for the occasion. At the termination of the cake or flower ceremony, the new maiden is now made to sit on the dais whereon she was hitherto standing, and with her eyes closed she is required to take chance-like any of the several articles placed before her on the plantain leaf. If she chances to catch the kadjan leaves or the style, it predicts that her first born would be a son; if she touches any of the other minor articles before her, it predicts that her first born would be a daughter. This being done, all the articles before her are removed and put into her lap. She is now asked to bend, and, whilst in that uncomfortable attitude, the elderly females present, who have been previously supplied with the sacred grass (kusha), and a quantity of milk in the palm of their right hand, come forward one by one, and each in her turn pours the contents of the palm over the bending form of the maiden, chanting at the same time versicles to the effect: "Be mother either of a son or daughter."

The new maiden is next presented with an admixture of plantain and milk, which she quaffs with grateful feelings towards the givers and prostrates before the audience to crave a blessing. This penultimate ceremony over, the guests present form themselves into a circle and indulge in singing lustful songs, accompanied with a loud clapping of their hands. The long chapter of the ceremonies thus ended, a distribution of *pan supari* is then made. It is a fitting conclusion to so painful and elaborate a ceremony, and reminds the assemblage that it is time to take leave of the festive group and to relapse into the hum-drum of every-day life.

The first year FUNERAL EXPENSES of a PARSEE of the LAST CENTURY (1763).

BY MR. BOMANJI BYRAMJI PATELL.

THE Gujrati document, a copy and translation of which I am going to lay before the Society this evening, is 130 years old. It is a memo. of the funeral expenses for the first year after the death of a leading and venerable Parsee gentleman of Bombay, Mr. Rustamjee Dorabjee Patel, who was my great-great-grandfather, and who died on the 12th of April 1763, aged 96. I hope this document will be found interesting from different points of view.

Firstly, a modern Parsee will have from it a picture of the funeral ceremonies of his co-religionist of the last century when funeral and marriage feasts played a very prominent part in their social life. From the number of plantain leaves mentioned in the document as used for the feasts it appears that, allowing for wastage and breakage, about 1,000 persons were feasted by a well-to-do Parsee on the *Chcharum*, or the fourth day after death of a deceased relation.

Secondly, those who are interested in the problem of " The Rise in Prices " will find in this document several important items for the comparison of prices. For this purpose I give below a table comparing the prices of some articles of food as given in this old document with their present prices. My authority for the present prices of the different articles is the schedule of prices placed at the Crawford market in the beginning of this month : —

Names of articles.		Prices in 1763. Rs. a. p.		Prices in 1898. Rs. a. p.		
Rice, 1 fara	... ...	2 4 0		4 8 0		
Wheat „	... ...	2 12 0		5 4 0		
Juvar „	... ...	1 6 0		3 0 0		
Gram :,	... ...	2 8 0		3 8 0		
Arad „	... ...	2 2 0		5 4 0		
Ghee, maund 1	... ...	7 12 0		13 8 0		
Sweet oil „	... ...	3 12 0		4 14 0		
Molasses „	... ...	1 0 0		2 12 0		
Mutton, lb. 1	... ...	0 2 0		0 2 6		
Eggs, 20	... ...	0 4 0		0 8 0		
Gourd, score 1	... ...	0 14 0		4 8 0		
Pears, dozen 1	... ...	0 1 0		0 3 0		
Pomegranates, dozen 1	...	0 4 0		0 9 0		
Plantain leaves, 100	...	0 8 0		1 0 0		

We find in this document prices of rice, wheat and juvar which even now form the staple food of the country and of gram. It is the prices of grain that generally help staticians in determining the comparative rise and fall of general prices, and so the above table comprising the se will, I hope, be found useful to those interested in this question.

In the vegetables and fruits, though we find several articles named, we find data for the comparison of only three articles, *i.e.*, gourds, pears and pomegranates. Among other articles of food we find the prices of *ghee* or clarified butter, sweet oil, molasses, eggs, plantain leaves and mutton.

Thirdly, the document is interesting, as it gives us data to compare the wages of Parsee servants or waiters who attended public or private feasts. The wages per day then was five annas, and now it is one rupee. So the wages for grinding corn was six annas per fara, and now one rupee and one anna.

Lastly, what attracts the attention is the professional fees of the priests. The fee for the recital of the *Vendidad* prayer in 1763 was annas 8, and now it is Rs. 5, and for *Ijashni* prayer it was one and a quarter anna, and now it is one rupee.

I cannot resume my seat with out offering my hearty thanks to my friend Shumsool Ulma Jeevanjee Jamsetjee Mody, B. A., for assisting me in compiling the footnotes of this paper.

પટેલ રૂશતમજી દોરાબજી ગુજરાછે સંવત ૧૮૧૯ નાં વરખે
ચય્તર વદ ૧૨ વાર શનેઉ રોજ આશામાન માહ ૬
શેરેવર (તા. ૧૨ મી આપરેલ ૭૬૩) ને રાતના
ગુજરા તે વારે ખરચા છે.

૨૨) અખ્ખી આનું વહચું તેના રૂ. ૨૨.

૧૧) ઘંઉ દૂરા ૪.

૧૧) જુંદો.

૨૧) ગુજરા તે દીને આપાછે.

૧ખા પા આમાજી.

૨) બેડા, પાંઉ, સુખડ ને ધોબાન.

આ નરીશાલને વહેચા.

૨) વરસાન નરીશાલને.

શા પાઆમોજી.

૮ાારૂા ઉઠાણા મધિ ખરચું છે.

૧૪ દોરીઆ. ૧) જમાને ફીને.

આ પટકો ૧) કરાખી કોરના.

૪૯૦ પીછોડી ૧) કરાખી કોરની.

ૐ૫૦ કરશીઆ ૨) તથા કાંશીઆ ૨).

૪૬૨ા થાલી ૨) કાંસાની.

-૧ ગોરા રતલ ૨.

૬) બાઘડી ૧) કોરી.

૧) બેડો.

હારડી ૧) કેરવાની.

૨) ફુલ પાન તથા પરચુટણ.

૧) કરાતી ૨.

૪ન શદરાનાં રોલા ૨૪.

(બીજું લખેલુ ઉઠાઈઝિ ખરાબ થયલુ છે.)

૧૦૫૮૦ ચોઠાંને ધીને ખરચા છે.

૨૨) ધંઉ ખાંડી ૧.

૨૦૫૦ ચોખા ખાંડી ૧ા.

૪ા કેરી ટોપલા ૩.

૧) મસાલો.

૪ાા ધંઉની દલામન.

૬ાા૪૦ દોચી.

૨) લાકરાં.

૧) મેજ.

૨૩૫૦ ધીર્ઈ મન ૨ાા.

૧) પાથનનું ભાડું.

૪ા ગોરા રતલ ૪૨) તથા સુરી તથા કબેજ.

૪૪૦ મજુરને.

૪ા પાતરાં ૧૫૦૦.

૬૫)૬૫ દશામાંના ખરચ.

૧૪૮૦ ધીર્ઘ મન ૫૪૮ રીર.

૭)૬૫ બદામ વરીઆાલી ને ખસખસ.

૬૫૦ તેલ મન ૧) ૪ રીર.

૩) કેરી કાચી.

૩)૨૦ રાધી કુરી ૪) હેલ શુદ્ધાં.

૧૦ા૫૦ ગોરા રતલ ૮૭ કલેજ તથા સુંડી.

૨) પાતરાં કેળના ૪૦૦.

ꞏરાદરા ગોળ મણ રાદ રીર.

૨) પરચુટન.

૧૫૪૮ઞા વારાણુ દશામાનાં.

ધાદરા કાંથીઆ ૭.

ખ઼ા ૨૫ કરશીઆ ૧૦.

રા તરામરી ૨ꞏ

ꞏ꞉ા૪૦ મજુર જન ૨, દર રꞏ૧૨૦ લેખે.

૫૭)૧૫ માથીરા ઉપર ખરચ કીધા.

૭) આખ઼ા ખાંડીઞા

ધા૫૦ ધીર્ઘ મન ꞏ꞉ા ૫ રીર.

૧ઞા꞊ ગોરા રતલ ૧૦૦ તથા કલેજ ૨) તથા સુડી રુꞏ

ૐ)૭૫ મેજ.

અ પાતરાં કેળનાં ૬૫૦.

ૐ)꞊ ધંહુની દરામન દૂરા ૩) ની.

ꞏꞏꞏ꞉ા ઇંડાં નંગ ૪૦.

ઇ) તેલ મન ૨ꞏ

૩)૩૬દાસીકુરી આા.

ખ઼ા પરચુટન પીરોજાખ઼઼ે ખરચા છે.

ꞏꞏꞏ꞉ા૬૦ મજુર ૩ દર રꞏ૧૨૦ લેખે.

૧ꞏꞏ૫૦ ખીજ મહીનાની ખાજ.

ઇ) ગોરા રતલ ૩૨.

૨) ધીર્ઘ રીર ધ꞉ꞏꞏꞏ.

ꞏ૫૦ મેજ.

૫) પરચુટન.

રણાઉઆ તરીજ મહીનાની ખાજ રોજ આસામાન માહા આ-
દર મષિ મેજ કરાવી તેના ખરચ થચ્મા.

ા૧ા મેજ શરવે ચીજ લીધી.

ગ૧૮ા ખજુર.

ગ૭ નાળીઅેર.

ગા૧૨ કેલાં.

ગ૬ શેરડી.

ગ૫ અપ્પરાત.

ગ૬ દરાખ.

ગ૬ કેવડા.

ગ૮ પેર ૪.

ગ૧૬ દાડમ ૨.

ગ અનેનાશ.

ગ૮ ખદામ.

ગ૭ પરાતાં.

ગ૬ ફુલ.

ગ૪૬ ચોખા તથા દાલ તથા ધહુ મળીને.

ાા ધીઈ શેર ૯.

ા પાતરાં કેલનાં.

ગ ૩૫ શાખ રતલ ૩૬ હેલશુખાં.

ગ ૫ મેથીની ભાજી.

ગ ૪૦ શાગડીવાલાને.

ા આશીદાદ આપીછે મેજ કરાવી.

આ પરચુટન અંધારને ખુરદો.

ાા ખમનદાર અંધાર.

ાા ફરામજી રશાતમજી.

ાા કાવસજી ફરામજી.

ાા નવરોજદાર પાવડી.

૧ા ચોથા મહીનાની ખાજ.

૧ા૮૫ પાંચમા મહીનાની ખાજ. ખીચરી ખીધી.

ગ૨૫ અરડ પાચ્મેલા ૯.

ર ધીઈ શેર ૭.

૨‖ તેલ.
૨‖‖ કાકડી ચીભડે.
૨। માછલી.
।‖] ૫૦ પાતરાં આલુનાં.
।‖‖ શાખ ૨તલ ૯.
। ૨૦ દાખી.
। ૧૫ તુરીઆં.
] ૭૦ મેજ.
] ચોલ મન ‖।
।·૫ પરચુટણ.
૨૮‖‖ ૫૫ છમથીની ખાજ.
  ‖‖‖ ૫૦ ચોખા ફરા ૩.
  ૮‖‖ ધી઼ મન ૧.
  ૨‖‖ ૫૦ તેલ મન ।‖‖·
  ·। કાંદા.
  ·‖ ૫૦ મેજ.
  ·‖ કેશાં.
  ·‖ ૭૫ નાળીઅેર.
  ૭] ખરા રૂ] દર રૂ. ૨ ષેૠ.
  ] લીખાન થુખડ.
  ।૩૦ પરચુટણ.
આ સાતમા મહીનાની ખાજ.
આ આઠમા મહીનાની ખાજ.
૪] નવમા મહીનાની ખાજ.
૩] દશામા મહીનાની ખાજ.
૫। અગીઆરમા મહીનાની ખાજ.
૧૫૮૫ા વરશીનો ખરચ.
  ૨] મરી.
  ] ૫૦ ખાના ઝઈ.
  ૨૦] બહુ ફરા ૧૦૦.
  ૨૫૫૦ ધી઼ મન આદ રીર ખરશાન ખાદ ૧૨ રૂ. ₩
  ૨। ચોખા ફરા ૨.

૧ૈ ચણા ૪રા ૪.

૫) આઈું.

ૈૌ ચોખા ૭ૌૈૈમન.

૪) બહુની દલામન.

૮ૌ અચ્ચારના ધડા ૫.

રૌૌ જુઆર ૪રા ૨.

૧ખૌૌ ૧રૌૌ તેલ મન ૫૮ રીર ખારદાન બાદ દર રૂ. આ૫ૂ.

૧૫ રોચી કુરી ૧૩.

૫) કાંદા.

ૌ૬૦ લશન.

૨) લાકડાં વાડીમધે રાંધવાનાં.

૫) મેજ.

ૌૌ ગોલ.

ૌૌૌ ખાંડ.

૫ૌ૨૦ આકડો હેલ શુધાં.

ૐ ૫ચ્ચુટ્ટ્ણુ ચુરેૈ.

૫ૌ૪૦ મજુર રાતના તથા દીરાના મલી જન ૧ૌ.

૨) વરચીને દહાડે ગીરા.

ૌૌ ઈંડાં નગ ૬૦.

ૌૌૌૌ ૨૫ કેરી પાતીૌૌ

૧ૌૌૌૌ પાંતરાં કેલનાં નગ ૨૩૦૦.

ૌ ૫રચ્ચુટન.

ખધા જ઼ુમધે ખરચ રૂ. ૬૭૬ૌૌૌૌૌ

૨શાતમ૬ુરૌૌ ગુજરા છે તેનાં ઉૌૌ આંનાંમધે આવુ છે તેહનાં.

૮ૌૌ વંદીદાદ ૬૩

૨૩ૌ બાખ ૨૩

૨૩ૌ૪૦ ૫ૌૌજશાની ૩૦૬.

૧૨ૌૌ૪૬

[Translation of the above.]

The Funeral expenses of Parsee Rustamjee Dorabjee Patell who died on the 12th of April 1763 :—

	Rs.	Qrs.	Reas	Rs.	Qrs.	Reas
Akhiàna [1] :—						
Wheat, Fara 4	11	...	...	...	...	...
Copper Coins	11	..	...	22	...	...
The expenses on the day of death—						
Pàyàmoji [2]	15	2	...	...	...	...
Shoes [3], Bread [4], Sandal and Frank						
incense [5]	2	...	...	...	...	...
Annuity to the Corpse-bearers	2	...	...	...	...	...
Payamoji to the Corpse-bearers [6]	1	2	...	21	...	...

---

* 100 Reases make one quarter, and 4 quarters make one rupee.

[1] *Vide* "The Funeral Ceremonies of the Parsees, their Origin and Explanation, by Mr. Jivanjee Jamsetjee Mody, B.A. (*Vide* Journal of the Anthropological Society of Bombay, Vol. II., No. 7, pp. 407.) It was a custom in Bombay about 70 years ago that when a Parsee died, all the priests in the town went to his house to take a part in the *Akhiàna* ceremony and all of them were paid in coins and wheat. In 1873 the Parsee Punchayet resolved that only those priests who were specially invited should attend.

[2] ‫میزد‬ ‫پای‬ *i.e.*, the wages of attendance on foot. This is the fee paid to the priests who go to the Tower of Silence with the funeral procession. As in the case of the *Akhiàna* ceremony, so in the case of *Payamoji*, formerly all the priests in the town attended, but subsequently it was resolved that only those who were specially invited should attend.

[3] The Corpse-bearers are sometimes supplied by the family with clean white suits of clothes, and they are asked to put on their new shoes, for which they are paid.

[4] Bread for the dogs which are kept at the Towers for the *Sag-deed* ceremony (Journal of the Society, Vol. II., No. 7, pp. 412, 420).

[5] For the sacred fire, that is perpetually burning in the *Sagdi* (Fire-house) at the Towers.

[6] Formerly the Corpse-bearers were paid by the family of the deceased. This and the above two items show the ways in which they received their wages. When their demands began to grow exorbitant, the Trustees of the Parsee Punchayet started in 1860 a public fund to pay monthly stipends to the Corpse-bearers. The late Mr. Rustomjee Jamsetjee Jeejibhoy, with his characteristic generosity, headed the list with a liberal sum of Rs. 7,000, and paid the losses for the first 3 years. The fund now stands at Rs. 3,64,702. Out of this fund altogether 48 men are engaged on monthly stipends varying from Rs. 34 to Rs. 20. These men have to offer their services at any place between Colaba

	Rs.	Qrs.	Reas	Rs.	Qrs.	Reas
Oothumna expenses[7]—						
1 *Dorio* for *Jāmā*[8]	14	...	...	...	...	...
1 *Putko*, with gold embroidered borders ...	2	2	...	...	...	...
1 *Pichodi*, with gold embroidered borders ...	4	1	60	...	...	...
2 Metallic water-jugs and 2 water-pots ...	4	...	50	...	...	...
2 Metallic trays	4	1	62½	...	...	...
2 lbs. Mutton	...	1	...	...	...	...
1 Turban	6	...	...	...	...	...
1 Pair of shoes	1	...	...	...	...	...
1 Rosary of amber	...	...	...	...	...	...
Flowers, betel leaves and miscellaneous ...	2	...	...	...	...	...
2 Sacred threads	1	...	...	...	...	...
24 Pieces of white cloth for sacred shirts[9] .	44	1	...	...	...	...
(A portion of the paper is here eaten away by the worms, so the writing is not legible[10].)				86	2	62½
Cheharum expenses [11]—						
Wheat, khandi 1...	22	...	...	...	...	...
Rice, khandi 1¼	20	2	50	...	...	...
Mango, baskets 3...	4	2	...	...	...	..
Spices	1	...	...	...	...	...
Wages for grinding wheat	4	3	...	...	..	...
Gourd	6	3	40	...	...	...
Fuel	2	...	...	...	...	...
Fruit	1	...	..	...	...	...

and Bandora. The nominal fees that are now charged for carrying each corpse and which now go to the fund are as follows :—

	Rs.	a.	p.
Adults	5	0	0
Grown-up children	2	0	0
Infants	1	4	0

[7]   *Vide* Journal of the Society, Vol. II., No. 7, pp. 434.

[8]   This and the following articles of clothes and utensils are necessary for the *Shiāv* and *Bāj* ceremonies, Vol. II., No. 7, pp. 439

[9]   As in the case of the *Akhiānā* and *Paxamoji*, so in the case of the *Oothumna* ceremonies, formerly all the priests in the town attended, and they were paid in cash and clothes, *i.e.*, a sacred shirt to every priest present.

[10]   This perhaps is the amount distributed among the priests.

[11]   *Vide* Journal of the Society, Vol. II., No. 7, pp. 439. Formerly the Parsees used to give as large feasts on funeral occasions as Hindoos now-a-days. All the articles under this head were purchased for such a feast, and for the sweets prepared for such an occasion. The number of the plantain leaves (1,500), on one of which each man is served with his meal, shows that the family of the deceased must have invited a large number of the adult population of the Parsees to this funeral feast of the fourth day. The list of the expenses of the funeral feast of the *Varsi* (Shalroz), *i.e.*, the day of the first anniversary of the deceased, which comes at the end of this document, gives a still larger number of the plantain leaves used on the occasion. It shows that a still larger number

	Rs.	Qrs.	Reas	Rs.	Qrs.	Reas
Ghee or clarified butter, maunds 2¼ ...	23	1	50	...	...	...
Hire for *Pathars* is [12] ...	1	...	...	...	...	...
Mutton, 42 pounds, with liver and head ...	6	2	...	...	...	...
Wages of waiters [13] ...	4	1	40	...	...	...
Plantain leaves, 1,500 ...	7	2	...	105	1	80
Expenses on the *Dasmá* or the tenth day of the death—						
Ghee, maunds 1¼ and seers 8 ...	14	1	80	...	...	...
Almond, variali and poppy seeds ...	...	...	65	...	...	...
Sweet oil, maund 1 and seers 4 ...	6	1	60	...	...	...
Mango ...	3	...	...	...	...	...
Gourd, 4 scores with cooly hire ...	3	...	20	...	...	...
Mutton, 80 lbs., with liver and head ..	10	2	50	...	...	...
Plantain leaves, 400 ...	2	...	...	...	...	...
Molasses, maunds 2¼ and 6 seers ...	2	1	62½	...	...	...
Miscellaneous ...	2	...		...	...	...
Utensils on the 10th day [14]—						
Metal pots, 7 ...	9	1	62½	...	...	...
Metal jugs, 10 ...	4	3	25	...	...	...
Large metal, 2 ...	2	1	...	...	...	...
Wages of two waiters at 1 quarter and 20 reas per head ...	...	2	40	61	...	65

was then invited. Perhaps it was a feast of the whole community. The consideration of this number brings us to the question of the Parsee population in Bombay in 1763. From the record of the census of the year 1816, it appears that the Parsee population then was 13,155 in all. From this it appears that in 1763, which is the year of the document, i.e., about 53 years before the first authentic census, the Parsee population must be very less. In the public feasts of *Gáhombárs* now at Bombay, where the whole community is invited to attend, the average attendance comes to about 6,000 in all. The expenses come to about Rs. 750.

[12] These are long pieces of linen carpets for guests to sit on while taking their meals.

[13] Looking to the number of guests, the number of waiters which, calculating at the rate of 5 annas per head (which, as it appears from a subsequent item was the rate of the wages of the waiters at the time), was sixteen, is a small one. But as in the towns of Guzerat now-a-days, so in Bombay about 50 years ago, the near relations and friends of the host generally took a great part in serving the guests.

[14] It was an old custom that utensils of domestic uses were placed where the sacred ceremonies were performed, and were subsequently sent as presents to near relations.

Expenses on the *Māsisā*, or the 30th day of the death—	Rs.	Qrs.	Reas	Rs.	Qrs.	Reas
Rice, ¼ khandi	9	...	...			
Ghee, ¼ maund and 5 seers	9	2	50			
Mutton, 100 lbs., 2 livers and 2 heads ...		2	50			
Fruit		...	75			
Plantain leaves, 650	3	1	...		...	...
Wages for grinding 3 faras of wheat		...	50			...
Eggs, 40		2	...			
Sweet oil, 2 maunds	8	...	...			
Gourd, 3¾ scores	3	...	30			
Miscellaneous expenses by *Piroja*[15]		3	...			...
Wages of 3 waiters at 1 quarter and 20 reas per head	...	3	60	50		15
Expenses of the second month day, *i.e.*, of the 60th day after death[16]—						
Mutton, 32 lbs.	4	...	...			
Ghee, 6¼ seers	2	...	...			...
Fruit	...	1	50			..
Miscellaneous	5	...	...	11		50
Expenses of the third month day, *i.e.*, of the 90th day after death[17]—						
Fruit—						
Dates			18½			
Cocoanuts		1	7			
Plantains		2	12			
Sugarcane		...	6			
Walnuts	...		5			
Grapes			9			
Kevrá flowers			9			
Pears, 4			8			
Pomegranates, 2			16			
Pineapples			...			
Almond			8			
Pistachio			7			
Flowers			6	...	...	...
Rice, dhall and wheat	1		46	...	...	...
Ghee, 6 seers	1	2		...	...	...
Plantain leaves	1			...	...	...
Mutton, 36 lbs., with cooly hire	6		35	...	...	...
Vegetable, fœnugreek			5	...	...	...
Presented to *Sagdiwalla*			40	...	...	...
Presented to priests	9	2		20	2	37½
Expenses of the fourth month day				11	...	...

---

[15] *Piroja* was the name of the widow of the deceased.

[16] It is usual to perform a few ceremonies on that day of the month on which the death occurred, for 12 months, *i.e.*, on the 30th day after death, on the 60th day, on the 90th day, on the 120th day, and so on up to the end of the first year, *i.e.*, twelve times during the first year.

[17] The death occurred in the month *Sheheriver*, *i.e.*, the sixth month of the Parsee year. So the third month after death was *Ádar*, which is a month dedicated to Fire, so the expenses on this day are a little higher than the preceding and succeeding months.

22

	Rs.	Qrs	Reas	Rs.	Qrs.	Reas
Expenses of the fifth month day.[18] Prepared						
Khichdi—						
Arad (a kin 1 of *Dāl*), pali 9	1		25			
Ghee, seers 7½	2					
Sweet oil	2					
Cucumber and chibhdoo (a kind of melon)	3					
Fish	1					
Aloo leaves	2	50				
Mutton, 6 lbs.	3					
Gourd	1	20				
Toorià (a kind of vegetable)	1	5				
Fruit		70				
Molasses, maund ½	1					
Miscellaneous		5	10	2		85
Expenses of the sixth month day [19]—						
Rice, fara 3	7	3	50			
Ghee, maund 1	8	3				
Sweet oil, maund ½	1	3	50			
Onions		1				
Fruit		2	50			
Plantains		2				
Cocoanuts		2	75			
Goats, 3 at Rs. 2½ per head	7					
Sandal and frankincense	1					
Miscellaneous		1	30	28	3	55
Expenses of the seventh month day				3	2	
,, ,, eighth ,, ,,				3	2	
,, ,, ninth ,, ,,				4		
,, ,, tenth ,, ,,				3		
,, ,, eleventh ,, ,,				5	2	
Expenses on the first anniversary of death—						
Pepper	2					
Dhana, Jiroo (kind of spices)	1		50			
Wheat, fara 10	20					
Ghee, maund 3½ and 6 seers	29	1	50			
Rice, fara 2	4	2				
Gram, fara 4	10					
Ginger	1					
Wages for grinding rice		3				
,, ,, ,, wheat	4					

[18] This month is the 11th month of the Parsee year, and is dedicated to *Behaman*, the angel presiding over cattle. So the Parsees generally about 50 years ago, and some even now, abstain from meat altogether during this month. So we find in the list of the expenses of this month a good deal is spent on the vegetables of the season. *Khichdi* is the name of a special dish prepared during this month.

[19] The expenses of the sixth month are also higher than the other preceding and succeeding months, the reason being that the sixth month after death is considered to be as important as the first.

	Rs.	Qrs	Reas	Rs.	Qrs.	Reas
Pickles, 5 jars	8	2	...	...	...	..
Jooar, fara 2	2	3	...	...	...	...
Sweet oil, mauud 5¼ and 8 seers	19	3	12½	...	...	...
Gourd, scores 13...	15		...	...	...	...
Onion	1		...	...	...	...
Fuel for cooking at the garden ¹⁰	2		...	...	...	...
Fruit	1		...	...	...	...
Sugar	1	2	...	...	...	...
A goat with the cooly hire	5		20	...	...	...
Miscellaneous expenses in copper coins ...	7		...	...	...	...
Wages of 17 waiters during the day and at						
night	5		40	...	...	...
Mutton on the anniversary day	2		...	...	...	...
Eggs, 60	...	2	...	...	...	...
Mango, basket, 1½	1	3	25	...	...	...
Plaintain leaves, 2,300	11	2	...	...	...	...
Miscellaneous	...	3	60	158	1	57½
Total expenses......	...		...	606	3	7½

Prayers announced in the *Oothumna* ceremony for the deceased Seth
Rustomjee ²¹ :—

	Rs.	qrs.	rs.
Recital of Vendidad prayers	81	2	0
Lákh, 23 ²²	23	0	0
Recital of the Ijashna, 308	23	0	40
	127	2	40

¹⁰ The garden alluded to here is the Manockjee Seth's *Vádi* in the Fort.
This building was founded in the year 1735 for the purpose of giving convenience
to the Parsee community to hold their public and private feasts. It is even now
a favourite place for the Parsees residing in the Fort to give marriage and
religious feasts.

²¹ It was a custom about 100 years ago that on the *Oothumna*, or third day
afternoon ceremony, friends and relations of the deceased declared that they
would get so many prayers recited for the benefit of the soul of the deceased.
The custom of announcing subscriptions to the different charity funds in honor
of the deceased has at present taken the place of the former custom.

²² Recital of a lakh of the *Ahunavara* or *Yathá Ahu Vairyo* prayer, which is
compared to the *Pater Noster* of the Christians.

On some ADDITIONAL FOLK-BELIEFS *about the* TIGER.

BY MR. SARAT CHANDRA MITRA, M. A., B. L.,

District Pleader, Chapra, Behar.

IN my paper entitled "On the Indian Folk-Beliefs about the Tiger,"[1] I have given some instances of popular and superstitious beliefs about the "King of the Indian Forests," prevailing among the various races inhabiting India and the countries adjacent to it. In the present paper I intend to gather together some additional forms of superstitious belief about the same animal, prevailing among the various Indian races.

There is a superstitious belief prevalent in one form or another among the various Indian races which forbids them to call evil things by their respective names. Whenever that particular thing has to be mentioned, it is alluded to by a roundabout way, in the belief that should it be called by its proper name, that evil will surely happen or that evil thing will surely make its appearance. Thus ignorant Bengali women would not mention the proper names of the thief (चोर) and of the snake (साप) during the night, from the dread that either a thief or a snake will appear in the house during the night. So whenever they have to allude to those two evils, they do so by using words which indirectly mean the same things. Thus if the word चोर or thief has to be named, they do so by calling him "*the unwelcome visitor*," or if the word साप or snake has to be used, they do so by calling it "*the creeping thing*" or लता.

An exactly similar form of superstitious belief, with regard to the tiger, prevails among the Canarese people of Southern India. They do not speak of the tiger by its proper name, but whenever they have occasion to use the name of that animal, they do so by using the Canarese words "*naie*" and "*nurri*," respectively, meaning "dog" and "jackal." They believe that, should they call the animal by its proper name, some one

---

[1] *Vide* "*Journal of the Anthropological Society of Bombay*," Vol. III., No. I., pp. 45—60.

of them is sure to be carried away by that ferocious monster. A curious instance of this belief has been recorded by Mr. G. P. Sanderson in his interesting work entitled *Thirteen Years among the Wild Beasts of India* (Edition, 1879), page 297 : " Whilst at dinner that evening, I heard voices and saw torches hurriedly approaching my tent, and could distinguish the words ' *naie* ' and ' *nurri* ' (' dog ' and ' jackal ') pronounced excitedly. *The Canarese people frequently speak of a tiger by these names, partly in assumed contempt, partly from superstitious fear.* The word ' *hooli* ' (tiger) is not often used amongst jungle-men, in the same way that, from dread, natives usually refer to cholera by the general terms of *roga* or *járdya* (sickness). The people were from Hurdenhully, a village a mile and-a-half away, and had come to tell me that their cattle had galloped back in confusion into the village at dusk, without their herdsman, who, we suspected, had fallen a victim to the tigress of Morlay." Again, at page 306, he says: " We had brought torches and men from Hebsoor, and after much calling that the tigress had been shot, voices were at last heard from different trees, lights began to appear, and watchers came from all directions, some shouting to us from the distance to let them come up and see the ' *dog.*' "

There is another silly superstitious belief prevalent in some parts of India, which is to the effect that each tiger is allowed by God one rupee per diem for his daily rations. The following instance of this belief is mentioned in the *Journal of the Bombay Natural History Society* : [2]

" In some places, too, there is a superstition that God allows the tiger one rupee a day for his food, so that if he kills a bullock worth Rs. 5, he won't kill again for five days. If it is worth Rs. 10, he won't kill again for ten days, and so forth."

" There is also another belief current among some Indian races, that the age of the tiger and the leopard can be determined

---

[2] Vol. III., No. III. (1888), page 153.

by an inspection of the lobes of the liver, the number whereof (*i.e.*, of the lobes) correspond with the number of years the tiger is old, being one lobe for each year the tiger has lived." But this is not anatomically true.

Sometimes a tiger is believed to enjoy the special protection of a deity who presides over the welfare of residents of the particular tract of country in which the animal commits his depredations. Mr. Sanderson gives an instance of this in his above-quoted work (page 307):

"From a long course of immunity from misadventure to himself the Don (name of the tiger) had come to be regarded as enjoying the especial protection of Koombappa of the temple, the great jungle-spirit; and it was universally believed that when that deity went the rounds of his jungles, the Don was chosen by him as his steed. The villagers had even made an effigy of the Don, respectably got up in wood and paint, and looking truly formidable, with a seat on the back, and on wheels, which they dragged round the temple and down to the river in solemn procession on feast-days. Though the Morlayites always entered with delight upon any hunts I organised, hardly any of them believed the Don (name of the tiger) would ever be shot."

Sometimes it is believed that when a person is killed by a tiger, his widow is supposed to be haunted by a devil which has to be exorcised away by the performance of religious rites. Mr. Sanderson mentions an instance of this belief at page 296 of his aforesaid work:

"The woman, with the strange apathy of a Hindoo, related what she knew of her husband's death without a tear. I gave her some money, as she would have to spend a small sum in accordance with caste usage *to rid her of the devil by which she was supposed to be attended on account of her husband's having been killed by a tiger, before she would be admitted into her caste's villages*."

The Canarese believe that the tiger scratches the bark of a tree, called the Bastard Teak (*Butea frondosa*) and called by them "*Muttaga*," because the tree exudes, on the slightest scratch, a sap of a blood-red color which the tiger thinks to be animal blood in which he delights.[3]

The whiskers of the tiger are, in some parts of Southern India, considered as a deadly poison and are singed off as soon as a tiger is killed. It is sometimes believed that, unless the whiskers are singed off, the spirit of the tiger will haunt the person who slew him, or that the slayer himself will be metamorphosed into a tiger in the next world. The small bone embedded in the muscles between the shoulder and neck of a tiger is also considered a charm.

In addition to those already given in my previous paper, I give a few more examples of superstitious beliefs entertained by the aboriginal tribes of India, with regard to the tiger. The Aryan settlers of Chota Nagpore and Singbhum believe that an aboriginal tribe named the Moondahs are great adepts in witchcraft, and can, at their own sweet will and pleasure, metamorphose themselves into tigers and other ferocious beasts for the purpose of preying upon their enemies.[*] Another tribe named the Katodis are looked upon by the Hindus with feelings of superstitious terror inspired by the belief that they can metamorphose themselves into the shape of tigers.[†]

The Zodiac of the Tibetans contain the twelve signs : mouse, ox, *tiger*, hare, dragon, serpent, horse, sheep, monkey, cock, dog, and pig. These are called *Lokhor Chuni*, or the animals by which the years of the cycle of twelve years are designated. The Tibetans calculate the years or determine the age of individuals by the cycle of twelve years, in which each year is named from a certain animal of the twelve signs commencing

---

[3] *Op. cit*, page 280.

[*] *Vide Trans. Ethnological Society of Lond.*, N. S. VI., p. 6 ; also J. A. S. B. for 1866, Pt. II., p. 158.

[†] Latham's *Descriptive Ethnology*, Vol. II., page 457.

with *Tag-lo* (*tiger-year*) and ending with Lang-lo (ox-year). These twelve signs, in combination with the twelve signs of the Tibetan zodiac, are also used in calculating the twelve months of the Tibetan year. Thus the new year of the Tibetans begins with the *Tiger* and is called *Horda-tang-po*. The Tibetans have a popular saying, namely, the *Horda-tang-po Tag-gi-da*, that is to say, the first month of the year is *Tiger's month*. These signs are also used in calculating every two hours of the day called "*Du-chhoi*," commencing from the dawn called "*Thorang*." The time between 3 to 5 A. M. is called *the hours of the Tiger*. The time of the hours of the break of day is called *Nam lang*, and that of *Nima shar* is denominated the hours of the hare which is really the beginning of the day. The Thorang or dawn comes at the end of these twelve divisions, which is the *Tag or Tiger*.‡

I have heard from a relative of mine who stayed in Gâyâ in Behar for a long time that, in the town of Gâyâ, there is a temple dedicated to the deity वाघेशी. The word वाघेशी is a mere Hindi corruption of the Sanscrit word वाघेश्वरी or the *Tiger Goddess*. The temple, I am informed, contains the brazen image of a tiger which is supposed to represent the deity. It is popularly believed there that tigers come during the night from the Barabar Hills on the other side of the River Poonpoon, which flows past the town of Gâyâ and knock their foreheads at the feet of the goddess by way of prayer that they may be allowed to prey upon human victims. It is said that, if the goddess grants their prayers, the tigers succeed in killing human beings during the year. If their prayers are not listened to, no human being falls victim to tigers during the year. In honour of the goddess, a fair called the श्रावनी सायेल is annually held in the Hindi month of श्रावन (Sanscrit श्रावण), corresponding to the months June, July of the English calendar, in the precincts of the temple of the Goddess वाघेशी. It is said that this fair

‡ *Vide Proceedings of the A. S. B. for 1800, pp. 5 -7.*

is held by way of supplication to the deity that she may not
listen to the prayers of the tigers and that human beings may
not fall victims to these ferocious beasts. It is also said that
pujahs are also offered to the goddess, during the fair, for the
aforesaid purpose.

This paper may aptly be concluded with a few other Bengali
proverbial sayings in which the tiger figures   There is a proverb
which runs to the effect that मावेरशिते वाघ काप or the cold of the
Hindu month of Magh (January and February) even makes the
tiger shiver, in allusion to the intense cold which prevails in
Lower Bengal in that month. A person with ferocious habits
like those of a ruffian is called a वाघाभालका लोक or a person with
the ways of *the tiger and the bear*. Sometimes the prefix वाघ
meaning a tiger is prefixed to the name of a person in Lower
Bengal to denote that the ways of that person are as ferocious
as those of a tiger.

ORDINARY GENERAL MEETING, held on Wednesday, the 26th July 1893.

Dr. P. PETERSON, *the President, presided.*

The Minutes of the previous Meeting were read and con-firmed.

The election of Mr. Sambhu Nath Sukul, as a Member of the Society, made in the last Meeting held on the 28th (June 1893) ultimo, was cancelled.

The following paper was then read :—

ON THE JEWS.

BY SURGEON LIEUT.-COLONEL WATERS.

THE Jews belong to the second or Semitic division of the great human family. They are unquestionably the most interesting of all people as regards the magnitude of the place they occupy in history. This, the Jacobite section of the Abrahamic race, which practically embraces all the inhabitants of Arabia and the parts adjacent thereto northwards, has appropriated to itself an overwhelming predominance in all that has formed the subject of historical writings ; and the fact may be taken to indicate that from the earliest of historical times they have manifested an intelligence superior to that of their neighbours and congeners. It is worthy of notice that the founder of this particular section of the Arab family, signalised his intellectual pre-eminence over his brother by taking advantage of that brother's urgent necessity ; and subsequently added to his reputation for selfish avidity by committing something very like a fraud on his father-in-law. It must not, however, from this remark be supposed that I, in any degree, share the views of those who are inclined to cast aspersions on Jewish integrity in general.

Sprung from the primeval human stock, which seems to have mainly inhabited the elevated plateaux of Central Asia,

the Semitic branch of the human family migrated south-
westward, there becoming stationary for a great length of time.
In this respect they stand out in contrast to the great Aryan
or Indo-Germanic tribes, which kept pushing westward till
further progress in that direction was barred by the littoral of
the Atlantic and German Oceans, respectively. But in this we
have nothing else than what we might expect, for the Jews
have ever been of a conservative turn, which, however, they
did not allow to stand in the way of such enterprise as gave
promise of advantage.

Learned Orientalists combine in the belief that the Jewish
language—Hebrew—is but a dialect of Arabic ; and support
this view with the assertion that theologians unversed in
the latter are unable to give a valid interpretation of many
passages of the Old Testament, which, of course, was originally written in Hebrew. Ethnographically the Jews have
not undergone much that is capable of specific differentiation
from the parent Arab stock. As a rule they are inclined
to be spare of body and of fair height. The Jewish facial
and cranial characteristics are those which usually belong
to high intelligence. M. Renan in his great classical work,
the People of Israel, speaks with great confidence as to the
race being in Biblical times at all events, particularly ill-
favoured, and seems to imply that the commanding height, and
comely person of Saul were the determining factors in his
being elected by acclamation first King of Israel. And in
like manner, M. Renan thinks, that David being of a " ruddy
and fair countenance," owed to this his phenomenal success : at
any rate, that it helped his remarkable address in gaining that
perfect mastery over his race, such as had neither before his
day nor since, been enjoyed by one man. The Jews of the
present day show every shade of good looks and bad, just like
the aliens amongst whom they mingle. For instance, the Jews
in Baghdad are among the fairest of mankind, the female Jews
of that quarter being specially fascinating both in face and

figure with a type of beauty of Hellenic character. The German Jews, on the other hand, embody, I should say, some of the most unlovely human physiognomy. A common mistake is to regard the nose as the feature most distinctive of the Jewish race. It is doubtless true, that a well pronounced nose is common among them, but so much may be said of most persons of striking or commanding individuality. It is said of the great Duke of Wellington that he had no reliance on the ability of a man who was not furnished with a big nose. No doubt, the rule warrants something like the view alleged to be held by that illustrious soldier; but surely this rule must be restricted in its application to the confines of Europe, for it is difficult for us to suppose that the no less distinguished Asiatic Captains, Attila, Ghengiz Khan, and Tamerlane, could have had the nasal characteristics, thought to be imperatively necessary for military genius in the West. Further, the Jew, though generally well endowed in this respect, has not as yet added military renown to his achievements. His line has lain quite in another direction which indeed, it is true, has become so intimately associated with the successful prosecution of military operations, that the *sinews of war* as the synonym of *money*, has passed into a proverb. But to return; the Jew, especially as seen in Europe, has undoubtedly a nose of magnitude, yet this is not his chief characteristic, inasmuch as it is not the least variable. What then is the most invariable element in the Jewish physiognomy? In my opinion it is most unquestionably the eye. The Jewish eye presents every shade of colour from black to blue, so the Hebraic organ of vision is not to be distinguished by its hue. Nor is it easy to explain in what the particular distinguishing peculiarity consists. The one word which most aptly characterises it is keenness; there is in it a look of eagerness of deep intensity; such an eye as bespeaks a fixed determination to gain some end; an eye such as is to be seen only in those persons of other race which bear a character closely approximating that of the sons of Jacob. It is signi-

ficant wherever seen of not only a desire, but a firmly rooted
resolve to succeed, and not often is it seen in Gentiles at all
events, as a concomitant of the milk of human kindness. It is
often a bright, even brilliant, eye, but seldom beautiful, lacking
softness; there is in it, however, a semblance of the latter
quality, but on close inspection this simulacrum of softness will
resolve itself into a significance which it would be disappointing
to analyse. It is possible that this keen alertness of look is
begotten of that necessity for watchfulness and circumspection
which devolve on those who have had a protracted struggle for
existence, and been for long the victims of the most relentless
persecution. Another very noticeable Jewish facial characteristic, is also connected with the eye. It consists in a thick *fleshy*
and often *drooping upper eyelid*; indeed, so marked is the
peculiarity in some of the children of Israel, that it amounts
to a disfigurement suggestive of paralysis In moderate
degree it is an attractive feature, in excess it is generally
speaking associated with sensual tendencies, and in so much
is repellent; naturally then we find the former condition most
common among the female, and the latter among the male
members of this race. The mouth in a less degree is also a
distinctive feature of the Jews, as compared with Europeans,
but it conforms to a very prevalent type of oral configurement
among Oriental races. The lips are thick, everted, and in
short of a *tout en semble* suggestive of the lower instincts. Of
course, for descriptive purpose, I have delineated roughly
the features, which are at least in some sense, characteristic,
as seen in their most marked and uninviting aspect; but
I by no means wish it to be understood that the Jewish
eye, mouth, and nose in general are unprepossessing. Far
from it. Like the rest of the Arab tribes the hair on the
cheek among the Jews is, as a rule, sparse, tending to an
abundant vigorous growth on the chin.

In common with his Arab brother the Jew is slow to pledge
himself, but having once passed his word, he holds it inviolate,

and in this respect the Jewish merchant has earned a high repute for commercial integrity; and it is in no way in conflict with the fact that he does his utmost, before entering into a bargain, to secure for himself the best possible terms. He thus merely draws on the resources of his high intelligence, throwing it as it were into the scales. It is interesting to note here, that to this day among the Arabs we have the persistence of a form of taking an oath, which was in vogue in Arabia something at least over three thousand years ago. Thus, when Abraham said to his servant " Put, I pray thee, thy hand under my thigh," he indicated that accompaniment and symbol of the most solemn ratification of an oath, which still obtains among the tribes of the Arabian peninsula. To give the passage in full—" put I pray thee thy hand under my thigh ; and I will make thee swear by the Lord the God of heaven, and the God of the earth, that thou shall not take a wife unto my son of the daughters of the Canaanites, among whom I dwell. But thou shall go unto my country and to my kindred and take a wife for my son Isaac—and the servant put his hand under the thigh of Abraham his master, and sware to him concerning that matter." Those who have had occasion to witness the Arabs dealing in horses will doubtless have observed the mysterious manipulation of fingers conducted under a handkerchief between the buyer and the seller. This is that convenient substitute for putting the " hand under the thigh " which is held to be sufficient for sealing minor covenants.

The interest which surrounds all connected with the Arabian peninsula, must ever endure among the Christian people of Europe not only as being the birthplace of their religion and the nursery whence all Western learning and culture emanated, but also on account of its wondrous plenitude of outcome in other directions. For instance, notwithstanding its proverbial aridity, it yet bears the finest breed of every kind extant within its borders. The Arab himself is the type of human excellence in intellect and physique. The Arabian horse is often declared to be the best horse in the world, but this requires qualification. An Arab cannot compare favourably with an English blood horse in endurance, far less in speed ; how then is the former validly better than his English descendant ? Thus, he is the best of his size among the equine species, this much· is certain. Then, similarly with regard to the Arab camel, deer, cow, dog, &c., down to the domestic fowl ; each is best of its kind.

The Jews, in early times, like their Arab kindred, seem to have held a low standard of morals. We are aware that prior to the great religious and social reforms effected by the Prophet Mahomed the inhabitants of Arabia wallowed in the deepest depths of moral depravity; infanticide was common ; and· so little did consanguinity stand in the way of union, that it defied even the conception of incest ; and to this deplorable state of society, it was therefore yet unknown as a crime. The conduct of Abraham in two critical episodes of his life shows that he breathed a moral atmosphere not less impure than his neighbours, and the fact that his wife Sarah was his half-sister indicates that he did not hold himself above the prevalent social standard. Then, again, we have it clearly recorded that King David of Israel, on the occasion of a scandalous domestic imbroglio, declared his willingness to give his peccant son Amnon, under certain circumstances, his daughter Tamar, Amnon's sister, to wife. From these instances we perceive that the Jews in marriage so trenched on the domain of consanguinity as to permit matrimonial union at least between non-uterine brother and sister, children of a common father. In the present day the Jews, though more addicted to marriages of consanguinity than other races, generally conform to the usage among the aliens by whom they happen to be surrounded. But still it would seem that with them matrimonial union between close blood relations is rather encouraged than forbidden. And the fact

that this system has not been conducive in the smallest degree
to either mental or physical deterioration reads an instructive
lesson to those who have inherited the long-prevailing notion
that such unions are productive of untoward results on the
issue in the shape of idiocy or insanity. That the Jews have
for thousands of years ordinarily restricted marriage within the
limits of blood relationship, and yet maintained their pristine
bodily and intellectual perfection, should go far to explode·the
old-fashioned belief which regarded the practice with appre-
hension. The late Sir James Simpson of Edinburgh, reasoning on similar lines to those I am humbly attempting to follow, instituted a wide and searching investigation, upwards of
thirty years ago, with the object of testing the validity of the
tenaciously held belief that marriage between first cousins was
to be avoided on the grounds that it was productive of idiocy
or insanity or scrofula in the offspring; and the result of this
inquiry was completely to show the fallacy of the assumption.
These ailments were found to have no partiality for the fruit of
consanguineous union. Further, it has recently been demon-
strated by experiment that " breeding in and in " has rather an
improving than detrimental effect on cattle, provided always
that both parents be free from taint of any kind. The Jews
in Baghdad evidently in advance of Western inquiry on this
point, have for something like half a century been engaged
in the scientific as well as common-sense endeavour to stamp
out that baneful disease consumption, by the social interdict of
the marriage of all persons so affected, and their efforts give great
promise of ultimately attaining so desirable an end. Likewise
giving play to the scientific instincts for which the race are eminent, they have been for the last thirty years prosecuting with
some success, an attempt by inoculation to obviate the disfigurement occasioned by the Baghdad boil—an erosive eczema of
specific character and protracted duration. By inoculation the
sore, should it occur at all afterwards, is much modified in character, and the resultant scar rendered void of offence to the eye.

The Jewish religion, like most others, has derived much from evolution. M. Renan perhaps goes further in the enunciation of this view than circumstances would appear to warrant. It is clear, however, from the Old Testament, an essentially Hebraic record, that the Jews regarded their Divinity Jehovah as being specially if not wholly concerned with Israelitish interests, to the neglect of all others. Jehovah, in fact, seems to have been regarded by them as much their own tribal deity as Baal and Ashtaroth were looked upon by their respective votaries. Indeed, it may be observed, that the Jews occasionally addressed their supplications to the deities of their alien neighbours, the devotion being referable to the matter of convenience, especially as to the accessibility of shrines or temples. Later, as the Jews rose in tribal importance and influence they concurrently widened the purview and enhanced the potentialities of Jehovah, til he attained the illimitable attributes — Omniscient, Omnipotent, and Omnipresent. They now closely approached that conception of the God of the universe which is held by all civilised peoples, only reserving a right to regard themselves as holding a first place in His consideration. They still laid claim to being the chosen people. The Jews have passed through the ages faithful to the God of Abraham, of Isaac, and of Jacob, to a degree that compels the most profound admiration, considering the innumerable disadvantages and disabilities to which through their religion they have all the time been subjected. Indeed, among the Western Nations amongst whom they have sojourned, their position up to as late as the middle of this century was almost complete social ostracism. But this is not so much a matter for surprise as might at first sight appear, for there are other examples of a faith being as it were fostered by persecution and made strong and vigorous by adversity. For instance, the Armenian Christians in Persia and Syria, the Chaldean Christians in Turkish Arabia, and the Zoroastrians in Northern Persia, have

21

stuck to the faith of their fathers throughout centuries of the most galling oppression. To the reflective mind this must ever be an enigma, for in general ethics and especially in moral tone and integrity these sectaries compare by no means favourably with their Moslem oppressors. It would almost seem then, especially bearing in mind the adverse circumstances which environed Christianity in its infancy, that hostile influences are indispensable to the growth and maintenance of religious faith. We have further examples of this in minor degree, in the tenacity with which the Scotch have held to Presbyterianism and the Irish to Roman Catholicism.

I have already made allusion to Jewish integrity, and would now add that from the ethical point of view they occupy a high position among people of all civilised nations. The Persian poet Saadi quotes in a celebrated couplet, what he alleges to be the dictum of the " wise men of old,"—that " a lie told with a good intention is better far better than truth that stirs up mischief." It may be said that the children of Israel do not despise this doctrine in covering positions of difficulty ; and who shall say that in this they are exceptional ? The question involved is one around which much fruitless debate has arisen, and its solution is a matter of such intricate complexity that only those expert in the study of moral Philosophy can be expected adequately to deal with it, and to these we should be content to leave it. In the conduct of business the Jews have ever shown a high standard of morality. There is, for instance, the case of the late Sir Moses Montefiore, who failed in business when a comparatively young man, and after the lapse of a long interval, called his creditors together and paid each in full with five per cent. interest. And there is the well-known story of the remarkable integrity shown by the first of the family of Rothschild to make a name in the world, who allowed the French troops to rob him of every penny of money, and all the valuables belonging to himself, yet preserved intact all he had in trust by burying it in his garden, where it was not

discovered by the plundering soldiery of the Great Napoleon.
Such instances have not been infrequent among the race in
question, and they have every right to be proud of the commercial renown born of multiplied examples of similar unsel-
fishness. The Jews may be called the princes of finance, and
this, according to the dictum of a great English thinker re-
dounds to their credit, for according to Professor Jowett " a man
cannot be more innocently employed than in amassing a fortune." There is this much further to the credit of the successful Hebrew as seen in England, and I believe, elsewhere in
Europe, that he does not leave his poor relations and depend-
ents to the tender mercies of State charity. The Jews, like
the Parsees, are justly celebrated for the charity they extend
to their co-religionists. Nor would it be doing them justice to
say no more, for their large-heartedness has time and again
been evinced in benefactions to the poor outside the pale of
Judaism. Of such we have innumerable instances. It fell to
my lot in Persia on entering on my appointment in the
British Residency at Bushire, in 1871, to be entrusted by Sir
Lewis Pelly with the dispensation of relief to the famine-
stricken inhabitants of the neighbourhood. The Lord Mayor
of London started a subscription for the purpose, and considerable
sums of money were from time to time sent to the Resident in
the Persian Gulf. The Jewish merchants of London not only
subscribed to the fund for the relief of the Persians in general,
but also started a separate subscription amongst themselves for
the special benefit of Persian Jews. That eminent philanthropist,
Sir Moses Montefiore, was the main figure in the latter charitable enterprise. Akin to the feeling of responsibility as to
the care of the poor, the Jews are highly endowed with natural
affection; this is particularly manifested on occasions of sickness
and bereavement. And so with regard to respect for age, especially as touching the manner in which they comport themselves in presence of parents or guardians. In this, however,
they but share the charcteristics of the Arab race in general,

amongst whom age has ever been held in reverence and honour. Indeed, in these very commendable qualities the semitic race show a distinct superiority to their Aryan neighbours.

The highest authorities on Hebraic literature and language, are inclined to regard Hebrew as deficient in much that lends charm to written thought and history, yet this disadvantage has not been such as to conceal the great power of imagery possessed by the Israelites, and thus it is that the grandeur and beauty of style and language of the book of the prophecy of Isaiah, have been, as held by those competent to judge, enhanced by its rendering into the fine old English of our Bible. Further, it will thus be explained, how the innate taste and culture of this most interesting people have gained much by their having recourse to European language for the expression of their thoughts.

And now let us glance briefly at the varied migration and vicissitude which brought about the proud position they now occupy in the learning, the culture, the commerce, and the politics of the countries of Western Europe, especially England. Their first contact with people of European derivation was in their many struggles with the Philistines, a Greek colony whom they met in the land which they believed was exclusively their own by divine promise. This was the first difficulty which they found hard to overcome in the shape of military adventure. The Philistines from their better acquaintance with the resources of invention as applied in warfare, had armed wheeled chariots which for long rendered them invincible to the Jews on the plains. The period of Egyptian bondage had left Israel in a helpless condition as to offensive military operations, and here it may be said that from the same source they were endowed with their best and worst elements of achievement, at one and the same time. Their bondage tended to give a twist to their sense of justice and honesty, all trace of which was slow to die out, yet their contact with the Egyptians at the same time gave them that stimulus to the cultivation of intellect which they have since turned to such marvellous account. It

is but fair to infer that Moses was not the only Israelite who
had become acquainted with all the "learning of the Egyptians."
It is probable, however, that the learning of Moses was incom-
parably superior to that of the people he led, not even excepting
his elder priestly brother. We have one striking incident in
the Exodus which at once points to this probability, and at the
same time suggests that it contributed largely to endow him in
the eyes of his followers with supernatural power. When he
descended from the Mount of Sinai carrying with him the
decalogue graven on stone tablets he found the Israelites, headed by his brother Aaron, in a state of idolatrous
relapse.—"And Moses' anger waxed hot, and he cast the tables
out of his hands, and brake them beneath the mount. And he
took the calf which they had made, and burnt it in the fire, and
ground it to powder, and strewed it upon the water, and made
the children of Israel drink of it." The water, no doubt, was
already in earthen vessels; and we know that the water of the
desert of the Isthmus in which the Israelites then were, is
intensely brackish, and that the result of the contact of gold
dust with such water would be the rapid formation of the
chemical product, chloride of gold, a salt which in its action
on the human economy, resembles cholera in its intensity of
cramping pain. We see then by this expedient that the
astute and learned Moses at one stroke punished his recalcitrant
followers, and impressed them with a deep sense of his own
dire potentialities, thus rendering them all the more amenable
to his future orders and injunctions.

The above interpretation of this incident in the Exodus must
not be understood to challenge Moses' leadership of the Israelites
being in the main, under divine governance.

After the successive Roman and Saracen occupation of the
Holy land the Jews migrated gradually westward and naturally
first set foot on the European countries bordering on the Medi-
terranean Sea, and thence emigrants wandered northwards and
westward by way of Germany and France, eventually forming a

Hebrew colony in England. All this while they were the victims of cruel hostility, the fruit of bigotry and malice. That knack of acquiring substance ever exemplified by this race from the time of their father Jacob, naturally begat towards them those sentiments born of jealousy and envy, which the indigent, the idle, the prodigal, and the improvident have at all times been prone to evince to the thrifty, the prudent and the provident, among men. In Germany the Jews for a long time enjoyed more privileges or rather laboured under less civil disabilities than elsewhere in Europe, but eventually they found their happiest home in England, where they were admitted by Cromwell. But after the protectorate their existence even in London was subject to occasional demands from the Sovereign in his need or his greed which pressed heavily upon them. The first European Sovereign, who granted complete civil and religious liberties to the Jews with all the rights of subjects, was to his lasting honour be it said, the first and great Napoleon, Emperor of the French. In England, it was only somewhat late in the benign reign of our present most gracious Sovereign that the Jews were incorporated among British subjects with unrestricted rights. It is interesting to note that whilst Jews were still ineligible for a seat in Parliament, members of that race and faith in India were among the most distinguished servants of the crown, eminent both in Civil and Military administration. It is further curious to observe that the Jews in England have in greater part espoused the views of the political party which was most opposed to their civil emancipation.

Notwithstanding all that is to the credit of the Jews as a race, such is the obdurate momentum of traditional opprobrium that not a few of them feel constrained to hide their Israelitish identity in an assumed name and faith. We thus find some of the oldest and most reputable British names adopted by them ; for instance, it is not uncommon to find people with a distinctly Semitic physiognomy under the very Celtic patronymics, Gordon, Graham, and Macdonald ; even the aristocratic name of Howard has been thus appropriated, in which however it is honored in comparison with the trick played it by the poet Pope in making it rhyme with coward, or that by the celebrated Mr. Buggins, who not only adopted the name, but also the ducal, titular distinctive Norfolk as a prefix. The Jews do not proselytise, yet by the number of them who have embraced Christianity, and by the fact that they permit marriage between themselves and Christians, the extent to which Israelitish blood pervades the population of Great Britain and its dependencies and colonies, and all other European countries except Russia, is altogether beyond calculation. Not improbably it is to be found in every rank of the European aristocracy and in numberless families among the Commoners where its presence is not even suspected. Nay, more, a Jewish strain has found its way to the throne of more than one European country, and wherever it runs it is a possession of price, the balance of evidence being in favour of the view that those who enjoy it are better rather than worse for it. It has given to England a statesman whom history will speak of as having only had one rival in the 19th century, one of the two pre-eminently distinguished Englishmen of his day. It has lent lustre to the Episcopate and given strength to the ranks of the clergy of the Church of England. It has given and continues to give men who adorn the English judicial bench and bar, and recruits to all departments of the public Civil and Military Services. It is found in the most select circles of literature, science, and art. The medical profession, has time and again been enriched by it, and to this society in general owes much of the relief from pain and suffering, that has accrued on the achievements of scientific research. To the Jews we owe the survival of science and especially of the medical profession, during the Middle Ages, and in more recent times we find them foremost among those who in the study of astronomy, have searched the serener altitudes of the heavens with critical inspection. In the wide and fertile domain of chemistry, they stand out prominently in the first rank of pioneers of analytical research, and have thus alone conferred countless benefits on mankind. Let us then withdraw from them that opprobrium with which they have too long been regarded, and replace it with sentiments of generous and grateful acknowledgment; for well doth it become us to pray that they may continue as heretofore to " run and not be weary :" " to walk and not faint."

ORDINARY GENERAL MEETING held on Wednesday, the 30th August 1893.

MR. KHARSETJI RUSTAMJI CAMA took the Chair.

The minutes of the previous meeting were read and confirmed.

The following donation was announced, and thanks voted to the donors:—

To the Library.

From Mr. DAVID HOOPER, Quinologist to the Government of Madras, Ootacamund; Index and Appendix to the Pharmacographia Indica, by Brigade-Surgeon William Dymock, retired, late Principal Medical Storekeeper, Bombay.

From the Anthropological Society of Great Britain and Ireland, A Journal Vol. XXII., No. 4 in exchange.

The following paper was then read :—

Note on the Use of Locusts as an Article of Diet among the Ancient Persians.

BY MR. SURUT CHANDRA MITRA, M. A., B. L.,
DISTRICT PLEADER, CHAPRA, BEHAR.

Among the *debris* found in prehistoric caves, the cloven bones of various mammals have been discovered, the presence whereof indicates that the dwellers thereof, viz., Palaeolithic

Man used not only to subsist upon the flesh of animals killed in
the chase, but also to feed upon the marrow of their bones which
they used to extract by breaking open the bones with their flint
hammers and stone-hatchets. Similar discoveries have been
made in the *Kitchen-Middens* of prehistoric peoples all over the
world, and it has been found that the shells of molluscous
animals form the major portion of these heaps of the kitchen-
refuse of the Palæolithic Age. These discoveries have led
Anthropologists to come to the conclusion that men in the
Palæolithic Age used to feed mainly upon the meat of animals
killed in the chase, eked out with a little fish they could catch,
and the berries of trees that flourished upon the earth in the
Pliocene and the Pleistocene Periods. Agriculture, as an art,
was unknown to Palæolithic Man. It is not until we come to the
Neolithic Age when the Mound-Builders, the Dolmen-Builders
and the Dwellers of the Lacustrine Villages of the Swiss Lakes,
flourished on the earth, that we find any remains of cereals and
other agricultural produce which land us on the firm ground
of positive evidence that these Neolithic Men lived not only on
the produce of the chase, but also earned their living by
following the more peaceful pursuits of agriculture. The
investigation by Professor Keller of the remains discovered at
the bases of these Lake-Dwellings has brought to light grind-
ing-stones, mill-stones, grains, breads, fruit, articles which
conclusively prove that Neolithic Men were not unacquainted
with the art of agriculture.

On coming to the latter end of the Quaternary Period when
we get the first traces of Historic Man, his dietary is found to
have been increased by the addition of new articles of food, and
the methods of dressing them for meals improved, whence is the
origin of the Art of Cookery. In this historic period—the Iron
Age—relics of the Palæolithic Man's dietary are found to
exist in some articles of food used by races of savage men all
over the world. Larvæ of insects, flesh of animals considered
unclean and unfit for food by civilized man, clay and such

25

other articles are still used as articles of diet by races of men grovelling in the lowest depths of savagery.

Among insects, the locust has, from time immemorial, been used as an article of food by man. In the Bible we first get the traces of its use as such by men of the Historic Period, in the story of St. John the Baptist, whose "meat" in the wilderness is said to have been principally " locusts and wild honey." There are also other passages both in the Old and the New Testaments (cf. Lev. xi. 22 and Matt. iii. 4) which prove that locusts were considered a delicacy by the Israelites and the Canaanites. In other countries of the East, these insects are eaten even at the present day. There are various ways of cooking them, of which the commonest is to tear off their legs and wings, extract their entrails, stick them in long rows upon wooden spits, and then roast them in the fire. Sometimes they are fried in oil, whereas, at other times, they are dried in the sun and ground in the mill into a flour-like meal of which bread is made in times of scarcity. These articles of diet, dressed in these ways, are considered bonne bouche and are devoured with the greatest gusto by the people who eat them. The Arabians eat them, prepared in the aforesaid fashions, even at the present day. The Bedouins of the Arabian deserts preserve them in salt, and, when undertaking long journeys, take a supply of these in their leathern sacks.

That the ancient Assyrians also used the locust as an article of diet is evident from the banquet scenes depicted on sculptures unearthed from the mounds of Kouyunjik on the Tigris wherein ancient Assyrian servitors are represented as carrying in their hands spits with rows of dried locusts. Among the sculptures on the left or west side of the Konyunjik Gallery in the British Museum, London, which illustrate the state of Assyrian art under the regime of Sennacherib, are " part of a series (Nos. 31-43) which originally lined the two walls of a long narrow gallery leading, by an inclined plane, from Konyunjik towards the Tigris. On the one side, descending the slope, were fourteen horses, led by grooms; on the other, ascending into the palace, were servitors bearing food for a banquet. The figures are somewhat smaller than life, designed with much freedom and truth, and, by comparison with the Panathenaic frieze in the Elgin Room, they may furnish a good point of view for estimating the capabilities and defects of Assyrian art No. 39, on which is seen a marshal or chamberlain with a staff, was originally placed, as here, at a projection in the wall. Amongst the attendants or servitors, represented on Nos. 41-43, *is one bearing in each hand a rod with two rows of dried locusts, which are to this day used as food by the Arabs.* The other attendants carry wine-skins, birds, pomegranates, and other fruit."[*]

In May 1891, a great flight of locusts passed over this district (Sáran). The locusts are known in Hindi as टिड्डी, تدّی In Urdu, the word is written in Persian character as such or *Tiddi.* I was then informed by the Hindus of this place, and also by my Persian teacher—himself a Mahomedan—that the Indian Mahomedans, especially those of the lower classes, eat these insects after having fried them in oil.

The Hindus of Northern India, as a class, consider the flight of locusts an ill-omen, in fact a visitation from God presaging famine or some other calamity to the country which is visited by these insects. As a consequence, they look with repugnance upon these insects. The lower classes of Hindus in Behar, who take flesh-meat and fish, do not eat this insect, nor do the Hindus of Bengal, who, without any restriction, take flesh and fish, even though the latter are in the habit of taking quantities of a minute crustacean—a kind of very diminutive-sized shrimp called in Bengali कुचा निगड़ी which very much resembles minute insects.

A similar superstition with regard to the locust also prevailed among the ancient Assyrians. Just like the Hindus of

---

[*] *Vide* "A Guide to the Exhibition Galleries of the British Museum, Blooms-bury." London: 1888, page 31.

Northern India, the ancient Assyrians also used to consider the locust an insect of ill-omen, boding evil to the place visited by it. In the Table-case B, placed along the middle of the Konyunjïk Gallery of the British Museum in London, and containing the smaller objects of Assyrian antiquity discovered in the course of the various excavations of the sites of ancient Assyrian cities, are exhibited terra cotta tablets referring to the language, legends, and mythology of the Assyrians along with selected specimens of Despatch or Report Tablets and letters. Among these tablets is one numbered 26, which records " a tablet of portents, describing what would be likely to happen if locusts enter a house," &c.[*]

The Ancient Persians were in the habit of taking locusts as an article of diet. By Ancient Persians are meant the inhabitants of Persia after they had been converted to Islam by the Mahomedan conquerors of that country. There is a passage in the Bustan by Sheikh Sádi, which clearly shews that this insect formed an item in the dietary of the ancient inhabitants of Persia. This passage occurs in حکایت در معنی رحمت برناتوان or the story about shewing compassion to poor در حال توانا_ے men by men in a state of affluence, contained in Book I., which is about Justice, Equity and Government. The passage is as follows :—

نه در کوه سبزی نه درباغ شنخ * .: ملخ بوستان خورد و مردم ملخ •

It may be thus translated into Urdu :

پها زون په سبزی نه باغون میں شنخ• .: ملخ کهاگلی باغ و خلقت ملخ•

The above Persian couplet may be thus translated into English :

" Not in the mountain, verdure ; not, in the garden, a branch ; The locusts ate the garden ; and men, the locusts."

Sheikh Sádi flourished about the end of the twelfth century and the first half of the thirteenth. Hence it is evident that the Persians of those remote times were in the habit of eating

[*] *Op. cit.* page 36.

locusts. Unfortunately Sádi does not tell us in what ways they were cooked by the ancient Persians. In the absence of such evidence it must be presumed that they were dressed in the same fashions as are prevalent at the present day in other oriental countries.

ANTHROPOLOGICAL SCRAPS.

" Proverb " writes in the *Madras Mail* :—

It is a belief, no doubt true, that proverbs always teach " the real people's speech," discover the " genius, wit, and spirit of a nation," and embody " its current and practical philosophy." South India is very rich in proverbs, and a minute observer can gather them from all sources, from the learned Pundit to the poorest cooly or woman vending vegetables in the street. A rough calculation made by workers in this direction goes to prove that the Tamil language contains no less than ten thousand proverbs. A common proverb is *Agati talaiyal poludu vidindadu* — *viz.*, the day dawned on the head of the unfortunate. This proverb is the outcome of the belief that the first face seen after rising in the morning governs the events of the day. Certain faces are carefully avoided as being extremely unlucky. " I saw the face of So-and-So, I am sure that this day will close on me with some blood wounds on my body " is a common saying among Hindoos. Sometimes great care is taken overnight to place near the head of the bed auspicious pictures, jewels, &c., on which the eye will fall the first thing 'in the morning. The person who has taken this precaution will probably rise up with his eyes closed, turn them in the direction of the pictures, &c., and then suddenly open them. In Malabar this looking at jewels, coins, &c., is elevated into a regular ceremony on New Year's Day. It is technically called the *Vishukkani*— *vishu* meaning the year, and *kani*, sight of—the (taking) sight of the new year. On New Year's eve all the gold coins available in the house, all the gold jewels, the looking glasses, all kinds of fruits, and everything considered to be good to look at, are placed in the room set apart for the worship of the household god, as well as flowers of the *Konnai* tree (*Cassia fistula*) and the berry of *Kovai* creeper (*Bigonia grandis*). All vegetables are also put in this room, care being taken that they are fully matured and perfect. Cocoanuts are broken into two pieces of the same size, and into each lamps are placed and lighted. The Karnavan, who is the head of the family, first opens this room between 4 and 5 A.M. on New Year's morn, and worships, with a lighted lamp in his hand, all these articles. Then every member of the house, one after the other, goes to the front of the room with his or her eyes shut and opens them when arrived at the proper spot to take a sight of the lucky goods. The Karnavan presents each with *Kainattu* (literally—the placing in the hand by extending both their palms into which the Karnarvan drops, something—coins, jewels, flowers, fruits, &c). After this ceremony the Malayalis take only one good meal during the day at 3 P.M., after a light breakfast of conjee-water in the morning. They do not generally eat at night. The meaning of this custom is that if they thus content themselves with only the conjee breakfast and one meal that day, they can be sure of these at least throughout the year.

This attributing the results of the events of the day to the first sight seen in the morning is a very old Aryan belief. It is not only restricted to the first sight in the morning, but also to such sights just at the time of any undertaking during the day. The meeting of bad persons—persons who are considered to be omens—while starting out on a journey, the sight of a falling star in the night, &c., are considered as heralding evil results. The fall of a star is supposed to be most unlucky, but looking at green trees is always supposed to be an effective remedy. The ancient Hindoo poets and modern superstition always explain this pheno- menon as the falling of good stars. Charitable persons of this world are supposed to live in the heavens as stars till their charity is all exhausted. This idea occurs in the oldest drama of India—*Michhakatika* or the *Toy Cart* where, in describing the fourth court of Vasantasena's house in the Act IV., the bronze cymbals are compared to the falling meteors. *Kshina punya iva gaganal, taraka nipatanti kamsya talah—viz.*, the bronze cym- bals fall (to keep up time) like the stars from the sky when their charity is exhausted. In the same drama, which is a store-house of authority for all ancient customs, the act of seeing a falling star is called a sin. In the beginning of Act IX., when the executioners are leading Charudattas, the hero of the drama, to the stake, to drive away the pressing crowds, one of the executioners exclaims :—" The Indra flag, which is being aban- doned after the ritual, the labour of cows, the falling of stars, the cala- mity of life,—*i.e.*, the death of good people—these four ought never to be witnessed." This belief in the malevolence of falling stars and the efficacy of gazing on green leaves is still very prevalent if not universal in Southern India. As looking on green leaves is supposed to expiate the sin of seeing a falling star, looking at the sun is supposed to avert bad omens. Boys always, whenever they happen to be polluted by the touch of unapproachable objects or persons, look towards the sun and say—"Sun-god, all pollution is to you and none to me." Grown-up persons also look at the sun when they see any bad omen on leaving their houses. That this idea was prevalent even in the 12th century A. D. in India is apparent from *Mudrarakshasa*, a drama by Visakhadatta, who flourished about that time. In the Act V. of that book, Siddharthaka, while starting on his pretended journey to Kusumapura, first meets a *Kshapanaka* (a Buddhist mendicant), which is considered to be a bad omen, and he at once says : *Katham kshapanaka agachhati tad yaran me asakunabhutam imasya darsanam tasmad aditya darsanena pratihanmi—viz.,* What ! a (Buddhist) mendicant comes towards me : and as long as the sight of this person remains an ill-omen, I shall avoid the evil effects of it by looking at the sun in the sky.

A most common method of trying to mitigate the evil effects of ill-omens is to return to the house or place from which the person started and to sit there for a few minutes till the effect of the bad omen has passed away, or to take a cup of water so that the second starting shall be deemed to be a fresh one. Even so to avoid the evil effects of an evil person seen first in the morning the practice is to go to sleep again and get up a second time. Several proverbs exist in Tamil and other Dravidian languages explaining this custom, and the one already quoted—"the day dawned on the head of the unfortunate"—is of special interest. The meaning of the proverb we have already given, and the following story is related to explain it : A certain King got up early one morning and directed his eyes towards the streets of the town ; everything was calm, for the day had not yet quite began, and all the people were asleep. No person therefore was to be seen except a beggar, who was engaged in picking up fruit-peelings, &c. The King saw the beggar and the beggar saw the King by accident. His Majesty turned again to his room, and while in the act received a knock on his head which began to bleed profusely. Suddenly he called his servants and ordered them to fetch the beggar whom he had seen and whom he pointed out. At once the poor man was brought. "Nasty wretch that you are," roared his Majesty, "I saw your face this morning and here is the result," pointing to his bleeding forehead. " I do not know how many of my subjects see your face thus every morning and suffer from broken heads · So instead of such a sinful man living in this world and causing the misery of so many people, it would be better that he lose his life and thus save so many from their miseries. We condemn you to the stake."

Thus spoke the King, and soon a thousand hands seized that unfortunate beggar to drag him to the stake. The man, though a beggar, was a ready wit. The sentence pronounced by the King had emboldened him and made him desperate. " My most noble Sovereign," said he, " I am condemned to the stake for having caused your forehead to bleed True, I curse my life. Very true. What is the use of this miserable being which your Majesty deems to cause the misery of so many of your inno- cent subjects. You know, Sire, that a condemned criminal has certain privileges. In justice I crave that those may be allowed to me, and that I be permitted to speak before I am dragged to the stake. Your Majesty saw early this morning this beggar and received a wound on your kingship's forehead. But this beggar saw your Majesty in the early morning, and as the result of it is now being condemned to the stake. So, I request humbly your Majesty to consider a little as to which of ours is the more sinful head." The King and the people were thunderstruck at this audacious reply. It was not without meaning, and admiring the boldness and the ready wit of the beggar, the King par- doned him. Thus ends the story which is related to illustrate the proverb, but the very story illustrates more the intelligent period in Hindoo history when such beliefs began to receive a shock. Because the hero happened to be a beggar he was thought a fit object for the calamity of the King being laid on his shoulders. But no one thought of abusing the King by the rule of such beliefs for having caused the greater calamity to the beggar until his Majesty had had it pointed out to him by that man. The exact meaning of the proverb as it is now applied is that it is always easy to attribute bad consequences to the weak, the poor, and the uninfluential, and excuse the strong, the rich, and the influential.

SUICIDES IN BOMBAY.

The number of suicidal deaths in Bombay during the past year was 93, of which 59 were males and 34 females. Amongst this number are included 16 insane persons, 11 who were tired of life from long continued illness, 8 who were delirious from fever, and 1 who drowned herself immediately on seeing her husband expire. This was a Brahmin woman of 20 years. Thirty-six of the ninety-three suicidal deaths are thus accounted for, leaving fifty-seven to be accounted for by other causes. As it would be tedious to show the cause of the whole of these fifty-seven deaths, we sub- mit a list of the chief causes arranged in the order of their frequency:— Domestic quarrels, 12; influence of mother-in-law, 5; debt, 5; ill-treatment of wife by husband, 4; after quarrel with wife, 3; after quarrel with husband, 3; disgraced by scandalous rumours, 3; because his wife absconded, 1 ; cut his wife's throat and then his own, 1 ; rain speculation, 1 ; and suspected of theft, 1. Domestic quarrels occupy a prominent place in the list. Some of these quarrels were of a trivial kind, such as a father scolding a grown-up son for keeping bad company; a husband pressed by his wife to provide her with means to go to her country; a father flogging his son for keeping bad hours; a man reproving a brother for contracting drinking habits; a quarrel with a son who supported his mother; a quarrel with a sister; a quarrel of a lad of 18 years with his father; a woman prevented by her husband from visiting her mother; a brother scolding his brother for absenting himself from his work; a wife with a bad temper who was often quarrelling with a mild husband; a husband refusing to give his wife money for household expenses. From the list of causes of suicide—chiefly by opium and by drowning—it will perhaps be thought that life is not so much valued here as it should be amongst intelligent communities. Although the whole number of what may be called domestic suicides in Bombay in any one year is not very great, the domestic relations of the classes who furnish these deaths are not of the happiest kind, even between parents and children, to say nothing of husbands and wives. The renowned "mother-in-law" was not so conspicuous for her love for her daughter-in-law during last year as in some previous years. Only five deaths of young wives are reported as being due to the mother-in-law influence. There is great difficulty in all such cases in drawing out the evidence even from the relatives and friends of the young wife. It is seldom that these relatives will disclose anything at all, for with remarkable coincidence they answer to the question as to the reason which caused the young wife to take her life is, "I know nothing about her domestic life." It is somewhat surprising that three deaths should have resulted from scandalous rumours. Many persons survive scandalous rumours with equanimity, even when these rumours are founded on a strong basis of truth. That comparatively ignorant persons should betray so much sensitiveness to the voice of scandal as to refuse to survive its croakings is remarkable enough, though in the three cases referred to they were all connected with supposed sexual depravity. In one case the husband of a child-wife of eleven years, who was foiled in his attempts at violence upon her, was so scandalized by the jeers of his neighbours when she was taken away from him by her friends that he put an end to his life by taking a poisonous quantity of opium. The case of the young Brahmin woman who drowned herself in a well in her own compound immediately after seeing her husband expire after a short illness, was remarkable. She was the constant and devoted attendant of her husband during his illness, and watched by his bedside continually and with great anxiety. Alarming symptoms only showed themselves about daybreak, after a night of constant watching, and the end came

26

quickly afterwards. Without a word or a sigh the wife walked straight to the well in the compound and threw herself in. She gave no warning of the immensity of her grief—a grief that choked her utterance and stifled her screams. The family suspected no desperate design, and allowed her to go out of the house. Had a friend restrained her movements for a few minutes until her grief had found relief in outward manifestation, there would have been no suicide.

THE JOURNAL

OF THE

ANTHROPOLOGICAL SOCIETY

OF

BOMBAY.

ORDINARY GENERAL MEETING, held on Wednesday, the 27th September 1893.

Mr. JIVANJI JAMSHEDJI MODI, *Vice-President*, presided.

The Minutes of the previous Meeting were read and confirmed.

The election of the following new members was announced:—

Colonel W. A. Salmon, Political Superintendent, Pahlanpur; Mr. John Marshall, Secretary, Chamber of Commerce, Bombay ; Mr. James Begbie, Bank of Bombay, Bombay ; Second Lieutenant A. Waller, Marine Battalion, Bombay ; Major W. B. Ferris, Bombay Staff Corps, Assistant Agent to the Governor-General, Amreli ; and Khan Bahadur Nawab Saiyad Nuruddin, Bo. C.S. and Nawab of Nasik, Acting District and Session Judge,Belgaum.

The following donation was announced and thanks voted to the donors :—

To the Library.

From the Anthropological Society of Great Britain and Ireland.—Journal Vol. XXIII., No. 1.

From Berlin—Zeilschrift for Ethnology for January 1893, Heft III. and IV.

From Zurich—Vierteljahrschrift der Naeturforschenden, Gesellshaft in Zurich.

The following paper was then read :—

On Some RUDE STONE IMPLEMENTS FROM BACK BAY,
MIDDLE COLABA, BOMBAY.

By Mr. FRED SWYNNERTON, Bombay.

BEFORE describing the flints, I will take the liberty of giving a brief glance at some " finds" made in Europe, which

27

appear to have occurred under somewhat similar conditions,
They are the well-known Danish Kjokkenmiddings or kitchen
middings, or as they are sometimes called the " refuse heaps,"
found along the coast of Denmark, and which contain vast
quantities of sea shells, bones of now-extinct animals and
worked flints and flakes. Associated with these are the " Coast-
finds" of the same country in which the remains are found
scattered over the shore itself. When this is the case, the
bones, &c., are found to be much injured by the action of the
sea. There appears to be some doubt among archæologists as
to whether the remains belonging to the "Coastfinds" were
originally deposited on the shore as we now see it—or whether
the sea has encroached on the land and so swept the contents of
some refuse heaps on to the shore where they are now found.
Sir J. Lubbock writes of one place at Bilidt on the Jsefjörd,
and, to use his own words, "this is one of the places at which
it would seem that the inhabitants cooked their dinners actually
on the shore itself, so that the shells and " bones " (and he
might have added "flints ") are much mixed up with sand and
gravel. This describes exactly the state of things on the shore
of Back Bay, if we substitute " flints," for " shells and bones ;"
but it may be that these flints will present an interesting study,
not to be explained by " finds " made elsewhere. I must thank
my friend, Dr. Gerson DaCunha, for being enabled to inspect
the " flakes " found by Mr. Sinclair, which are at present in
this Society's collection. These specimens, I find, are all of
agate or other pebbles, and I was surprised at their small size.
The flints from Sukkur, in Sind, also in the Society's collection are in general character and compositon (allowing for the
waterworn state of mine) very like some of those I have found.
There are no *implements* properly so called in either of these
collections, all being simple flakes and cores, undoubtedly very
ancient.

The worked stones found at Back Bay are plentifully

scattered along the shore for a quarter of a mile or so, and all
that portion of the shore where they occur is at present under
water at high tide, with the exception of one or two banks
only covered by extraordinary tides. On those banks some of
the best of my flints were found. The shore is principally lime-
stone, cropping up here and there through tracts of sand and
gravel ; the latter appearing to have been at one time covered
with mud, indurated lumps of which are still visible in places.
The stone, of which the flakes and implements are composed, is
in many cases a kind of very tenacious and close-grained white
or yellowish quartz. Lumps of it in its natural state may be
picked up anywhere on the shore. It flakes off more readily than
flint, though it is not quite so sharp when freshly broken.
Besides quartz, there appears to have been used black and white
flint, agate, and basalt, in fact any stone with a good cleavage
seems to have been used, though generally quartz and flint. The
delicate, sharp-pointed and keen-edged flakes found in such
enormous numbers where flakes occupy their original bed, have
not been found here—and this I consider is accounted for by
the action of the sea on such frail objects. But that long,
narrow, and delicately made flakes were used is proved by the
fractures on one or two "cores" I have picked up. I have found
only a few very small flakes, but fragments are numerous. The
larger worked stones are comparatively common. The implements I have found may be divided into the following recognized types :—" Flakes " (probably intended for cutting purposes). Flake "scrapers" (or flakes which bear traces of having been used for scraping wood or bone); " used up flakes " ;
" awls or borers " ; " skin scrapers " ; hatchets and hammers
(very rude). There are, beside these, several flakes which
when fresh and sharp may have served as spear-heads. Three
of these have notches chipped out of one side near the base, and
in this, resemble several broken flints which appear to have
been rudely chipped on each side of the base. Many of the

worked stones are not only of the rudest character, but are extremely worn away by the continual action of the sea. In some cases the evidence of their having been used as implements is very slight, being merely the small chips along the edges caused by friction against wood or bone. There is also to be taken into consideration the accidental chippings caused by the sea rolling them about; but even with all this, the general character of the flints which I exhibit is unmistakable, especially in those cases where hollows have been worn in the stone by the continual use of one particular part. I may here add that to detach even a small chip from flint, unless broken in the proper direction, is no very easy matter, even with an iron hammer. So I venture to assert that little of the chipping can be attributed to the work of the sea. The evidence of their antiquity is also present. Many of them bear the polish that age gives to fractured flint, newly broken flint being dull and lustreless. They bear also the characteristic stains produced by the colour of the surrounding earth in which they have long lain. " In ochreous sands, especially if argillaceous, they are stained yellow, while in ferruginous sands and clays they assume a brown colour." (Lubbock.) Many are in a very decomposed state, their surface being quite porous; so much so that ink or other moisture is immediately absorbed if applied when the flint is dry. This surface decomposition is very characteristic of the implements found in the "Drift" in Europe and gives evidence of high antiquity. The "skin scrapers" are here represented by one specimen, and it is a good type of the ruder sort found in Europe, especially of the "spoon-shaped" variety, that is being rounded at one end with a sort of handle, all formed of a single piece of stone. One figured on page 92 of Lubbock's "Prehistoric Times" is very like the one I exhibit and I may add that I found one almost identical in shape to this, in some Quarternary gravel near Rome, along with fossil teeth, and tusks of elephants, &c., though it was not so decomposed as this specimen. The "awls" or "borers" are represented by eight specimens. These implements, used no doubt for boring holes in wood, bone, or hide, are also of the rudest type, with the exception of one, which is chipped with considerable care to a sufficiently sharp point. Lubbock describes these implements as "rude pieces of flint, or flakes worked up at one place by a number of small chips to a point." " Though not very sharp they are pretty strong." There is another class of implements represented here by one specimen which I must notice. They have been found in considerable quantities in the refuse heaps and "Coast-finds" of Denmark, and have given rise to some controversy as to their real nature. Some maintain that they are axes of a rude form, while others, among whom is Professor Steenstrup, think they are far too blunt to have ever served as axes, and believe they were used as sinkers for fishing lines, because the Esquimaux use worked stones somewhat similar in form for that purpose at the present day. The flint No. 2 in my collection appears to be an example of these implements, but I will not be positive. They are described as "generally rudely triangular, with the cutting edge at the broader end, and vary from 2½ to 5½ inches in length, with a breadth of 1½ to 2½ inches. They are never ground, and the cutting edge though not sharp is very strong, as it is formed by a plane meeting the flat side at a very obtuse angle." (Lubbock.) I have seen specimens of these implements in Europe, and the one I exhibit, so far as I remember, gives their general type, and with all humility I suggest that they might have served very well if fixed in handles, for breaking shells off the rocks, or for raking in sand or gravel for sea shells. Two stone objects I have found are very unusual if not unique in form. The larger of the two has a square end, and is flat on one side and rudely bevelled on the other. The square end appears to me to bear marks of having been struck against some hard substance—it has a bruised look in fact. The other end is smaller and has apparently a groove worked around it about half an inch from the tip. Part of the tip has been broken off from the groove upwards. The groove may have served for fastening the stone to a handle, when it might have been used as a hammer (for breaking off " flakes " or shells, or as a club. The smaller specimen is more doubtful as it is so water-worn, but it also has a groove apparently worked right round, and altogether it looks very like a small tomahawk head. The square or cutting end is certainly strangely symmetrical if accidental. One or two of the larger flints exhibited may have been implements, and one appears to have its square end worn away quite flat, while another has notches chipped out on both edges, and the part which might have served as the point appears to have been fractured. To estimate the comparative age of the flints might seem ridiculous, and the question is rendered more difficult by a fossil tooth I found close to one of the more perfect flakes. This is, I believe, the first fossil belonging to a mammal found at Bombay, and it is, therefore, unique. I have not yet ascertained to what kind of animal the tooth belonged, but it bears on it evident marks of having lain in earth for some time, and possibly may have come out of the indurated mud I have before mentioned as occurring here and there on the shore. The tooth is undoubtedly stone, and the mud on it is also fossilized. One of the flints has also some semi-fossilized mud upon it, and might have come out of the same stratum as the tooth. It would be interesting to know whether the worked stones have been chipped on the shore when the latter was pretty much as we now see it, or whether they have lain in the alluvial matter forming part of the shore and have only comparatively recently been washed out by the sea. Do the flints belong to the same period as the fossil tooth? and have they come out of the same stratum? The tooth I may say was found on one of the higher portions of the shore about half-way between high and low water, where flints are numerous. In conclusion, I wish to point out that the old discoloured water-worn flint which has been re-chipped would seem to indicate a great lapse of time between the making of the old and newer specimens, even if we allow that some have been more protected than others by being buried in the earth. From this little circumstance I feel convinced that the same spot of land had been frequented by the· flint chippers for a considerable period. Attentive examination will show that the small reworked flint has been intentionally chipped and is not merely accidental—for to form a straight edge (such as we see in the newer chipping) a dozen blows, at least, must have been cleverly and deliberately dealt. I wish also to suggest that these flints might be classed with those of the " Coast-finds " in Denmark whatever their age may prove to be (though some are almost as discoloured as those from the " Drift " in Europe) and share with the Danish specimens the doubt as to whether they were chipped on the shore, or whether the sea has encroached on the land since their manufacture."

Note.—Since writing the above I have found several large worked stones which afford further and unmistakable proof (if any was wanted. to those who have studied rude stone implements,) that the Back Bay prehistoric people were in a very low stage of culture.

One of the specimens is a well formed hatchet found buried in the matrix (the sand, stones, &c.) out of which one corner of it projected. It is not waterworn. Its colour is a rich brown. The bulb of percussion is clearly defined. It measures 4¾ inches in length by 3 inches in width, and at its thickest part is ¾ inch. Out of the sides about the middle of the implement hollows have been chipped to facilitate fastening it to a handle. One of the sides has been delicately chipped straight to mprove the form of the implement. A slight projection has been chipped away on one face. Part of the other face retain's its natural rough surface. The cutting edge is a little worn and splintered. Altogether the workmanship of this implement; which is the best I have found, shews its manufacturer had not nearly arrived at that phase of culture, which is indicated by the beautifully chipped weapons of the Neolithic age,—and if it had been found in Europe it would probably be classed with the specimens of the older periods. However even now if fixed in a handle it would prove a formidable weapon.

Another flint closely resembles some of the smaller drift " haches " in general form. But the only secondary chipping it presents is near the

point, where some attempt appears to have been made either to sharpen
the point or to chip away a projecting ridge. This specimen is encrusted
with indurated sand under which its worn edges extend shewing that it
was in a worn state before it became embedded. Several other large
flints have been recently found by me,—one having one face rudely
worked into a disc or circular form,·-another is a hammer-stone probably used for breaking off flakes, and several others I have classed as
line or net sinkers.

Judging from a careful examination of all the specimens I have, as
compared with European implements, figured in Lubbock's "Prehistoric
Times," Evans' " Rude Stone Implements of Great Britain ;" and other
works and from my own little experience it would appear that by this
" find," we have clear evidence that at one time this part of India was
inhabited by people in as low a state of civilization as that of the Cave
men of Europe, though of course not necessarily belonging to the same
period.

PLATE.

TYPICAL IMPLEMENTS FOUND ON THE SHORE
AT BACK BAY, BOMBAY.

Fig. 1. (Half actual size.) Hatchet found buried in matrix, out of
which one corner projected. The bulb of percussion is on the
other side. This implement is *not* water-worn. Chipped at
A A, probably for convenience of tying to handle. Colour—a
rich brown.

Fig. 2. (Half actual size.) Worked stone, probably a rude hatchet
or club. The other side has no secondary chipping, but shows
bulb of percussion. It is not water-worn.

Fig. 3. (Half actual size.) Paleolithic " hache " type, much water-
worn. Minute secondary chippings at point. Part incrusted
with indurated sand or fine gravel, under which the worn edges
extend, showing it was worn before it became embedded.

Fig. 4. (Half natural size.) Paleolithic "hache" type, slightly
water-worn and incrusted with hard mud.

Fig. 5. (Half actual size.) Spoon-shaped scraper, much water
worn.

Fig. 6. (Actual size.) Type of borers found, not water-worn.

Fig. 7. (Actual size.) Arrow head, flake chipped to a point, and all along edges and at base. Slightly water-worn.

Fig. 8. (Actual size.) Hollow scraper, slightly water-worn.

Fig. 9. (Actual size.) Scraper. Not water-worn.

Fig. 10. (Actual size.) Smallest of three implements, with groove worked all round. Slightly water-worn.

Fig. 11. (Actual size.) Simple flake, slightly worn by use near point. Not water-worn.

Fig. 12. (Actual size.) One of several water-worn flakes, chipped on both sides near base.

ORDINARY GENERAL MEETING, held on Wednesday, the 25th October 1893.

MR. KHARSHETJI RASTAMJI CAMA, *Presided.*

The Minutes of the previous Meeting were read and confirmed.

The election of the following corresponding Member was announced:—

Mr. Sarat Chandra Mitra, M.A., B.L., Pleader, Judge's Court, Chupra, Saran District, Behar.

The following paper was then read:—

On AGHORIS AND AGHORAPANTHIS.

By Mr. H. W. BARROW, Bombay.

1. THE three MS. volumes of the late Mr. Edward Tyrrell Leith's "Notes on the Aghoris and Cannibalism in India,"

28

which the council of this Society entrusted to me for preparation, are, almost without exception, written in pencil, and a good deal of the writing has already faded and is difficult to decipher. By far the greater portion of the papers relates to the subject of human sacrifice and of cannibalism in India, and contains a vast amount of information thereon. As far as possible, however, I have left those subjects untouched and confined myself to the study of the question of the Aghori, or Aghoripanthi sect. For two reasons, I have in every instance cited the authorities for the facts stated. Firstly, on account of the perishable nature of these records, and secondly, to satisfy the doubts of those who are of opinion, that the Aghori or Aghorapanthi is a myth, or, who think, to quote the words of one of our most entertaining and learned local historians, that " the Cannibal and the Aghori are the creation of acute famine　*　*　* in the primary sense of the words　*　*　they have never existed nor do exist in India " and that even in the most circumstantial cases that have been brought to light neither date nor place has been quoted.†

The data upon which I have proceeded consists of random entries, jotted down as information was received from day to day by Mr. Leith on any subject connected with human sacrifice, cannibalism, and the doings of the Aghoripanthis. Consequently, the facts set forth below are found scattered here and there throughout the three volumes, and in order to group the various points dealt with in something like order and to marshal them into successive array and continuity, I found it necessary to go through the volumes several times.

Leyden in his *Language and Literature of the Indo-Chinese Nations* (see Asiatic Researches, Vol. X., p. 203) observed that it was surprising the singular customs of the Aghoripanth as an Anthropophagy in Bengal and other parts of India, had not been investigated, for that these people ate human flesh was a

---

† " Bombay and Western India."

fact which could not be easily called in question. It was
probably these observations, together with certain facts which
were communicated verbally to Mr. Leith by Surgeon
Lieutenant-Colonel T. S. Weir (*see* para. 25) which induced
Mr. Leith to apply himself to the study of this little understood
subject. In any case, when some years ago he settled himself to the work, although much was known regarding cannibalism in India, scarcely any recent information could be
said to be on record regarding Aghoris and Aghoripanthis
until he had gone through immense trouble in corresponding
with those best calculated to possess information on the matter,
including many distinguished officers of the Civil Service of
India, Military officers in Political employ, Native officers of
rank in the services of Feudatory States, as well as with pandits
and other learned Indian gentlemen. He received most
willing and courteous attention from those to whom he applied,
however, and by means of the assistance thus rendered, was
at length enabled not only to gather together a mass of really
reliable information regarding the past and present doings
of the Aghoripanthis, but to converse with two of them
in Benares and Allahabad, to ˙have others of the sect
examined elsewhere on his behalf, and to elicit from their
own lips many curious details of their esoteric doctrines
which naturally, are usually hidden from the view of the outside
world. He ascertained, that not only are these sectaries
numerous in Benares and other parts of India, but that within
recent years some of them have been seen in the streets of
Bombay, in the burning ghaut at Nasik and in other quarters
of Western India, notably on Girnar and Abu. It appears,
moreover, that in 1885 Mr. Kedernath Basu, the learned editor
of the *Berhampur Universe*, and one of the most valued
corresponding members of this Society, wrote to Mr. Leith
expressing the hope that Government would make searching
enquiries into what the writer designated "the black deeds
connected with the Aghoris" (*see Appendix* A), though he

added that he did not think much good could be done in the matter unless those enquiries were secret.

There are some well executed photographs of one of the Aghoripanthis examined by Mr. Leith, contained in the album of this Society's library. I may add that in April last, I heard from Surgeon-Major Kanoba R. Kirtikar, Civil Surgeon of Thana, that he had recently discharged an Aghoripanthi from Thana Jail.

The names of most of the gentlemen to whom Mr. Leith was indebted for assistance in this enquiry will be found in Appendix **B.**

Before proceeding, it is well to add that the details of the practices of this filthy sect are so interwoven with all branches of the enquiry that I have found it difficult to eliminate the narration of their abominable doings from the main enquiry, consequently, I regret that a great portion of this paper is of such a nature as to limit its publication to the pages of the Society's journal.

2. Although there are differences of opinion among the learned as to whether the *Vedas* authorised, or abrogated, human sacrifice, or whether it was introduced in later times by authors of works like the Kalikâ puranâ, *rudhirâdhiâya*, or the bloody chapter (*see* Colebrooke, H. H. Wilson, *the Indo-Aryan* of Rajendra Mitra, *Asiatic Researches*, Vol. XVII., p. 204 and paper by Rao Bahadur Gopalrao Hari Deshmukh*), the sanction to such sacrifice and to the sale of man's flesh is conveyed in unmistakable terms in the following texts (furnished by Mr. Kedernath Basu) :—

"The goddess remains satisfied for a thousand years with a human being sacrificed according to prescribed rites and ceremonies, and with three human sacrifices for a hundred thousand years. *Kamekshya Bhairari*, who is an emblem of myself, remains satisfied with human flesh for three thousand

---

* See Appendix C.

years. The (human) blood that is offered with Mantras always becomes ambrosia. The goddess eats both human head and flesh offered as a sacrifice. For this reason the wise should offer (human) head besmeared with blood (literally, "red head") in oblation, in *puja*, and (human) flesh in *homá* and *bhoyja* or food offering." (Tantra) *Káliká Purana*.

" In a different quarter the princes had begun to sell human flesh publicly."

Harshacharita, Chapter V.

" Human flesh is for sale—unwounded real flesh from the body of a man. Take it, take it."

(Sanskrit drama of *Málati Mádhara* by Bhavabhuti.)

There is abundant evidence of these sacrifices in the *Vedas* and other ancient books of the Hindus, and an obvious allusion to the Aghoris and their practices of sacrifice in this drama (Act V.) where Mádhava rescues his mistress from the Aghora Ghanta, and says, "Yadastu tudastu Vyápádayámi," *i. e.*, ".Happen what may I will slay thee" (before the goddess Chámmunda)[1]. Its author, who wrote in the 8th (Christian) century, evidently alluded to the Aghoris, and other Sanskrit authors of the 11th and 12th centuries constantly accused the Bhils and other hill-tribes of being addicted to the sanguinary worship of the Aghori with its human victims.[2] The Hindu sects who practice cannibalism in connection with their religious rites and ceremonies are the Aghorapanthis, Bauls, and Vamachárís or Vamis, known also as Kaulacharis or Tantrics.[3] The accurate and learned Professor, H. H. Wilson in his " Religious sects of the

---

[1] See Professor H. H. Wilson, "The Religious Sects of the Hindus " and the Religious sects of the Hindus by Sri Akshoy Umar Datta, Calcutta, 1289, Vol. 2, p. 98.

[2] Professor H. H. Wilson, " Asiatic Researches," Vol. XVII., p. 204, and " Religious Sects ' of the Hindus," Vol. 1, p. 282.

See also letter from Lt.-Col. Watson, Pol. Agent, S. M. Country, through Mr. Vesey Fitzgerald, also of the Political Department.

[3] Babu Kedernath Basu's letter to Mr. Leith, of 6th January 1885.

Hindus " Vol I, p. 233, says : "The pretended insensibility of the *Paramahansa* being of a passive nature is at least inoffensive, and even where it is mere pretence, the retired nature of the practice renders the deception little conspicuous or revolting. The same profession of worldly indifference characterises the *Aghori*, or *Aghorapanthi;* but he seeks occasions for its display, and demands alms as a reward for its exhibition.

"The original Aghori worship seems to have been that of *Devi* in some of her terrific forms, and to have required even human victims for its performance.* In imitation of the formidable aspect under which the goddess was worshipped, the practices were of a similar nature, and flesh and spirituous liquors constituted, at will, the diet of the adept.

* *   "The only traces of it now left, are presented by a few disgusting wretches who, whilst they profess to have adopted its tenets, make them a mere plea for extorting alms. In proof of their indifference to worldly objects, they eat and drink whatever is given to them, even ordure and carrion. They smear their bodies also with excrement, and carry it about with them, in a wooden cup, or skull, either to swallow it, if by so doing they can get a few pice ; or to throw it upon the persons, or into the houses of those who refuse to comply with their demands. They also for the same purpose inflict gashes on their limbs, that the crime of blood may rest upon the head of the recusants ; and they have a variety of similar disgusting devices to extort money from the timid and credulous Hindu.

---

* It may be credulity or calumny, but the Bhils and other hill tribes are constantly accused by Sanskrit writers of the eleventh and twelfth centuries as addicted to this sanguinary worship. The *Vrihat Kathá* is full of stories to this effect, the scene of which is chiefly in the Vindhya range. Its covert existence in cities is inferable from the very dramatic situation in *Bhava-bhuti's* drama, *Málati* and *Mádhav*, where *Mádhav* rescues his mistress from the Aghora Ghanta, who is about to sacrifice *Málati* at the shrine of *Chá Mundi*. (Act V. p. 83.)

They are fortunately not numerous, and are universally detested and feared."[4]

3. The French writer, M. d'Anville, alludes to the Aghori as "une espece de monstre," and observes it is a curious fact that the *Merdi Chor* or *Merdi Khor* should have been noticed by *Pliny*, *Aristotle* and *Ctesius* under nearly the same name, *Masti Chora*, whilst the Troglodytes of *Herodotus* and some of the people spoken of by Marco Polo were akin to the Aghori.[5]

4. The author of that extraordinary Persian book, the *Dabistân* or "School of Manners," writing probably about the middle of the 16th (Christian) century, gives a short but clear description of Aghoris who practised acts of "Atilia" or "Akhori." He says this sect originated at Goraknath, and he describes having himself seen one of them "singing the customary song" and seated upon a corpse, the flesh of which he ate when it became putrid[6].

5. M. Thevenot, whose travels were republished in London in the year 1687, alludes apparently to a community of Aghori cannibals who, during his time, were established at a place which he calls Debca in the Broach District. Although his veracity has been called in question, there is a tradition that in the village of Walwâd, on the Mahi river, cannibals resided a century or two ago.[7] In the early part of this century, there were several Aghorapanthis at Baroda where there were the ruins of a temple dedicated to Aghor-Eshwari-Mata ([8]), and

---

[4] Mr. Kederath Basu writing to Mr. Leith says, "Wilson's Religious Sect of the Hindus," is the best and most reliable work on Hindu sects that he (Mr Basu) knows of, the next best being Ward "On the Hindus."

[5] *Lt.-Col. J. Tod's Travels in Western India*, pp. 83-85.

See also the accounts of the Ogre or ghoul in *Burton's* translation of the *Alf Laylah Wa Laylah* or "Thousand Nights and a Night."

[6] See Appendix (D).

[7] Letter to Mr. Elliott, Resident at Baroda, from Kazi Shabudin, C.I.E., then Dewan of that State.

[8] Tod's Travels as above.

an Aghorapanthi Sthan still exists at a place between Ahmedabad and Kadi*, which is sixteen miles from Ahmedabad.

Lieut.-Col. J. Tod in his *Travels in Western India* (1839), pages 83—85, gives a vivid description of the Aghoris of his time, saying it was reserved for him to discover the extent to which the debasement of man could be carried by the doings of these people, which happily were too far below the attributes of human nature to be erected into a system. This outcaste of human nature is the jackal of his species, though even that reveller amidst graves and impurities, is cleanly in his habit compared with the Aghori * * by whom a dead man or a dead dog is viewed with equal indifference, or rather appetite and * * who does not hesitate to feed on the excretions of nature. Our author passed the gopha or cave of the most celebrated of these monsters, who was long the terror and the loathing of Mount Abu and its neighbourhood. His name was Futteh Poori. After having embowelled whatever came in his way, at an advanced age he immured himself in his cell, and so readily were the commands of the maniac obeyed, that when he gave the order, the mouth of the cave was built up and he was left entombed. There were still several of these wretches inhabiting the caverns of the mountain at the date of Col. Tod's visit, from which they seldom emerged in open day. Col. Tod was told by a native gentleman that a short time previously, when he was conveying the dead body of his brother to the burning ground, an Aghori crossed the party and begged to have the corpse, saying it "would make excellent chatni." So great were the superstitions regarding the Kálka Shrine on Mount Gírnár, that when Col. Tod insisted on visiting the dread spot, the Guicowad's agent, Lalla Joshea, gravely imputed an attack of lameness that the traveller suffered from, to his profanity in this matter. The legend was, that when a sacrilegious visitor was foolhardy enough to

_____
* Statement of Rao Bahadur Gopalrao Hari Deshmukh of Bombay to Mr. Leith, 7th July 1885.

set out on his journey, he was sure to be joined by a stranger, who after a while disclosed her identity with the dread Mother herself. But the actual stranger was a murderous Aghori, and Ogur Sikra itself was called after a mardi-khor or man-eater, one Gazi, who occasionally quitted his mountain lair for the plain to indulge his appetite. The last time he was seen, a live goat and a vessel filled with shráb were placed before him. He tore up the animal with his teeth and nails, gorged, drank and slept among the offal, awoke again, gorged and drank and then returned to the forest (page 333).

6. That *Aghoris*, *Aghorapanthis*, and kindred sects long continued to terrorise the people in different parts of India by the exhibition of their flagrant indecencies, and the enormity of their crimes, is amply shown by *Sherring* in his *Hindu Tribes and Castes* (Vol. I., page 269; Vol. II., page 339), the *Revelations of an Orderly* (selections "Calcutta Review"), Vol. III., page 315 (Benares, 1849), the *Topography of Assam*, Calcutta(⁹) (1837); *Professor H. H. Wilson's* Works, Vol. I., page 233 (¹⁰); the *People of India*, edited by Forbes Watson and John W. Kaye, London, Vol. II., No. 94; *Lieut.-Col. Tod's Travels in Western India*, p. 383; *Ward's Hindoos*, Vol. 2, p. 373; the N.-W. P. *Gazetteer*, Punjab Census Report of 1881, Vol. I., p. 286 (¹¹) and by other authorities. (¹²). Norman Chevers in his *Medical Jurisprudence for India* remarks that in any other country but India, the Agorapanthis would be regarded and treated as dangerous maniacs.

So intolerable were their misdeeds, that their regular worship was long since suppressed by Government.

7. The Aghoris and Aghorapanthis borrowed their creed

(⁹)   Appendix D.
(¹⁰)   See para. 2 above.
(¹¹)   Appendix D.
(¹²)   See Professor H. H. Wilson as above.

from the Paramanhansas,([13]) but though human sacrifice forms no part of the ritual of the last named, yet among Jogis and others the belief is prevalent that human victims are required and are still sacrificed in the performance of the bloody rites of the sect or sects of Aghorapanthis, the flesh of the sacrificed being partaken of by those who murder the victims, especially in remote and lonely spots at Girna and Abu. (See Appendix A, and para 11.)

The initiation ceremony of the true Aghori is said to be very terrible, and only performed in full, in lonely spots. It is first necessary for the candidate to be an Atit or religious ascetic, forbidden to marry ; he is required to learn the mantra and to perform ceremonial observances for twelve years before becoming a perfect Aghori.([14]) The Aghorapanthi of to-day has, to some extent, at any rate, to content himself with making the initiation ceremony of the neophyte, as indecent and filthy as possible, as will be found by a reference to Appendix F.

Agorapanthis are generally regarded as cannibals and many old men living near the Benares Takya ([15]) have seen them eating man's flesh, whilst they affirm that the custom is still in force. When Aghorapanthis are drunk, they will seize hold of corpses that drift to the bank of the river and bite off pieces of flesh. Even at the present day they admit that their sect do eat dead man's flesh(*) and one of

---

([13]) *Religious Sects of the Hindus*, by Shri Akshoy Umar Dutt. Statements of Mr. Kedernath Basu in letter to Mr. Leith, and as above. See also statements further on, of Colonel West, extract from Lieut.-Colonel *Tod's Travels in Western India* Statement of Gosains, &c.

([14]) Lt.-Col. Watson and Lt.-Col. West as before.

([15]) Statement of Hari Singh, a Kshatri cultivator of Benares, made to Mr. Leith at Benares, 1st January 1885. Hari Singh cited the names of Ishwari Singh, Bisear Singh, and Nankir Ahir, the oldest inhabitants of the district, as to the cannibalism of Aghoris, *see* also Norman Chever's Medical Jurisprudence.

(*) Ramnath (Jogi) Aghori.

them, in Benares, offered to point out to Mr. Leith one or
two of the number who eat it. He added that he (the
Aghorapanthi) had himself eaten such flesh, at Jaunpur,
and on another occasion,([16]) and that he would swallow some
more if Mr. Leith would give it to him! This cannibal added
that Agorapanthis do not care to feast on corpses thrown into
the Ganges for fear of being beaten by the people, and
because they prefer to get money and wood at the burning
ghauts. Their religion prompts them to eat corpses,([17]) and
so does hunger.([18])

8. If at initiation, an Aghorapanthi refused to eat human
flesh he would be dismissed by the guru as unfit for his
calling,([19]) but on the other hand, a chela who has eaten the
refuse food of his guru, who has himself fed on man's flesh is
not called on to perform acts of cannibalism, the partaking of
the refuse being equivalent under the circumstances to the
chela's tasting such flesh. ([20]) ([21])

At times when thinking of what they have been ordered to do
by their gurus, they become frenzied and rush at a dead
man's corpse in order to devour the flesh.([22]) On other
occasions, as already shown, they swallow it at the masans or
burning ghauts, in order to acquire the knowledge of jadu.([23])
Sherring, in his *Hindu Tribes and Customs*, relates that newly
initiated Aghoris used to be sent to Ashtbhuja, the shrine of
a famous goddess, six miles from Mirzapur, where they
practised incantations until they imagined they had acquired

·([16]) Statement of Bharanath Agherapanthi of Benares, as above.

([17]) Statement of Raghunathdas of the Ramanandi sect.

([18]) See statement of Jamnaram Agorapanthi and of Raghunathdas ; statement to Mr. Leith, 7th April 1885, of Mr. Hardevram Nanabhai, Vakil, of
Bombay, and of Rao Bahadur Gopalrao Hari Deshmukh.

([19]) Jamnaram Aghoripanthi's Statement to Mr. Leith, 4th January 1885.

([20]) ([21]) Bharanath Aghoripanthi.

([22]) Ramnath (Jogi) Aghori Guru. Statements to Captain Malcolm
Meade, Political Agent, Bhopal, 1885. Also of Baladin Badrunath Trivate,
a servant of Mr. Hardeveram Nanabhai, Vakil of Bombay.

([23]) Statement of Pundit Nilkantrao.

the power of the Goddess Aghor Mukhi whom they worshipped.([24])

9. As a matter of fact there was a curious case at Kolhápur some years ago, in which one of the fraternity was tried for murdering a boy who was sacrificed with a view to finding out hidden treasure by magical incantations. While in jail the man horrified every body by ostentatiously tasting his own excrement and urine, but he showed he was not above human weakness when the capital sentence was confirmed, as his fortitude quite gave way and he showed abject cowardice.([25])

Another horrible case, unconnected with magic, and arising from mere blood-thirst, apparently, occurred at Neriád, one day in June 1878, when Ranghavdas Ramdas Agorapanthi of Dwarka, a mendicant, staying at the temple of Sitaram Laldas, seized a boy of 12, named Shankar Ramdas, who was playing with two other boys, threw him down on the ontla of the temple, ripped open his abdomen, tore out part of his entrails, and, according to the poor little victim's dying declaration, began to eat them. The other boys having raised an alarm the monster was seized. When interrogated by the magistrate as to whether he had committed the crime in order to perform *Aghor Vidya*, the prisoner said that as the boy was *Vibshan* he had eaten his flesh. He added that if he had not been interrupted he would have eaten all the entrails. He was convicted, but only sentenced to transportation for life. The High Court, however, (West J., and Pinhey J.,) altered the sentence([26]) and ordered the prisoner to be hanged.

Of the monstrous brutality of Aghorphanthis to human remains, the following passages from the proceedings of British law courts are striking examples : —

([24]) See Appendix D. (Sherring) ; see also statements made to Col. West.

([25]) Letter to Mr. Leith from Lieut.-Col. West, Political Agent, Kathiawad, dated Jetpur, 5th December 1884.

([26]) Bombay High Court Proceedings, 3rd October 1878.

On the 25th March 1862, Mr. Brodhurst, afterwards the Honourable Mr. Justice Brodhurst, convicted Deoki Ram Aghori, at Ghazipur, under Sections 270-297 of the Indian Penal Code and sentenced him to one year's imprisonment for having offered indignity to a human corpse. The prisoner, a drunken, homeless man, was found carrying the remains of a putrid human corpse along a public road. He was throwing the brains from the skull on to the ground and the stench of the corpse greatly distracted the people. Here and there he placed the corpse on shop boards and on the ground. Separating pieces of flesh from the bones he ate them and insisted on begging. The account he gave of himself was that he was a disciple of Fakira Aughar and resident at Mauzah Kakrahat, Shahabad. He was 18 years of age and for 5 years had been a disciple of Fakira in Zamania. As to the corpse he found it on the river side the previous day and ate some of the flesh. He added that he ate corpses whenever he found them.

At the Rohtak Court, on 11th April 1882, Ramdial, Aghori, Chela of Bhanidas Jogi, was convicted and sentenced by the magistrate to six weeks' imprisonment for offering indignity to a human corpse (Section 297, Penal Code): the prisoner having dug up the corpse of a little girl and devoured part of the flesh thereof.

A man who said his name was Hardgal, but refused to give the name or residence of his guru, was convicted, July 1884, and sentenced by Mr. J. S. C. Davis, Assistant Superintendent of Dehra Dhun, to imprisonment for twenty-two months and a half, under the terms of Sections 297 and 267 of the Indian Penal Code. The prisoner had opened a newly filled in grave, taken out the body of a Hindu girl who had died of small-pox and carried off the body to his hut to which it was traced by the father of the deceased. The distracted parent was horrified at seeing other human remains in the hut, and the prisoner pulled from his own bundle two hands and some pieces of flesh. His defence was that his guru had ordered him to collect 100 hands and 100 human skulls. The prisoner in his statement to the Court said he frequently ate human flesh when hungry.

On the 29th December 1884 Mr. Ishan Chandra Sen, Deputy Magistrate, convicted one Krishna or Kinto Das Babajee, mendicant, in the Magistrate's Court, Berhampore, under Section 290 of the Indian Penal Code of committing a public nuisance by eating the flesh of a human corpse at the cremation and bathing ghat in that town. Mr. Kedernath Basu who was one of the witnesses for the prosecution saw the accused exhume with his chimta, or tongs, portions of a half burned corpse and then eat some of it. Accused afterwards placed pieces of the flesh in an earthen pot which he carried away with him. He ate the flesh before all the people who were bathing or carrying water, and evidently desired to be regarded "as a saint or great man." On a previous occasion Mr. Basu saw this beastly creature eat the vomit of a dog and expose his naked body to the public. Another Hindu gentleman deposed to seeing the accused eating the remains of a corpse and to hearing him cry out loudlly. "I take Mohamgso (human flesh)." The Court fined the offender Rs. 15 with the option of 15 days' imprisonment.

10. In this connection I may add that on 13th May 1885, Captain (now Major) Meade and Mr. King came across a man at a place called, I believe, Sotia Bhopal, who was eating carrion in the bed of a stream. He was quite naked and covered with thick hair.

Colonel Saurin Brooke, who was then Deputy Commissioner of Khundwa, C. P., and who after a long service recently retired, informed Mr. Leith it is difficult to get information about the Aghoripanthis in the Central Provinces, though there is no doubt they do practice cannibalism, not habitually, but on initiation and at other times.

Sir Michael Filose of H. H. Scindiah's service, met two Aghorpanthis some years ago on the occasion of a fair at

Ujjain, one of whom said his nath was at Mount
Girnar. They came from Jaipur and Jodhpur, respectively, and
were heard invoking the names of Bherunddea (a form assumed by Shiva when he carried off Narsingha) and Kalidevi.
They said they did not worship idols, and denied that they
ate human flesh.([97])

11. The Head-Quarters of the Aghorapanthis appears to
have always been at Mount Abu and the Girnâ hills,([98]) but
the caves in which they reside are in the wildest and most in-
accessible parts of the hills. A number of them who reside
at Girnâr have such an evil reputation that the authorities do
not like Europeans to go there, except with an escort.([29]) As
recorded by Colonel Tod above, it was at Abu and its neighbourhood that the noted Aghoris, Kherajpuri and Futehpuri
resided, as also Lalgir, Deogir, and Kuputgir, Gurus of the
sect. According to one authority([30]) these three last mentioned also frequented Girnâr. A tomb or platform in memory
of Lalgir exists at Hinglaj, and his name was held in great
veneration by another Guru, Gangagir, who before smoking
tobacco and ganja used to invoke Lalgir's name. Two of
the successors of these men were said to be living recently, on
the Girnâ clump, one on the Jogania hill, and the other on
the Bhim Guppa or Bhim Cave.([31])

A Bramachâraya now alive says that he has seen them, and
a devotee named Shivadâsji, used to say, that formerly an Aghorapanthi lived in the cave near Patharchati. Aghorapanthis
usually reside in the depths of the jungle, but sometimes visit
human habitations.([32])   Generally they conceal themselves

([17])   Letter from Sir Michael to Mr. Leith, 29th March 1885.

([18])   Mr. Chaina Mall, letter, 26th June 1885.

([19])   Lieut.-Colonel West, as before, also letter from Lieut-.Colonel Watson
as before.

([30])   Pandit Nilkuntrao, as before.
Statement of Bhagwandas, Bhairaji.

([31])   Raghunathdas's statement to Mr. Leith, 5th April 1885, in Mr. Leith's
bungalow.

([32])   Lieut.-Colonel Watson as above.

at Girnâr. There are numerous caves in which during the hot
season devotees live in the neighbourhood of the villages of
Oosrut and Shergaum, the last of which is the most remote on
Abu. It is on the N.-E. end near Sirhoi, and about double the
distance of Oosrut from Abu. Shergaum has very seldom
been visited by Europeans, and when a few years ago Mr.
Shanahan, a retired Conductor of the Public Works Department,
and who is, or was, till quite recently, probably the oldest
European inhabitant of Abu, made his way to this village, he
was told that no European had been there since Major Roberts
visited the place about 1840. Mr. Shanahan shot some
crocodiles in the Langraij talao which, on being found dead by
Aghorapanthis (or Waghoris), were devoured by them. These
people are described by him as a tribe of carrion eaters
who feed on dead bodies, human or otherwise, and all kinds of
filth, who formerly and still, it is commonly believed, by the
people, whenever they have the chance, kidnap children, carry
them away to their haunts and devour them. His own opinion
was, that if cannibalism still exists among these wretches at Abu
it is practiced in the caves near Shergaum ; the villages about
the base of the hills or the grassia huts among the hills on
the other side of the Railway being possibly the places from
which children or other weak defenceless individuals are
carried off.([33]) Some of these caves contain evidence of recent
occupation. The account given by a Gosain who has frequently
been at Abu and Girnar, and resided at Satpura Boira,
coincides remarkably with the above. He said Aghorapanthis
live on Girnâ, but keep themselves concealed. They
attend the Shivarâthi fair on Girnâ as Gosains along with
other Gosains * * * The name of the Aghorapanthis
at Girnâ are Somwargir, whose Guru is Motigir,([34])
Mangir, whose Guru was Sarvangir. The former lives near

([33]) Statement made by Mr. Shanahan to Major W. C. Wyllie, then
First Assistant Political Agent, Rajputana.

([34]) Statement of Raghunathdas as before.

the Kálká Temple, which is situated a little below the Sisaband Shikra or peak. About ten years ago another Aghora-panthi arrived from Abu and went to live on Kali dongri. The temple is still held in the same awe that it was nearly three-quarters of a century ago when visited by Colonel Tod as mentioned in para. 6. The superstition is that since the curse pronounced by the goddess no one has dared to enter the temple, not even a priest. If he ventured to do so he would never return alive. No other religious sects live near, and the temple is in a very wild and secluded spot " abounding in tigers." An imaginative pilgrim who has been to the neigh-bourhood says that the man who ventures in the vicinity of the temple is killed : if by Kálká she only sucks his blood "as one would suck a mango,'" if by an Aghorapanthi the flesh is eaten as well.(³⁵) The Máta of Mataji Sikra is Ambika Máta not Kálká Máta, and can be visited by any one. Mátaji's Temple is six miles from Kálká temple.

Dattátrya was the guru at Girnár. He is worshipped as the Avatár of Siva, and was an Aghoripanthi. His murat (idol) has only one face, not three. It is a stone idol in human shape, not a tomb, and is on a platform. There is no representa tion of a dog near it.(³⁶)

12. A man relates that a báwá came from the Barda hills to the village of Lángad, under Junagad, and carried away a kunbi of that village, whom he kept with him for four years. The báwá used daily to carry off and eat an entire goat, and whenever he was unable to find one used to threaten to eat the kunbi, who is said to be alive now, and to be the patel of Langad.(³⁷)

Another man affirms that a báwá who lived near the Dámo-dhar Khund in the Girnár, used to dig up and eat corpses,

(³⁵) Ragunathdas as above.
(³⁶) Statement of Jamnarám, Aghorapanthi of Allahabad, made there to Mr. Leith, 4th January 1885.
(³⁷) Lieut. Col. Watson, through M. P. Fitzgerald.
30

and that he tried to do so with the corpse of a Pardesi, who had been buried there, but the cannibal was driven off by the dead man's friends who watched the grave. The same authority says that a person in his own family died, and that they took the corpse to the burial ground at night. While he and another were watching the corpse, a bâwâ appeared and gazed eagerly at the corpse. The friends of the dead man were alarmed, but just then other members of the family came up, and the bâwâ who had come from Joganis hill, fled away towards Mount Raivata.[38]

13. On rare occasions the Aghoripanthi presents himself in a more amiable light, as when he contents himself with honest milk diet, thus :—A grihastha of Junagad relates that an Aghoripanthi used to visit the grihasta's grand-father's house and ask for goras, i. e., a vessel of curds. If the goras were given him he would devour the entire contents (i. e., several pounds) and if he were given molasses he would swallow from 10 to 16 pounds thereof, and then depart.[39] Fortunately, these greedy people do not seem to trouble Junagad now.

14. A gentleman who was well known in the city of Bombay, and who is so frequently quoted from in this paper, had a most unpleasant experience of an Aghorapanthi at Nassick, one day about the year 1880. This gentleman, the late Rao Bahadhur Gopalrao Huri Deshmukh, informed Mr. Leith that on that occasion he (the Rao Bahadur) accompanied the corpse of his grandson to the burning ghat (Talkute ghat). The men who supplied the wood for the pyre advised that the family of the deceased should remain at the pyre until the corpse was ontirely consumed; as otherwise the Aghorapanthi who was present, would snatch away the remains and eat them. The Aghoripanthi was dressed as a Gosain and carried two or three skulls.

---

(38) Statements made to Lieut.-Colonel West.
(39) Lt.-Col. Watson as above ; Lieut.-Col. West.

Mr. Deshmukh saw another Aghoripanthi at Rutlam in 1834, and a third in Bombay, in Null Bazar, on 5th July 1885, who was also dressed as a Gosain and carried three skulls in his hand. He was sitting in the verandah of a native shop begging. He had copper money in a skull. People had collected round him. He was smeared with ashes on the forehead, and had a mark in red lead (Shindur) between his eye-brows.

At Benares these objectionable people live at both the burning ghats on the Ganges, i. e., at the Jalsam ghat, near Asi, and at the Masan ghat, and are supposed to number between one hundred and two hundred. They get their living by alms obtained from the relatives of those whose bodies are burned there, and are considered loathsome and impure. They also frequent the Aughar Nathke Takya (resting place, literally, pillow, of the head, Aghorapanthi) where some of their dead are disposed of.([40])

15. It is in the city last mentioned where the Aghorapanthis are most commonly met with, and the horror with which they are regarded at this day, is graphically told by Mr. Kedernath Basu.([41])

Some years ago the present Dewan of Junagad, Rao Saheb Haridas Vicharidas, came across a troublesome Aghorapanthi, and the method he adopted in freeing the neighbourhood of the unwelcome visitor is amusingly told by the Rao Saheb.([42])

16. Regarding the origin of the Aghoris, the following curious legend is related by Baladin Badrinath Trivedi : "Sankara Achárya had four chelas whom he instructed in magic. Being about to visit a country beyond the sea, he requested his chelas to follow him in whatever way they liked

---

([40]) Verbal statement made by Pandit Rama Shankar Misra, Deputy Collector of Benares, to Mr. Leith, Christmas, 1884.

([41]) See Appendix A.

([42]) See Appendix E.

best. Three of them took ship, although they were acquainted with *mantras* which would cause the waters to recede and thus enable them to travel overland. The fourth chela, named Jetha, however, made use of the *mantrás*, and consequently arrived at his destination before his fellow disciples. Thereupon Sankara Achárya cursed him for his arrogance in employing such magic means without first obtaining his Guru's permission. By this curse, the followers of Jetha were doomed to perpetrate deeds most repugnant to human nature, and hence acquired the name of Aghoris.†

17. The Aghori, generally, is regarded as all that is terrible and hideous, filthy and formidable. His real worship is that of *Devi* in her most terrific form, and he must make himself as dreadful and formidable as possible ; his wand is a human bone or staff set with bone, his drinking vessel, the upper half of a human skull. The *Devi* is made as hideous as human imagination and contrivance can make her, and her worship requires human victims.(⁴³) One authority is of opinion that originally the true Aghoris were a superior sect, (⁴⁴) of very holy saints " possessed of miraculous powers" as shown in a passage of the *Maha ama* relating to them as follows :—" My own body is terrible. The atoms are terrible. Fire is terrible, the wind is terrible, water is terrible. the other is terrible. Whatever is terrible gives me pleasure."

18. Another learned person, Pandit Rama Shankar Misra, is of opinion that the reason why in former times the true Aghori resorted to the burning ghâts was in proof of his indifference to worldly things and the desire of meditating on the vanity of wordly matters ; but this scarcely coincides with

† Statement of M'. Harlovrim Nánábhai, Vakil, as before.

(⁴³) Lieut.-Col. Watson, Pandit Ramasankar Misra, as before. Letter through Mr. F. W. Porter, Collector of Benares, 19th June 1885. Professor H. H. Wilson, Vol. I., p. 233.

(⁴⁴) Mr. Chaina Mull, Octroi Superintendent, Amballa Cantonment. Letter to Mr. Leith, dated 25th June 1885.

the terrible attributes of the Aghori recorded in Sanskrit and other writers I have quoted.

. 19. The modern Aghorapanthis follow in all respects the tenets and usages of the Aghoris, though one writer holds that the true Aghori need not make cannibalism an essential of Devi worship([45]) : a true Aghori is very rare now.([46]) Those who are commonly met with nowadays deduce their origin from Kiner Ram and Kâla Ram (the Guru or spiritual guide of Kiner Ram) who resided in Benares about 150 years ago.

20. Other religious devotees disdain to mix with Aghora-panthis and say they would never talk with them knowingly, as otherwise they would be turned out of their own sect. When Aghorapanthis talk to other religious people they pretend to be ordinary gosavis and to worship Devi.([47]) Many are impostors and cannot be distinguished from gosa-vis.([48] to [51])

21. Some Aghoripanthis have the audacity to pretend that although they may accept whatever is offered to them, they are forbidden to ask alms, the falsity of which is shown in the fact that most of their monstrous atrocities are perpetrated with the object of extortion.([52])

22. There are many variations of the meaning of the word Aghori, but the modern representative of the sect, as we see, are generally known as Aghorapanthis, who, according to one

---

([45]) *Religious Sects of the Hindus*, by Babu Akshoy Umar Dutt. Calcutta, 1299. (Bengali) Vol II., p. 98.

([46]) Jamnarâm, as before. Pandit Ramsankur Misra.

([47]) Statement of Raghunathdas, as before.

([48-51]) Statement made, 31st January 1886, to Mr. Leith, in his bungalow, by Bhagwan, a Dher, who, formerly a " Khutah-wallah " in Mr. Leith's service, became a Bhairagi and changed his name to Bhagwandas.

([52]) Bishwarnath, Aghori of Ghazipur, Mr. Jagundranath Roy, as per letter from Mr. Roy to Mr. Irvine, B. C. S., 1st February 1885.

Census Report, Central Provinces, 1881, Vol. II., p. 30. N.-W. Provinces *Gazetteer*, Vol. VI. p. 657. Punjaub Census Report, 1881, Vol. I. Huri Singh.

authority are " Ghoris " a degenerate branch of the original
sect.([33]) Of the Aghorpanthis there appear to be two branches
with different customs: one *Shuddh* or pure, the other *Malin* ·
or dirty, who are the eaters of abominations, but it is difficult
to describe what the differences are, although it is obvious
that Aghoris, Aghorapanthis, Kápalikás, Bauls, Paramahansas,
Bahikatha and perhaps, also the Kalingjas or Kuking Kjas,
have at times been taken the one for the other. According
to the *Dabistán*, to which I have already alluded, it was the
act of *atilia* or *akhori* from which the Aghori derived his
designation, but a living Aghoripanthi([44]) contends that
" Aghori " means one who is solitary, separate, distinct from
other men. The similarity of the term *Merdi-chor* or *Merdi-
khor*, *Masti-chora* to that of *Aghori* is alluded to in para. 3.

As to the connection between this word and the term
" Ogre " it is worthy of remark that one of the places resorted
to by Aghorapanthis is called " Oghur Sikra" after an Aghori
(see para. 5), and that the sthan at Tatta is to this day known
as " Ogar-ki gádi " (see Appendix H). Another term for
these people is Waghori (see para. 11). The word signifies
also "one who is terrible "([44]) " without fear," ([44]) and is a
title of Shiva of whom Aghoris are followers ([47]) and in honour
of whom they recite shlokas.

They are also known as "Sur-bhang " *i.e.*, head turned by
" bhang"([48]) " Wâmmargi," " Cowll,"([44]) " Aughor," and
"Augor" may be synonymous, but " Aughor " and " Aughar"

---

are not.([⁶⁰]) Some authorities, however, differ on this point, though it would seem that Aughars are considered to be a respectable class, whilst Aghorapanthis are universally detested.([⁶¹]) It is thus difficult to define· the difference between Aghorapanthis and kindred people.

The learned Pandit Ramashankar Misra, in allusion to the Aghorapanthi Baranâth, wrote to Mr. Leith as follows : " He is not a Yogi, to my thinking. He is a Sanyasi of the Aghorapanthi sect. A Yogi by religion cannot be a Sanyasi. An Aghori is what he is and nothing more. He is what the tenets of the Aghoripanth require him to be. Augar or Aughar cannot be a sub-division of the Jogi tribe or sect. Kanphatis are certainly Jogis, but to call an Aghori a Jogi, seems to be very awkward and ridiculous. No doubt Shiva is held in veneration both by Jogis and Sanyasis, but this cannot lead to the inference that a sub-division of the latter must be contained in the former. I do not know Mr. Ibbetson's authority when he divides Jogis into Kanphatis and Aughars, but I must say, I have nowhere found this division, and to my thinking, Mr. Ibbetson possibly has been led astray by popular and erroneous ideas given to him by his unlearned Court officials. The Kanphati, so called from his ears having been bored, is no doubt a respectable ascetic, but an Aghori is an object of dread and loathing. I am not aware that Augar or Aughar has any other signifi-cation than the one commonly given, and if this is so, Mr. Ibbetson has not much truth in his assertion that Augars, rather Aughars, belong to the Jogi sect. I might as well add that at the present time there are no typical and true Aughars, but all the same, those that are, cannot be classified under the Jogi tribe simply because they happen to hold Shiva in venera-tion, and that some outward bodily decorations of theirs tally

---

([⁶⁰]) Babu Jogendranath Roy of Ghazipur, in letter to Mr. Irvine, B. C. S.
([⁶¹]) Mr. Chaina Mull as before. See also Mr. Dentil Ibbetson, B. C. S.,
letter to Mr. Leith, 13th July 1885.

with those of Jogis. Augars are Aughars though degenerate, and they must be taken as such."

23. As to their worship some profess to adore Agoreshwari
Mata (referred to in para. 24), some Sitala Devi, others
Parnagiri Devi, "who presides at Pali beyond Ajmere and
is regarded as the tutelary deity of ascetics,"(**) others
Kali, whose temple is in Calcutta, whilst others again have
other deities. According to some Sunyasis, Aghorapanthis
at Girnár only worship the sun. At times, when speaking,
they chant a mantra beginning "Jog-i-Jog." Bháránath
did so when conversing with Mr. Leith. At funerals, they
cry "Ram" for the reason that Máhádev likes to hear that
word called out by the followers of a corpse, in the ashes of
which he loves to roll. This word forms the initials of the
Trimurti, *Ra* for *Ragha*, *Ah* for *Vishna* and *Ma* for *Máhá-
deva*.(**) While boasting of their powers, Aghorapanthis sometimes break out into wild imprecations.(**) Regarding their
superstitions, they pretend that *bhuts* or *pisachas* fly from
their presence "ten miles" away.(**) Their least offensive
offerings are wine, sweets, milk, but sometimes they include
bhang "and everything." (**)   Some, when seen with spirituous liquors, instead of making a parade of drinking it, as
most of them do, pretend that they are about to turn the
strong drink into milk.*

24. All the castes can become Aghoris(**) whose
divisions are the same as those of the Hindus.(**) Any Shaivas
can become Aghoris but not Vaishnavas. One Brahmin

(**) Jámnáram, Ragunathdas, Bháránath as before.
(**) Jánáram's interviews with Mr. Cockburn. Appendix J.
(**) Mr. Jogendranath Roy's letter as before.
(**) Bhárànath.
(**) Bis swanath Aghori's statement to Mr. Jogendranath Roy of Ghazipur.
* Mr. Hardeveram Nanabhai, Vakil, as before.
(**) Babu Nadiachund Dutt.
(**) Ramnath (Jogi) Aghor, Statement to Major M. Meade, Political
Agent, Bhopal, March 1885.

accounted for his becoming an Aghoripanthi by saying that he quarrelled with his father and left home.([**]) About fifty years since several Jains of Surat became Aghoripanthis.([70]) One of the reasons assigned for men thus becoming converts is that the Aghoripanthi can, at will, assume the shape of bird, quadruped, fish or insect.([71]) Another is, that he has the power of bringing back to life a corpse of which he has eaten([72]) by the act of going to sleep for some hours after his cannibalism, and then vomiting on the fragments of the corpse([73]). Any one desirous to become a member of the order must, after initiation by a qualified Guru, study the mantras relating thereto to be found in the *Vedas,* but those who profess to know it refuse to communicate the mantra save to the man who really desires to study it.([74]) In Western India the original patroness of the order is said to have been Aghor Eshwari Mata represented as "lean famine" the all-devouring, and many years ago the remains of her temple were still existing at Baroda or in the Baroda territory,([75]) as related in para. 5.

25. The greater numbers of the Aghorapanthis, it is obvious, are mere rapacious, shameless mendicants, who, by the terror of their attributes, horrible appearance, and the threat of eating human ordure and urine, if their demands are not complied with, still contrive to prey upon the credulity of

---

([**])   Jamnaram.

([70])   Statement of Mr. Madhavara Mehtaji, School Master of Surat, to Mr. H. N. Vakil.

([71])   Colonel Watson, as before.

([72])   Statement made to Mr. Leith as to the superstitions regarding these people, by Mr. Chagunlal Gigabhoy, clerk to Mr. Mulji B. Barbhaya, Solicitor of Bombay.

([73])   *See* Religious Sects of the Hindus.   Statement made to Mr. Leith, by Raghunathdas, resident of Satpura Bhoira (cell), Girnár, as before.

([74])   Lieut.-Col. Watson.

([75])   Lieut.-Col. Tod.

31

the ignorant or timid.([76])   About thirty years ago one of these wretches, even managed to get into the presence of H. H. Maharajah Khanderao, Gaekwar of Baroda, and horrified H. H. by actually diving into a basket of night-soil and swallowing some of the contents.([77])   Aghorapanthis will make a bravado of carrying such filth about with them, and of obeying the calls of nature in public, especially that of vomiting([78]) as alluded to in the preceding paragraph.

26.   The five Makárs are : — *Madya* or wine, *mánsa* or flesh, *maithuna* or sexual intercourse, *mala* or excrement and *mutra* or urine.   It is said that Aghoripanthis in some way add to these.([79])   They pretend to defend their monstrous doctrines by saying there must be something in cannibalism, and that if human ordure makes hard and barren land fertile, in the same way the feeding on such filth will render the human body fertile and the mind capable of meditation.   Mere eating and drinking depend on inclination.([80])   A thing once tasted cannot be forgotten.   The less degraded, however, admit that a man who professes that he is saved by eating ordure must be mad.   Eating human flesh and "dead moles" is another

---

([76])   Pandit Rama Shankar, Sir Michael Filose, Census Reports of the Central Provinces, 1881, Vol. 2, p. 311 ; of the N. W. Provinces, 1881, Vol. 2, p. 311 ; Basti District, Vol. VI., page 657, also Appendices to this paper and Sherring as before.

([77])   For this fact, which is not mentioned in Mr. Leith's papers, I am indebted to Surgeon-Lt..Col. T. S. Weir, who had it from one of his subordinates, the late Mr. Thompson formerly an officer of the Gaikwar's Army, who was present at this sensational scene.

([78])   See Pandit Ramashankar Misra as before, through Mr. Porter, B.C.S. Ditto of Bharanath Ragunathdas, see also Sherring.

([79])   Ramnath (Jogi) Agorapanth's statement as before.

([80])   Bisnawarnath Aghori's Statement to Mr. Jogendranath Roy as per letter from the last named to Mr. Irvine, B. C. S., Feby. 1885.

See also Rao Bahadur Gopalrao Huri Deshmukh, Pandit Rama Shankar, and Sherring as before.

matter, but should be done in secret as should the offices of nature, otherwise the Aghorapanthi is seeking to extort.([⁸¹])

27. Notwithstanding the astounding wickedness of their tenets the Aghoripanthis have the audacity to claim for them that they are the doctrines of equality and humanity.([⁸²]) In their eyes all castes are equal, and they make no distinction between what is good and what is bad. One God has created all Aghoripanthis, Mohamadans, Fakirs and Sunyasis ([⁸³]) but indifference to all that is should be the all in all of the Aghoripanthi's existence.([⁸⁴]) No one really has a father or mother, " it is all mere accident." ([⁸⁵]) The God of the Aghoripanthi is he who has no father or mother. The Aghoripanthi does not worship images ; except God, he reverences no one but his Guru whom he is bound to obey.([⁸⁶]) He has no care in life, eats whatever he comes across,([⁸⁷]) sleeps anywhere and, in fact, walks into a well if one comes in his way. He has no scruples about anything,([⁸⁸]) but should subdue his natural tastes by eating human flesh and filth, the carrion of reptiles, anything. He should also drink spirituous liquors, the object of all being the attainment of that perfection of wordly indifference which is expected of every Sunyasi or Jogi intent on salvation.([⁸⁹]) Celibacy is

---

(⁸¹) Bisnawarnath, see also letter from Mr. Mande, B. C. S., to Mr. Leith, 4th May 1885, and Magrath's Census Report, 1872.

(⁸²) Bisnawar Nath, as before.

(⁸³) Ramnath (Jogi) Aghori, as before.

(⁸⁴) Pandit Ramasunkar Misra.

(⁸⁵) Ramnath Jogi's statement, as before.

(⁸⁶) Jámnaram.

(⁸⁷) This is denied by Ramnath, who says that until a chela has been twenty-four years in the fraternity he must eat only from Hindus. After that, all things are lawful and the chela may accept food from the hands of Hindus, Mussalmans, and Christians. Kanphati Aghoripanthis eat the flesh of kine, swine, or dead men.

(⁸⁸) Raghunathdas.

(⁸⁹) Pran Krishna Rai, Deputy Magistrate and Deputy Collector, Pooren, letter 13th May 1885, to Mr. Porch, B. C. T. Bháránath, as before. Pandit Ramshankar Misri, as before.

strictly enjoined,([90]) and if an Aghorapanthi marries the effect
of the mantra is lost on him, and he can no longer change his
shape. A true Aghorapanthi has full command over his
passions, and one of them said to Mr. Leith, "Jub mooj hai
ihtilam hota hai tub main mani kha jata hoon." It is adimitted
that this rule as to celibacy is not always followed,([92]) and
the proof of this laxness of discipline is found in the official
Census Returns for 1881, which enumerate 93 (51 male and
42 female) Aghoripanthis in the Central Provinces and 2,121
males and 1,046 females in the N.-W. P. (Azimgarh District).
In the Ballia District there were 68 of whom fully half were
women.

28. These people go on pilgrimage to different places for
puja (worship), nahayet (bathing), and darsan (visiting
tombs). One man([93]) states that he has visited Pasupathi-
nâth in Nipal for puja, and Pali for darsau, and that he has
performed Sakti workship at Kálighát in Calcutta. When
Aghoripanthis go to Shivaratri fair at Giruár they are with
gosains.([94])

29. For the most part, Aghoripanthis lead a wandering
life, are without homes and prefer to dwell in holes, clefts
of rocks and burning ghâts.([95]) They do not cook but eat
the fragments given them in charity as received, which
they put, as far as may be, into the cavity of the skull they
carry about with them.

30. A chela cannot become a Guru until twelve years after
his own Guru's death. At the installation of a Guru there is a
feast, and other Gurus place the new Guru on the gádi. He
does not change his name.([96]) The Ghazipur Aghoripanthis

([90]) Mr. Chaina Mull.
([91]) Bhárinath's statement.
([92]) Ramnath Jogi.
([93]) Jamnaram.
([94]) Ramnath, Jogi and Hari Singh, as before.
([95]) Pandit Lakshmi Shunkar Miari.
([96]) Jamnaram.

under Hari Rám do not make many chelas, but the followers of Kenerám are said to admit them without limitation of
numbers. The difference between these two divisions is, that the
followers of Kenerám do not use gerna (coloured clothes), and
that they carry earthen pots (bhamkah) and rota (sticks).[97]

The bodies of chelas who die in Benares are thrown into the
Ganges, but the dead who die well off, are placed in coffins,
and many Aghoripanthis have been interred in the Augarnath
ka Takaya there.[98] As a rule, Aghoripanthis do not care
what becomes of their bodies[99] ordinarily, bodies cannot be
buried in the Sthans. Those bodies that are buried, are
placed in the grave sitting cross-legged, not lengthwise.[100]

31. All the Gurus keep dogs which may be of any colour,
and are said to be maintained for purposes of protection.[101]
The dogs are not all pariahs of the streets, although some
Gurus are followed by three or four when on pilgrimage.[102]
Occasionally the dogs seem to be regarded with real affection
by their strange masters.[103]

32. The Aghoripanthi is believed to hold converse with
all the evil spirits frequenting the burning ghâts, and funeral
parties must be very badly off who refuse to pay him something.[104] In former days he claimed five pieces of wood at
each funeral in Benares; but the Doms or Dumras interfere
with his perquisites, and in some cases only let him carry off the
remains of the unburned wood from each pyre.[105] When
angered and excited Aghoripanthis invoke Kala, Kalikadevi
or other deity and threaten to spread devastation around

[97] Mr. Jogendranath Roy, 1st February 1885.
[98] Huri Singh, as before.
[99] Bharanath and Jamnaram.
[100] Ramnath.
[101] Bharanath.
[102] Jamnaram.
[103] Sir Michael Filose.
[104] Notes by Mr. Cockburn, as before.
[105] Huri Singh, and Bharanath, as before.

them·([106]) Even among the educated classes who should know better (*see* Appendix I) they are dreaded, and as an instance of the terror which they create among the ignorant it may be mentioned that in the Lakhnao district it is believed that if alms are refused them the Aghoripanthis will cause those who refuse, to be attacked with fever.([107])

33. On the other hand, their good offices may secure benefits, as in the case of a zemindar of Muzaffernagar who, being at Allahabad, refused to eat a piece of human flesh offered to him by an Aghoripanthi who thereupon threw the flesh at the Zemindar's head, on which it stuck. The zemindar afterwards became so exceedingly wealthy that he had difficulty in storing his wealth.([108])

34. In Benares and elsewhere they are not allowed within the precincts of temples, nor are they permitted to stand outside private houses. Their principal hunting grounds are the burning ghâts.*

35. From various causes the practices of Aghoris, Aghoripanthis, Kápálikas, Paramhansas, Bauls, and Báhikathas have been confounded one with another in some instances, and I have given a brief notice of the last mentioned sects in Appendix (G). In Appendix H an account will be found of the Mâths or Sthans of the Aghoripanthis, the names of their Gurus, and so on. Appendix J is a description of the manner in which Aghoripanthis dress, and wear their caste marks together with some other interesting details.

([106]) Sir Michael Filose.

([107]) Mr. Hardevoram Nanabhai Vakil.

([108]) Punjaub Notes and Queries, Vol. III. 351,

* See also statements of Sir Michael Filose, Mr. Hardeveram Nanabhai, Pandit Rama Shankar, and Appendices.

APPENDICES.

APPENDIX A.

It would seem that it is at Benares where the Aghoripanthis are most frequently seen now, and the detestation with which they are still regarded in Bengal is shown in the following account of them by Mr. Kedernath Basu, Editor of the *Universe*, Berhampur, near Murshidabad. * " The Aghorapanthis are determined cannibals. They kill stray persons and eat them whenever they find an opportunity." He then quotes a letter from his tutor and friend Babu Khirodechandra Rai Choudhuri, M. A., who states that in the last week of December 1872 he went to " do " Delhi and that on the 22nd of that month he visited Asoka's Sat Ferozeshah-ki-kotta. " I attempted," says Mr. Khirodechandra, "to examine the building that supports its base. That building is in ruins   *   * The house is three storied and has a large number of rooms. In one of these rooms, hardly lighted up by the rays of a winter sun   *   * I found flowers, vermilion and a *cherágh* (or earthen lamp) of red colour with wicks   *   * I concluded that the lamp was lighted that night or the night previous. I had read Bankim Babu's Kapal Kundalá before that and hastened out as soon as I possibly could. On returning to town and addressing with elderly residents of the place, I was told that the ruined house was seldom visited by travellers in the day time and hardly ever at night and was the rendezvous either of dacoits or of Aghoris. I think the latter was the more probable surmise. The gentlemen told me that the Aghoris if they could catch me would have killed me for religious purposes. That Aghoris do so, is well known in India. I hope Government will take proper measures to protect travellers in such places." Mr. Kedarnath Basu went on to express the hope that Government would make searching

---

* Letter to Mr. Leith, dated 6th January 1895.

enquiries "into the black deeds connected with the religion of
the Aghoris," though he did not think much good could be
done unless those enquiries were secret, " because the Hindus
are such a superstitious set of people that if they get an inkling
of the Government prying into the religious doings of their
sects they will take every precaution to thwart it."

APPENDIX B.

(*Authorities referred to in para. I*).

Colonel Barr, formerly Resident, Baroda.

Hon'ble Mr. Justice Brodhurst, Allahabad.

Babu Nadia Chand Dutt.

Mr. William Cockburn, formerly of Benares.

Mr. Chaina Mull, Octroi Superintendent, Amballa.

Major Curzon Wyllie, 1st Assistant Agent to the Governor-
General's Agent, Rajputana.

Mr. Elliott, C. S., Political Department.

Mr. P. Fitzgerald, Political Department.

Sir Michael Filose, H. H. Scindiah's service.

Mr. Forman, C. S., District Judge, Shikarpur.

Rao Bahadur Gopalrao Hari Deshmukh, of Bombay.

Rao Saheb Haridas Viparidas, Dewan of the Junagad State.

Mr. Hardevram Nanabhai, Vakil of Bombay.

Hari Singh, a cultivator of Benares.

Mr. W. Irvine, B. C. S., Ghazipur.

Mr. Denzil Ibbetson, B. C. S.

Mr. Jogendranath Roy of Ghazipur (Pleader).

Mr. Kedernath Basu of the Berhampur " Universe."

Captain (now Major) Malcolm Meade, Political Agent,
Bhopal.

Mr. H. Maude, Ben. C. S.

Mr. Porter, B. C. S., Collector of Benares.

Mr. Porch, B. C. S.

Pandit Nilkantrao, Deputy Inspector of Schools, H. H. Scindiah's territory.

Prankrishna Rai, Deputy Magistrate and Deputy Collector, Poorea.

Mr. H. Rivett-Carnac, B. C. S.

Pandit Rama Shankar Misra, Hony. Deputy Collector of Benares.

Mr. Shanahan, formerly of the Public Works Department.

Kazi Shahabudin, C. I. E., formerly Dewan of Baroda.

Major (then Captain) R. C. Temple, formerly Cantonment Magistrate, Amballa.

Lieut.-Colonel Watson, Political Agent, Southern Maratha Country.

Lieut-Colonel West, Political Agent, Kathiawad.

And the following Aghoripanthis :—

Bharanath of Benares.

Jámnáram of Allahabad.

Bisnarwar Nath of Ghazipur.

Ramnath (Jogi) Aghori. .

Also Raghunathdas of the Ramanandi sect, and Bhagwandas, Bhiragi.

APPENDIX C.

The Hindu religion mostly consists of sacrifices, so much so that even the burning of a human corpse is called *antyeshti* (the final sacrifice). There is hardly any commandment of the Vedic religion which is not attended with sacrifice of one kind or another * * Those sacrifices that profess to be based on custom and not on any works of *rishis* (sages) must have been originally practiced by the aboriginal races whom the Aryans conquered, and must have been subsequently incorporated by the Aryans into their sacrificial observances

32

as the unavoidable result of their contact with the non-Aryans.
The Aryan sacrifices are again divisible under two heads : the
Vedic and the Tantrick * * * It is said that the Vedas
were revealed by Brahma, the last of the Hindu Trinity. It
is curious to note that his worship is prohibited throughout
India except in * * * Brahma Pashkar near Ajmere,
and Brahma's Khed near Idwi. The reason assigned for this
prohibition is, that when he was once appointed an arbitrator
in a dispute, he spoke a lie, and was punished for it by Siva
with the prohibition of his worship in the form of an idol. The
Rig-Veda declares that the sacrificial fire was first kindled by
Brahma's son, Manu, who corresponds to Noah of the Christian
Bible (*Rig-Veda*, V. 1. 11. and V. 2. 1.) The reason why
I identify Manu with Noah, is that like Noah, Manu is said to
have been saved by God at the time of the universal deluge
* * According to the *Sankaravijaya* which gives an
account of Sankarácháraya's life, that great philosopher is
said to have supported the performance of sacrifices on
the ground that they were commanded by the Vedas. It
is said that many Jains came to him to dispute the position
of the Vedas, being a revelation, on the ground that they
were cruel to animal life ; but Sankaráchárya vanquished
them all in a controversy and maintained the sacred
character of the Vedic teaching. Buddhist and Jain Pandits
fought against Brahmans for nearly 1,500 years and
prescribed the Vedas and the caste, the former because they
were cruel to animal life, and the latter because it maintained inequality among men. Their heresy so prospered
for a time that Brahmans were obliged to acknowledge
Buddha as one of the *avataras* or incarnations of the deity, but
somehow or other the projected revolution was not successful
in the end, and the religion of mercy known as *dayá-dharma* was
crushed in India * * Some Hindu authors have conceded
that if a man desires to perform a sacrifice the goat should
not be a living animal but one made of rice flour. The question

is still debated with considerable vehemence by *Smárta* and
Vaishnava Bráhmans, but the *Smárta* Bráhmans yet continuo
to perform their sacrifices with living animals. *   *   *
*   *   *   *   The *Tantrik* sacrifices cannot be performed
without meat or liquor *   *   Even Bráhmans are found
among the performers of these sacrifices *   *   The performers of Tantrik sacrifices do not observe caste *   *.
Their sacrifice is called *bali-dána*, which consists in cutting the
head of the animal intended to be sacrificed. The authorities
which they follow are *tantras, rahasyas,* and *yamalas,* and also
some *puránas;* for instance, the Káliká Purána contains a chapter
on sacrifice. It is called *rudhirádhyáya* or the bloody chapter.
It recommends victims for a sacrifice, from a human being
down to a sheep. Their religious rites are very immoral and
cruel, and yet they attract several followers, owing to the high
pretensions of supernatural power held out to devotees *   *
Some writers attempt to elevate this system to the rank of the
Vedas. But the practices of this sect are so strongly condemned by the orthodox that persons wishing to perform
Tántrik sacrifices are obliged to perform them at night with
great secrecy and in places not frequented by people. This sect
is more numerous in Bengal, Kashmere, and Dravida than
elsewhere. Durga, Chandi, Káli or some other goddess is the
object of worship. In all Vedic sacrifices animals are killed
by suffocating them, in Tántrik sacrifices they are decapitated.
The Vedic mode of killing preserved the blood of the animal in .
its body, while the Tántrik mode allowed it to run out. In
course of time the Vedic and the Tántrik ceremonies became
mixed, so that in the later ritualistic works called *prayogas*
and *paddhatis* they came to be set down side by side. I was
for several years engaged in the investigation of the Tántrik
system of sacrifice as laid down in their works. I have given
the result of it in my book called *Aga maprakása* in Gujrathi.
It has been translated into Marathi by Mr. Krishnarao

Nawalkar. It has been largely quoted from by Professor Sir
M. Monier Williams in his work *Religious Thought in India.*
Mr. Nawalkar has also translated the work into English,
and intends to publish it. Non-Aryan sacrifices are not
founded on any religious work, but rest solely on custom.
Buffaloes, sheep, fowls, &c., are promised to idols at different
shrines, such as those of Káli, Khandobá, Biroba, Bhaváni,
Bahirobá, Sitala, &c. They are carried on according to custom
or the advice of the temple priests. In India there are numerous
temples where animals are sacrificed in great number. The
temples of Káli in Calcutta, Durgâ in Benares, Vindhya Vásin
at Mirzapur, Bhaváni at Kondanpur and Tuljapur, will suffice
as examples. Besides every village has a *jatrá* (a fair) held for
the prosperity of the village. At such a fair buffaloes-and sheep
are sacrificed. These village *jatras* are called Lakshmi-
Kárya. The proceedings of a recent *jatrá* are reported in
the *Dnyanodaya,* a Bombay weekly, of the 26th August 1886.
It is stated that twelve buffaloes and many sheep were killed
before the idol, and that the ceremony lasted for two weeks.
I know of several villages in which these *jatras* are held, and
buffaloes are slaughtered in a very cruel manner. The belief
that prosperity in a calling cannot be attained unless these
sacrifices are performed, is general among the villagers. In
the village of Khavlee, near Wai, in the Satara District,
it is usual to take off the heart of the animal before it
is decapitated. In other places, the blood of the animal
sacrificed is sprinkled over all the fields, in the belief that such
sprinkling produces fertility. In some places, the head of the
animal is kept for several days before the temple with a lamp
burning on it. Bheels, Kolis, Mahars and other aborigines
are very particular about the performance of these sacrifices.
There are various superstitions connected with these sacrifices.
It is believed that the lamp burning on the severed head of
the animal, if removed and buried, carries prosperity to the

village of its burial ; and accordingly attempts to remove such lamps stealthily are often made by inhabitants of neighbour-ing villages. The people of the village are accordingly seen guarding the lamp with sticks and arms and preventing any one from taking it away.

The non-Aryan sacrifices require no priest, for there is no written ritual. The ritual is regulated by custom handed down from generation to generation. As in every village, so in every fort, there is some deity which must be satisfied by an offering of some live animal. It appears that when forts were built, human beings were sacrificed. It is common to meet a Maharin's place near the gate of a fort. At one of these forts which I saw, I was told that a female of the Mahar caste was buried alive there, and I saw the place worshipped. A buffalo is selected for a sacrificial offering to goddess Bhavani, because, according to a *Puranik* account, she killed a demon named Mahishasura who had the form of a buffalo, and it came to be believed that on that account the killing of that animal would be very acceptable to her.

These superstitions are very strong and ancient. All sacrificial worship is founded on some error or misconception of the true nature of God. The light of knowledge will dis-place the error and teach what is proper and right, but, till this consummation takes place, sacrifices, Aryan and non-Aryan, will prevail.

Sacrificial worship is one of the three modes of worshipping the deity, recognised by the Hindu religion. They are called *Karma* (sacrificial religion), *jnâna* (philosophical religion) and *bhakti* (devotional religion). The first system, which I have already described, supposes gods to be expecting offerings of food from man, and offering him in return the good things of this and the next world.[1] It has its foundation mainly in

---

[1] Bhagavad-Gita, ch. III, v. 11.

revelation, or the *Samhitas* and *Brâhmanas*. The second system of worship, or the philosophic religion, is based on the *upanishads* and the *sutras* of the founders of the six orthodox schools of philosophy, called *darśinas*. The followers of this religion accept reason as their principal guide. They scorn the idea of sacrifice as childish, and say that if a sacrificer goes to heaven, he will return after he has lived out his merit and will be born again. They maintain that a sacrifice, though recommended by the highest authority, is cruel and barbarous and is not intended for this *Kali-yuga*. They transfer the merit ascribed to sacrifices in Vedic times to other acts of piety, such as ablution in sacred rivers (snâna), gifts (dâna), visits to shrines (yâtrâ), and repetition of God's name (bhajaua). They inculcate that a man going to bathe in the Ganges performs a horse sacrifice at every pace of his journey. They never perform any sacrifice but contemplate the infinite power of God and His identity with human soul. The third system or the devotional religion teaches that God is personal and wants physical worship. It is founded on the *Mahâbhârata* and on *Puranas*, particularly the *Bhâgavata*. The founders of the four Vaishnava *Sampradâyas* (sects) and saints like Chaitanya, Nityânanda, Ekanâtha, Tukârâma and others, belong to this religion and teach faith in God and His parental goodness. These are called *bhaktas* and *sâdhus*. They do not believe in sacrifices or philosophy; they inculcate fear of God and the necessity of worship and of faith in His goodness. They abstain from animal food, falsehood, and immoral practices of the *tântrika* sacrifices.

(*Abstract of paper by the late Rao Bahadur Hari Deshmukh on "Hindu Sacrifices" read before this Society, 20th Oct. 1886.*)

This paper is not referred to in Mr. Leith's notes, but I have included it in the appendix as elucidating the question of human sacrifice.

APPENDIX D.

The author of the *Dábistán* says "the sect of Yogis know no prohibited food * * They also kill and eat men * * * There are some of this sect who having mixed their excretions and filtered them through a piece of cloth, drink them and say such an act renders a man capable of great affairs, and they pretend to know strange things. They call the performer of this act *Atilia* and also *Akhori* * * They have all originated from Gorakhnath."

"The author of this work saw a man, who singing the cus-tomary song, sat upon a corpse which he kept unburied until it came to a state of dissolution and then ate the flesh of it : this act they hold extremely meritorious." He goes on to state that the followers of this sect prostitute their barren wives to the performers of such acts (Ibid.), p. 156." (¹)

Sherring in his Hindu Tribes and Castes.—Volume I., p. 269, under the head "Aghori," says :—"This is the name of a flag-rantly indecent and abominable set of beggars who have ren-dered themselves notorious for the disgusting vileness of their habits. Prowling about in the pursuit of their miserable calling, which, however, is one of the most successful in India, they will take no denial. In case of refusal of alms they will besmear themselves with filth and eat the most loathsome garbage in the presence of the persons who withhold money

---

(¹) *Dábistán*, Vol II, p. 129 (translated from the original Persian by David Shea and Anthony Troyer. Paris and London, 1843).

The supposed author of this extraordinary work, Moshan Fani is thought to have died about A, D. 1670. Sir William Jones who brought the work to light says "it contains more recondite learning, more entertaining history, more beautiful specimens of poetry, more ingenuity and wit, more indecency and blasphemy than I ever saw collected in a single volume." There is no reference to the *Dábistán* in Mr. Leith's papers, but I have quoted this passage from my own copy of the book as which a most reliable authority.

from them. They are a pest of native society. The Aghoris deduce their origin from Kira Râm and Kâlu Râm (the guru or spiritual guide of Kira Râm) who are supposed to have lived in Benares about one hundred years ago. Hindus of all castes may enter the order. On induction their bodies are first shaved and they are sent to Ashtbhuja, Mirzapur, the shrine of a famous goddess, six miles from Mirzapur, where they practise incantations until they imagine they have acquired the power of the goddess *Aghor Mukhi*, whom they worship and whose tenets they observe   *   *   *
    *   *   The Aghoris eat all kinds of food including the carcases of jackals, cats and other animals which die of themselves."

In another passage (Vol II., p. 334) he adds : The Aghori or Sar Bhangi are described as being wanderers and like the gosavis, and as being a kind of conjurors pretending by tricks to produce milk, liquor and so forth from their mouths. They carry human skulls in which they mix up urine and gur or sugar, and drink the same as a dram, by doing which and by squatting before houses for purposes of nature, they extort gifts from people glad to be rid of the horrible nuisance of their presence. They are believed to be gang robbers.

In the " *Revelations of an Orderly*," *Selections* " *Calcutta Review*," *Vol. III., p.* 315 (*Benares* 1849), the writer describes the most loathsome sight at the burning ghauts, to be the Aghoris, going about *in puris naturalibus*, carrying fresh human skulls off which they had previously eaten the flesh and from which they had afterwards with their fingers scooped out the eyes and brains. Their food, the first thing that offered, whether putrid corpse, cooked food or ordure. With matted hair, blood-red eyes and body covered with filth and vermin, the Aghorapanthi was an object of terror and disgust, who looked rather a wolf ready to destroy and devour his prey than a human being. The writer saw a wretch of this fraternity, eating the head of a putrid corpse, he howled and pointed at the writer and then scooped out the eyes from the skull and ate them. The "orderly" had his matchlock with him " and was within an ace" of putting a ball into the monster's head. On another occasion, an Aghori who had previously been convicted of rape, assault, almost amounting to homicide, and vagrancy, was apprehended whilst violently intoxicated carrying a huge Malay kris, a blow from which would have been death. He was ordered to find heavy security, but afterwards was released, consequent on the superior wisdom of the Appellate Court. The writer proceeds to protest against the Government of the day for tolerating the existence of Aghoris and asks whether such miscreants should not be imprisoned for life, pointing out that the precepts of Islam would sanction the wholesale slaughter of such monsters, whilst unfortunately some Hindoos looked upon them with veneration.

In the *Topography of Assam*, Calcutta 1837, by I. M'Cosh, page 87, it is stated that the temples in that country were prolific in faquirs and other vagrants who strolled about the country in the most disgusting state of filth and nakedness. Aghorapanthis or eaters of dead men's flesh were occasionally met with amongst them. "During my residence at Goalpura, two men of that caste were caught gnawing the flesh from a human bone and taken up by the police. They were sent to me by the Magistrate to have my opinion as to their sanity. One of them was not exactly *compos mentis*, but the other was of sound mind and told me he has been in the habit of eating human flesh for many years. It was once the custom with these carrion cannibals to walk about the bazars picking a putrid thigh bone with the object of extorting money from the inhabitants who preferred paying them a few pice to get rid of the annoyance; and it was even considered justifiable to shoot them like wild

33

beasts whenever they were found.   One of the above men came
from Beauliah and was on a pilgrimage to Gohatti.   The other
was an Assami barber."

Ward in his Hindoos, Vol. II., p. 373, describes these mendicants as "born in the western parts of Hindoostan" and as
eating the abominations already referred to in order to extort
alms.

Aghorapanthis or Aghoris are a class of people who frequent
the ghauts at Benares, though they are occasionally to be found
in other parts of India, and have been met with even in Assam.
They are ogres (indeed the similitude of the word to Aghoris
is noticeable) and effect a practical philosophy which disbelieves
in the existence of any difference between things and asserts
that all distinctions depend on the imagination.   A cuff or a
kick is as immaterial to them as a blessing.   Hindoos, however,
look on these wretches with veneration, and none dare to drive
them from their doors.   They are among the worst of the many
turbulent and troublesome inhabitants of Benares, and there is
scarcely a crime or enormity which has not on apparently good
grounds, been laid to their charge.   (Here follows a quotation
from Málati and Máhdava by Bhavabhuti who wrote in the
8th century, "Now wake the terrors of the place," &c., Act V.,
Scene I.   (*The people of India, Ed. by Forbes Watson and John
W. Kage, London, 1868, Vol. II., No. 94.*)

The regular worship of the sect (Aghori) has of course been
long suppressed, but a few disgusting wretches still extort alms
by the practice of what they are pleased to call its rites.   They
eat and drink everything down to ordure and carrion.   With
the former they smear their bodies or pelt the people who refuse
to grant their demands.   They inflict gashes on their limbs that
crime of blood may rest on the head of the recusant.   Nor are
these the only repulsive devices by which they draw cash from

the always-credulous and often timid Hindu. "One of them at Gorakpur," writes Buchanan, "shocked the people so much that they complained to Mr. Ahmuty, then Judge, who drove him out as a nuisance." In the present day a Magistrate would probably apply to an Aghori those sections of the Criminal Procedure Code which relate to vagabonds. And it is perhaps the fear of such treatment which prevents the sect from practising its rites under the eye of the police. But in Buchanan's day, its chief, who lived at Benares, gave instruction to many respectable persons including Brahmans and Rajputs, while in one district (Basti) the principal land-holders had a strong hankering after the doctrines of the sect.—N.-W. P. Gazeteer, Basti District, Vol. VI., p. 657.

In the *Punjaub Census Report*, 1881, Vol. I., p. 286, Mr. Denzil Ibbetson says:—The Aghori or Aghorapanthi is an order which has happily almost died out. My figures show 316 only, but I have been told by an intelligent native that he can remember that in his youth they were common objects wandering about the street stark-naked leading a jackal by a string, smeared with blood and human ordure, and carrying the same substances in a human skull with which to bespatter him who refused them alms.

_____

APPENDIX E.

Rao Saheb Haridas Vibaridas, Dewan of Junagad, says : "While at Wadhwân, I had come across a Bawa (gosai) about fifty years old, having a robust constitution and a fearful look. I saw him walking in the bazar with the arm of a dead human being in his hand, and some other parts of the same in his jholi (bag). He had a bottle of liquor in his other hand. I saw him drinking liquor at first, and then eating a part of the dead arm. He then again drank liquor. I put him some questions. He would not answer them, but became angry and unruly. I had him arrested and shut up in the Bazar guard chowki. He cursed me and exclaimed that I should die within six months.

All round me feared that I must die when such a jogi cursed me. But I told him in the presence of many people that. I would deposit Rs. 500 with a shroff, and if he would try his best in honour of his guru that I must die within three days the shroff would pay the money after my death. He said he did not commit an offence as he was only taking out dead bodies from the graves and eating them. I told him it would never do: he must take oath that he would not eat such things any more. He became more unruly and I put him in chains. Three days after he became meek as a lamb and prostrating himself before me, assured me that he would henceforth never eat such flesh, and I turned him out of Wadhwan territory.*

The State records of Rewah afford an equally good story.† Some years ago when Maharajah Bishnath Singh was Chief of Rewah, a man of the Aghori caste went to Rewah and sat dhurma on the steps of the palace; having made ineffectual demands for alms, he requested to be supplied with human flesh, and for five days abstained from food. The Maharajah was much troubled, and at last, in order to get rid of his unwelcome visitor, sent for Ghunsyam Dass, another Aghori, a fakir, who, for some years had lived in Rewah. Ghunsyam Dass went up to the other Aghori and asked him if it was true that he had asked to be supplied with human flesh. On receiving a reply in the affirmative, Ghunsyam Dass said : " Very well, I too am extremely partial to this form of food ; here is my hand, eat it and I will eat you," at the same time he seized the other's hand and began to gnaw at it. The Aghori on this became much alarmed and begged to be excused. He shortly afterwards left Rewah and was not heard of again while Ghunsyam Dass was rewarded for his services. His descendants are still living in Rewah, but do not practise cannibalism.

---

* Letter to Lieutenant-Colonel West, December 1884.
† Letter from Colonel Barr to Mr. Leith enclosing this translation.

APPENDIX F.

Initiation.—At Christmas 1884, Mr. Leith was informed verbally by Pandit Lakshmishankar Misra, M. A , Professor of Physical Science, Government College, Benares, that about the year 1864, he was present at the initiation ceremony of one Siyram, a Brahmin Pundit, aged about 35, at the Aghornath-ki-Takya in that city. Strangers were allowed to be present. There are several tombs built of brick and mortar at the Takya. At the largest tomb there was a bottle full of dâru or fermented liquor, distilled from Mahwa flowers, and some skulls were scattered about the place. A few spectators were present, but of the Aghorapanthis, only the Guru, or master of the Takya and the candidate. The Guru blew a conch (Shanka) and some hired musicians played music of the rudest types. The Guru then micturated into a human skull and poured it on to the candidate's head, which was then shaved by a barber. After this the candidate drank the dâru and ate food brought by the Guru, consisting of meat, cakes of flour and pulse which had been previously collected as alms from various persons, including those of the lowest castes. In such a case Brahmins would send food to the Takya, instead of giving it at their own doors. The candidate next put on a langoti of an ochre colour known as bhagwa, the sacred colour worn by all ascetics and religious mendicants. He also took a stick in his hand.

This experience of the learned Pandit is borne out by the statement of an inhabitant who had known the Takya for 45 years, and who added that at the ceremony * the Guru and the chela sit down, and the Guru repeats mantras into the ear of the chela, which no one else can hear. The Guru cuts off the chela's shendi or top knot. The chela drinks his own

---

* Statement made to Mr. Leith, 1st January 1885, in Benares, by Hari Singh, Khatri, cultivator.

urine and some of the spirit as also refuse food which has been given to him in charity. If human flesh and ordure is eaten at the Benares initiation, it is believed that that is done secretly.

An Aghori, residing in Allahabad[1], who was initiated at Mattra, as part of the ceremony, drank his Guru's urine. The slokas recited by the Guru were as follows :—

" Ulti Kopri Cir Jetha ang bajarka gao bicha karna mai chalao Aughor mere Sâth."'

The Aghori added that he had heard of other Aghoris eating human flesh, though he has not seen them doing it. The skull is given to the initiate to drink out of, but in some cases it is not awarded until twelve months after the initiation.

At some initiations the novice is only required to drink country liquor[3] and the head is merely shaved,[4] but on the other hand he is required to eat human flesh as part of the ceremony.[5] Two necklaces are placed round the neck, one of boar's tusks and the other of the vertebra of the cobra.

---

[1] Jamnaram Aghorapanthi who stated that he was born a Brahman and became an Aghoripanthi as he thought the sect was a good one. This man was examined at considerable length by Mr. Leith, on 4th January 1895, and gave a great deal of valuable information.

[2] Captain R. C. Temple, then Cantonment Magistrate at Amballa, wrote these words as follows :—

"Ulti Khopri, Sir Jata, Aung-bajr ka ghàs, Bajog Karna main chala Aughor mere sath "

Which he thus translated :—

"With skull up-side down, and matted head of hair and strong body wounded, I wander about alone and the Terrible one (Shiva) is with me."

[3] Statement of Mr. Jogendranath Roy of Gazipur, dated 1st July 1885, and addressed to Mr. Irvin, B. C. S.

[4] Statement of Bharanath, who, however, confessed that he drank urine when so inclined !

[5] Statement of Jamnaram.

APPENDIX G.

Kápálika Vrata, or worship of the terrific forms of Siva and Durga,[1] of which a vivid description is given in the *Prabodh Chandradaya* or Moon of Intellect.[2]

In a scene between a Digambar and a Kápálika, or carrier of a human skull: the latter, on being questioned, says: "O! Digambar, hearken to our rites.

" After fasting we drink liquor out of the skulls of Brahmans: our sacrificial fires are fed with the brains and lungs of men mixed up with their flesh, and human victims covered with the fresh blood gushing from the dreadful wound in their throats, are the offerings by which we appease the terrible god ' (Maha Bhairava.[3]) '" On being reproached for using these horrible rites by a mendicant and another Digambar (Sadhu), the Kápáliká in wrath cries out: " Thou unholy man, who art lower than the heretics; thou that shavest thy head, thou chandal, who pullest out the hairs of thy body, thou deceiver, I contemplate the Lord of Bhavana, the principal god who creates, preserves and destroys the fourteen worlds, whose glory is both revealed in the *Veds* and displayed in his works. The might of our religion is such that I control Hari, Hara, and the greatest and most ancient gods. I stop the course of the planets in the heavens. I submerge the earth in water with its mountains and cities, and I drink up the waters in a moment." On being interrupted in this eloquent discourse by the Digambar's telling him he has been deceived, the Kápáliká cries out: "Profane man, dost thou denominate the great god juggler? The wickedness of this fellow is not to be endured (draws out his scimitar). I will appease with the blood springing from his divided veins and

---

[1] H. H. Wilson's Select Specimens of the Hindus. London, 1871, Vol. 2. *Malati and Madhava* ; as before.

[2] J. Taylor's translation. London, 1812.

[3] Whose sanguinary tenets are contained in the Kalika Purana.

bubbling through the wound, the consort of Bhag, and the assembly of the demons summoned together by the sound of the Damani." (Raises his scimitar and advances towards the Digambar.)

———————

Hiuen Thsang, the Chinese pilgrim, who visited India in the first half of the 7th century of the Christian era, wrote of the Kápálikás as a sect who decorated their heads with wreaths of skulls, carried skulls round their necks and lived in caves or rocky " schluchten" (Larsen, Vol. 3, p. 691). He also speaks of the Ku-king-kja, a sect who wore filthy clothes and ate refuse food and rotten flesh, and were of the most extremely repulsive appearance (p. 692).

———————

Sherring, in his Vol. 1, p. 270, writes that the Kápálikás are a class of devotees who adopt the *muntra* or sacred text of the female deity Kâli. They are somewhat similar in their habits to the Aghoris, but not as shameless and abominable. They eat flesh and drink spirits, but refrain from eating dead carcasses.

———————

John Garrett in his *Classical Dictionary of India* (Madras, 1871, p. 315) under the heading *Kápáliká*, * says : " His body is smeared with ashes from a funeral pile, around his neck hangs a string of human skulls . . . his hair is wove into the matted braid, his loins are clothed with a tiger's skin, a hollow skull is in his left hand . . . and in his right he carries a bell which he rings incessantly, exclaiming aloud : ' Ho Sambhâ Bhairava' (Ho! Lord of Kali).''

——— ———

As to the Paramahansas, Edward Moor, in his *Hindu Pantheon* (London, 1810, p. 352), describes them as being epicurean cannibals, to whom the human brain is the most

———————

* " Walking, " the word signifies one who carries a human skull.   John Taylor's translation of " *Prabodh Chandrodaya.*"   London, 1812.

delicious morsel, but he may have confounded them with Aghorapanthis. Professor H. H. Wilson writes that Moor was wrong in attributing cannibalism to the Paramahansas; Mr. Kedernath Basu concurs with Professor Wilson, and cites the *Religious Sects of the Hindus,* by Sri Akshoy Umar Dutt, Calcutta, 1289. Although the Aghoris and Aghorapanthis have borrowed their creed from the Paramahansas, human sacrifice forms no part of the ritual of the last named sect.

Of the Paramahansas, it is said that when a learned man is called Paramahansa it may be rendered by " a great phœnix." Hansa and phœnix were both symbolical of the sun (Dr. Kera). Royal As. So.'s Journal, Vol. VI., p. 237 ; and Edward Moor, in his *Hindu* Pantheon (London 1810) says that in Vol. IX. of the *Asiatic Researches* he found the word applied to ascetics of the orthodox sects in the last stage of exaltation.([1])

The Bahikatha is described by *Sherring,* Vol. 1, page 270, as being another class of beggars as notorious and as much feared and shunned as the Aghoris. On presenting themselves before a house and asking for aid, should their importunity not be attended to, they begin to cut themselves about the head and body inflicting deep gashes and stabs ; this they continue until in sheer horror, and consternation the family thus addressed give them every thing they demand.

The Bauls[2] have a peculiar ordinance called the " Chari Chandva Bheda" or the four moon consummation. " Blood semen, excrements and urine " are the four moons. As these are inherited from their parents, they say, they are not to be

---

[1] See also, letter through Mr. Porter, B.C.S., from Pandit Ramasankar Misra, Honorary Deputy Collector, Benares.

[2] *Religious Sects of the Hindus,* by Ashoy Kumar Datta.

34

thrown away, but must be taken back into the system, and they eat and drink human and animal ordure and voidings, semen, blood. Their religious practices abound in obscenities so great that they cannot be detailed.

APPENDIX H.

The Maths or Sthâns of the Aghoripanthis and the names of their gurus are as follows :—

Abu, (¹) Allahabad, Mr. Leith's note is that the math is at Daragunj (Guru, one Bishcharâm, formerly an Ahir of the Shudra caste of cowherds and having two chelas, one a small boy). Balanath. (²) Augharkittali, in the dominion of H. H. the Guikowar about 100 miles from Baroda. Balanath (³) Buddhagaya, (⁴) near Patna, Buxar (⁵) (shut up because the guru in charge married and was excommunicated in consequence, Ghorukpur(⁶) Goraknath Kamatta, Girnâr, (⁷) the guru is Bujenath Lalgiri, Aghori, whose temple is that of Datta-trya (⁸) is the chief deity of the Aghorapanthi. There are about five maths here (⁹).

Ghazipur, (¹⁰) Biswarnath is the guru apparently. Hinglaj(¹¹) "in the west, where the sun sets," this is also described as 'situated beyond Hydrabad in Sind." Hariapur, (¹²) near

---

(¹)   Statement of Bharanath Aghoripanthi and Bhagwandas, Bairagi.
(²)   Ditto of Jamnarám, Aghoripanthi, made to Mr. Leith, in Allahabad, 4th January 1835.
(³)   Statement of Bharanath.
(⁴)   Ditto   Ditto.
(⁵)   Ditto   Ditto.
(⁶)   Jamnaram's Statement.
(⁷)   Ditto   Ditto.
(⁸)   Statement made to Mr. Leith, December 1884, and January 1885, at Allahabad by Bharanath.
(⁹)   Statement of Mr. H. N. Vakil, as above.
(¹⁰) Mr. Jogendrenath Roy.
(¹¹)   Ditto   Ditto.
(¹²) Jamnaram's Statement.

Ghazipur. This is Kalaram's math. ([¹]) Hardwar. ([²]) Jaunpur, ([³]) near the Ramghât Mâsanghât or burning ground ; and adjacent to the Sakaldea Railway Station. Jaunpur is between Benares and Ghazipur. This is Habbaram's math. ([⁴]) Hinglaj, a place of pilgrimage for Hindus from all parts of India, is close to the Aghor or Hingol river and in the territory of the Jam of Las Beyla. It is about two days' journey from the small port of Ormâra and more than 150 miles from Karachi † Ramghur (Keneram's math. ([⁵])

Pali, near Ajmere, ([⁶]) via Jeypore, Ujain,([⁷]) Tatta, Ogharki gadi. ([⁸]) Here the goddess Hinglaj is worshipped but whether by Aghoris, is doubtful, ([⁹])

Benares.—Three maths. Bharanath Aghorapanthi, in his statements to Mr. Leith in December 1884, and January 1885, claimed to be guru of Augharnath Katrakya and said that one Jain Augor Râm was guru of the Krimkhand math. The guru of Kiveram's math or "Kinaramgadi " is Hariaram, who has about fifteen chelas. This guru was formerly a Brahmin Pandit.

Other maths are mentioned, but I have not included these as they are not so fully described as the foregoing.

([¹]) Note by Mr.Leith.'
([²]) Barnath's Statement.
([³]) Jamnaram.
([⁴]) Note by Mr. Leith.
† The *country of Baluchistan.* London, 1877. A. M. Hughes, (*see* also *The People of India,* 1872, and *Hart's pilgrimage* in the Proceedings of the Bombay Geographical Society, Vol 3, p 77.) Also Journal Royal A. S. Vol II. p. 172 for an account of the Kaprias, whose holy land is Hinglaj.
([⁵]) Statement of Ramnath (Jogi) Aghori, to Major Malcolm Meade, Political Agent, Bhopal, 1885.
([⁶]) Jamaram.
([⁷]) Mr. Jogendranath Roy, through Mr. Irvine, B. C. S.
([⁸]) Mr. W. Forman, E. C , District Judge, Shikapur.
([⁹]) *Note* by Mr. Leith. Statements of Bharanath and Janaram, as above, and letter from Prankrishna Rai, Deputy Magistrate and Deputy Collector, Poona, to Mr. Porch, B. C. S., Magistrate, 13 May 1885.

APPENDIX I.

An English officer who served in Kathiawad and Guzerath in the earlier part of the present century, informed Colonel Todd that at a Jatra held at Girnâr, an Aghori, on making his appearance had puja done to him by the pilgrims who clad him with shawls, turbans, &c. He sat for some time, and at length with an idiotic laugh, sprang up and darted into the forest. (¹)

APPENDIX J.

As to the manner in which the modern Aghorapanthi decks himself out, a very good idea may be formed from the portraits now in this Society's room. They are of Jamuaram, so often referred to and were taken at Allahabad by Mr. Rust, for Mr. Cockburn, who with Mr. H. Rivett-Carnac, rendered such valuable assistance to Mr. Leith. Jamnaram was in the habit of smearing himself over with ashes from the funeral pyre, but as the photographer kept no stock of such ashes on the premises, Jamnaram was prevailed on to daub himself with chalk and prepared himself to represent Mahadeva.

As to the marks on the forehead, the trident (trisul) T is the weapon of Mahadeva (Shiva), whilst the rainbow (Dhanish) ≡ ≡ is the symbol of Vishnu. The worshippers of Mahadev, besides a dot, representing the moon (which rests on the head of Mahadev), draw on their foreheads, in two lines, the bow of Vishnu, whilst vice versâ the Vaishnavas wear the trident of Mahadev. Mr. Cockburn was not able to get any satisfactory explanation on this point, but was of opinion that the Vaishnavas and Shivaites have distinct religious ceremonies. It may be that although they worship Mahadev or Vishnu only they are conscious of the unity of Brahma, Vishnu and Mahadeva.

(¹) Lieut.-Col. Todd's Travels in Western India, p. 383.

The "Rudráksh" necklace worn by Jamnaram signified the "Eyes of Mahadev," from Rudra, his name, and "Aksha," eyes. Mahadeva, the god of destruction, devils, demons and ogres and of magic generally, is described as having a snake round his neck as well as snakes in his hair, and hence Shivait Jogis work their hair into long rolls. So, too, Mahadev is shown as covered with human ashes in which he loves to roll and disport himself; Mahadev's other necklace, representing the 108 skulls of his deceased mortal consorts, whom he used to decapitate until Sarasati had sense enough to persuade him to make her immortal. He also holds a skull in one of his hands. The rings on Jamnaram's necklace were only in token of his visits to shrines. He had the bones of a snake round his neck and carried a skull in his hand.

The Rudráksh seeds are supposed to bear marks resembling the human face. Sometimes, Aghorapanthis are seen with necklaces of human teeth. In this case it would not be surprising if the boar's tusk referred to the *Varáha* or boar's incarnation of Vishna. The pig's tooth is a necessary requirement in Jádu, involving a converse with demons, which is the particular department of Mahadeva, and practised only by Shivites. Jamnaram was decently dressed in the tawny yellow colour of Mahadeva. He wore three necklaces round his throat. On this necklace, strung with the beads, were two Mahadeva rings; (2) a necklace of the bones of the Nága Tripud (cobra); (3) brass chains, from which was suspended a boar's tusk in copper. On his right arm Jamnaram wore a Mahadeva bracelet. On his left arm was slung a bag used for carrying a skull, and in his left hand he was holding a skull. He said, the cobra necklace, the boar's tusk necklace, and the skull were all symbols of his being an Aughur or Aughurpanthi. He took off his jacket to show Mr. Leith and Mr. Cockburn (who took him to Mr. Carnac's house) that he had *Dwarkanáth* symbols burnt into the flesh of the forearm, the conch, the mace, the lotus, and the wheel. When surprise was expressed at his bearing Vishnu's emblems, he being a *Sivaite*, he smiled and said that he went to Dwarkanath, and that there he was told to have the marks burnt in, and he did so. In reply to further questions he said the Mahadeva bracelets come from Pasuppati Nath's shrine in Nipal, and that they were there given to him " by the Raja." All Brahmins and Sàdhus who visit that shrine receive such bracelets, but Chamars and low castes do not get them. A pilgrim to the shrine might be given two or three, and could bring them away and give them to Brahmins or Sadhus who had not been to the shrine. The bracelet when used at a wayside shrine is taken off the arm and used in puja. The puja thus performed is as if performed at Pasupathinath. He would not sell his bracelet or necklace, which latter was given to him by his guru. The bracelet had 32 different emblems of the gods (deobas) on them. He did not know their names.

This statement as to the necklaces coincides with those of two witnesses, not Aghorapanthis (¹) who state that Aghoris paint the skulls, they carry all over, so as to conceal what they really are, as otherwise such Aghorapanthis would be driven off. (²) The statement of a jogi from Girnar was to the same effect, and he added that some Aghorapanthis wear sumra bead (white stone) necklaces from Hingluj.(³) It is customary for

Aghorapanthis to have their backs branded thus ⌐⌐ (⁴)

The guru being on the gadi does not wear the sect mark, the chelas who go begging, do. The boar's tusk necklace and

---

(¹) Raghunathdas as before. Bhagwandas ditto.
(²) Raghunathdas.
(³) Mr. H. N. Vakil.
(⁴) Jamnaram.

cobra skeleton necklace are not worn by gurus. The Sanyasit and Aghoris wear small white beads which they get as Hinglaj.

The Aghori, whose photograph is given in the "People of India," Vol. 2, No. 94, is represented with only a long loin cloth with striped border, a skull in right hand and a bottle (English) in left, a stick with a carved handle tucked under his right arm, head apparently shaved and a horizontal Shiva caste mark on forehead.

THE JOURNAL

OF THE

ANTHROPOLOGICAL SOCIETY

OF

BOMBAY.

ORDINARY GENERAL MEETING, held on Wednesday, the 29th November 1893.

MR. KHARSETJI RASTAMJI CAMA took the Chair.

The Minutes of the previous Meeting were read and confirmed.

The following paper was then read :—

On some SUPERSTITIONS *regarding* DROWNING *and* DROWNED PERSONS.

By MR. SARAT CHANDRA MITRA, M.A., B.L.,

Pleader, Judge's Court, Chapra, Behar.

ANTHROPOLOGISTS have come to the conclusion that the principle of animism has its origin in the belief that every locality has its presiding spirits. This stage of belief is principally the characteristic of savage races, and still survives as relics of primitive faith among peoples who have now adopted the amenities of civilization. Primitive men believed that every mountain, rock, and valley, every well and stream and lake, is the abode of some spirits. This belief again originates from the association of the idea of personal life with that of motion, just as the swaying of a tree appeared to the mind of

35

primitive man to be a proof of personal life like the flight of
birds or the movements of animals. This idea became gradually developed, and, in conjunction with dreams during sleep,
reminiscences of the dead and accidental associations of
motionless objects with motion (as a rock in the midst of a
rapid or eddy), gave rise to animism or spiritism. Primitive
man was awe-struck at the majesty and grandeur of a mountain, and, inwardly reflecting that such majesty and grandeur
can only belong to spirits or beings superior to himself,
believed the mountain to be the local habitation of the same
beings.

Relics of savage animism are still to be met with among
civilized races, such as the mountain-worship of the Japanese,
the well-worship as prevailing in the different counties of
Great Britain and Ireland, and the river-worship of the
Hindus. The Ainos, who are the aboriginal inhabitants of
Japan, profess " the rudest and most primitive form of nature-
worship, *the attaching of a vague sacredness to trees, rivers, rocks,
and mountains,* and of vague notions of power for good or
evil to *the sea, the forest, the fire, and the sun and moon.*"
This belief still survives among the modern Japanese who
worship mountains. Miss Bird says (page 108 of Vol. I. of
her work) : " Mountains for a great part of the year clothed
or patched with snow, piled in great ranges round Nantaisan,
their monarch, are worshipped as a god." At page 122 of
the same volume, she again says : " The mountain peak of
Nantaisan is worshipped, and on its rugged summit there is
a small Shinto shrine with a rock beside it on which about
one hundred rusty sword-blades lie—offerings made by
remorseful men whose deeds of violence haunted them till
they went there on a pilgrimage and deposited the instruments of their crimes before the shrine of the mountain-god."

In the same manner, primitive man believed that every river
has its presiding spirit, and instances of this belief are still to

---

[1] Miss Bird's *Unbeaten Tracks in Japan*, Vol. II., p. 94.

be met with among peoples of savage culture. The Tshi-speak-
ing peoples of Africa believe in a great spirit Prah which presides over rivers, and to whom they offer human sacrifices,
one adult male and one adult female, in the belief that the
spirit can do harm to the people through the agency of the
rivers. By the principle of substitution, offerings of flowers,
fruits, sweets, cereals and incense which the Hindus of Bengal
offer every year to the Ganges, Brahmaputra, Padma, Nerbudda and other rivers, have become substituted for the human
sacrifices which are offered by savage peoples to the great
river-spirit.

Traces of the belief that every river, sea, and other bodies
of water have presiding spirits, and that they require human
sacrifices, are to be found even at the present day in the shape
of various superstitions about drowning and drowned persons,
which are prevalent among civilized peoples. Hence is the
reluctance displayed by some peoples to save a man from
drowning if he falls into the river or the sea. In the
Solomon Islands, when a man falls into the river and is
attacked by a shark, he is neither helped out of the water nor
is he assisted in warding off the attack of his marine assailant.
If the person anyhow manages to escape from the bloody
fangs of the shark, his fellow-tribesmen again throw him
into the water so that the shark may make a meal of him.
This they do under the impression that the victim is destined
to become a sacrifice to the river-god.[2] Another form of
this antipathy to saving a drowning man obtains in Scotland,
and has been recorded by Sir Walter Scott in his novel entitled
" The Pirate." In that story the peddler Bryce refused to
assist Mordant in saving the life of the shipwrecked sailor
from drowning and even rated him roundly for attempting
to do such a thing. I will reproduce the conversation which
took place between the two, because it shows the motive for
not assisting a man from getting drowned. Bryce said: " Are

---

[2] Codrington's *The Melanesians*, p. 179.

you mad? You that have lived sae lang in Zetland to risk the saving of a drowning man? Wot ye not if ye bring him to life again, he will be sure to do you capital injury?" The origin of this belief is stated by some to be the idea that the person rescued from being drowned would, some day or other, inflict mischief on the man who saves his life. Others say that it has its foundation in the belief that, as rivers and seas are entitled to get human sacrifices, the presiding spirits of those bodies of water would wreak their vengeance on those who prevent them from getting victims, as is illustrated by the item of folklore from the Solomon Islands or by that prevailing in the Orkneys and Shetlands. It is said that "among the seamen of the Orkney and Shetland it was deemed unlucky to rescue persons from drowning, since it was held as a matter of religious faith that the sea is entitled to certain victims, and if deprived would avenge itself on those who interfere."[3]

The superstition that the water-spirit, if despoiled of his victim, would wreak vengeance on the person who deprives him of the sacrifice due to him, is prevalent in one form or another, among many races in various parts of the world. It existed among the sea-faring population of Great Britain and Ireland and especially among those of Cornwall. The sea-faring community of France, the boatmen who ply their vocation on the River Danube and the common peasant folk of Russia also share in this belief. Formerly a superstitious belief was current amongst the Bengalis that a water-spirit in the form of an old hag—called जलं बुड़ी—haunts tanks and ponds and, when any person goes thereto, she fetters that person's feet with an invisible chain. The victim was allowed to go wherever he liked, dragging the invisible chain, so long as the daylight lasts, but as the shades of evening begin to fall, the जलंबुड़ी begins to withdraw the chain, and, therewith, the victim is gradually drawn within the waters of the tank and ultimately drowned therein. . This superstition which

---

[3] Tudor's *The Orkney and Shetland*, p. 176.

could formerly be always heard from the lips of credulous
gaffers and gammers, is now fast vanishing away before
the progress of English education and enlightenment, and
now only lingers as a relic in the threat with which Bengali
infants are frightened, namely, that, should they become
naughty, the মরা ভূতী will catch them and take them away.
Another mythical being named জক্ষ was believed to exist in
Bengal formerly. It was supposed to guard hidden treasure
and to reside in tanks. It was also said in respect of this
being that if anybody went to take the treasure in charge of
the জক্ষ, he was dragged into the water by that spirit and
killed by being submerged into it. This bit of folklore is
also disappearing. The Siamese believe in a water-spirit
called Pnuk who, they say, seizes those who go to bathe in
the water and drags them into his habitation thereunder.
The Sioux Indians entertain a similar belief in a water-demon
whom they call Unk-tahe and who, they believe, kills men
by dragging them underneath the water, in a way similar
to that of the Siamese spirit. The Kamschatkadales refuse to
help a drowning man out of the water, on account of some
similar superstitious scruples. If such a man was anyhow
rescued, no one of his fellow-tribesman would allow him to
enter his house or give him food, but on the other hand,
would take him for one who is dead. The Chinese also display a similar sort ·of reluctance to save a drowning man,
because they believe that the spirit of the drowned man
hovers over the water till it succeeds in killing a fellow-
creature by dragging him underneath the water and thereby
drowning him. It is also popularly believed by the Hindus
of Bengal that the spirits of persons who have come by their
deaths from drowning, haunt the tanks and wells in which
they have been drowned. Persons are afraid of going to
such tanks and wells, after night-fall, from a superstitious
dread that the ghost of the drowned man would be sure to
appear to him, or some other evil would happen to him. The

waters of such tanks and wells are considered impure and unclean until those receptacles of water are re-consecrated, and thus rendered pure, by performing some होम or sacrifice or some *Jagna*. Like the Bengalis, the Japanese also consider the water of wells wherein persons have been drowned, as impure. Miss Bird, at page 184 of Vol. I. of her above quoted work, says: " I have passed two wells which are at present disused in consequence of recent suicides by getting drowned in them." There is a belief current among the people of Bangalore in Mysore that the spirits of those persons who have been drowned, possess women.[*]

There are some omens which are superstitiously believed to prognosticate death from drowning. Before the days of the Suez Canal, ships used to come to India by the route round the Cape of Good Hope. European sailors believed that a phantom ship, which they called the " Flying Dutchman," used to sail near the Cape and would appear to passing vessels in times of storms. Sailors believed that the vessel which sighted the " Phantom Ship " would surely come to grief, and all the crew on board the vessel would be drowned. Captain Marryat has founded the plot of his novel *The Phantom Ship* upon the legend of the " Flying Dutchman." There is a superstition in Bengal to the effect that, if a single female rides in a boat in which there are male passengers only, it is believed by the lower classes of Bengalis-that the boat would come to grief and the passengers drowned. To obviate this evil, the single female passenger must tie a knot in her cloth remembering the name of another female. I once saw a curious illustration of this superstition. In May or June 1884, I had occasion to go over to Seebpore on the other side of the river Hooghly. I hired a boat from the Colvin's Ghat, Calcutta, and was crossing the river. While in mid stream, the

---

[*] " Note on a Mode of Obsession, which dealt with the belief in a part of Bangalore in the Possession of Women by the Spirits of Drowned Persons," by F. Fawcett, in the *Journal of the Anthropological Society of Bombay*, Vol. I., No. 8.

wind began to blow a regular gale, and the boat was toss ed to and fro. My fellow-passengers began to tell me that the rough weather was the consequence of the presence of a single female who was a passenger in the same boat with us· On a previous occasion also, while going to Seebpore, I was accompanied by a single female—a relative of mine—and, when stepping into the boat, I saw her tie a pice in a corner of her cloth, remembering the name of another female, as there was no other female passenger in that boat. This she did to obviate the consequences of the popular belief that a boat with a single female passenger would come to grief. There are also the Bengali superstitions that women who have got children must not put water into a vessel containing lime after taking their meal, otherwise their children will get drowned.[5] Also a person, who dreams that he is drowned in mire, ought to know that such dream prognosticates an early death to him.[6] The Bengali Hindus also believe that those persons who have got convolutions of hair (peculiar growth of the hair in a spiral form which is called in Bengali चुलेर पाक), are sure to get drowned. I came across a curious instance of this superstition lately. In the beginning of August last, a nephew of a Bengali pleader of the Chupra Bar got drowned while bathing in the River Saraju, which flows past this town. While on a visit of condolence to the bereaved gentleman, another Bengali gentleman—also a pleader of the local Bar—asked one of the uncles of the drowned boy whether the deceased had got a convolution of hair in his head. On being informed that he had got one, the gentleman told us all that when the deceased had got such convolution of hair he was sure to have died by drowning. The aforesaid gentleman also informed us that his second son had also got a similar convolution of hair, and that he was afraid lest he (his son) also get drowned. He further told us that in consequence

---

[5] and [6] *Vide* items Nos. 150, 155, and 189, in paper " On Popular Superstitions in Bengal," published in the *Journal of the Anthropological Society of Bombay*, Vol. I., p. 345.

of his son's possessing such convolution, he did not allow him (his son) to go to bathe either in a tank or in the river.

There are also certain processes, which, if had recourse to, would prevent a person from getting drowned. The performance of certain religious ceremonies are also supposed to have the same effect. Sailors believe that if a portion of the caul which covers the face of some children at the time of birth, be worn as an amulet round the neck, the person wearing it will not get drowned. In Bengal, it is sometimes believed that if a person accidentally eats ants along with sweets or other eatables, he will not get drowned. When a person is about to go to a distant part of the country and will have to cross rivers, the Hindus of Bengal, previous to the person's starting on his journey, offer *pujahs* to the goddesses of the rivers Ganges, Brahmaputra, Padma, Nerbudda, &c., &c., so that any mishap may not occur to him in the river. In our own family at Calcutta, I have observed similar *pujahs* offered to the family idol Nârâyana (who in this case is supposed to represent those river-goddesses), before any member of the family undertakes a journey to a distant part wherein he will have to cross rivers, simply for the purpose of appeasing the river-goddesses, who will, therefore, preserve him from all accidents in the rivers. The Bengal boatmen cry "*Badar*," "*Badar*," when a boat is in danger of capsizing, in the belief that doing so would cause the vessel to reach its destination safely. The Ainos, who are the aborigines of Japan, believe that if they throw the images of their gods, which are nothing but wands and posts of peeled wood, whittled nearly to the top, from which the pendent shavings fall down in white curls, into rivers, streams, rapids, and other dangerous places, they will be able to cross them safely.[1] The Japanese worship a god who, they believe, saves men from drowning and accident. They have also an amulet which saves persons from drowning.

---

[1] Bird's *Unbeaten Tracks in Japan*, Vol. II., p. 95.

Miss Bird says: " The amulet which saves from drowning is a certain cure for choking, if courageously swallowed."[8] The Kakhyens of Burma worship a Nat called the *Khakoo Khanam*—the god of water—on the occasion of anyone getting drowned. They also worship another Nat, named the Ndong Nat (Aing-peen Nat of the Burmese)—the god of the outside of Home—who, they believe, resides in the house, but *is worshipped by them outside if one of the family is killed by drowning.* The Mahomedans, when undertaking journeys by water, utter, as a protective from drowning, the following formula, which is contained in Surah Nooh of the Koran :—

بسم الله مجربها و مرسها ان ربي لغفورا لرحيم

The whole may be transliterated in Roman character thus, " Bismillâheh Majrihâ O Mursâhâ innâ rabi-il-ghafur ur-rahim." The origin of this custom is contained in the following legend, which may be thus narrated in Urdu :—

قصہ طوفان حضرت نوح علیہ السلام کا مشہور ہی پر مختصر یہ ہی کہ طوفان شروع ہوا حضرت نوح علیہ السلام ہر ایک جانوروں کا ایک ایک جوڑا اور بیا ہے رقصوں کے ساتھ کشتی میں سوار ہوۓ باقی لوگ حتی کہ ایک لڑکا حضرت نوح علیہ السلام کا بھی برمسبب نا فرمانی کے غرق ہوا تمام روۓ زمین دریا ہوا درخفوں اور پہاڑوں سے جب (۴۰) چالیس گز پانی بالا ہوا اہل کشتی شدت باد اور کثرت امواج سے بد حواس اور زندگي سے مایوس ہوۓ حکم الهي ہوا بسم الله مجربها و مرسها ان ربي لغفورا لرحیم جو کوئي ورد زبان کریگا حق تعالی اوسکي سب مشکلات آسان کریگا الله تعالی نے اپنی اسم کے برکت سے اونکو ڈوبنے سے اور طوفان موقوف ہوا [9]

The legend in Urdu may be thus translated into English:—

" The story of the Deluge of the Patriarch Noah—on whom be peace—is well known. The long and short of it is that when the Deluge commenced, the Patriarch Noah took a pair of each kind of animal, and thence repaired with his nearest relatives to the Ark. The rest of the people, as also a son

---

[8] *Op. cit.* Vol. I., pp. 379 and 380.
[9] Anderson's *Mandalay to Momein*, p. 457.

of the Patriarch Noah, were drowned on account of disobe-
dience. The whole of the earth was flooded. And when the
water rose to the height of 40 yards above the trees and
mountains, the inmates of the Ark, on account of the terrific
storm and the fury of the waves, became senseless with fear
and despaired of life. Then God ordered : "Bismilláheh
Majrihâ O Mursâhâ innâ rabi-il-ghafur ur-rahim."[10] Whoever
will utter these words, the Almighty God will deliver him from
all difficulties. *The Almighty God will, by reason of the Benign
Influence of His Name, preserve him from drowning.* And the
storm was allayed."

The Russians also believe that saving the life of a drowning
man excites the wrath of the water-spirit. An illustration
of this item of Russian folklore is given by Mr. Barry, in his
novel entitled "Ivan at Home," which is descriptive of Russian life. Once upon a time, a drunkard fell into the water
and disappeared. Some spectators who stood close by on the
shore did not show any inclination whatever to save the drowning
man. The man was drowned. The villagers held a court of
enquiry to investigate into the matter of that man's death from
drowning. In the course of the enquiry it was elicited that
no cross had been found on the neck of the deceased. The
village Daniels, who sat to enquire into the matter, quickly
returned the verdict that the man had got drowned because
he had no cross upon his neck. The fisher-folks of Bohemia
also display a similar kind of reluctance to save a man from
drowning, under the impression that the presiding spirit of
the water would get angry at thus being deprived of his
victim, give him bad luck in fishing and soon get him

---

[10] This formula may be translated into Urdu as follows :—

ساتھ نام الله کے ہی چلنا اوسکا اوسکا اور نهرنا اور نهرنا اوسکا لعقیق کے رب میرا
البتہ بخشی والا اور مہربان ہی •

The above may be translated into English thus : "The moving and stopping
(of this boat, *i.e.* Noah's Ark) depends upon the influence of the name of God.
For, in truth, our God is, preeminently, a Pardoner of sins and Merciful."

drowned. The same superstition also obtains in Germany, and, when a person comes by his death from drowning, the German-folks say : " The river-spirit claims his annual sacrifice," and cometimes also, "The nix has taken the drowned man." Mr. Jones, in his "*Credulities Past and Present*," offers an explanation to the effect that "a person who attempts to rescue another from drowning is considered to incur the hatred of the uneasy spirit, which is desirous, even at the expense of a man's life, to escape from its wandering." Dr. Tylor, in his "*Primitive Culture*," explains the superstition by saying such reluctance is only a relic of the ancient belief that the water-spirit very naturally used to get angry on being deprived of his intended victim, and, consequently, bore ill-will towards the person who ventured to do so, and would try to wreak vengeance on him at the first opportunity.

There is another class of popular beliefs as regards the time when the body of a drowned man would float up. In past times, it was popularly believed that the body of a drowned man would float up on the ninth day. This belief is prevalent in the county of Durham, as we are informed on the authority of Mr. Henderson. Sir Thomas Browne, the author of the *Hydriotaphia* and the *Religio Medici*, has also discussed this popular belief in his *Pseudodoxia Epidemica*.

In ancient times, people believed that the spirits of those persons who had been drowned in the sea, wandered for one hundred years, owing to their corpses not having been pro-perly buried with all the rites of sepulture. Relics of this belief are to be found even at the present day. The belief still lingers among ignorant fisher-folk in some parts of England that the spirits of those sailors who have been drowned by shipwreck frequent those parts of the shores near which the shipwreck took place, and some of them even assert that they have heard the spirits of the drowned sailors " hailing their own names." Hunt, in his "*Romances in the West of England*," refers to this belief and says that fisherfolks are afraid of walking in such localities after night-fall. This belief is similar to the Bengali superstition, described above, that the spirits of drowned persons haunt those tanks and wells in which they have been drowned, and has its counterparts among other races of people all over the world.

Lastly, there are some curious popular beliefs about the methods by which the corpses of drowned persons may be discovered. One of these methods is to tie up a loaf of rye-bread in the shirt of the drowned person and set it afloat in the water near the place where the person was drowned. It is believed that the loaf of bread would float until it reaches close to the spot where the body of the drowned person lies and then sink at that spot. The *Indian Mirror* of Thursday, the 29th September 1892, gives the following account of a search, in the aforesaid way, after the body of a drowned boy:—

" A novel method was adopted at Springfield, Illinois (United States of North America), in searching for the body of a drowned boy. The searchers tied up a loaf of rye-bread in the lost boy's shirt and set it adrift in the water above the place where the lad was drowned, the theory being that the loaf would float until it came close to the body. The package in this case is said to have floated until it reached a certain point when it suddenly sank. The boy was found within a few feet of the spot."

This belief is to be found in various other modified forms in many other countries of the world. Another modification of this belief consists in floating a loaf weighted with mercury, which is believed to float at once towards, and stand over, the spot where the corpse lies. A writer in an American paper gives the following instance of this belief: " Some years ago, a boy fell into the stream at Sherborne, Dorsetshire, and was drowned. The body not having been recovered for some days, the mode of procedure adopted was thus : A four-pound loaf of best flour was procured, and a small piece cut out of the side of it, forming a cavity, into which a little quicksilver was poured. The piece was then replaced, and tied firmly in its original position. The loaf thus prepared was thrown into the river at the spot where the body fell, and was expected to float down the stream till it came to the place where the body had lodged. But no satisfactory result occurred." In another form, this belief is also prevalent among the aboriginal Indians of North America. Sir James Alexander, in his work on Canada, says : "The Indians imagine that in the case of a drowned body, its place may be discovered by floating a chip of cedar-wood, which will stop and turn round over the exact spot. An instance occurred within my own knowledge, in the case of Mr. Lavery of Kingston Mill, whose boat overset, and himself drowned near Cedar Island ; nor could the body be discovered until this experiment was resorted to." The writer in the American paper, from whom I have quoted above, says: "Not many months ago a man was drowned at St. Louis. After search had been made for the body, but without success, the man's shirt, which he had laid aside when he went in to bathe, was spread out on the water, and allowed to float away. For a while it floated, and then sank, near which spot it is reported, the man's body was found." Another modification of the theory of the discovery of a drowned man's corpse by a loaf, is current in Brittany. When a man gets drowned in Brittany and his corpse cannot be recovered, a lighted taper is stuck into a loaf of bread, which is then set adrift in the stream. Wherever the loaf of bread stands over still, there, it is believed, the corpse lies underneath the waters. Another modification of this belief consists in tying round a wisp of straw, a strip of parchment having on it some cabalistic letters written by the parish priest, and setting it afloat in the stream. Wherever it will stop still, there, it is believed, the body is sure to be found. A correspondent of the *Notes and Queries* (English) says that the corpse of a drowned person was recovered by this means.

In some other countries, a living animal is employed for the purpose of recovering the body of a drowned man. It is believed that the animal will either cry out or sink at the exact spot where the corpse lies. In Norway, the people searching for the body take a cock with them in the boat and row with it hither and thither. It is believed by them that Chanticleer will crow out when the boat reaches the spot where the body of the drowned man lies. In a similar manner the Javanese, or the inhabitants of Java, throw a living sheep in the water, when the corpse of a drowned man is to be recovered. They believe that the spot where the sheep will sink is the place where the dead body is sure to be found.

On the CEREMONIES PERFORMED by the KABIRPANTHI MAHANTS of the SARAN DISTRICT, on their INITIATION as Chelás and on their SUCCESSION to the MAHANTSHIP.

BY MR. SARAT CHANDRA MITRA, M. A., B. L.,

Pleader, Judge's Court, CHUPRA, Behar.

IN the district of Saran, there are many maths (मठ) or monasteries presided over by their spiritual heads—the Mahants. These Mahants are all *Kabirdhás* (कबिरदास) or followers of Kabir and practise the tenets promulgated by that famous religious. reformer. They belong to two classes, *viz.*, the *Sanyásis* (सन्न्यासी) and the *Gharbásis* or Grihabásis (घरबासी or गृहबासी).

The Sanyâsîs, who usually have the title of *Parbats*, entirely withdraw themselves from the world, cut off all connection with their respective families, and live a strict life of celibacy within the precincts of their *maths* or monasteries. The Gharbâsîs have usually the titles of *Gîr, Atith, Purî* or *Bhârathí*, and are house-holders, living with their families and children in their *maths*. These latter are, by reason of their being house-holders, considered as of inferior rank by the Sanyâsîs or Parbats who do not partake of food touched by the *Gîrs, Atiths, Purîs* or *Bhârathís*. On the other hand, the Gharbâsîs (the Gîrs and others) will eat the remnants of food partaken of by the Sanyâsîs or the Parbats.

The Kabirâhâs or Kabirpanthí Mahants enlist *chelas* or disciples from all castes, and eat, as some say, with all castes also. The ceremonies observed at the time of becoming *chela* or disciple are as follows :—Firstly, the would-be disciple's head is shaved by a barber, and a lock of hair called the *tik* (टीक) is left on the centre of the crown of the head. The *Guru* or the spiritual preceptor then cuts off this tuft of hair, and also takes off the उपनीत or the sacrificial thread which is worn by the would-be disciple. The lock of hair and the sacrificial thread are buried underneath the ground. Homa (होम) is then performed by a Brâhmana priest. No *mantra* is given at this time to the disciple. The *chela* is then invested with *garuá busan* गेरुवा वसन or cloth dyed in red ochre. Some say *bije* (विजे) or a feast is also given at that time. Mahants and *chelas* or house-holders also attend the ceremony of becoming *chela*. No other ceremonies are performed at that time. After becoming a *chela*, the disciple ceases to be a house-holder, continues to live in the *math* and serves the presiding *Mahant* who is his *guru* or spiritual preceptor.

When a Mahant dies, his corpse is interred in the ground four days after his death. A *Samâdhi* is erected over his grave. Four days after the Mahant's death, *i. e.*, on the day of his burial, the ceremony of Dudhrot (दुधरोट) or the Milk-and-

Bread ceremony is performed. On this occasion, the attending Mahants are fed on milk and bread.

The deceased Mahant, during his lifetime, usually selects the most worthy amongst his *chelas* or disciples to succeed him after his death. If he does so, the Mahant-elect performs the Bhândârâ ceremony of his deceased preceptor one year after his death and invites the Mahants of the neighbouring *maths* to be present on the occasion of the performance of this ceremony. The attendant Mahants confirm the nomination, by the deceased Mahant, of the Mahant-elect by giving him *chudders* or linen sheets on the occasion of the Bhândârâ performed by him in commemoration of his deceased *guru* or preceptor. But if the deceased Mahant dies without having selected, during his life-time, a successor, the Mahants attending the Bhândârâ of the deceased nominates the principal and the most worthy among his *chelas* or pupils as his successor and instals him (the nominee) on the *guddi* of Mahantship by giving him *chudder*. With reference to the election of Mahants, Babu Shâmâ Charan Sarkâr, a recognised authority on Hindu Law, says :* " Generally, the usage or custom of Mahanths is that the Mahanth or principal of any *math* or monastery states his principal and most worthy pupil to succeed to him at his decease ; that after his death the *Mahanths of other similar institutes* in the vicinage convene an assembly of the order and perform his Bhândârâ or funeral obsequies at which they generally confirm the nomination made by the deceased and instal the pupil he selected as his authorized successor. * * * *. But where a Mahant dies without appointing a successor, there his successor is selected generally from amongst his pupils by the Mahants convened at his Bhândârâ and invested with the Mahantship of the *math*. * * *. In short, the installation of the successor by an assembly of Mahants at the obsequies of the deceased *Mahanth* is in all cases indispensable and conclusive ;

* *Vide* Vyâvasthâ Chandrikâ, Vol. I., page 222.

and consequently the appointment of a successor by the late
Mahanth is not final so long as it is not confirmed by the
Mahanths convened at the *Bhândârá*."

The ceremonies performed at the Bhândârâ, which is performed one year after the Mahant's death, may be described
as follows : A *kalas* (कलस) or earthen jug full of water and
crowned with mango leaves, and rice in a separate pot, are
placed on a *mandala* made of powdered rice upon a *vedi* or
platform of earth. Homa (होम) is then performed by a Brâhmana priest. Then the *Achârya Guru* of the *math* gives
mantra to the would-be Mahant (*i.e.*, whispers the sacred formula to him), and he is thus initiated as a Sanyâsî. Some say
a flagstaff is planted at the *math*, and the mahant-elect's head
is shaved. Then every one of the mahants* of the neighbourhood, who may be present there, give the newly-elected Mahant a mahanti *chudder* or linen sheet and two rupees in cash.
After this, Brâhmanas are feasted. Subsequently to this, the
Parbats are feasted. Then the lower castes, beggars and other
people are fed. Some say that, at the conclusion of the Bhândârâ ceremony, a *surathâl* or a record of the proceedings at
the *Bhândârâ* is written out and attested by respectable witnesses. On the day next to that in which the *Bhândârâ* is
performed, the newly-elected Mahant bids farewell to the
invited Mahants who might have attended the ceremony, by
returning them double of what they had given to him, *i.e.*, four
rupees and two chudders. The Mahants are prohibited from
uttering the names of their *Achârya Gurus* who initiate the
former as Sanyâsîs.

---

* According to some, the Atiths and Girs, who are householders, are not fit
to give mahanti chuddor to the Parbats.

ORDINARY GENERAL MEETING, held on Wednesday, the 20th December 1893.

MR. KHARSETJI RASTAMJI CAMA, took the Chair.

The Minutes of the previous Meeting were read and confirmed.

The following donations were acknowledged and the thanks voted to the donors :—

To the Museum.

From MR. W. R. SANDFORD, Madras Railway Podaung, Prehistoric Pottery, Weapons, &c., found in graves in the Nilgiri Branch of the Madras Railway.

To the Library.

From the Bombay Natural History Society—Description of the people of India (Pope).

The following paper was then read :—

FURTHER NOTES *on the* CHOWK CHÂNDÂ, *and the* PANCHAMÎ VRATA.

By MR. SARAT CHANDRA MITRA, M.A., B.L.,

Pleader, Judge's Court, Chapra, Behar.

IN a previous paper entitled "*On Vestiges of Moon-Worship in Behar and Bengal,*"* I have given an account of the *Chowk Chândâ* day of Behâr, which corresponds to the *Nashta Chandra* day of Bengal and falls on the fourth day of the light half of the moon in the month of Bhâdon (August-September). In that paper, I have tried to shew that the ceremonies observed on this occasion are mere survivals of moon-worship in the two provinces of Bengal and Behar. The legend which I have narrated therein as having given rise to the superstition of not looking at the moon on the *Chowk Chândâ* and the *Nashta Chandra* day, is slightly incorrect. The correct version thereof

---

* *Vide* the *Journal of the Anthropological Society of Bombay,* Vol. II., pp. 597-601

is given below, as also an account of some additional ceremonies observed by the Hindus of Behâr, especially of Sârun,
on this occasion.

The correct version of the legend, whereon the superstition
connected with the *Chowk Chândâ* day in Behar is based, is
given in the सप्तपञ्चाशत्तम अध्याय or Chapter LVII. of the प्रेमसागर
(*Prem Sâgara*) which gives an account of the life and exploits
of Krishna (श्रीकृष्णजी.)

The chapter opens thus :—

श्रीशुक्रदेव जी बोले कि महाराज ! सत्राजितने पहले तो श्रीकृष्णचन्द्र को
मणि कि चोरि लगाई, पीछे भूठ समझा लज्जित हो उसने अपनि कन्या सत्य-
भामा हरि को ब्याहसी । वह सुन राजा परीक्षितने श्रीशुकदेवजी से पूछा कि
कृपानिधान !

सत्राजित कौन था, मणि उसने कहां पाई ? और कैसे हरिको चोरि लगाई ।
फिर क्योंकर भूठ समझ कन्या ब्याहसी । वह तुम मुझे समझाके कहो । श्रीशुक-
देवजी बोले कि महाराज ! सुनिये मैं सब समझाकर कहता हुं । * * * † *.

The chapter thus concludes:

इतना कथा सुन राजा परीक्षितने श्रीशुकदेवजीसे पूछा कि कृपानिधान श्रीकृष्ण-
जी को कलङ्क क्यों लगा सो कृपाकर कहो । शुकदेवजी बोले राजा ।
चांद चौथ को देखियौ, मोहन भादौं मास । तातें लग्यौ कलङ्क यह, अति मन
भयौ उदास ॥

और सुनौ

जो भादौं कि चौथ को, चांद निहारे कोय । वह प्रसंग श्रवननि सुनें, ताहि
कलङ्क न होय ॥ इति । *

The above may be thus translated :

Srî Sukadevajî said : O great king ! Satrâjit charged Srî
Krishnachanda first with the theft of a jewel ; and subsequently
finding his accusation to be false, he was ashamed, and gave
his daughter Satyabhâmâ in marriage to Hari. Râjâ Parîkshit
asked Srî Sukadevajî, " O abode of mercy ! who was Satrâjit,
where did he get the jewel, and how did he accuse Hari of
theft, and afterwards finding the accusation false, in what

---

† The passages are extracted from the edition of the प्रेमसागर in Hindi,
published by Nrityalâl Sil of Ahîrítolâ, Calcutta, in Saka 1796. The chapter
in question is contained in pp. 178-183 of that edition.

manner did he give his daughter in marriage? Explain the circumstances to me." Śrî Sukadevajî answered : "O great king ! be pleased to listen, and I will explain all the circumstances." (Then Sukadeva narrates the story which may be thus briefly stated :

Satrâjit of the family of Jadu, having performed a very difficult religious penance in honor of the Sun-god, obtained from the latter a jewel named *Syamantaka*. One day Satrâjit, having put on the jewel, went to the court of the Jadavas who greatly admired the brilliancy of the jewel, and thought the Sun-god was coming to see Śrî Krishnajî. But Krishna explained that it was Satrâjit with the jewel on his arm, and not the Sun-god, that was coming. After this, Satrâjit frequently used to come to the Yadava Court with the jewel on his neck. One day, the Yadavas told Krishna to take the jewel from Satrâjit and give the same to king Ugrasena, as it was fit only for a king. Krishna requested Satrâjit to give the jewel to Ugrasena. Having heard this proposal, Satrâjit went to his brother Prasena and informed him of Krishna's request. At this Prasena was angry and, snatching the jewel, put it round his own neck ; and, arming himself and mounting a horse, went a-hunting. While in pursuit of a deer, he came to a large cave wherefrom a lion came forth and killed Prasena, his horse, and the deer, and carried off the jewel into the cave. A bear named Jâmbûbâna, seeing the brilliancy of the jewel, killed the lion, carried off the jewel, and went with it to his wife who gave it to her daughter. The child used to play with it.

In the meantime, the followers of Prasena, not having found him in the forest, came and informed Satrâjit that they had not been able to trace the whereabouts of Prasena. On hearing this Satrâjit began to suspect that Krishna might have killed his brother for the sake of the jewel and carried it off. He also informed his wife of his suspicion about Krishna's complicity in the theft. She, on the other hand, told his female companions and servants about her husband's suspicions about Krishna. Now the matter, having got noised abroad, reached the ears of the female members of Krishna's family, who, thereupon, began to blame the latter and speak ill of him. Hearing this, Krishna went to the Yâdava Court and told Ugrasena, Vâsudeva and Balarâm that he had been accused of killing Prasena and carrying off the jewel Syamantaka ; and craved their permission to go and search for Prasena and the jewel in order that the disgrace might be effaced.

Then Krishna, with the companions of Prasena, and some of the Yâdavas, went in search of them. When Krishna, in the course of his quest of the lost jewel, came near the cave, he went inside it, and, having found the jewel therein, began to wrestle with Jâmbubâna. Jâmbubâna, coming to know that the person wrestling with him was no other than the lord Krishna, expressed to the latter his wish to give him his (Jâmbûvâna's) daughter Jâmbuvatî in marriage. Krishna granted permission. Then Jâmbûvâna, having performed the ceremonies prescribed by the Vedas, gave his daughter in marriage to Krishna and gave her the jewel Syamantaka as a part of her dowry. Krishna, having returned to the court of the Yâdavas, sent for Satrâjit and, when he came, informed him that he had falsely accused him of the theft of the jewel, and then made it over to him. Being very much ashamed at having falsely accused Krishna, and being desirous of atoning for the sin incurred thereby, Satrâjit expressed his wish to give the jewel, his daughter Satyabhâmâ, to Krishna. Then Satyabhâmâ was married to Krishna with all the necessary ceremonies.

Raja Parîkshit interrupted Sri Śukadevâjî in this part of the story, and enquired : " O abode of compassion ! *kindly explain, why the suspicion and calumny of the theft were fastened upon Sri Krishnajî.*" Śukadevajî replied : " Râjâ ! *Mohan* (*Krishna*) *had seen the moon, when it was four days old in the month of Bhâdoñ ; hence the infamy of theft got fastened to the*

*name of Krishna who was very much frightened and dejected on
account thereof. And, further, listen to me that, should anybody
see the moon on the fourth day of the light half of Bhâdoñ, the
infamy will be wiped away on hearing this discourse.*"

Those, who are rendered sinful by looking at the moon on the
Chowk Chândâ day, are absolved from the sin by throwing ढेला
or brickbats on to the thatches of other people, and, thereby,
getting abused in return ; or by hearing the discourse contained
in the fifty-seventh chapter of the *Prem Sâgara.*

On the day next to the *Chowk Chândâ, i. e.,* on the fifth day
of the light half of the moon in the month of Bhâdoñ (August-
September) falls the पञ्चमीव्रत (Pañchamî Vrata). Those who
perform this *Vrata* have to remain fasting the whole of the
day. In the evening they have to cleanse their teeth with
दातन (or sticks for cleansing the teeth with) made of the
branches of a shrub called चिड़चिड़ी. It is a plant which has
ovate leaves and grows in profusion in waste places during the
rains. After cleansing the teeth, the performers of the *Vrata*
have to break their fast by taking भवेंसी का दही or tyre (curdled
milk) made of buffalo's milk ; and तिनाकेभात or boiled coarse
rice, तिना being a kind of coarse rice of a red color.

The Hindus of all classes and shades of belief, believe that
women become impure during the menstrual period. Hence
the Hindu Shâstras prohibit the contact of men with women
during this period. Those persons, however, who are rendered
impure by contact with women during this period, are absolved
from the sin and the consequent impurity by the performance
of the पञ्चमी व्रत. I do not know whether this व्रत is performed
in other places than the Sâran district.

ORDINARY GENERAL MEETING held on Wednesday, the
31st January 1894.

MR. JIVANJI JAMSHEDJI MODI, B.A., *Vice-President*, in the
chair.

The Minutes of the previous Meeting were read and confirmed.

The election of the following new member was announced :—
Brigadier-General M. H. Nicolson, Bombay Army, Commanding at Deesa.

Mr. Kharsetji Rastamji Cama and Mr. W. S. Millard were
elected Auditors, to audit the accounts of the Society.

The following paper was then read :—

On the RITE of HUMAN SACRIFICE in ANCIENT, MEDIÆVAL
and MODERN INDIA and OTHER COUNTRIES.

By Mr. PURUSHOTTAM BALKRISHNA JOSHI.

BY no nation on the face of the earth is life considered so
sacred as by the Hindus, and there is no faith which enjoins
on its followers so strictly the observance of the principle of
non-destruction of life as Hinduism.   The most fundamental
doctrine of Brahmanic Hinduism is *Ahinsa paramo dharmah,*
which means that non-destruction of life is the best of religions.
The Sixth of the Ten Commandments of the Christian Scriptures says, " Thou shalt not kill," but the first and the most
important of the Commandments of the Hindu Scriptures [1] says,
" Thou shalt not kill any living creature," and this doctrine of
humanity is carried to such an extent that with certain classes
of the Hindus not only the life of man and the life of animals
are sacred, but even the life of the minutest of insects and of
the smallest of plants and trees are holy.   Such being the case
it will be naturally presumed that inhuman and barbarous

---

[1] अहिंसा सत्यमस्तेयमकामक्रोधलोभता । भूतप्रियहितेहा च धर्मोऽयं सार्वलौकिकः:
The universal religion consists in (1) abstaining from killing living beings;
(2) in speaking the truth ; (3) in refraining from anger, (4) covetousness,
nd (5) fornication ; and (6) in benevolence to all living beings.

practices like the offering of human victims must be foreign to the religious instinct of the Hindus not only of the present day, but even of the Vedic and Puranic periods. But if one were to peruse carefully the religious literature of the Hindus, he will be surprised to find numerous traces of the practice of human sacrifice in India.

Rig Veda, the earliest of the four Vedas of the Hindus, does not contain any distinct trace of this revolting rite. I am inclined to believe that to the pious Rishis who composed and chanted the admirable hymns of the Rig Veda, and whose offerings consisted, for the most part, of the juice of the Soma plant or pieces of sacred wood, or the three principal products of the cow, this horrible ritual was unknown, and that they became acquainted with it after they had settled among and mixed with the Dravidian and other aboriginal races. The region which gave birth to the hymns of the Rig Veda is supposed to have extended from the valley of Kabul to the banks of the Ganges, but the country in regard to which they supply the most data is the region of the Five Rivers—the Punjaub.[1] Gradually, the Aryan invaders advanced eastward and took possession of the fertile soil of Hindustan proper,· and at the time of the Brahmanas they appear to have advanced still further. On the east and south they came in contact with the tribes which inhabit the shores of the eastern sea and the other side of the Vindhia mountains.[2] As the Aryans advanced still further in India and settled in the parts inhabited by the Dravidian and other native races, they appear to have adopted good many practices of the tribes conquered by them.[3]

[1] Barth's Religions of the Hindus, p. 38. Also compare the following in Manu smriti :—परस्वनीदृषद्र्याँदैवनयोंदॅन्तरम् । तं देवनिमितं देसं नबावतँ प्रभुमैा॥ कर्हशेवं च मन्स्याक पंचाला: शूरसेनकाः। एव बाब्राभिदेसो वे नबावतांदनंतरः ॥
The Institutes of Manu, ch. II.

[2] Aitareya Brahmana, VII., 18, 2.

[3] Compare the following :—
We see in the incorporation into Brahmanic body of the dark-skinned Tulu Brahmans and Kaveri Brahmans of Kurg that Brahmanism sometimes accommodated itself more to the customs of the conquered races than one would infer from the rigorous custom of caste—(Paul Wurm. Gesch. der indisch. Religion, Basel. 1874, p. 7.

The subject races in turn also adopted the customs and usages
of the conquerors, and in this way the work of assimilation
continued for centuries together. In several parts of India,
particularly in the Hindustan, and north of the Deccan, the
assimilation has been so complete that a very large proportion
of these races has become indistinguishably blended together
with the race of the invaders. In his work on the "Religions of the Hindus," Barth observes that some of the goddesses
of the Hindu religion which sanction bloody sacrifices are of
Dravidian origin. I fully concur with the above view, and
believe that if we accepted this view we can fully account for the
traces of human sacrifice which we find in the sacred literature
of the Hindus, particularly in the **Puranas** and the Tautras of
Shaktism. The rite of human sacrifice was, no doubt,
intimately connected with the worship of the Mothers or
Matris and probably with the cultus of Shaivism in its
primitive stage. To this day the most powerful of the
divinities of the Dravidian and other aboriginal tribes are the
Mothers. They are innumerable, but the most important of
these is the goddess Káli who is known by various other ap-
pellations, such as Kalika, Chandi, Chamunda, Maha Maya,
Girija and Vindhyawasini. The last three names are worthy
of notice, as they distinctly show that the goddess was originally a deity of the mountaineers.

I have already observed that the Rig Veda Sanhita contains
no traces of human sacrifice. Purusha Sukta, or the 90th
hymn of the Rig Veda Sauhita, is considered by a few scholars
like Dr. Haug, to be a distinct trace of the practice of human
sacrifice among the Hindus of the Rig Veda period. In his
tract on "The Origin of Brahmanism," p. 5, Dr. Haug says:
"According to the position which is assigned to it in the
Yajur Veda (where it is found among the formulas
referring to human sacrifice) the hymn appears to have been
used at human sacrifice." But here we should not lose sight
of the fact that the whole hymn is an allegory, and that it is so,

33

will be clearly perceived from the sixth verse of it, which says: "When the gods performed a sacrifice with Purusha as the oblation, the spring was its butter, the summer its fuel, and the autumn its offering." Moreover, the hymn does not appear to belong to the ancient portion of the Rig Veda, inasmuch as nowhere in the Sanhita we come across any reference to the four castes of the Hindus except in this hymn. This hymn appears in the Yajur Veda Sanhita and also in the Atharva Veda, and by many it is considered a later addition to the original hymns of the Rig Veda Sanhita. Dr. J. Muir is distinctly of this opinion, and he believes that it was adopted as a part of the ceremonial at a later period when the immolation of human beings had ceased to be otherwise than formal and nominal. Colebrooke in his Miscellaneous Essays (I. p. 309), considers that the hymn has decidedly a more modern tone and must have been composed after the Sanskrit language had been refined and its grammar and rhythm perfected. Professor Max Muller concurs in this view. In his "Ancient Sanskrit Literature," p. 570, the learned Sanskritist observes that "the hymn is full of allusions to the sacrificial ceremonials, it uses technical and philosophical terms, it mentions the three seasons in the order of *Vasanta* Spring, *Grishma* Summer, and *Sharada* Autumn, and that it contains the only passage in the Rig Veda where the four castes are mentioned."

From the above it will be perceived that the hymn is a modern addition to the Sanhita of the Rig Veda. But, for the sake of argument, even if it be supposed that it is as ancient as the other hymns of the Rig Veda Sanhita, this circumstance does not support the theory that it is a relic of human sacrifice. What does the hymn say ? Does it not describe the *virat* nature of the Creator ? And when it says of the Purusha as possessing a thousand heads, a thousand eyes, and a thousand feet, are we to understand that there was a wonderful being who had in reality a thousand heads or a thousand eyes and an equal number of feet? Would it not be more rational to take the word *sahasra*, a thousand, to mean infinity, and the whole to signify that the Purusha was omnipotent, omniscient and omnipresent? In fact, the whole hymn is symbolical like the Psalm LXXX of David's Psalms, and should never be taken in its literal sense.

The first positive mention we have in the ancient Hindu religious books of this cruel rite is in the Aitareya Brahmana[1] of the Rig Veda. Here, we are told that a certain king of the family of Ikshwaku named Harischandra had no son. As it is considered a disgrace among the Hindus to be without a son, Harischandra made a vow to Varuna, the god of water, that if a son be born to him he would sacrifice the child to the god. Accordingly a son was born to him and he named him Rohita. From day to day the father postponed fulfilling his promise to Varuna on the ground that the child was not fully grown up. In course of time Rohita grew to manhood, and his father perceived that he could no longer delay the fulfilment of his vow. He, therefore, asked Rohita to prepare himself to be sacrificed. Rohita objected to be killed, and ran away from his father's house. In the meantime, the father was afflicted with dropsy. For six years Rohita wandered in the jungles, and there at last he met a poor Brahman named Ajigarth who consented to sell one of his sons named Shunashepa for a hundred cows. Rohita consented to pay the price and took Ajigarth and his son to his father, the king. Shunashepa was now bound to the stake and was about to be sacrificed to Varuna when, at the suggestion of Vishwamitra, he repeated seven hymns from the Rig Veda, and he was thereby set at liberty.[2]

---

[1] There are 7 hymns in the first book of the Rig Sanhita which Shunas Shep is believed to have recited when he was about to be sacrificed. But H. H. Wilson is strongly (and I should say rightly) of opinion that they cannot be associated with a human sacrifice.

[2] The legend of Shunashepa is narrated at great length in the Mahabbarata, Anushasanaparva Section 3; and with a slight variation we find the

The above legend, no doubt, leads us to believe that at the time of the Aitareya Brahmana human sacrifices were, in exceptional cases, practised or at least tolerated, though it is true that even in the Aitareya Brahmana we have no positive evidence of the actual sacrifice of a human being as in the story of king Somaka to which I propose to revert hereafter. In the Vajasneya Sanhita[1] of the White Yajur Veda as well as in the Taittiriya Brahmana of the Krishna or Black Yajur Veda there is a long passage which refers to Purushamedha or man-sacrifice. This passage begins with the words "*Brahmane Brahmanam alabhate, Kshatrayá Kshatriyam,*" &c., *i. e.*, to Brahma, a Brahman is sacrificed, to Kshatra (the god of Kshatriyas?) a kshatriya ; and it is supposed to describe the different kinds of human victims appropriate for particular deities. Dr. Rajendralal Mitra has given this passage in full with its variations and English translation in the second volume of his Indo-Aryans (*vide* pp. 80-89), but it is too long to be quoted here as it covers nearly nine pages of the volume.

Purushamedha was generally performed for the attainment of superhuman power, and could be celebrated only by a person of the Dwija, twice-born castes. The Shatapatha Brahmana gives a full description of the Purushamedha rite. But there we find that the offering of a human victim is only formal or emblematic, as the victim as well as the animals that are tied or are supposed to be tied to the sacrificial posts are

same tale mentioned in the Devi Bhagnawat. (*Vide* chapter VII., Sections 14-17.)

[1] With reference to the passage (in the Vajasneya Sanhita) which enters into most details about human sacrifice. Paul Wurm (Gesch. der indisch. Religion Basel. 1874, p. 56) holds that this should be held in an allegorical sense, and he observes, that although at the time when the Brahmanas were composed human sacrifices occurred, yet their Aryan origin is still not proved. A repugnance on the part of the Aryans to human sacrifice is shown in the Sabha Parva of the Mahabharat v. 861, where King Jarasandha is about to slay in honor of Shiv certain captured kings and Krishna represents to him that such an offering is unheard of and displeasing to the gods.

left unslaughtered¹ after they are consecrated by turning flaming brand round them. According to the Shatapatha Brahmana (vi., 2, 1, 39) Shyaparna Sáyakáyan was the last who consecrated the erection of the altar by the sacrifice of a human being.² Human victims were (or rather believed to have been) sacrificed not only in the Purushamedha or man-sacrifice, but they were required also in the Somayaga and the Ashwamedh sacrifices. But while we have in the legend of Shunashepa (Aitareya Brahmana) a presumptive testimony that in those days the rite of human sacrifice was practised by the Hindus, on the other hand, in the same work, we meet with a passage which greatly tends to weaken the value of the presumption in favour of the practice. In this passage we are told that once upon a time the gods killed a man for their sacrifice, but that part in it which was fit for being sacrificed went out and entered a horse. The gods therefore killed the horse. But the part fit for being sacrificed went out and entered an ox. The gods then killed the ox. But in this case also the part fit for sacrifice went out and entered a sheep. The gods therefore killed the sheep. But when the sheep was killed the part fit for being sacrificed went out and entered a goat. The gods then killed the goat. But the part fit for being sacrificed went out and entered the earth. The gods then surrounded the earth, and then the part turned to rice. Hence rice became fit for being used as offering, and from this time all the animals from whom the sacrificial part (Medha) had gone out became unfit for sacrifice, and consequently unfit to eat. This leads us to suppose that the practice, if it did prevail at one time in India, was undergoing a modification even in the period of the Aitareya Brahmana. But if we accepted this passage as a proof of the modification that was gradually taking place in the rite, we cannot satisfactorily explain the necessity of sacrificing animals

---

¹ Rajendralal Mitra's Indo Aryans., II, 98.
² Barth's Religions of the Hindus, 53.

like the horse and the goat in the *Ashwamedha*, the *Somayaga* and other big sacrifices of the Hindus—a custom or religious privilege which has been observed by the Hindus from time immemorial, and which is still observed as is proved from the incident of a sacrifice recently performed by a rich Brahman at Alibag. In truth, the testimony in the Vedic Sanhitas and the Brahmanas, both in favour of and against the practice, are so very conflicting and self-contradictory that it is impossible to say definitely to what extent the rite was observed in ancient India.

Leaving the epoch of the hymns and the Brahmanas, as we approach the mediæval period of the great epics, the Puranas and the Tantras, we find abundant testimony to prove that the rite was known and tolerated by the Hindus in India. In the story of king Somaka and his son Jantu narrated in the Mahabharat, we have a distinct proof of the actual celebration of a human sacrifice. This is perhaps the only detailed record of a human victim being actually killed and sacrificed by a Brahman, and the evidence it furnishes is so strong and convincing that I am at a loss to conceive how so shrewd an observer as the late learned Dr. Rajendralal Mitra in his paper on human sacrifices in ancient India published in the second volume of his Indo-Aryans, omitted to notice this important incident. The story is interesting, and I think it will not be out of place if I give it here in full. It is narrated *in extenso* in the Vanaparva of the Mahabharat (sections 127-128) and is as follows:—

There lived a certain king named Somaka, descended from the family of Puru. Being desirous of getting a son he had espoused to himself one hundred wives. And although he did all in his power that a pious Hindu could do (by way of rites and ceremonies) to beget a son, he was not blessed with one, and for a long time he continued a sonless man. However, when he had grown old and was endeavouring every means in his power to obtain a son, a son was born to him, and he named

him Jantu. Now Jantu became an object of joy to all the
hundred wives of the king, and every one of them fondled him
and caressed him and gave him whatever things he desired.
One day it so happened that an ant stung the boy at his hip
and he felt the pain so much that he screamed loudly. The
mothers on hearing the boy scream, were all frightened and
they came near him and began to cry. Thus there arose a
tumultuous noise, which was heard by the king, while he was
sitting in his court with his ministers and family priest. The
king, therefore, made enquiries about the cause of the noise,
and his attendants informed him of what had happened.
Hearing this, the king got up and hurried to the harem and
there soothed his son. He then returned to his court and
sat with his ministers and family priest. Here Somaka
sighed and grieved that he should be so unfortunate as to have
only one son and that, too, weak and sickly. Addressing the
priest who was close by, the king said : " O ! Brahman, I married
these hundred wives after a careful selection with the object
that I may have many sons. But none of them had any issue
for a long time, and one of them has now borne this single
son who is so weak. Day by day I am advancing in years,
and so are my wiyes, and to all of us this boy is as dear and
precious as the very breathe of our nostrils. In these circumstances, will you please tell me of any ceremony (whether
great or small, good or evil) by the performance of which I
may get one hundred sons?" The Brahman replied as follows :
" Yes, there is a rite by the performance of which a hundred
sons may be obtained. But can you perform it ? If you will,
I shall explain it to you." Hearing this Somaka replied
that whether the rite be good or bad, meritorious or otherwise,
he would perform it, if by doing so, he could be the father of
a hundred sons. And he requested the priest to explain the
rite to him. Hereupon the priest said : " O ! monarch, allow
me to prepare a big sacrifice, and you must be prepared to
sacrifice your only son in the holy fire. And when you have

done so, within a short time a hundred sons will be born to
you. For, as soon as the mothers smell the fat of **Jantu**
thrown in the holy fire, they will all be *en ceinte* and will give
birth to brave and powerful sons.'

Somaka accordingly allowed the Brahman to perform the
requisite sacrifice. The royal priest now prepared the sacrifice, and was going to offer Jantu as a victim, when the mothers
objected to this cruel deed and forcibly took the boy away.
They all were smitten with grief, and holding Jantu firmly
by the hand they wept bitterly. But the royal priest heeded
them not, and seizing the child by his right hand, he snatched
him away from the weeping mothers, took him to the sacrificial hall, killed him, and offered his fat as an offering to the
sacrificial fire. And when the king's wives felt the smell of
the child's fat they grieved and fainted. And lo! as soon as
this happened, all of them conceived, and after the lapse of ten
months each of them gave birth to a handsome son. Jantu was
born of his former mother and he became the pet of all of them.
And lo! on his back there appeared a mark of gold, and he was
superior to all the other sons in wisdom and valour. In
course of time the family priest breathed his last, and soon
after the king followed him. But it so happened that the
king was carried to heaven and the priest to hell. And when
the king saw his priest cast in a hell of fire, he asked him the
cause of this, and he replied that that was the punishment meted
out to him for his having officiated at the human sacrifice.
Hearing this Somaka went to Dharmaraja (the celestial
dispenser of justice) and asked him to allow him to suffer the
pangs of hell in lieu of his priest whom he requested him to
liberate. But Dharmaraja would not condescend to this; and he
said that every man was himself responsible for his own acts,
good or bad, and that he must reap the fruit of his good deeds
or suffer punishment for his wicked acts, and that no substitute
could be allowed in the case. But the king was not satisfied
with this, and he told Dharmaraja that he must go to heaven

with the priest, and if that was not possible he would fain prefer to reside in hell with his friend and suffer the pangs with him, as he himself was a participator in the act for which the priest was punished. The lord of hell consented to this and allowed Somaka to stay with his friend, and share his sorrows, until the term for which the priest was doomed to perdition was over. The king, therefore, stayed there with his priest, and when the prescribed period was at an end, he was set at liberty together with the priest, and both were admitted tb the regions of the immortals.

The legend of Somaka is highly valuable as testifying to the actual celebration of a human sacrifice by a Hindu king and his Brahman priest. But while it proves that the rite was occasionally practised in India, it at the same time indicates that the rite was not observed as a religious duty or sacred obligation, but that it was resorted to on extremely rare occasions for the acquisition of worldly comforts, and never for the attainment of spiritual bliss. On the contrary, we perceive that it often interfered with the spiritual happiness of the performer, and paved his way to perdition. Had it been otherwise, the priest who advised the celebration of the rites killed the victim, and offered his fat to the holy fire, would not have been condemned to a hell of fire after his death.

As we come to the epoch of the Puranas and the drama of the Hindus we find a radical change in the mode of the sacrifice. Here (in the Puranas) the rite of Purushamedha is utterly discarded. By this time the teachings of Buddhism, and more especially of Jainism, had spread far and wide in India, and they were not without their influence on the followers of the religion of the Vedic Rishis. The Jainas argued that their religion was superior to that of the Brahmans because it did not sanction the destruction of life or slaughter of animals for sacrifice, which the Vedic religion of the Brahmans countenanced. The Brahmans now saw that in the doctrine of *Ahinsa* or respect for life, the Jainas possessed a very

powerful weapon of argument, and that until they armed themselves with it, they could not be able to put down successfully
the heresy of their opponents. The Smritis and the Puranas of
the Brahmans, therefore, not only prohibited Purushmedha, but
they strictly interdicted the performance of several other rites
and acts like the killing of a cow *gawálambha*, the offering of
flesh to the manes *palapaitrukam*, and the procreation of a son
on an elder brother's wife *devarát sutotpatti*, all of which
were, hitherto, freely permitted and practised.[1] But though the
celebration of *Purushamedha* was now interdicted, the rite of
human sacrifice did not become obsolete. On the contrary, it
found an outlet and affinity in the more congenial soil of the
cultus of Shaktism. The Puranas while discarding human
sacrifice as a Vedic rite, either permitted or connived at its
performance in the worship of the non-Vedic deities like
Kali or Chamunda. Kali, as has been already observed, was
one of the principal deities of the Dravidians, and the work
of assimilation of the two races had, by this time, become so
complete in several parts of India that some of the deities of
the aboriginal races came to be the deities of the conquerors
and *vice versd*, and the result of this fusion was that works
like the Kalika Puran and various Tantras and Mahatmyas
sprung up in Sanskrit to sing the praises of these goddesses,
to extol their exploits, and to show their ways of worship.
Of all the works which treat of the worship of the goddess
Chamunda and the other goddesses or mothers, the Kalika
Purana is probably the most important, though it is decidedly
more modern than some of the Tantras of that cultus. It
contains about ninety-five chapters, out of which the fifty-
seventh chapter gives most disgusting details of the way in
which the *narabali* or human victim should be sacrificed.

---

[1] अमिहीनं गवालम्भः संन्यासः पलपैतृकम् । देवराच सुतोत्पाषिर्कलौ पंच विवर्जयेत् ॥
i.e., in the Kali age the following should not be practised, viz.: (1) the maintenance of a perpetual holy fire, (2) the slaughter of cows, (3) assuming the
garb of an ascetic or Sanyashi, (4) offering flesh to the manes, and (the
procreation of a son on an elder brother's widow.

In that chapter various birds and animals are mentioned as fit for being sacrificed to the goddess Kali, such as crows, camels, crocodiles, goats, hogs, and buffaloes, but of all these the offering which pleases the goddess most is *nara-bali* or human sacrifice which is, therefore, styled *atibali* or the highes offering. In the same work, further on, it is stated that by the offer of a human victim (it must be a male and never a female) sacrificed in the prescribed manner, the goddess rests satisfied for one thousand years, and if three men be sacrificed to her at once, she remains contented for a period of one hundred thousand years. According to this Purana, the best place for performing this sacrifice is that which is not frequented by human beings, and the best time, *nishitha samaya* or the time of midnight. And certainly the goddess who (as will be shown hereafter) was a patron-deity of thieves and malefactors, could not choose time and place more convenient to her votaries for the performance of such diabolical rites.

In some of the dramas of Sanskrit poets like Bhavabhuti, we come across scenes which clearly indicate that human victims were offered to the goddess Chamunda by her votaries, for the acquisition of superhuman powers. Thus, in the fifth act of Bhavabhuti's *Málati Mádhav*, we find that Málati is taken before the goddess Chamunda by two persons named Kapalkunda and Aghoraghanta for the purpose of sacrificing her to the goddess. The former of these, as it appears from his name, belonged to the sect of the Kapálikas or the bearers of human skulls, and the latter, to the sect of the cannibals known as Aghoris. Before killing the victim Aghoragbanta addressed the goddess as follows :—*Chámunde bhagavati mantra sádhanádá ruddishtám upanihitám bhajasıca pújám*, i. e.! " O, illustrious Chamunda! accept the worship placed before thee, and which was promised for the attainment of powers for using charms and spells." Repeating these words he raises his sword to kill Málati, when suddenly her lover Mádhava appears on the scene, and rescues her from the hands of the villains.

The Bhágawat Puráṇa is decidedly the champion-Purana
or the *Puraṇa par excellence* of the doctrine of *Ahinsa* or nou-
destruction of life; but even here we find traces of the existence
of the ritual of human sacrifice among the votaries of the
goddess Chamunda or Káli. From the legend of Jada Bharata,
mentioned in the 5th part of Bhágawat, we learn that the
goddess Kali was a patron-deity of thieves and freebooters, and
that her worship required the immolation of human victims.
Jada Bharata, we are told, was one of the nine sons of a
pious Brahman descended from the family of the sage
Angiras. His father, knowing it full well that it is the father's
first duty to give his sons the best education possible, tried
his best to make his son Jada Bharata well-versed like his other
sons in the Vedic lore. But Jada Bharata, or stupid Bharat, as
his name indicates, showed no inclination to learn, and the father
died without his desires to make his son a learned man being fulfilled. After his father's demise, his brothers seeing that he acted
like an idiot, sent him to work in the fields. But here also he never
cared to work and often used to stay and wander in the jungle.
Once upon a time, it so happened that a certain king of thieves
and freebooters came to the forest, with the object of propitiating the goddess Bhadra Kali by the sacrifice of a human
victim, in order that a son may be born to him. But,
through some accident, the victim got himself released and fled,
and though he was pursued by the king's followers, owing to
the darkness and late hour of the night they could not re-
capture the victim. But, while they were wandering in this
way through the forest, they accidentally came to the spot where
Jada Bharat was sitting in an erect posture, surrounded by animals like deer and hogs. Thinking he was a person fit to be
offered to the goddess they bound him with a rope, and carried
him to the temple of Bhadra Kali. There they bathed and
consecrated him according to their rites, dressed him in new
clothes, decked him with ornaments and garlands of flowers,
daubed his forehead with red lead, fed him sumptuously, and

having taken with them things requisite for the ceremony, such as incense, lighted lamp, red lead, leaves and sprouts of trees, fruits and flowers, brought him in procession before the image of the goddess with the beating of drums and the singing of songs. Now, the priest of the king of robbers with the object of pleasing the goddess with the blood of the man, took out a sharp-edged sword that was charmed with the mystic incantation of Bhadra Kali, and was about to strike the victim with it, when the goddess, highly displeased at the outrageous and unusual act of the wicked thieves in bringing an innocent Brahman to be sacrificed to her, suddenly came out of the image, and with a terrible cry, pounced upon the villains, and cutting their throats with the sword, she drank the hot blood flowing therefrom in the company of her attendants. After getting themselves intoxicated with the bloody drink, the goddess and her retinue sang loudly, danced, and played with the heads of the thieves as if they were so many balls!

Before we pass on from the mediæval to the modern India we must not omit to notice two other kinds of human sacrifice which were common in India in the middle ages. They are:—(1) the burning of the widow on the funeral pyre of her husband, commonly known as the custom of Suttee, and (2) the act of self-immolation by a votary before the image of a deity with the object of compelling the deity to satisfy the votary's demands. Both these acts were voluntary and are not sanctioned by the Vedas. The custom of widow burning was widely known and practised in India. It is sanctioned by the Hindu Smritis, and we have numerous instances of it in the Puranas, the Mahabharata, and other religious works. Alexander the Great is said to have noticed its existence among one of the tribes of the Punjab ; and had it not been for the existence and supremacy of the British rule in India the custom would have been still in vogue in this land. In some of the obscure parts of India, like Nepaul, the custom is still practised, and I am informed that a few years ago, when the late Sir Jang Bahadur, the Prime Minister of Nepaul, died, his widow burnt herself with his corpse. A best illustration of the practice of self-immolation before the image of a goddess, is furnished in the story of King Chandrahas who, because the goddess Chamunda would not restore his brother-in-law to life, was going to offer his head to the goddess, when the goddess suddenly made her appearance, stopped him from committing the bloody act, and restored his brother-in-law to life. The story is related at considerable length in the Jaimini Ashwamedhá.[1]

In modern India, or India of authentic history, we meet with two principal modes of human sacrifice, *viz.* : (1) the Brahmanic rite observed by the followers of Shaktism, and (2) the non-Brahmanic rite practised by the Khonds and other aboriginal races. In parts of India, like Bengal and Behar, where the worship of the Shaktis predominated, the former rite was more commonly observed than elsewhere.

In the Bombay Presidency where the teachings of the followers and preachers of the Vaishnavite cultus of *Ahinsa* or non-destruction of life have cast into background the worship of the blood-thirsty mothers, the rite was not much practised among the Brahmanic Hindus except the Karhadas. It is a well-known fact that the Karhada Brahmans were accused of offering human victims to their *Kuladeri* or family goddess; and my learned friend, Professor Agarkar of the Fergusson College, Poona, tells me that the Karhadas are still suspected of perpetrating the act, and that in the out-lying parts of the Deccan, an orthodox Brahman of the old type would not dine at the house of a Karhada for fear of being secretly poisoned. In the transactions of the Bombay Literary Society (Vol. iii., p. 93) Sir John Malcolm gives the following account of the practice of offering human victims said to be prevalent among the Karhada Brahmans : " The tribe of Brahmans called Karodi had formerly a horrid custom of annually

---

[1] *Vide* Jaimini Ashwamedha (in Sanskrit), Chapters 50-57.

sacrificing to their deities a young Brahman. The *Shakti* is supposed to delight in human blood, and is represented with three fiery eyes and covered with red flowers. This goddess holds in one hand a sword and in another a battle-axe. The prayers of her votaries are directed to her during the first nine days of the Dassara festival, and on the tenth a grand repast is prepared to which the whole family is invited. An intoxicating drug is contrived to be mixed with the food of the intended victim who is often a stranger, whom the master of the house has for several months treated with the greatest kindness and attention, and often, to lull suspicion, given him his daughter in marriage. As soon as the poisonous and intoxicating drug operates, the master of the house takes the devoted person into the temple, leads him three times round the idol, and on his prostrating before it, takes this opportunity of cutting his throat. He collects, with the greatest care, the blood in a small bowl which he first applies to the lips of the ferocious goddess, and then sprinkles it over her body; and a hole having been dug at the feet of the idol for the corpse, he deposits it with great care to prevent discovery. After this the Karhada Brahman returns to his family and spends the night in mirth and revelry, convinced that by his blood-thirsty act he has propitiated the goddess for twelve years. On the morning of the following day, the corpse is taken from the hole in which it had been thrown, and the idol deposited till next *Dassara* when a similar sacrifice is made." It is generally believed that this horrible custom was forcibly put a stop to by the Peshwa Balaji Bajirao, who ruled the destinies of the Deccan from 1740 to 1761 A. D. In the Deccan human victims were offered to the *Sthánadevta* or the spirit of the place whenever some difficulty was encountered in the construction of a hill fortress, or when a supposed hidden treasure was to be dug out. The headman of a village on the lower plateau of the fort of Lohagad in Sholapur belongs to a family who gained the Patelship of the village by offering at the close of the 18th century a married couple of his family to be buried alive under the principal bastion of the fort. Human sacrifices were common in Bengal till the close of the eighteenth century and Ward gives minute details of the ritual observed on such occasions.[1] First a *Yadnya mandup* or sacrificial hall was prepared consisting of sixteen posts, six of *bilwa* six of *khadir* and four of *udumbar*. A golden image of a man and an iron one of a goat were prepared and placed in the hall, and so also golden images of Vishnu and his consort, and silver ones of Shiv and Garud. Goats and sheep were tied to the different posts of the sacrificial hall, and to the post of *khadir* the human victim was tied. The holy fire was kindled by means of a flint or a piece of glass. The priest called Brahma sat on a seat of the *darbha* grass at one corner of the altar with an alms dish in his hand and consecrated the *yadnyapatras* or sarificial utensils. Another priest called *hota* performed some other minor rites, and then offerings were made to the *Dashadigpalas* or the ten guardians of the ten directions, the *nav grahas* or the nine planets, to Rudra, Brahma, Wastupurusha, and Vishnu. After this, in the name of the gods mentioned above, was made the burnt sacrifice with the flesh of the animals tied to the posts; and this was followed by the sacrifice of the flesh of the human victim. The victim to be offered to the goddess Kali must be of good appearance, and must be washed and fed with holy food. He must also be kept aloof from flesh and women, adorned with garlands of flowers, and smeared with gandha or sandal paste.[2]

In Malabar, in the Presidency of Madras, at a shrine of the goddess Bhagawati (another name of Kali) near Manar in Tiruval a pregnant woman was every year publicly sacrificed till 1743 A. D. Subsequently the rite was performed at night and since then a sheep is substituted for the human victim.[3] In Coorg human victims used to be offered to the goddess Bhadra Kali, the patron deity of thieves, and in South Mysore it was not uncommon to pro-

---

[1] Ward's Views of the Hindus, II., 48.
[2] Maurice's Indian Antiquities, VII., 646.
[3] Madras Journal. Lit. and Sc. IX., 361.

pitiate the blood-thirsty goddess Chamunda with the blood of human victims. According to Rice (Rice's Mysore II, 228) this rite was tolerated and practised in Mysore till the year 1760, when it was stopped by that unscrupulous adventurer, the famous Haidar Ali.

Of the non-Brahmanic rites practised by the aboriginal races of India, the most noteworthy instances are found among the Khonds of Orissa, who little more than sixty years ago, used to perform human sacrifices accompanied by the most revolting features. The rite varied in details in different localities. In Goomsur the sacrifice was annually made to Taddo Pennoor (the Earth-god) as a propitiatory offering to obtain favourable crops. It was essential that the victim should be a Khond boy under seven years of age and bought for the purpose. He was clothed and fed at the public cost. For a month prior to the sacrifice there was feasting and dancing round the victim, who was called Meriah and was adorned with garlands. The day before the rite, he was stupified with toddy and was bound sitting at the bottom of a post, bearing the peacock as effigy of the god. The crowd danced round to music, and invoked the Earth-god to grant good crops in return for the offering. They then addressed the victim as follows : " We bought you with a price and did not seize, and now we sacrifice you according to our custom and no sin rests with us." Next day, the Meriah being again intoxicated and anointed with oil, each person touched the anointed part and wiped the oil on his head. All then marched in procession round the village and its boundaries, preceded by music, carrying the victim in their arms. On returning to the post, which was always near the village idol called Zecari Penoo, a hog was sacrificed and the blood allowed to flow into a pit prepared for the ceremony. The victim was then seized and thrown in, and his face pressed down till he was suffocated in the bloody mire. The priest then cut a bit of flesh from the body and buried it near the three stones as an offering to the Earth-god. All then followed the priest's

example, and carrying the pieces to their own villages buried
them near their village idol and their village boundary.
In some parts of Orissa, the most common method of sacrifice
among the Khonds was to bind the Meriah between two planks
or bamboos, one being placed across the chest the other across
the shoulders. These were first of all firmly fastened at one
end, the victim was placed between them, the other ends were
then brought together and tied, and the victim was thus
squeezed to death.[2] The Gonds of Nagpur used to offer human
victims to Bhimsen, their god of rain. The ceremony was
called the rite of Bhimsen, and it was considered of so much
importance by the people that without its performance no
Dravidian act of moment was complete, without it no festival
was celebrated, no altar consecrated, no cradle or tomb ceremony performed, no act of reaping or sowing, of war or peace,
was undertaken. As a rule, on all these occasions the ceremony
of Bhimsen was performed when a Brahman lad, well-fed
and brought up for the purpose, was sacrificed to the god
Bhimsen. According to Martin (Eastern India, iii, 169)
Bhimsen is a very common object of worship in Mithila and
still more so in Nepal. The Rajputs and the higher Shudras
seem to have the utmost regard for his memory ; and songs
concerning him are in every one's mouth.

In some parts of India, one occasion on which a human
victim was required to propitiate the spirit of the place, was
the accession of a new chief on the throne. A trace of this is
seen in some States of Rajputana in the custom which requires
that in order to avoid future mishap the new chief's brow
should be marked by a low-caste man with the blood of his
thumb. According to Col. Dalton, among the Bhuiyas of
Kunjhar in Bengal, a certain family holds land on condition
that whenever a new chief succeeded to the gadi, the family

---

[1] Major-General Campbell's Wild Tribes of Khondistan, Lond. 1864,
pp. 54, 55.
[2] Ibid. 57.

should allow one of its members to be sacrificed. At the present day whenever a new chief is to be installed, a member of the family comes forward, throws himself before the chief and then his neck is touched with a sword. The would-be victim then disappears for three days and then comes back as if miraculously restored to life.

The excavation of a well or the search for a supposed hidden treasure required the offer of a human victim. The lower classes of the Hindus still believe that whenever a difficulty is experienced in the sinking of a well, or in the construction of a bridge, or in the discovery of a supposed hidden treasure, the work can be facilitated by the offer of a human victim to the guardian spirit of the place. A case illustrating this belief occurred in one of the villages of the Madras Presidency in 1885, and was reported in one of the local papers there.[1] According to this report a certain Mahomedan purchased some landed property in Calvetty in a court-sale and proceeded to build a small house on it for his habitation. Having discovered that there was no good drinking water within his compound, he hired coolies and ordered them to sink a well in a suitable place. The work accordingly proceeded. When about twelve feet of earth had been excavated, the workers struck upon a huge copper vessel. Intimation was at once given to the owner, and he at once hired more coolies and let down strong ropes and ladders into the pit for the purpose of raising this vessel, which was believed to contain secreted wealth. However, the most strenuous efforts were of little avail, and the cauldron seemed to sink lower and lower as the sand and clay around it were dug away. The work of excavation was still continued without abatement, until there was a rush of water from all sides of the pit, and the coolies, fearing consequences, got them lifted out. By this time thousands of Moplas had gathered on the spot, and the owner proposed to hold a council to decide how he should proceed to get at the wealth which

---

[1] Vide "The Times of India" of 26th September 1885.

fortune had placed in his way. Accordingly twelve men were called aside, and after shutting themselves up in a room they proceeded to clandestinely deliberate on the matter. After a great deal of discussion, the conclusion was arrived at that the wealth had been probably deposited in the spot in question by some of the old Dutch inhabitants of Cochin, and as they usually made a human sacrifice before burying their wealth underground, so that the dead man's spirit might haunt the place and guard the treasure, a second sacrifice was necessary before the treasure was unearthed. The victim to be sacrificed was also described. He should be some old decrepit and diseased man whose life in this world was a burden and who would willingly pass away to make room for others. A person answering to this description was then procured, and under the influence of some drug was forced into giving his consent, which, after that influence had passed away, he withdrew. The Moplas not to be outdone attacked his house one night, and finding that the doors and the windows were too strong to force open, they got upon the roof, and removing the tiles proceeded to enter, when the affrighted man inside raised a cry which attracted his neighbours and thus foiled the attempts of the wicked intruders.

In many other countries of the world besides India, the rite of human sacrifice appears to have been practised ; and in some parts of Asia and Africa, human victims are still offered by the wild races. According to Shway Yoe,[1] as late as the year 1880 A. D., human victims were offered in Burmah, and it is stated that ex-King Theebaw of Burmah (in the year 1880), with the object of making the foundation of his new palace secure and the palace impregnable, planned to bury alive about five or six hundred human beings under the foundation of the palace, but for some reason or other, the plan failed. Dr. Rajendralal (in his Indo-Aryans, II, 69) thinks that the Persians were perhaps the only nation of ancient times who did not indulge in human sacrifice. But we have a historical testimony which proves that

---

[1] Shway Yoe's "The Burman," II, 207.

even the Persians in the time of Xerxes offered human victims;
for we find that in Xerxes' expedition into Greece, the Persians
buried alive nine boys and nine girls, probably with the object
of propitiating the Mother Earth.[1] In China about a century
ago human victims were sacrificed to the spirits of ancestors;
and now human figures drawn on painted paper are offered.
According to Gray[2] as late as the year 1795, the Chinese used
to place a man and a woman in the tomb of their Emperor.
In ancient times all Japanese funerals required the sacrifice of
human victims. About the time of Christ servants used to be
buried alive in Japan, but subsequently one of the Japanese
kings named Suinin ordered the cruel custom to be discontinued and substituted the burial of figures of clay.[3] In
Madagascar human victims were sacrificed on various occasions, but one of the most important occasion on which the
offering of such victims was necessary was the laying of the
foundation of the royal palace.[4] In most of the countries of
Africa one of the occasions which required the sacrifice of
human victims was the funeral of a chief. The celebrated
African traveller, the late Dr. Livingstone, states that in South
Africa when a chief dies the Negroes kill his servants in
order that they may be able to join their master in the next
world.[5] In Central Africa when the king of Dahomey dies
there are tremendous massacres, and every year a fresh batch
of messengers is sent to him.[6] The ancient Greeks and Romans
offered human victims to their divinities. The Greeks generally offered their victims to the god of rain, while the Romans
sacrificed young boys to Mania, the mother of ghosts. The
Germans offered human victims every ninth year to Odin, but
the victims as a rule were prisoners of war, slaves purchased

---

[1] Maurice's Indian Antiquities, II, 170.
[2] Gray's China, I, 314.
[3] Reed's Japan, I., 55.
[4] Sibree's Madagascar, 304 5.
[5] Livingstone's South Africa, 318.
[6] Tylor's Primitive Culture, I, 462.

iu markets or criminals sentenced to death; while the German priestesses slaughtered prisoners in cold blood and foretold future events from their blood.[1] In the eleventh century the Danes offered ninety-nine men, horses and cocks to appease their deities.[2] The Franks sacrificed women and children to the spirits of the water while crossing a river; and the Druids of Great Britain sacrificed human victims to their gods in a most cruel manner, often burning them in wicker baskets.[3]

Of all the nations of the world probably the native races of America indulged largely in the performance of this horrible rite. In Mexico children were sacrificed by the people to their divinities every year, and the number of victims thus offered was very large. In Colombia human victims were often offered to the sun-god. The victims were generally prisoners, and their blood was sprinkled upon stones on high hills or mountains. The prisoner to be sacrificed was first made senseless by administering him a poisonous drink, and was then escorted with music, singing and dancing to the place of sacrifice. Here he was requested by the friends and relatives of the dead persons to carry their messages, and then he was duly sacrificed, his blood being sprinkled on the stone as mentioned before.[4] Among the Aztecs of Mexico the celebration of every important festival required the immolation of human victims; but the largest number of victims was sacrificed when a new monarch was installed on the throne or when a new temple was consecrated. The number of victims sacrificed by these people in ordinary years was reckoned at from twenty to fifty thousand, but on extraordinary occasions, such as the consecration of the temple of Huitzilpotchli (in 1486 A. D.) it rose to a hundred thousand.[5]

From the above it will be perceived that the rite of human sacrifice was in vogue at one time or another in most of the

---

[1] Tacitus' Germany, II, 297.
[2] Mallet's Northern Ant 114.
[3] Mitra's Indo-Aryans, II, 83.
[4] Orient. 1884, p. 117.
[5] Prescott in Mitra's "Indo-Aryans." II, 62.

countries of the world ; and if we take into consideration the unpolished habits and customs of the people in different parts of the world in earlier times, and their crude ideas of God-head, it is not a matter of wonder that such revolting practices should have prevailed everywhere. With all savage or uncivilized races we find that fear of the spirit of the dead is at the root of all their bloody rites and ceremonies. All ailments, all untoward occurrences, and all accidents were, in the primitive stage of society, attributed to the machinations of the malignant spirits of the dead, and to avoid all these evils it was deemed necessary that the spirits should be kept contented. With this view all things of the dead, including his wife and servants, were buried or burnt with him. The sacrifice of *Suttee* (which primarily could not have been a voluntary act), no doubt, had its origin in this notion, and the more sublime idea of " self-sacrifice through love or affection" came into existence at a later period. Sir Alfred Lyall has truly observed that " in India at least one can distinctly follow the evolution of the ghosts of the men whose life or death has been notorious into gods ; and wherever the belief can still be found in an elementary or indigenous state, or wherever they appear to have grown up spontaneously, some of the principal deities can be identified with the spirits of departed humanity."[1]. To search for illustrations in support of the above, we need not go far. In the rite of Bhimsen which requires the sacrifice of a human victim, and a brief account of which has been already given in this paper, we have a distinct proof of it. Bhimsen is supposed to have been the same as Bhimo-devo, a local king who brought the Khonds under subjection. This king appears to have been subsequently deified by the Khonds, and to please his malignant spirit, they sacrificed human victims.

In the majority of cases, the deities to whom these bloody offerings were made in India, were the *Matris* or Mothers,

---

[1] Sir Alfred Lyall's " Natural Religion in India," p. 26.

and the Kalika Puran gives a detailed description of a number of them. Nowhere, whether in India or elsewhere, we find that these bloody rites were performed with the sublime object of attaining spiritual bliss. We find that almost everywhere the object was to gain wordly comfort, whether it be to obtain wealth, to be blessed with a child, or to ward off sickness, or to secure the stability of a castle or a palace, or to discover a hidden treasure. Even in the midst of the Hindu civilization of the epoch of the Brahmanas, we find that the Purushameda was performed for the attainment of supremacy over all living beings, and not for attaining *mukti* or salvation, as in the case of other *yagas* or sacrifices of the Hindus. That the object was invariably selfish is best illustrated by the legend of Shunashepa, where the father condescends to sacrifice his own son to Varuna in exchange for a paltry sum of money, or a hundred head of cattle.

ANTHROPOLOGICAL SCRAPS.

The following remark appeared in the *Pioneer*, dated 13th January 1894, on the paper read by Mr. W. H. Barrow, Municipal Secretary, Bombay, on the Aghoris and Aghorapanthis, before the Ordinary Monthly Meeting of the Anthropological Society of Bombay, held on the 25th October 1893 :—

CANNIBALISM IN INDIA.

In a recent issue of the *Pioneer* a correspondent referred to three manuscript volumes of *Notes on the Aghoris and Cannibalism in India* bequeathed to the Anthropological Society of Bombay by the late Mr. Tyrrell Leith, and quoted cases in which the eating of decayed human flesh by morbid devotees had been proved. " Mr. Leith," the correspondent, observed, " actually held converse with two of this sect in Benares and Allahabad, and appears to have put it beyond reasonable doubt that within recent years some of them have been seen in the streets of Bombay, in the burning ghaut at Nassick, and in different parts of

Western India, notably on Girnar and Abu. Mr. Barrow added that Dr. Kirtikar, the Civil Surgeon of Tanna, had recently discharged one of them from Tanna Jail."

When examining some records in my office lately I came across a case which proves that the horrible form of cannibalism investigated by Mr. Leith still exists in the North-Western Provinces. Though the details are gruesome and repulsive, it is, I think, worth while to publish them. A knowledge of the depths of savagery which underlies Hinduism is essential to a right comprehension of the social and political problems of India. In the case referred to, the evidence for the prosecution consisted of the testimony of two Europeans, Mr. Madden, Permanent Way Inspector on the Oudh and Rohilkhand Railway, and Mr. Tyres, a Sub-Engineer at Narore. I quote Mr. Madden's deposition in full.

" QUEEN-EMPRESS

versus

RAGHUBIR DAS.

Charles W. Madden, witness, on oath :—

" ' I am Permanent Way Inspector, Oudh and Rohilkhand Railway. I reside at Rajghat. About five weeks ago I gave a small picnic to some friends. For this purpose we went to Karan Bas. With three of my friends I went in a boat to a silt bank, a kind of island in the river, where the accused lives. On the island there is a platform on which the accused sits. It is surrounded by palings of bamboo with skulls on the top.

" ' There was lying on it a freshly-cut human head. After some little time I saw this accused take up the head, and tear from it pieces of flesh, which he swallowed. I saw him take two mouthfuls of the flesh and then I went away, as this made me feel sick. The head looked as if it had been hacked off the trunk. On many occasions I have seen cut-off human heads at the accused's place. I never, however, saw him cut off heads. Once I there saw on a bamboo a head that was quite fresh and blood dropping from it. Near it there was a bloody axe.

" ' On the occasion of the picnic Mr. Tyres saw what I did. I did not speak to accused further than to say Salam. There must have been several hundred skulls about the accused's place. One of my companions, a Mr. Johnson, spoke to accused, but I do not know what he said.'

" *Cross-examined by accused.*—' The accused caught up the head by the ears, and thus ate it. His face got all covered with blood. I can swear that he did this of his own free will. No one forced him to do so.

41

No violence of any kind was offered to him while I was present by any one. Before me he took the head up twice, and each time took a piece of flesh from it.'

" *Cross-examined by pleader of accused.*—' With me were four boatmen, those of Mr. Tyres.' "

Mr. Tyres fully corroborated Mr. Madden's evidence. The prisoner first set up an absurd defence that the Europeans had thrust the head into his mouth, and then denied that he had touched the head at all.

Mr. Lambe, District Magistrate of Budaon, decided the case on the 16th February 1888, and had no hesitation in convicting the monster under Section 297, Penal Code, of offering an indignity to a human corpse, and in inflicting the most severe punishment that can be awarded by law, namely, one year's rigorous imprisonment.   •

On appeal it was argued that no offence had been committed, inasmuch as no intention to insult the religion or wound the feelings of any person was proved, but Mr. Ross Scott, the Sessions Judge, held that accused must have known that the feelings of the European spectators would be wounded by the horrible spectacle, and, on the 7th April 1888, dismissed the appeal. The record was called for and examined by Government.

No case could have been more conclusively proved. It is shocking to think that a monster so foul should, owing to the imperfection of the law, escape with a year's imprisonment, and that he should have had a chance of escaping punishment altogether. Inquiries have been ordered and proceedings will be taken if Raghubir Das has resumed his ghastly performance.

V. A. S.

Extracts from the late Mr. Edward Tyrrell Leith's Manuscript Notes on the subject of—

" THE DOG IN MYTH AND CUSTOM."

Liebrecht,
Page 17.

    Liebrecht (Felix) Zur Volkskunde Heilbroun 1879, Grimm has pointed out that not only the physical but also psychical resemblances of animals to man, led naturally to human qualities being attributed to animals and animal peculiarities to men. The boundary lines were swept away

*Tylor's Primitive Culture.
Vol I.

by the imagination of primitive races.° Tylor says the same of modern savages. Hence we have myths of men turned into animals and animals into men, and the whole doctrine of transmigration of souls.

Thus the Dog who cohabited with *Tinneh*, the first woman, changed at night into a handsome youth.

See also the legend of the *Dogrib Indians* (Gervas, p. 169) and Muller. Amer. Urrelig, p. 65.

> Bancroft's Native Races, Vol. III., p. 507.

The Ferve Islanders have a legend that once a year Sea Dogs are changed to men.

> Liebrecht, p. 17.

The Bear and the Wolf are, according to the belief of the American Indians, children and consorts of the first woman, and in both forms the great spirit is conceived as embodied.

> Muller's Amer. Indians, p. 123.
> Liebrecht, p. 18.

The American Indian legends are given by *Muller*.

> Muller's Amer. Indi., pp. 61, 108, and 134.

The Irish legends are in Gervas of Tilbury.

> Gervas, p. 64.

The Turkish legends in Gibbon.—The founder of the Turkish race is fabled to have been a *She-Wolf*. Hence the animal is depicted on their banners.

> Gibbon, Decline and Fall, Ch. 42.

The *Tonkawas* (west of the Mississippi) believe their original progenitor was descended from Wolves, and hence a dance of men disguised as Wolves, who disinter a live member of the tribe apparently buried for the purpose.

> Liebrecht, p. 19.

The *Tugus* or Dulgass tribes trace their descent from a *She-Wolf* and the Soa-gin (Ka oche) or Tell (chili) from a Princess who cohabited with a *Wolf*.

> Liebrecht Zur Volks Kunde, p. 17.

The Batachi (a Mongolian Chief) claimed to be descended from a blue *Wolf* and a white doe. The *Tonkious* were descended from a wolf and the Mongols from a grey *Wolf*.

The Dog and Wolf are interchangeable in Myth (see Marmharst Germ. Myth, p. 198) The *Eskimo* myth is that a woman had intercourse with a dog and bore him many children. (*Rink*.)

The Aleutians trace their descent from *Dogs*.

The Ainos believe they are descended from a beautiful woman and a huge dog. (*Lindau*.)

The Chippeway Indians come from a *Dog's skin*.

The black *Kirgis* (*Kara-Kirgis*) in the mountains of Lake Issik-Kul and in Khokand derive their names from the circumstance that they come from 40 maidens (*Kirk Kige*) who returned from an expedition and found their parents, and cattle gone and home destroyed. They saw a *red* dog in the neighbourhood with whom they had intercourse and from these the tribe sprang. Journ. As. VI., emme Ser. 2-311.

Liebrecht Zur Volks K., p. 20.
Among the Islands to the west of Sumatra is *Pulo-Simalu,* which according to the Myth has been peopled by the descendants of a banished woman and a *dog,* which she brought with her (Waitz. Anthrop., Vol. v., p. 33).

Ib.
* " *Santhsai (Affairs of Indian) Book XII, fol. 27.*
Klaproth cites a passage from a Chinese work* (Nouv. Journal As.. Vol. 12, p. 288). " In the kingdom of *Dogs,* the men have the form of *Dogs,* their heads are covered with long hair, they are undressed, and their language resembles the barking of *dogs.* Their women belong to the human race and understand the Chinese language. Their dress is made of sable skins. This race lives in caves. The men eat raw food, but the women cook it. The women contract marriages with *dogs.*" *Klaproth* mentions, also, a similar tale among the *Mongols.*

Ib.
There is an Armenian work which relates of women living with *Dogs* and bearing offspring by them. Of these, the male resembles the father and the female the mother.

Ib.
The same myth appears among the people of the *Jeji* river.

Ib.
In *Tufan,* in *Thibet,* the Hiognu (Huns) were descended from a *dog.* (Z. F. Ethnol., Vol. I, p. 55.)

Ib.
Attila, the Hun, was born of a *Dog.*

Liebrecht Zur Volks K., p. 21.
Grimm (Deutsche Sagen Berl. 1816 (No. 515, 535, 571) relates the myth regarding the origin of the family of the *guelphs* from 9 or 12 boys born at one birth, who are hence called blind whelps or puppies.

Liebr., pp. 21, 22.
The *Turks* bear on their banner the *wolf* as ancestors of their race, and North American Indians have the *wolf* as cognizance of their tribe.

Ib., p. 22.
In the myth of *Romulus and Remus,* the she-wolf is the mother of the twins, and as such originally a Luperca (i. e., a Bitch). The father is *Faustules* (i e., Faunus Lupercus, or a *Dog*).

See Prenner Hestia-Vesta, p. 389, etc. Liebr., p. 22.
*Liebrecht, p. 22. (Note). A bitch also suckled *Cyrus.*
The *Lares* (*Luperci*) whose mother was *Acca Larentia* (*Fauna Luperca*) were portrayed in *dogs'* skins, and accompanied by dogs. This shows they had originally the form of *dogs.* The *Lares* were the souls of departed ances-

tors worshipped in the households as tutelary deities, and
these souls must have been originally conceived as *dogs.*
The idea of the *dog* as ancestor is the origin of this.

The form of a *Dog* was assumed by *Apollo* when he begot   Liebr., p. 22.
Telmissos, and by *Krimissos* when he begot *Akestes.*

Dogs were sacrificed at the *Luperealia.* This was   Liebr. page
originally an offering to the *Lares,* and dogs were probably   22, p. 23.
in the earliest times also eaten, as among the people of
Arkansas who worshipped the *dog* and ate it at the festival
in its honour; also in Huanca, in *Peru,* a *dog* was worshipped
in the temple and after being fattened was eaten. (Z. f.
Ethno., Vol. I., p. 56.)

According to Liebrecht, it is not surprising, after the   Ib., p. 23.
above facts, that one meets with the *dog* in connection with
the under-world and the souls of the departed.

The DOG appears on many sarcophagi. As Psychopom-
pos and Disposer of the Dead, the Dog appears in ancient
Persian conception.

Justi says that Dogs guard the path to the world beyond,
and that such is a belief common to the Aryan races, of
which traces are to be also found amongst the Hindus.
Greeks and Teutons, 'and that the gaze of the Dog drives
away evil spirits.

Also the North American Indians and New Zealanders
know the DOG as the guardian of the under-world.

To this connection with the under-world is to be ascribed,
the idea of the DOG being a spirit seer and announcing
deaths by barking.

In a certain connection with the souls of the 'deceased
appear the Armenian *Arâlez* or *Arlez* (*i. e.,* licking continually
completely), of whom it is related that they were a class of
supernatural beings or divinities BORN *of a Dog,* whose
function it was to lick the wounds of warriors fallen on the
field of battle and to recal them to life.

To return to the *Romulus* myth, we have seen that the   Liebrecht
Twins were most 'probably imagined as descended from   p. 24.
dogs, and that nothing despicable was associated with such
an idea. Among other races, the same belief existed, and not
only did they boast of such descent, but such was attributed
to kings like a Hila, and divine beings as the *Aralëz.* The

Dog also appears as a king among some nations, *i. e.*, according to Liebrecht as incarnate deities.

Liebrecht continues that in the same way as *F. B ichere* explains in Hartman's article the custom of the *Fungi* or in some similar way, may the old Norse legends be explained, according to which the Norwegian King *Eystein*, gave to the people of *Throndheim* the Swedish King *Adils* to the Danes, and the Swedish King Gumear to the Norwegians a Dog for their king   These myths acquired a totally different meaning later, when they had ceased to be understood.

breoht,   The honor in which the Dog was held in ancient days is
25.   shown by the names of famous heroes, in which it appears, *e. g.*, Hunding (Dog's son) in the *Edda*, and there still exist old noble German families of Hund or "Hundt." The same may bo said of the family of "Wolf." (Guelph.)

THE JOURNAL

OF THE

ANTHROPOLOGICAL SOCIETY

OF

BOMBAY.

THE EIGHTH ANNUAL GENERAL MEETING was held on
Wednesday, the 28th February 1894.

DR. P. PETERSON, *President, in the Chair.*

The Minutes of the previous Meeting were read and confirmed.

The election of the following new members was announced :—
Lieutenant C. Pollard, Royal Canadians, Wanowri Lines, Poona,
and Messrs. Luzac and Co., Publishers to the India Office,
opposite the British Museum, London.

The following office-bearers were elected for the ensuing
year :—

PRESIDENT.

Mr. H. A. ACWORTH, I. C. S., Barrister-at-Law.

VICE-PRESIDENTS.

Hon. Mr. JUSTICE JARDINE, I. C. S.

Mr. H. W. BARROW.

Mr. KHARSETJI RASTAMJI CAMA.

Hon. Mr. JAVERILAL UMIASHANKAR YAJNIK.

COUNCIL.

Ex-Officio Member.

Dr. P. Peterson, M. A., Ph.D., Past President.

42

Ordinary Members.

Mr. H. H. Risley, I. C. S.

Rev. D. Mackichan.

Surgeon-Lieutenant-Colonel G. Waters.

Mr. Jivanji Jamshedji Modi, B. A.

„ C. E. G. Crawford, I. C. S.

„ Purushotam Balkrishna Joshi.

„ Bahamanji Behramji Patel.

„ Basil Scott, M. A., Barrister-at-Law.

„ Nasarwanji Jivanji Readymoney.

„ Darab Dastur Peshotan Sanjana.

Surgeon-Major K. R. Kirtikar.

Mr. Denzil C. I. Ibbetson, I. C. S.

Major R. C. Temple, B. S. C.

General and Literary Secretary.

Dr. J. Gerson da Cunha.

Foreign Secretary.

Mr. O. S. Pedraza.

Treasurer.

Captain W. P. Walshe.

Curator of the Museum and Librarian.

Mr. H. M. Phipson.

The Treasurer's report showing the financial condition of the Society up to 31st day of December 1893 was read, confirmed, and adopted.

The report of the Council was then read and adopted. It contained the following information :—

Number of Members.—At the commencement of the year there were 182 Life and Ordinary Members and 10 new members were elected during the year. The names of 24 members were struck off owing to deaths, resignation, &c., &c., thus leaving 168 members on the roll at the close of the year.

Meetings.—During the year 11 Ordinary Meetings were held.

List of Papers read during the year.

1. Address of the Retiring President, Mr. H. H. Risley, on the progress of Anthropology in India.

2. Notes on two Behari Pastimes, by Mr. Sarat Chandra Mitra.

3. On the name-giving ceremony of a new born child, by Mr. Tribhuvandas Mangaldas Nathubhai.

4. On some curious customs among the Kochs, by Mr. Kedarnath Basu.

5. On Dakkhina Raya, by Mr. Kedarnath Basu.

6. On the first year's Funeral Expenses of a Parsee of the last century (1763), by Mr. Bahamanji Behramji Patel.

7. On Hindu Ceremonies observed in the Madras Presidency, by Mr. Mahomed Sufther Hussain.

8. On some additional Folk beliefs about the Tiger, by Mr. Sarat Chandra Mitra.

9. On the Jews, by Surgeon-Lieutenant-Colonel G. Waters.

10. On the use of Locusts as an article of Diet, by Mr. Sarat Chandra Mitra.

11. On some rude stone implements from Back Bay, by Mr. Fred. Swynnerton.

12. On the Aghoris and Aghorapanthis, by Mr. H. W. Barrow.

13. Further notes on the Chowk Chanda and the Panchami Vruta, by Mr. Sarat Chandra Mitra.

14. On the rite of Human Sacrifice in Ancient, Mediæval, and Modern India, by Mr. Purushotam Balkrishna Joshi.

Journal.—The second, third and fourth numbers of Vol. III. were published during the year.

Donations.—A number of books and articles of Anthropological interest were received by the Society during the year.

HONORARY TREASURER'S REPORT

For the Year 1893.

STATEMENT A.

ANTHROPOLOGICAL SOCIETY OF BOMBAY.

STATEMENT SHOWING THE NUMBER OF SUBSCRIBING MEMBERS.

Remaining on 31st December 1892	182

Add—

Admitted from 1st January to 31st December 1893...	10
	192

Deduct—

Struck off on account of Deaths	5	
Resignation, Removals, &c., &c.	13	
Retired from India	6	
		24
Number of Members remaining on the 31st December 1893		168

(Signed) W. P. WALSHE,
Honorary Treasurer.

ANTHROPOLOGICAL SOCIETY OF BOMBAY,
Bombay, 31st December 1893.

STATEMENT

Statement showing the Receipts and Expenditure of the

RECEIPTS.	Rs. a. p.	Rs. a. p.
Balance with the Bank of Bombay on the 31st December 1892...	....	969 8 3
Balance in hand of Treasurer on the 1st January 1893 (remaining from previous year)	10 0 0	
Amount realized by Cash Sale of Journals, &a.	48 8 0	
Amount of Subscriptions received during 1893, as per Statement C	1,520 0 0	
Amount received from the New Oriental Bank (in Liquidation)	153 11 11	
		1,732 3 11
ADVANCE ACCOUNT.		
Remaining in hands of the Honorary Curator from year 1892	....	13 1 6
Total...Rs.	....	2,714 8 8

Examined and found correct.

(Signed) K. R. CAMA.

„ W. S. MILLARD,

Auditors.

B.

Anthropological Society of Bombay during the year 1893.

EXPENDITURE.	Rs. a. p.	Rs. a. p.
Clothing to Peons	8 0 0	
Establishment	777 13 8	
House Rent (for 13 Months)	650 0 0	
Stamps (including Post Cards and Postages on Journals and letters, &c.)	50 11 9	
Dead-stock	17 13 0	
Printing Charges	188 0 0	
Stationery and Binding Charges	26 5 6	
Miscellaneous Charges	76 4 4	
		1,789 15 10
BALANCE.		
In the Bank of Bombay	....	924 8 10
Total ..Rs.	....	2,714 8 8

(Signed) W. P. WALSHE,

Honorary Treasurer.

ANTHROPOLOGICAL SOCIETY OF BOMBAY,

Bombay, 31st December 1893.

STATEMENT

Statement showing in detail the Amount of Subscriptions
received and the Balance

	Rs. a. p.	Rs. a. p.
Balance remaining to be recovered from previous year	......	910 0 0
AMOUNT PAYABLE FOR 1893 AS UNDER :		
Members, Life.		
4 Life Members remaining on Roll from previous year (by whom no further subscriptions are due)	......	
Members, Annual.		
(Special Subscriptions.)		
1 His Highness the Nizam of Hydrabad (Deccan) (Annual Subscription, Rs. 100)	100 0 0	
1 His Highness the Nawab of Junagad	15 0 0	
Raja Murli Manohar Bahadur	15 0 0	130 0 0
Ordinary Subscriptions.		
170 Members continuing from previous year ...	......	1,700 0 0
3 Members from whom no Subscriptions are due for 1893	......	......
Elected during the year.		
10 New Members elected up to 31st October 1893	......	100 0 0
Subscription of two Members received during 1893 in advance for 1894, as per contra ...	......	20 0 0
Carried over ..	......	2,860 0 0

C.

payable for the year 1893, and also showing the actual Amount remaining to be recovered.

AMOUNT OF SUBSCRIPTIONS ACTUALLY RECEIVED, AS UNDER:	Rs.	a.	p.	Rs.	a.	p.
Members, Life.						
3 Life Members remaining on Roll from previous year	......					
Members, Annual.						
(*Special Subscriptions.*)						
1 His Highness the Nawab of Junagad ...	15	0	0			
1 Raja Murli Manohar Bahadur	15	0	0			
Ordinary Subscriptions.				30	0	0
108 Ordinary Members	......			1,080	0	0
3 Ordinary Members from whom no Subscriptions are due for 1893	......			....		
Subscriptions for 1894 paid in advance by two Members in the year 1893	.. ...			20	0	0
From Outstanding Subscriptions.						
For the year 1888. Ordinary Members...	10	0	0			
For the year 1889. Ordinary Members	30	0	0			
For the year 1890. Ordinary Members	50	0	0			
For the year 1891. Ordinary Members	80	0	0			
For the year 1892. Ordinary Members	220	0	0			
				390	0	0
Total Actual Receipts during 1893......	......			1,520	0	0
Carried over...	......			1,520	0	0

43

STATEMENT

	Rs. a. p.	Rs. a. p.
Brought forward...	......	2,860 0 0
Total...Rs.	......	2,860 0 0

C—*continued.*

	Rs. a. p.	Rs. a. p.
Brought forward...	......	1,520 0 0
By Amount written off by reason of Deaths (Rs. 60), Resignations (Rs. 20), Temporary absence from India (Rs. 30), Retirement from India (Rs. 100)	......	200 0 0
BALANCE.		
Remaining to be recovered from 1 Member for 1888...	10 0 0	
Do. do. 3 Members, 1889...	30 0 0	
Do. do. 8 do. 1890...	80 0 0	
Do. do. 12 do. 1891...	120 0 0	
Do. do. 19 do. 1892...	190 0 0	
Do. do. 62 do. 1893...	710 0 0	
		1,140 0 0*
Total...Rs.	......	2,860 0 0

* Of this amount, Rs. 160 have since been recovered.

(Signed) W. P. WALSHE,

Honorary Treasurer.

ANTHROPOLOGICAL SOCIETY OF BOMBAY,

Bombay, 31st December 1893.

After the adoption of the report, thanks were voted to
Captain W. P. Walshe, the Honorary Treasurer, for the clear
and lucid way in which the accounts were kept by him and for
his exertions in collecting the arrears of subscriptions.

Thanks were then voted to Mr. Kharsetji Rustomji Cama
and Mr. W. S. Millard for their kindness in auditing the
accounts of the Society.

The following Presidential Address by Dr. P. Peterson, the
Retiring President, was taken as read :—

GENTLEMEN,—My first duty this evening is to thank you, as
I desire to do most heartily, for the compliment you paid me
when you elected me your President for the year that has now
expired. The position is one which I felt it to be a great
honour to be called upon to fill. My other task is to make
what small returns I can to you by the following contribution
to your proceedings. I am an amateur anthropologist; and I
have not thought it possible for me on this occasion to serve
the interests of our Society, as some of my predecessors in this
chair have done, by reviewing the recent progress of the
science, or pointing out the direction in which it may be that
new fields are to be won. You elected me, I take it, because
I am a Sanskritist ; and I have chosen rather to lay before you
from a Sanskrit book, venerable for its antiquity, a bundle of
customs relating to a subject in which anthropologists must
always be keenly interested, in the hope that my description
of things as they were in the r spect referred to in this land
upwards of two thousand years ago may throw light on, and
receive light from, other anthropological data. My subject is
marriage. I propose to go over with you the form for the
solemnization of matrimony, as that stood in Southern India in
and before the year 500 A. D. My text is the Grihya Sutra,
or household prayer-book, of Apastamba, as that has been recently put before us in a masterly monograph by Dr. Winternitz, the learned assistant o. Professor Max Müller, in the
work of preparing a second edition of that scholar's Rig Veda.

Without further preface let me ask you to imagine yourselves standing with me at the beginning of the auspicious day that has been fixed on for a marriage in that far-off time.

Apastamba dismisses in two short rules a part of the ceremonial which is treated at greater length by other authorities, the formal request, namely, for the bride, addressed to the father on behalf of the suitor by a deputation of his friends.

1. "Let him send a deputation of friends, learned in the Veda, to woo the girl on his behalf."

2. "When he dismisses them on this errand let him say the following verses : 'Go happily forth according to our design; take the best road to the house of those from whom you are to ask a girl in marriage for me. May Indra take pleasure in our alliance, seeing the soma plant. Thornless and straight be the paths along which my friends go to seek a wife for me. May Aryaman bring us together; may Bhaga bring us together ; may our alliance be blessed of you, O gods.' "

The next rule pre-supposes that the suit has been heard and accepted, and shows us the young couple face to face.

3. "When the bridegroom catches sight of the girl let him murmur to himself this verse : 'O God Varuna, grant to this woman the blessing that she may not prove fatal to her brother ; O God Brihaspati, grant to her that she may not prove fatal to her husband ; O God Indra, grant to her that she may not prove fatal to her son ; O God Savitri, do thou bless her.' "

This is the first of a set of precautions taken in this old ritual to prevent the woman from bringing evil into the house with her. This is a fear which is stated with great bluntness in another text, where the husband is directed, before consummating the marriage, to recite over his unhappy wife five verses of this kind ; "Agni (O God Fire), Thou art the expiation of the gods : I, a Brahmin, entreat thy protection. The substance which dwells in her that brings death to her husband, that extirpate in her." This is repeated with death to her children, to the cattle, to the home, to her husband's good name, substituted for the first evil deprecated. Then he is directed to empty the waterpot, into which the oblations have been poured with each single prayer, over her head with the following comprehensive invocation : " The evil substance which dwells in thee that brings death to thy husband, death to thy children, death to cattle, death to the home, death to my good name, that I change into one that brings death to thy paramour. Thus live with me to old age." It is gravely added that a wise man will avoid the wife of a Brahmin, knowing that this curse is not ineffectual.

This is followed in Apastamba by a rule to a similar purpose.

4. " Let him look her straight in the eyes, saying to himself this verse: ' Let thine eye be not unkindly, be not fatal to thy husband, be beneficent to my cattle, well-minded, well-bodied : be a mother of heroes and dear to the gods ; bring good luck to us two-footed and four-footed alike.' " The first adjuration here is obviously directed against the evil eye. Next follows a very curious development of the same idea.

5. " Let him take a piece of darbha grass between his thumb and fourth finger, and pass it lightly between her eyebrows, saying; ' Let this be the evil in thee that might be fatal to thy husband,' then throw the wisp of grass over his shoulder."

6. " If there be occasion, let him say this verse ; ' They weep for the living, though no evil has befallen her : they are wrong: let those who have prepared this feast for the delight of the spirits departed, and for the joy of the husband about to embrace his wife, think rather of the long-enduring bond.' " From other sources we know that Apastamba's somewhat oracular ʋᴏᴵᵉ.there be occasion" means " if the bride cries." For both and beᵢ.layana and Sankhayayana the same verse is prescribed or housch...asion when the bride cries at the moment of going cently put be s incumbent on the bride to weep.

nitz, the learnᵉes us to a large crop of analogies. Winter-work of preparing...qualification that it is as obligatory on the bride to weep in the Germany of to-day as it was in the India of Asvalayana. That is not the case with us in England now, whatever it may have been a generation ago. It is the case in India still. "The final moments are scenes of great sorrow, real or affected. The mother weeps violently and noisily; the women of the family beat their breasts as if the girl were going to her death; and the girl herself, who one would think was glad enough, puts in a sympathetic whine, which she stops on the slightest occasion. Meanwhile the bridegroom stands by and looks foolish." (*Punjab Gazetteer*, Delhi District, 1883-84, p. 50 fg.) In modern Greece the bride breaks out into loud wailing, and struggles as if to be allowed to remain. It is then the rule for the bridesman to say, "Let her stay, she is crying"; and equally the rule for the bride to exclaim through her sobs: "Take me away from here, but let me cry." The idea that this is a survival of marriage by capture must not be pressed. After all it is natural that the bride should cry; and even she who felt no sorrow might think it desirable to simulate it out of deference to public opinion. But this matter, put by Apastamba at the beginning of the ceremony, has in other hands taken us well-nigh to the end. Let us go back to the moment when the two are standing face to face, and he has successfully conjured the evil eye.

7. "Let him now turn to the Brahmins and say: 'Oh Brahmins, the evil must be conjured away; do you draw water, and bring it that she may bathe? Draw the waters that will avert death from her husband.'"

Now follows a complicated ceremonial, each act of which has its own verse.

8. "Let him now put upon her head a round pad woven out of darbha grass and say: 'Let the people quickly go round about the fire of God Aryaman while the mothers-in-law and the brothers-in-law look on.'"

9. "Next, let him take the yoke of a bullock-cart, and place it so that the right of the two openings is exactly over this pad,

and say: ' In such an opening of a barrow, in such an opening of
a chariot, in such an opening of a yoke, O spouse of Sachi, God
Indra, didst thou thrice purify Apala, and gavest her a body
glorious as the Sun.' " Here, of course, we are entirely at a loss
to account for the reference. We can only repeat the legend
as it has come down to us. According to that Apala was a
maiden afflicted with white leprosy. No one would marry
her. Minded to worship Indra, she one day went down into
the river to bathe. She was carried away by the stream, and
there came floating towards her a branch of the soma plant.
Crushing it with her teeth, she offered the sap to Indra.
Pleased with the sacrifice the god poured water through the
three holes of a wagon, a barrow, and a yoke, and with this
thrice purified his worshipper, who shone then like the Sun.

10. " Into this opening let him put a piece of gold, and say :
' The gold bring thee luck; the waters bring thee luck ; the pole
of the cart bring thee luck; the yoke-hole bring thee luck ; the
waters purify thee an hundredfold, and bring thee luck. Join
. thy body to thy husband.' "

11. " Then let him take the water and pour it over her [that
is over the piece of gold, through the opening in the yoke, and
so on to the head crowned with the darbha grass] and say :
' There is a stream of water, bright like gold, pure and
making pure, that flows forth free from all things evil; it
has power to purify an hundredfold ; may God the Creator
purify thee with it. There is a stream of water bright like
gold, pure and making pure ; in it Kasyapa was born, and the
God of Fire: yea, it concealed the very God of Fire within
its womb, may it bring thee good luck and prosperity. Through
the midst of it goes King Varuna, spying the righteousness
and the unrighteousness of men ; it held Agni in its womb;
may it purify thee. The many gods that are in heaven find
nourishment in it ; it held Agni in its womb ; may it purify thee.
May it look upon thee with a kindly eye; may this its body

touch thy skin for good to thee ; may this water, dropping fat, pure and making pure, bring thee all good.' "

There is no more venerable record of the antiquity out of which all in this room have sprung than the verse here which tells of the waters that are above the firmament, in the midst of which King Varuna walks spying the righteousness and the unrighteousness of men.

12. " Let him now put a new garment upon her and say, ' O Thou that hearest praise, may these my hymns encompass thee, as this garment encompasses this woman.' "

13. " Then let him gird her with one of the ropes that tie the oxen to the cart, while she says, ' Hoping for joy, children, good luck, I reverently worship Agni, and gird my body.' "

This ends the rule for the bride's purificatory bath, which is full of puzzling as well as interesting details.   It seems highly probable that the placing the opening in the yoke over her head has taken the place of an actual drawing the body of the girl through that or some similar aperture.   Such a rite of purification occurs elsewhere.   In Hanover, for example, when the bride has arrived before her husband's house, she remains seated in the cart while two rungs are being taken out of the ladder used for descending.   Through the aperture thus form- ed she is carried, seat and all, and so borne into the house. Elsewhere the bottom is knocked out of a basket, and the young men in the company put the bride through it, putting it over her head, after which the girls present do the same for the bridegroom.   The idea is the same as in the case of the passage at Walkeshwar through which you can pass in such a way as to leave your sins behind you.

14. " Let him now take her by the right hand, and lead her before the fire on the altar, saying ' May God Pushan lead thee from henceforth ; may the twin Asvins bear thee in their chariot; come to my house that thou may'st be its mistress ; and as my wife lead my devotions.'   After which he must spread a mat west of the fire in such way that the points of the blades of grass

44

point to the north ; on this they must sit, the bridegroom to the left and the bride to the right."

15. "Here let him make the usual oblation to Agni and Soma saying 'Soma got thee first; the Gandharva got thee second; thy third spouse was Agni ; thy fourth this man. Soma gave thee to Gandharva, Gandharva gave thee to Agni ; riches and sons has Agni given to me, with this woman.' "

We have now arrived, after due service of oblation, at the central point of the ceremony, which in India, as in Rome and England, consists in the solemn joining together of the hands of the pair. The next five rules deal with this.

16. " Now let him take her right hand in his right hand : the palm of his hand must be turned downwards, and the palm of her hand must be turned upwards."

I need not stop to dwell on the analogies to this among western branches of the one nation. Unless I am mistaken I have seen the officiating priest at English weddings interpose to get the two hands into the position here indicated, in the rare event of the two not falling of themselves into what is the natural position. Winternitz says that that is often seen in Germany. There follow 'some subtleties which we are ignorant of. Perhaps they never had an equal place with the joining hands itself.

17. " If he wishes to have only daughters, let him take hold of her four fingers only.

If he wishes to have only boys, let him catch her by the thumb.

If he is indifferent in this matter, let him take her by the hand up to the back of her thumb and the hair on the back of the hand."

There follows now what must be looked on as the original of our " I M. take thee N., &c."

18. " Clasping her hand let him say ' I take thy hand that thou mayest be the mother of fair offspring to me, that with me for thy husband thou mayest see old age ; the Gods

Bhaga, Aryaman, Savitri and Purandhi have given thee to me to tend my family altar. Round it they once stood as the first of those that marry; here Murdhanvat, the son of Subhru, first shone out before the gods. O Sarasvati, protect my altar, thou art the giver of good luck and all good things. May Airamma of the golden hand, he who goes through the world a purifying flame, knit thy heart to mine.' "

In one of the texts we have the rule which is still observed among us, namely, that the name of the bride must be introduced into the formula, " Let the bridegroom say, what is your name? And let her tell her name." Then let the bridegroom say " By command of God Savitri, with the arms of the twin Asvins and the hand of Pushan, I take thee (here naming her) by the hand. He must be looking west and she looking east. He must stand ; she must sit."

If this part of the ceremony is familiar to us in Europe what follows is absolutely unknown to us. I refer to the seven steps.

19. " Now let him make her, standing to the north of the fire, take seven steps to the north or to the east. She must put her right foot foremost." The verses for the seven steps are as follows :

For the first : Vishnu lead thee one for sap.

For the second : Vishnu lead thee two for strength.

For the third : Vishnu lead thee three for holiness.

For the fourth : Vishnu lead thee four for well-being.

For the fifth : Vishnu lead thee five for cattle.

For the sixth : Vishnu lead thee six for the seasons.

For the seventh : Vishnu lead thee seven for the seven sacrifices. With the seventh step, as is well-known, the marriage is irrevocable. It is marked out by the following prayer.

20. " When she has taken the seventh step let him say, ' The seventh step is taken : be my friend : the seventh step is taken, be thou my friend and I will be thine. May I win thy friendship. May I never be separated from thy love, nor thou

from mine. May we be one ; joined in love, prosperous and like-minded, dwelling together in peace and prosperity. Grant that I may be able to bring our hearts together, to bring our works together, to bring our thoughts together. Thou art thou, I am I ; I am I, thou art thou : I am the Heaven, thou art the Earth; I am seed, thou the holder of the seed ; I am mind, thou art speech ; I am a Sama verse, thou art a Rig verse. Be true to me, and bear me a man child. Come, my beloved, bear me a goodly son.' "

What are the seven steps of this old-world formula? Does not Shakespeare tell us:

" One man in his time plays many parts,
His acts being seven ages."

The rite is a beautiful symbolism of the joint life that lies before the two ; and the simple but passionate words in which the husband is directed to express his heartfelt wishes have not yet, I think, lost their power to move.

The marriage, now complete, must immediately be sanctioned by sacrifice and worship. Remember that our own marriage service ends with the note that it is convenient that the new-married persons should receive the Holy Communion at the time of their marriage, or at the first opportunity after their marriage. What is made matter of convenience for us was obligatory on the ancient Aryan. The next twelve rules have to do with this solemn sacrifice. The new-married pair, joined together in the sight of the gods, proceed to offer the first, as it is hoped, of a lengthening line of mutual daily praise and prayer.

21. " When the preparations for the burnt-offering are complete, let him lead her round the altar-fire, keeping it to the right."

22. " Let them then sit down as before (the bride on the bride-groom's right), and in that position let him make sixteen oblations, each oblation accompanied by its proper verse. During the whole of these oblations she must not loose her hold of him."

The idea that spiritual influence can be communicated from man to man if they are in touch with each other, and not otherwise, has cropped up again in modern times. Witness some of the proceedings of the spiritualists. In the same way the rich man who has a sacrifice performed to his order is directed to lay hold of the officiating priest during the whole of the ceremony. In the present case the act is of course symbolic of the one flesh that has been made out of two.

23. "Next let him lead her to the north of the altar-fire, and cause her to put her right foot on a stone placed there, and say, ' Tread on this stone, and be firm as it : tread down our foes, be victorious over our foes.' "

These two ceremonies go back to the Vedic times, and are continued in the India of our own day.

24. "Let him then direct her to put her hands together so as to form a cup-like hollow. Into this sacrificial ladle he must put a layer of clarified butter, on the top of it roasted grains of corn, and then a second layer of sacrificial clarified butter."

According, however, to some authorities, it is her brother who should do this for her.

25. "Let him now throw this offering into the fire, and say : ' Hear the prayer this woman utters as she makes her oblation—Grant that my husband may have long life : may he live a hundred autumns. ' "

26. "Let him again lead her round the altar-fire, keeping it to the right, and say : ' In the beginning they brought Surya to thee with bridal pomp ; do thou now, O God Agni, give to husbands the woman with offspring. Give, Agni, the wife with life and splendour ; and may her husband see length of days ; may he live for an hundred autumns. May we rise over all our enemies, as over a flood, by thy help.' "

27. "Let him as before [using the same verse] make her tread upon the stone."

28. "Next, let him again offer a burnt-offering, and say : ' The maidens have worshipped the divine Aryaman in the form

of fire; may that good god set her foot free from her father's house, but not from her husband's: may he establish her firmly there.'"

29. "Again, let him lead her round the altar-fire, keeping it to the right, and repeating the proper verses: again let him cause her to tread with her right foot upon the stone, to the same verse as before: again let him make a burnt-offering, and say: 'Thou, Agni, art Aryaman (the giver), forasmuch as thou givest to our young maidens a heavenly name: they anoint thee, as a firm planted tree with butter, because it is thou that makest husband and wife to have one mind.'"

30. "Last of all, let them again walk round the altar-fire, keeping it ever to the right, and repeating the proper verses."

This ritual, as will have been seen, consists of four well-defined parts—the taking fire to witness, the offering of the husband, the offering of the wife, and the treading upon the stone. It seems likely that all four symbolic acts, which are absent from none of the Grihya sutras, though these differ much in detail, are part of the original Indo-Germanic rite. Of the importance attached to the witness of fire there is an amusing illustration in Vatsyayana's Kamasutra. That author, learned in the lore of love, gives six prescriptions for running away with a girl, whose parents will not consent to an orthodox marriage. In the case of all six he dwells on the importance of having a fire handy, that the man may make offering, and that the pair may walk thrice round it. When that has been done it matters not how soon the parents of the young lady become aware of what has gone on " for it is the uniform opinion of the sages that marriages performed before fire turn not again." There are traces of this part of the rite even in England, where in some parts it was the custom, perhaps is, for the whole bridal party to walk round the church, keeping it to the right. It was part of the Roman ceremonial. In South Germany, the bride is said to be still solemnly conducted thrice round the pot-hanger in the middle of the room. The Slavonic bride has to poke up the fire, and throw a penny into the flame. In Bohemia the bride is led to the fire-side, and made to throw three hairs plucked from her head into it. In Croatia and Servia she is led thrice round the hearth, on which a fire must be burning.

The sacrifice is over, and with it that part of this ancient marriage rite which fell to be performed in the father's house. The moment has come for the going away.

31. " Let him now unloose the girdle with which he had bound her, and say, ' I loose thee from the noose of Varuna with which the kindly god Savitri bound thee : in the lap of the creator, in a world of good, I make ready for thee a fair dwelling place with thy husband. I loose from thee this noose of Varuna with which the bounteous Savitri bound thee : in the lap of the creator, in a world of good, I establish sure thy husband and thee."

The meaning of this part of the ceremony is clear enough. The time is at hand, or has come, when she is to " forget her father's house."

32. " So saying, let him lead her, or cause her to be carried out." One friend goes with them from the old house to the new, the god in whose sight they have plighted their mutual troth.

33. " Raking the fire on the altar into a pan, they bear it behind the pair."

34. " And this fire they must keep ever burning."

35. " Should it go out, it must be kindled again in one way only ; by rubbing two pieces of wood against each other."

36. "Or fire may be brought for the purpose from the house of some learned Brahmin."

37. " Moreover the wife or the husband must fast during the whole of any period that this fire is not burning."

38. " Or he may bring a burnt-offering, and say the appropriate verse, in which case he need not fast."

39. " As he props up the wagon let him say, ' The Earth is

supported by truth; the heavens are held up by the Sun: through righteousness the Adityas stand firm, and Soma is fixed in highest heaven.' "

40. "As he yokes the two oxen let him say, 'There is a god that is mighty wherever oxen draught cattle have to be spanned; we invoke him at every fight; we call our friend Indra to help us.' "

41. "He must yoke the right animal before he yokes the left."

42. "As she places her foot in the wagon let him say, 'Here is a chariot gay with kinsuka flowers, made of salmali wood, of the colour of gold, well made, and with fair wheels: step into it, O wife and go on thy way to the world of immortality, let the bridal procession go forward that it may be well with thy husband. Mount higher and higher, destroying the foes; mount on thy husband's head, and be lady of the house by reason of thy children. Rule thy father-in-law; rule thy mother-in-law; bear rule over thy sisters-in-law; bear rule over thy brothers-in-law.' "

According to other authorities the father must sit down and take his daughter in his lap, out of which she is to be taken by her husband. Compare the Roman custom according to which the bride had to be taken from her mother's embrace. In the same text the bridegroom is directed to say, as he takes the bride out of her father's lap, "May the gods we worship send back whence they came the illnesses that are wont to follow in the train of the marriage procession of the bride." To return to Apastamba:

43. "Let him take two threads, one blue and the other red, and lay them down across the track, so that the right wheel will go over the blue thread, and the left wheel over the red one. As he does this, let him say, 'Blue and red are the two, and the witchcraft that is in her cannot pass them: her relations will now prosper, her husband is in bonds.' "

44. "As the cart moves over the two threads let him say,

'May the gods we worship, &c. (as above), let no waylayers,
lying in wait, attack the bridal pair: passing along well-built
roads may they overcome all danger and see their foes flee before
them. I have entered on the well-made road, sure and prosperous, a road on which a hero takes no harm, nay, even
makes himself master of the goods of others.'"

45. "And when they pass by bathing-places, posts, or cross-
roads, let him say, O twin Asvins, do you, rejoicing in my
house grant to your worshipper riches and ten goodly sons;
make our liquor pleasant to drink, O Lord of Glory. Drive
away the wicked post that stands in our way." This last
verse furnishes perhaps a good example of the way in which
this old ritual, and all rituals, are put together. The formulæ
are not composed *ad hoc*; but are chosen from existing material.
In the present case it is the second part of a verse already old
which has won for it a place in this prayer-book.

The cross-road has not yet lost its terror for the ever young
mind of man. Only yesterday we read of the memorial to Con-
vocation of certain clergymen in England who regret the loss
of what they call the "salutary horror of the act of self-destruc-
tion" engendered by the burial of the corpse without Christian
rites at the cross-road. The symbolic barring of the way by
the two threads is curious. Two things are mixed up in it. It
is a bar, but not intended to be an effectual one, to the passage
of the bridal pair. This may be a remnant of marriage by
capture. It has analogies all over Europe. In France the
procession is brought to a stand for a moment by a rope
stretched across the streets. In Bohemia a chain is used in the
same way, having in the middle a great loop of silk, or a rope
adorned with flowers. In Texel a broom or a beam of wood
is laid across the road; in the Rhineland a chain of flowers.
In Aargau as soon as the bride, seated in the cart, has reached
the end of her native village, the young man and maidens of
the place bar her way with sticks, chains and ropes. It
is the business of the bridesman to cut a way through this

45

barricade with the bridal sword. The commentator says that the posts that are adjured are posts fixed firm in the earth for cattle to rub themselves again. Well-made roads were few in those days, and such as did exist were not well lighted. What is the origin of man's reverence for and fear of a cross-road ? Gautama classes them with temples of the gods as venerable things you must never put on your left. All that can be conjectured is that it has something to do with the burial of the dead. For the rite for suicides is a survival in their case of what was a wider practice. Pausanias, for example, tells us that the Greeks chose cross-roads by preference as a place of burial. So do the Slaves of to-day. This, of course, carries us back only one step. We do not know why the cross-road seemed to our fathers a ground to be chosen to take their rest in. But the practice may well have given to the cross-road the reputation it still enjoys. The dead are there ; and the dead know how to resent any want of respect shown to them by the living.

On the other hand, the gates that are to be burst open for the bride are to close again at once and for ever against the train of awful influences she will bring with her if the merciful gods do not send these back whence they came. This idea is clearly expressed in the verse said by the husband as the wheels of the cart go over the two threads.

46. "If they come to a river and must take boat, let him say, 'May this lord of the forest [the boat] take us to the further shore in safety; may the stream be easy to cross that we may see length of days and good luck.' " In the commentary he is directed to take up his position behind the boat and look down its length while he says this verse. The next precept is extremely amusing.

47. " She must not look at the crew."

The crew are the first strange men she has met or been thrown in contact with since she passed from her father's charge to that of her husband's ; and no time is lost in warning her that her eyes must henceforth be for her husband only. In another text the very natural rule is given that if they come to a deep place she is to shut her eyes.

48. "When they are over let him say, ' O God Indra, so may we reach the further shore of evil, and live in the light happily.'" Two European analogies can be cited. In Scandinavia care is taken to avoid, if possible, the passage of a stream between the church and the house. It means danger from evil spirits. In Slavonic countries the bride must be carried across any bridges that are in the way, if she is to escape great suffering, and even death, in childbirth. I omit certain expiatory rites and verses which are now prescribed for the event of some ill-omen actually happening which it proves impossible to avert, such as passing a cemetery, the breaking-down of the cart, &c. The feeling that hitches of this last kind are evil and foretell evil has not yet passed away.

49. "As he points out the house to her, let him say, ' Look with a reverent friendly eye at our procession and at this house with all that it contains; may God Savitri make the whole goodly show a blessing to your husband.'"

The commentator explains that the whole goodly show means the presents and ornaments of all sorts with which the friends of both bride and bridegroom have filled it. The exhibition of presents then is a rite of immemorial antiquity; and there is something to be said for this form of it, under which the bride does not as with us fly straight away from it, but finds all her treasures of the sort already decorating her new house.

50. "As he unyokes the oxen, the right one first, let him say, ' Your loving kindness, O twin Asvins, givers of all good things, has come into our hearts, you have granted us our hearts' desire: watch over us, O Lords of Glory, may we enter this house enjoying the friendship of Aryaman. May the gods Savitri, Brihaspati, Indra and Agni, Mitra and Varuna ever protect us : may Tvashtri, Vishnu, and the God of Love that shall give us children, unyoke you.'"

The solemn moment has come in which the bride must put her foot for the first time into her new home. That is not to be done lightly. The husband goes in first by himself, and makes the preparations stated in the next rule.

51. "Let him spread out in the middle of the house the skin of a bull putting the neck to the East and the hairy side uppermost, and say : 'Spread the skin for a protection and guard for this woman ; Oh Sinivali, grant that she may bear children here, and enjoy Bhaga's good-will.' Then let him cause her to enter with her right foot foremost and saying this verse : ' I enter, but not so as to bring death to my husband, this happy and kindly house, that shall be full of children, full of goodly children, it will nourish me, dropping butter : I enter it and am glad at heart.' She must pass the threshold without threading upon it." The bull's skin is a puzzle. The right foot foremost we have already had. But the precept that the bride must put her right foot and not her left first into her new home is in full force in many parts of Europe to this day. In the Upper Palatinate the bride must put her right foot foremost the whole of her marriage day, " that she may not fall from her marriage vow, but remain good and brave." In Bohemia she is warned to enter the church with her right foot foremost. The Albanians and the Slaves agree in directing her to enter her new home in this way.

In the Roman rite the bride was carried over the threshold by the bridesman, while the pronuba warned her not to let her foot come in contact with the stone. I have myself seen the same thing done in Scotland. How is it all to be explained ? The Anthropological Society must tell us. Is the bride carried across the threshold to ensure her against a stumble on the threshold of her new home and her new life ? Or is that too a remnant of the time when the weeping victim of men's violence was borne, an unwilling prey, into her husband's house ? Is she directed not to step upon the threshold because under it brownies and fairies live, who will avenge an insult to it? In Germany it is still believed that the souls of the departed are under the threshold. In building a new house care has to be taken not to tread on it, for that is apt to hurt the poor souls. The threshold is a place of burial among primitive people.

As a solemn joint sacrifice was the last part of the ceremonial in the father's house, another sacrifice is the first thing in the husband's house. I omit the details of this, merely noting that the fire used is the fire that has been carried all the way behind the pair, and that again the wife is directed to lay hold of her husband during the whole of the sacrifice. Then follows a symbolic act of great interest.

52. " Let him now place in the lap of his wife the son of a woman who has borne sons only, all of whom are alive, and say, ' It is by Soma that the Adityas are strong; it is by Soma that the earth stands fast; Soma's high place is in the lap of all these stars.' Let him give fruit to the boy, and say: ' Be fruitful, and may she shine in the world by her children.' Then [when the boy has gone] let him say: ' May the desire of my heart be granted to me in this house by your children born of thee; be wakeful here to keep my house; unite thy body to thy husband; keep my house for me when thou art an old woman. Lo! here is a wife who promises me good luck; come together and see her; give her good luck and then go your ways.' After this let him sit silent with his wife until the stars rise."

All this is extremely interesting. In the Punjab to this day a boy is placed in the lap of the young wife. The boy-bridegroom's elder brother sits down, opens her legs, and takes the bridegroom between her thighs. The bride sits similarly between the bridegroom's thighs, and takes a little boy into her lap. But, what is even more interesting, is the fact that in many widely separated parts of Europe, a similar custom prevails. In Corsica a child is put in the bride's lap; she tenderly kisses it, and then is herself embraced by the bye-standers who say : God give thee luck ; three boys and one girl. The Slavonic people do the same, and have a proverb which explains the details in the Corsican blessing. A son, they say, is the house's pillar; a daughter is an evening meal for a stranger. So the Albanians believe that an owl sitting on a house means that a death is about to take place there, or that one of the inmates is about to be delivered of a daughter !

Apastamba, curiously enough, knows nothing of another use, which flourishes to this day in every branch of the now wide-dispersed Indo-Germanic family. You will have guessed that I refer to the practice of throwing rice over the newly-married pair.

53. "When the stars are up let them rise, and go outside, and walk towards the East or towards the North. Let him point out to her the pole star and Arundhati [one of the Pleiades] and say : [for the pole star] 'Thy dwelling standeth sure ; thy seat is immoveable ; thou art firm, and firmly established : thou art the post round which the stars revolve, like oxen treading corn ; protect me against all who would do me harm.'

[For Arundhati] 'When the seven sages fixed Arundhati fast as the first of the Krittikas, the other six owned her as their queen : may this my wife ever prosper more and more, may she be another [the eighth] Krittika.' "

The seven sages are the seven stars of the great bear : the Krittikas are the Pleiades. The seven sages had the seven Krittikas to wife. Arundhati was seventh in rank, but shone pre-eminently as a true and faithful wife, and was rewarded for that by the primacy among the Pleiades bestowed upon her. You see, then, that Arundhati is for Apastamba what Sarah was for the compilers of the Christian Marriage Service, the model of a true and faithful wife. This part of the rite has not yet died out in India. Kearns' account of the marriage ceremonies of one of the communities of Southern India he treats of, ends with the words: " The couple then unite their hands and walk round the altar three times, tread upon a grinding-stone, look up in the sky at a star, and enter the room. Near Vasishtha (who is in lat. 60 N) is a small star, representing his wife Arundhati. Astrologers watch carefully their motions, because their influences are variously modified; and whatever new married couple see them in an auspicious conjunction or position, they are sure to live happily together for a hundred years." (Moor, *Hindoo Pantheon*, p. 87.)

Here let us leave our Indo-Germanic pair. I think you will agree with me that the picture is a pleasing one. The joys and the pains of the day are over, and the two stand alone together in the clear moonlight, looking up into heaven, and praying that, as Arundhati called Vasishtha lord, and trusted in the gods, so this woman, by divine assistance, may secure for her husband and herself a long, a happy, and a virtuous life.

ORDINARY GENERAL MEETING, held on Wednesday, the 28th March 1894.

MR. H. A. ACWORTH, President, in the Chair.

The Minutes of the previous Meeting were read and confirmed.

The election of the following new member was announced :—

Mr. Muncherji Framji Khan, Merchant, Chundanwady, Bombay.

The following donations were announced and thanks voted to the donors :—

To the Library.

From the Anthropological Society of Great Britain and Ireland—A Journal, Vol. XXIII., Nos. 2 and 3. From the

Asiatic Society of Bengal—A Journal, Vol. LXII., Part I.,
Nos. 2 and 3, 1893.

The following paper was then read :—

CHARMS or AMULETS *for some* DISEASES *of the* EYE.

By MR. JIVANJI JAMSHEDJI MODI, B. A.

FAITH in the virtue of charms and amulets is common to
almost all nations and all ages. The belief has been prevalent at one time or another, among almost all countries. It is
a common belief in many countries, even now, that the mere
carrying of certain medical preparations or plants on the body
of a person, has the power of healing diseases. They say that
similar faith has not entirely ceased in England even at the
present time.

Pieces of parchment with passages from the Bible were carried
about by the Jews on their bodies as amulets, and they were
known as phylacteries. Pieces of paper with passages from
the Koran are carried about by the Arabs under the name of
Tâviz (amulets). One very often comes across such amulets
among the Hindus. The subject of this paper is a similar charm
or amulet prepared by a respectable Parsee family at Nowsaree
for a complaint of the eye known as ૪ુંદ (ulcer of the cornea).
The charm is known there by the name of ૪ુંવાનો દોરો *i.e.*,
the thread for the ulcer of the cornea. A large number of
people afflicted with that complaint go to Nowsaree from
adjoining villages to take the charm from the Parsee family.
Later on I will also give the text of a Persian amulet with
passages from ancient Avesta texts. The use of that amulet is
enjoined generally for all kinds of eye complaints.

As an instance of the still surviving belief in the virtue of
amulets, is mentioned the case of the anodyne necklace
which is made up of beads formed from the roots of bryony
and which is suspended from the necks of infants with the
object of helping the process of their teething. It sometimes
happens that the particular plant, used in the charm, is believed

to possess the medicinal properties of curing a particular disease if taken internally. The popular belief, then transfers the efficiency of internal application to mere external application and turns the medicinal plant into a mere charm or amulet. How far that is true in the case of the charm I am describing this evening, I leave it to medical members of our Society to determine.

The plant whose root I have placed on the table for the inspection of the members of our Society, is known at Nowsaree as વાર મોગરી (vâr mogrô), and is used, as I have said, as a charm or an extraordinary cure for a complaint in the eye known as ૪ૐ. It is identified by Dr. Lisboa as "Jasminum Pubescens," coming nearer to "Jasminum Rottlenarum." Dr. Lisboa says, that its uses are not known, and that, like the flowers of all Jasminums, its flowers are more or less scented.

They say that there lived in Nowsaree, about 50 years ago, a Parsee gentleman, named Sorabjee. One day a fakir happened to pass by his door and was pleased with his looks. To show him his liking for him, he taught him a cure for the ulcer. He showed him the plant in the adjoining gardens and fields and asked him to follow the following instructions to make the application of the plant perfectly efficacious as a cure. He also said that the cure could only be produced by Sorabjee or some male members of the family in direct line of descent from him.

The person who is in the direct line of male descent from Sorabjee has to go to the place where the plant grows on a Saturday evening and invite the plant for the next morning. "તને આવ્જીમાવ" is the Gujarati phrase used at Nowsaree for the invitation. The process of this invitation consists in placing a few grains of rice at the root of the plant and saying "I will take you away to-morrow for the cure."

The man must go to the plant early in the morning the next day, i.e., Sunday, before washing himself and dig out the root. The root, after its being dug and cut out from the plant, must, on no account, be allowed to touch again the mother earth. It

46

must be dried and not allowed to touch any wood. It must be
kept suspended from a wall by a nail. Women in their menses,
men after their wet dreams, and persons in the state of such
temporary uncleanliness must, on no account, touch these roots,
otherwise they lose all their so-called medicinal properties.

To prepare the thread, it is necessary that the yarn must
have been prepared by a spinster. Some say that it is necessary to do so on the ધતીવીાદ મ day. Seven threads of the yarn
are woven into one which is then put round the root, so as to
pass thrice over it.

If the patient has the ulcer in the left eye, he is to put on
the thread on the right ear and vice versâ. Before so putting
it on, the smoke of frank-incense must be passed over it.

The person carrying the thread for the patient should take
care not to put himself in any state of uncleanliness. Again, the
patient must on no account let it fall on the ground or on his
bed. If it falls on the ground he is to send for quite another
thread. If it falls on a sleeping bed it must be again submitted
to the process of passing the smoke of frank-incense over
it. It must be immediately removed when the patient is free
from his complaint, otherwise it may further spoil the eye.
The family which inherits the right of producing the
medicinal properties in the above-described manner is
prohibited from charging any fees to the patients for preparing
the threads. But they sometimes ask the patients to feed the
dogs of the streets, as an act of charity in return for the cure.
It is said that hundreds of men of all religions from the adjoining villages go to Nowsaree to take the thread so prepared, for
the patients afflicted with ulcers in their villages. It is very
noticeable that in India while at times illiterate people of
different religions knock one another's head for their so-called
zeal for their religion, at other times they resort to the priests
of the hostile communities for the sake of charms and
amulets. It is not rare for a Hindoo to go to a Mahomedan
Moola, a Parsee Mobed or a native Christian Padre, nor is it

rare for a Mahomedan, a Parsee or a Christian to go to a Hindoo Brahamin, and so on, to fetch from him a charm or an amulet blessed by incantations from the scriptures of that very religion which they seem to hate with words and sometimes with blows.

The invitation to the plant in the above case on a Saturday evening, to be prepared to be taken away for the ulcer the next morning, seems to be something like an invitation to the spirit of the tree. It reminds us of the belief in the transference of a disease to a tree or to the spirit in the tree. In Eunemoser's History of Magic (Vol. II., p. 206) we find the following reference to the belief which is somewhat akin to the invitation to the plant in our above story of Nowsaree.

" Amongst the forms of adjuration we find the commencement thus, " Twig, I bind thee; fever now leave me." Westendorp relates the following Netherlands practice: " Whoever has the ague, let him go early in the morning to an old willow tree, tie three knots in a branch, and say, 'Good morning old one! I give thee the cold; good morning, old one!' He must then turn round quickly and run off as fast as he can without looking behind him."

This belief in the transference of a disease to something else reminds us of the so-called cure for another complaint of the eye, known as the અાંજણી (stye).

The best remedy believed in, for curing this, is the knocking at midnight, at the door of the house of a man who has two living wives. While doing so he has to utter these words, " અાંજણી ઘર બાંજણી. અાજે મને તો કાલે તુને"

i.e., Stye! you are the breaker (of the peace) of a house. To-day it is my turn, to-morrow it will be yours."

This cure for the અાંજણી reminds us of another cure for the same. The mere application of a dried bomaloe or Bombay duck upon the stye is believed to be efficacious, because the અાંજણી (stye) is said to be of the Brahamin caste (બ્રાહ્મણની જાત). And as the Brahamins, being strict vegetarians, shudder at the

sight of fish, so the stye being a Brahamin by caste, will shudder at the sight of the bomaloe and will immediately leave the
eye of the patient on the application of that [fish. (Compare
the following:—

"A singular remedy is adopted against dyspnœa or fainting,
which they call 'mountain sickness.' This they (the Kirgese)
represent to themselves under the form of a young lady, before
whom they utter to the patient, the most obscene and disgusting expressions, thinking thereby to shock the lady's modesty
and drive her away."—*Chinese Central Asia. Vol. I., p.* 124, *by
Dr. Lansdell*).

The above story, of a charm for the eye prepared by a
respectable Parsee priestly family at the direction of a fakir,
naturally leads us to inquire if there are any strictly Parsee
charms or amulets for the eye spoken of in the old Persian books.
We find nothing on the subject in the older books, but the later
Persian Revâyats give a Tâviz or an amulet for curing all
general complaints of the eye. I have taken the text of
this amulet from the manuscript copy of the Revâyat-i-Burzô
Kavám-ud-din belonging to Mr. Edalji 'Kersaspji Antia,
Zend teacher at the Sir Jamshedji Madressa. The text gives
the following instruction as to how the amulet is to be put on

بر دست چپ بستن تا درد چشم دفع شود بواج بهرام ایزد گرفتن
و بشتن

i.e., "To be tied on the left hand until the complaint of the
eye is cured. To tie and untie it with the Bâj of Beheram
Yazad."

The text of the amulet.

(¹)·۱۹ویللڈ سوسلس یس اکبا ۰ئی یکس ۰ئبی
سکیدده بیو ۰ئیی یار یر ۰ئرہی ۰ئدم دمن سمم ۰سدیخ ۰سیو-

(¹)   We find these sentences also in the Pâzand portion of the Vanant yasht.

[Four lines of Avestan/Pazand/Pahlavi script, with interlinear Persian notation]

Translation.

"In the name of God. In the name of the strength and splendour of Fredun the son of Athawyân. We praise the swift-horsed Sun. We praise the immortal, glorious and swift-horsed Sun. We praise the strong-eyed Tishtrya. May (so and so, *e. g.*, Ader Cheher the son of Ader Cheher), by virtue of the strength and power of the splendour of Fredun, the son of Athawyân, by virtue of the strength of the northern stars be healthy in body. May it be so. May there be good life and good marks. May it be good. May it be so."

The text of the amulet is written in a mixture of Avesta and Persian characters. Again it is written in Avesta, Pazand and a little of Pehelvi. It does not seem to be the production of a iterary man, versed in the sacred books.

Now, it is worth inquiring why Hvarê Khshaêta (the Sun), Tishtrya (the star Sirius) and Fredun, the well-known monarch of the Peshdâdyan dynasty, alluded to by Sir Walter Scott in his Talisman, are mentioned in this Persian amulet or talisman.

The reason why the Sun, the star Tishtrya (Sirius) and other stars are mentioned in the amulet for the eye, seems to be

---

(¹) This and the next sentence are taken from the Khurshed Nyâish.

(²) Here must be written the name of the patient. *e. g.* Ader Cheber son of Ader Cheher.

that the old Persian books of the Avesta use a metaphorical
language in which these luminaries are represented as possessing good strong eyes. Poets very often compare eyes with
the sun, the moon, the stars and such heavenly bodies. For
example the Sun is spoken of as the " bright eye and monarch
of the world." So the Avesta speaks of the Sun and the Mithra
as the eyes of Ahura Mazda ·ﺳﻮﺳ· . ﻭﺩﺩﺭﺟﻰﺳﻼﺟﺩﻭﺩﺭﺟﺩ ﺭﺳﻰ)

(ﻛﻮﺳﻰ، ﻩ· .ﻣﺩﻭﺩﻻﺩﻣﻰ yaçna LXVIII —22). Mithra the god of

light is said to be the possessor of ten-thousand eyes-ﻣ ﺭ)) ﺩﻻﻣﻣﻰﺩ

ﻩﻯ ﻣﻋﻣﻭﻣﻰﺭ yt. X. 7). The star Tishtrya is said to possess good

strong eyes (ﻩﻯ)ﻣﻋﻣﻭﻣﻰﺭﺩﺭ)ﻻﻭ Khurshed Nyâish 7).

Now the reason why the name of Fredun is mentioned in
this amulet is, that to this renowned monarch of the Peshdâdyan dynasty of ancient Iran, are attributed by later traditions
the supernatural powers of curing many diseases by charms and
amulets. This Fredun is the Thraêtaona of the Avesta who is
compared with the त्रित of the Vedas. He is spoken of in the
Fravardin yasht (yt. XIII—131) as having discovered some
cures for fevers, snake-bite, &c. The Pehelvi Dadastan-i-Dini
alludes to this when it refers to him as a person knowing all kinds
of medical cures. (ﻣﺭﻋﻻﻭ ﺭﻣﻭﻩ ﻩﻭﺭﺭ ﻻﻭ XXXVII—
35.) The Pâzand portion of the Vanaut Yasht alludes to this
fact. Mirkhond in his Rauzat-us-safa speaks of Fredun as
being very friendly to physicians and as being an ardent student
inquiring into the nature of human constitution.[1] Later
books say that it is owing to his connection with all kinds
of medicines and cures that the name of Fredun is mentioned
in various Persian charms and amulets,

---

[1] Shea's Mirkhond. p. 172

I beg to lay on the table for the inspection of members a ring which is the property of Dowager Lady Ruttonbai Jamshedjee. It is intended to be used as a cure for the ulcer in the cornea of the eye. It is made of a kind of stone having on one side the form of an eye with the eye-ball and the white of the eye clearly marked. This amulet is enjoined to be passed over the eye several times every morning by some person other than the patient, and it is believed to lessen the ulcer or the opacity of the cornea gradually.

ORDINARY GENERAL MEETING held on Wednesday, the 25th April 1894.

Mr. KHARSETJI RUSTAMJI CAMA, *Vice-President*, took the chair.

The Minutes of the previous Meeting were read and confirmed.

The election of the following new members was announced:—

Mr. Kaliandas Keshavdas, B.A., 43, Manoredas Street, Fort, Bombay. Mr. Harilal Harshadray Dhruva, B.A., LL.B., Judge, Naosari, and Mr. Ochchavram Nanabhai Haridas, B.A., LL.B., Solicitor, Malabar Hill, Bombay.

The following donations were announced and thanks voted to the donors :—

To the Library.

From the Royal Asiatic Society, Ceylon Branch. A Journal Vol. XI., No. 41.

From Berlin—Zeitschrift Fur Ethnology for 1893 Heft **VI.** The following Paper was then read :—

A few ANCIENT BELIEFS *about the* ECLIPSE *and a* FEW
SUPERSTITIONS BASED ON THOSE BELIEFS.

By Mr. JIVANJI JAMSHEDJI MODI, B.A.

THE last eclipse of the Sun on the sixth of this month has
suggested to me, the subject of my paper this evening. Sitting
on the veranda of my house the previous evening, 1 heard
a few mill-hands talk various things about the phenomenon
and about the customs to be observed on the occasion. I
thought that an inquiry into the belief of the ancient Persiant
about the cause of the eclipse, a comparison of that belief with
the beliefs of other ancient nations, and an enumeration of
the superstitions based on those beliefs, would form a fitting
subject for a paper before this Society. Hence this paper.

The ancient Aryans and the different nations that
descended from them held a belief that the eclipse was the
result of a fight between a hostile power and the Sun or Moon
as the eclipse happened to be solar or lunar. Though according to Sir Monier Williams, Arya-bhata who lived in the fifth
century after Christ, knew the true theory about the cause of the
eclipse, the Mâhabhârata points to a similar belief among
the ancient Hindoos. Dowson thus describes the belief. (¹)

" Râhu is a Daitya who is supposed to seize the sun and
he moon and swallow them, thus obscuring their rays and
causing eclipses. He was son of Viprachitti and Sinhikā.
and is called by his metronymic, Sainhikeya. He had four
arms, and his lower part ended in a tail. He was a great
mischief-maker and when the gods had produced the Amrita
by churning the ocean, he assumed a disguise and insinuating
himself amongst them drank some of it. The sun and moon
detected him and informed Vishnu, who cut off his head and
two of his arms, but, as he had secured immortality, his body
was placed in the stellar sphere, the upper parts, represented

<hr>

(¹) Dowson's Classical Dictionary of Hindu Mythology. The word R. hu.

by a dragon's head, being the ascending node and the lower parts, represented by a dragon's tail, being Ketu the descending node. Ráhu wreaks vengeance on the sun and moon by occasionally swallowing them." The same story is referred to in the Vishnu Purana. Thus it is the fight between the Daitya Ráhu and the sun or moon that causes the solar or the lunar eclipse. According to Pictet (¹) it is this story that has given the Sanscrit word ráhugráhai its secondary meaning of eclipse. The same authority gives different myths of the same kind prevalent in other nations. The Mongols have taken this belief from the Indians with this difference, that among them Arachu has taken the place of Ráhu. The Scandinavians say that there are two wolves Sköll and Hati which always run after the sun and the moon. Hati which is also known by the name of Mánagarwr (the dog of the moon) will in the end devour the moon. It is this tradition that has given rise to the Burgundian phrase " May God save the moon from the wolves," which is used ironically for a distant danger.

The ancient Greeks at one time believed that Diana or the moon once fell in love with Endymion, the beautiful shepherd when he once slept unclothed on Mount Latmos and that the lunar eclipses were due to her absence from the Heavens to pay her frequent nocturnal visits to her lover on the earth.

The Romans believed that the sorcerers and magicians, especially those of Thessaly, had the power to bring the moon down to the earth from the heaven to aid them in their enchantments and that the eclipse was due to this attempt on the part of the magicians. The Chinese belief about the eclipse is thus described by Lewis Le Comte.(²) "All nations have ever been astonished at eclipses, because they could not discover the cause of them ; there is nothing so extravagant as the several reasons some have given for it ; but one would wonder that the Chinese, who as to Astronomy may justly claim seniority over

---

(¹) Les Origines Indo-Européennes Tome II., p. 85.

(²) A complete History of the Empire of China. by Lewis Le Comte, Jesuit, pp 70 and 487.

47

all the world besides, have reasoned as absurdly on that point as the rest; they have fancied that in heaven there is a prodigious great dragon who is a professed enemy to the sun and moon and ready at all times to eat them up. For this reason as soon as they perceive an eclipse, they all render a terrible rattling with drums and brass kettles till the monster frightened at the noise lets go his prey . . . . . While the astronomers are in the tower to make their observations the chief Mandarins belonging to the Lipon fall on their knees in a hall or court of the palace, looking attentively that way, and frequently bowing towards the sun to express the pity they take of him or rather to the dragon to beg him not to molest the world by depriving it of so necessary a planet." The same author later on thus describes what he saw during an eclipse.

"The Chinese were terribly alarmed, imagining that the earth was going suddenly to envelope in thick darkness. They made a hideous noise all abroad to oblige the dragon to be gone. It is to this animal that they attribute all the disappearances of the stars, which come to pass, they say, because the celestial dragon being hunger bit, holds at that time the sun or moon fast between his teeth with a design to devour them." (¹)

Coming to the belief among the ancient Persians we find no reference to the eclipse in the oldest writings of the Avesta. Among the Pehelvi books we find the Dinkard only saying that the moon shines with the light of the sun. (²) It is the Dadistan-i-Dini (³) that attempts to explain the cause of the eclipse. The sixty-eighth question in that work runs as follows :

ﭘﺮﺳﻦ ﺯﻣﺎﻧﻪ ﭘﺎﺳﺦ ﻭ ﺑﻪ ﭼﺮﺍ ﺧﻮﺭﺷﻴﺪ ﻭ ﻣﺎﻩ

ﺧﻮﺭﺷﻴﺪ ﺳﺘﺎﺭﻩ ﺍﯼ ﮐﻪ ﮐﯽ ﻭ ﻣﺎﻩ

(¹) A complete History of the Empire of China, by Lewis Le Comte. Jesuit p. 187
(²) Dastur Pehelvi Vol. I. 316.
(³) S. B. E., Vol. XVIII. West's Palahavi Texts, II. Ch. 69

When something catches hold of the Moon or Sun, what is
the cause (vahâné) of it? and from what does it always catch
hold?

The reply is as follows:—

[Pahlavi script text, eleven lines]

Translation.

" Two opaque (avin) dark faces (or bodies) move and revolve
far below the sun and the moon. When in the usual revolution of the sky, they pass below the sun or below the moon,
it (*i. e.*, one of the two opaque bodies) becomes a covering
and stands as a curtain ([Pahlavi]) over the sun. Thus it is

that the sun or the moon is not seen. Of both these opaque bodies one is called the head and the other the tail. Their motion is explained in the calculation of astronomers. However, in standing in the way of, and in covering those luminaries, they do not thereby (actually) raise a covering over those luminaries. From (the fact of) the luminaries being, in a place pure and free from opposition, and from (the fact of) the (two) concealers (of light) being far below them, there results no diminution of light in those luminaries, except this, that their light is concealed from the world, and that their all-adorning energy of supplying light to the earth during that time is incomplete."

It appears from this passage that the ancient Persians believed that the eclipse was caused by two opaque dark bodies interfering between us and the luminaries, that these dark bodies moved much below the luminaries, and that their cutting off, of the light of the luminaries was temporary. We do not find in the Dadistan-i-Din-any clear reference to the two opaque dark bodies as being distinctly hostile to the sun and the moon, but the following passage in the Shikand Gumanik Vijar shows, as Dr. West says, that these bodies were hostile to the luminaries :

"And these two fiends that are greatly powerful who are opponents of the planetary sun and moon move below the splendour of (those) two luminaries."(²)

The idea of there being some heavenly bodies opposed to other heavenly bodies is not entirely foreign to Persian belief.

---

(1) The text published by Dr. Hoshang and Dr. West, p. 139, ch IV. 46.
(2) S. B. L. XXIX. Dr. West.

According to the Zadsparam (¹) some heavenly bodies are said to belong to the good creation, and others, for example, the planets, to the evil creation. Again, there is another thing to be noticed in the Mâhabhârata version of the cause of the eclipse and the Dadistan-i-Díni version. One of the two interfering dark bodies is spoken of in the Dadistan-i-Dini as the head (sar) and the other the tail (dûmb). So in the Mâhabhârata, Râhu's body being cut into two pieces by Vishnu, his upper parts were represented by a dragon's head and his lower part by a dragon's tail.

Not only do these references in old books point to a belief in a fight between a hostile power and the luminary as the cause of the eclipse, but as Pictet points out, the very words for eclipses in different nations point to that belief. For example the Persians speak of the eclipse as گرفت ماه‌تاب or آفتاب گرفت i.e., the capture of the moon or the capture of the sun.(²) The Pehelvi word)٣()٢) vakhdûntan used in the above passage of the Dadistan-i-Dini is also a synonym of Persian 'giraftan' and means "to catch hold of, to seize." The Sanscrit ग्रहण which has come to mean an eclipse in Gujarati has also the same primary meaning. According to Pictet ' camman,' the old Irish word for eclipse, signifies ' combat.'

Again a few proverbs of different nations also point to the belief that a fight with a hostile power was the cause of the eclipse of the luminary. For example, the tradition of a fight between two wolves and the sun or the moon being the cause of the eclipse, has given rise to a proverb among the Burgundians which is used ironically for a distant danger but which literally means " May God save the moon from the wolves." The Tamils also hold the belief of the fight and so we find in one of their quartrains, illustrating ' generosity

---

(¹) S. B. E. V. West's Pehelvi texts I., ch. III., 4.

(²) Vide the word گرفت in Dr. Steingass's Persian-English Dictionary.

to fallen foes', a reference to this belief. An old quartrain says :—

" Worthy men, when they behold where foes are foiled, themselves too feel sore-abashed and do not hasten on to crush them. Behold the strong invulnerable dragon draws not near the moon (to swallow it) when it is in its tender crescent days."(¹) Again take our common Gujarati proverb ꠱ꠣ꠰ꠣ ꠣꠣ꠱ꠣ. When two persons begin a quarrel we generally say ꠱ꠣ꠰ꠣ ꠣꠣ꠱ i.e., the eclipse has commenced.

We will now speak of some of the eclipses immortalized in history, as having produced, by a superstitious belief in them, marvellous changes in the destiny of great men and great armies.

Eclipses were generally regarded by almost all the ancient nations as precursors of some events of great importances. Herodotus supplies us with some instances. When the famous bridge over the Hellespont was completed by the Persian king Xerxes, the occurrence of an eclipse of the sun struck the monarch with alarm. "At the moment of departure," says Herodotus, " The sun suddenly quitted his seat in the heaven, and disappeared, though there were no clouds in sight, but the sky was clear and serene. Day was thus turned into night ; whereupon Xerxes, who saw and remarked the prodigy, was seized with alarm, and sending at once for the Magians, inquired of them the meaning of the portent.

They replied—" God is foreshadowing to the Greeks the destruction of their cities; for the sun foretells for them, and the moon for us." So Xerxes thus instructed, proceeded on his way with great gladness of heart."(²)

According to the same authority it was a solar eclipse that had frightened the Spartan general Cleombrotus into recalling

---

(¹) Naladyár. Four Hundred quartrains in Tamil by G. Pope. p. 155.
(²) Rawlinson's Herodotus, Bk. I , Ch. 37.

his army from the task of building the wall at the Isthmus. (¹)
Again it was an eclipse, known subsequently as the " Eclipse
of Thales," being predicted by him, that had frightened the
two fighting nations the Lydians and the Medians, into
entering into some terms of peace. (²)

Malcolm, who believed that Cyaxares the Median king spoken
of by Herodotus, was the same as Kaikáoos of Firdousi, points to
a passage in the Shâh-nameh (³) as referring to this above eclipse
predicted by Thales of Miletus. In the expedition of Kâoos to
Mazenderan, according to Firdousi, Kâoos and his army were
' struck with a sudden blindness which had been foretold by a
magician." Malcolm says, that the predicting magician is
no other than Thales of Miletus and that the blindness was
nothing but the darkness caused by the eclipse. (⁴) I think it
is a far-fetched comparison of events suggested to Malcolm
by his zeal to find striking resemblances between the events
of the reigns of the two monarchs. If Firdousi's account of
the phenomenon refers to anything, it is to a sudden volcanic
eruption.

From Tacitus we learn that Drusus the son of Tiberius made
use of the occurrence of a lunar eclipse, which occurred during the
time of a revolt by three Roman legions under his command, to
frighten his soldiers and thus to suppress the revolt. Tacitus
thus describes the event, " The night that followed seemed big
with some fatal disaster when an unexpected phenomenon put an
end to the commotion. In a clear and serene sky the moon was
suddenly eclipsed. This appearance, in its natural cause not
understood by the soldiers, was deemed a prognostic, denouncing
the fate of the army. The planet, in its languishing state,
represented the condition of the legions ; if it recovered its
former lustre, the efforts of the men would be covered with

(¹) Bk. IX., 10.
(²) Bk. I., 74.
(³) Vuller I., p. 328.
(⁴) History of Persia, Vol. I., p. 515.

success. . . . . . The crowd in the meantime stood at gaze: every gleam of light inspired the men with joy, and the sudden gloom depressed their hearts with grief. The clouds condensed and the moon was supposed to be lost in utter darkness. A melancholy horror siezed the multitude ; and melancholy is sure to engender superstition. A religious panic spread through the army. The appearance in the heavens foretold eternal labour to the legions and all lamented that by their crimes they had called down upon themselves the indignation of the gods. Drusus took advantage of the moment." Tacitus then describes at some length how Drusus by promises and by the terror caused by the eclipse, subdued the spirit of the insurgent soldiers (Annals Vol. I., 28) (¹).

Plutarch, in his Lives (²) refers to several eclipses which had agitated the minds of great men and great nations in antiquity. An eclipse of the sun at the time of the death of Romulus had greatly agitated the minds of the Romans. An eclipse at the time when Pericles was embarking for an expedition against the Pelopnesians had frightened the pilot and his men. "The whole fleet was in readiness, and Pericles on board his own galley when there happened an eclipse of the sun. This sudden darkness was looked upon as an unfavourable omen and threw them into the greatest consternation. Pericles, observing that the pilot was much astonished and perplexed, took his cloak and having covered his eyes with it, asked him, "If he found anything terrible in that, or considered it as a sad presage ?" Upon his answering in the negative, he said, " Where is the difference between this and the other, except that something bigger than my cloke causes the eclipse ? " (³)

In the last Macedonian War, the Roman Consul Æmilius Paullus, predicting the occurrence of an eclipse, by his superior knowledge of Astronomy, prepared his soldiers for the event

---

(¹) The Works of Tacitus by A. Murphy. Vol. I.
(²) Plutarch's Lives, translated by J and W. Languorus, Vol. I . p. 88.
(³) Ibid, p. 299.

and cheered them up while the phenomenon spread terror and alarm in the Macedonian army. According to Livy, it was Sulpicius-Gallus, a general of the Consul, who predicted the eclipse. The event is thus described. " An eclipse of the Moon, it was known to Sulpicius, would occur that night, and he thought it prudent to prepare the soldiers for it. When the eventful moment arrived, the soldiers went out indeed, to assist the moon in her labours, with the usual clamour of their kettles and pans, nor omitted to offer her the light of their torches ; but the scene was one of amusement, rather than fear. In the Macedonian camp on the other hand, superstition produced the usual effect of horror and alarm ; and on the following day the result of the battle corresponded to the feelings of the night." According to Plutarch, the Consul, Æmilius Paulus, sacrificed eleven heifers to the moon and several oxen to Hercules on that occasion. (¹)

When Dion was preparing an expedition against Dionysius of Syracuse, an eclipse of the moon alarmed his soldiers. Miltas, the diviner, " assured them that it portended the sudden obscurity of something that was at present glorious; that this glorious object could be no other than Dionysius, whose lustre would be extinguished on their arrival in Sicily." (²)

In the expedition of the Athenians led by Nicias against the Syracusans, a lunar eclipse retarded the retreat of the Athenians.(³) " Everything accordingly was prepared for embarkation, but in the night there happened an eclipse of the moon, at which Nicias and all the rest were struck with a great panic, either through ignorance or superstition . . . . . . They looked upon it, therefore, as a strange and preternatural phenomenon, a sign by which the gods announced some great calamity . . . . . . Supposing the eclipse a prodigy, it could not, as Philochorus observes, be inauspicious to those who wanted to

(¹) Ibid Vol. I., p 450.
(²) Ibid Vol. III., p. 392.
(³) Ibid Vol II . p. 242.

18

fly, but on the contrary, very favourable; for whatever is
transacted with fear, seeks the shadow of darkness; light is the
worst enemy. Besides, on other occasions, as Anticlides remarks
in his commentaries, there were only three days that people
refrained from business after an eclipse of either sun or moon;
whereas Nicias wanted to stay another entire revolution of the
moon, as if he could not see her as bright as ever the moment
she passed the shadow caused by the interposition of the
earth."

Now we come to the question of the different customs and
usages observed by different people at the time of the eclipse, (a)
either with a view to help the luminary in his supposed
difficulty, (b) or to threaten and frighten his supposed opponent,
so as to force him to slacken his strong grasp of the
luminary.

To help the luminary in his difficulty, some resort to self-
sacrifices, offerings, or prayers. For example, the Mexicans
fasted during the eclipses just as our Hindoo friends do.
But it is difficult to determine exactly, what it was that led
people to fast during the eclipses. Perhaps it was a pious
desire to participate in the grief of the luminary that was
supposed to have been attacked by an opponent. Some are
frightened into fasting, lest the extraordinary event may bring
some mischief during the process of eating. Again, it is
possible the origin of the custom may be due to the desire of
undergoing a little privation in order to avert a greater mishap.
It is a little sacrifice to propitiate the powers to avert a greater
danger. The latter view is illustrated by a custom of the
Mexican.women, who, they say, maltreated themselves on such
occasions, while their young girls got themselves bled in their
arms. This belief of the Mexican women, brings us to some of
the observances observed by Indian women on such occasions.
Women who are *enceinte* are advised to lie down during the
eclipse, so as to avoid coming under the shadow of the eclipse,
lest the evil influence of Râhu might overtake them and their

children in embryo. They, as well as their husbands, must avoid cutting or breaking anything during the time of the eclipse. If they do not do so, their future children are affected some way or other. Children with cut ears or defective parts of some members of the body, are sometimes pointed out to us, as the result of carelessness, or obstinacy on the part of the parents in not properly observing this rule of abstaining from cutting or breaking anything during the time of the eclipse. The ancients believed in the influence of the moon on women. The moon had all feminine characteristics, and was therefore a female goddess while the sun possessed the male characteristics. The sun and moon as such, represented the creating and conceiving powers of nature. That being the case, it is not surprising to find women, especially those in the state of conception, ready to show in various ways their sympathy in the grief of the luminary when attacked by a supposed opponent. Among the customs observed by the ancient Romans, we find a peculiar mode of helping the luminary to get out of his supposed difficulty. It was the custom of lighting torches and candle-sticks and of pointing them to the sky to recall the light of the eclipsed luminary. Plutarch refers to this custom in his life of Æmilius Paullus. ([1])

Again the custom of raising cries and creating noise and bustle, with a view, either to help the luminaries in their hours of trouble, or to frighten their adversaries, seems to be very old. It was prevalent among the Romans of the first century after Christ. As pointed out by Pictet, Juvenal in his well-known satire on women refers to this custom when he says ([2]):—

"Such a power of words falls from her, you would say so many pans, so many bells were being struck at the same time. Let no one henceforth fatigue trumpets or brasses; single handed she will be able to succour the moon in labour." As

---

([1]) Plutarch's Lives translated by Langhorne, Vol. I., p. 450.
([2]) Juvenalis Satiræ, by Lewis Satire, VI., 440-43.

Lewis observes, this was due to the old Roman belief referred to above, that magicians and witches were endeavouring to bring the moon down from heaven to aid them in their enchantments and that she could be relieved from her sufferings by loud noises, the beating of brass, and the sounding of trumpets, produced to drown the voices of the enchanters. They say that the home of this custom of creating a noise with trumpets at the time of the eclipse, was ancient Egypt where Isis the moon was honoured with the play of drums and trumpets. It is usual, even now, to see that in some of the Native States the appearance of the new moon is announced with a flourish of trumpets and a play of drums. Tacitus also refers to this custom among the Romans. Describing the lunar eclipse which occurred during the time of the revolt of the three Roman legions in the time of Emperor Tiberius, he says " In a clear and serene sky the moon was suddenly eclipsed . . . . . . To assist the moon in her labours the air resounded with the clamour of brazen instruments, with the sound of trumpets and other warlike music " (¹).

The custom was prevalent even in the middle ages. It is said that "the people of Turin used to greet eclipses with loud cries for which St. Maximus of Turin who lived in the fifth century after Christ had to rebuke them. Two centuries later St. Eloi is said to have preached against this superstition." According to Birgman the Mongols also made loud cries, to save the luminaries from their enemies. The custom is still prevalent to a certain extent. Mr. Child (²) says of the Siamese that at the time of the eclipse " guns, crackers, gongs. and other instruments of rattling and confusion innumerable, are brought into requisition to frighten the fabulous monster Râhu from his effort to swallow the sun or moon." The Siamese resort to this custom also on the occasion of their new year's day to expel evil spirits from the precincts of the city

(¹) The Annals of Tacitus Bk. I., 28. Translated by A Murphy, Vol. I.

(²) The Far East Asia. . . Five Years in Siam. by J L. Child, p 261.

and thus to bring about prosperity and happiness. Pictet says
that this custom is still prevalent among the Greenlanders and
also among several tribes of Africa.

In India this custom is said to be more or less prevalent
in several parts ; but on this side of the country, the principal
means believed to be efficacious and therefore adopted to
relieve the luminary is to present offerings and to give alms
in charity. Hence it is not uncommon to see Hindoo women
throw તીલ તાંદૂર (i.e., seed and grain) high in the air towards
the luminary supposed to be in affliction, with the words
છોડ ગ્રહણ, છોડ ગ્રહણ i.e. Leave your grasp. The words very
often heard in the Bombay streets announcing the commencement of the eclipse, viz., દીએ દાન છૂટે ગ્રહણ tend to the same
belief. It is generally the lower classes such as the Mângs
and the Dhers that go about in Bombay streets, uttering the
above words, and asking for alms. The presence of these lower
classes is accounted for by the following story which is on its
face a corrupted version of the original Mâhabhârata story
given above. I give the story as narrated to me by a Hindoo
mill-hand on the evening preceding the last solar eclipse.

Rama on his return from Lankâ, after the victorious fight
with Râvan, gave a feast to his victorious army. Mâhadev and
Pârvati were serving the meals. Mâhadev drew the attention of
Pârvati to the presence of a low class Mâng in the assembly
and asked her to be careful, and to serve him the meals
from a distance. This drew the attention of Râm who slew
the Mâng boy for daring to go there to mar the sacredness of the feast. The mother of the boy took up the head,
placed it in a basket and tried to resuscitate it with fresh water.
With the basket containing the head of her lost son, she goes to
the gods and goddesses to ask for her meals. In turn she goes
to the sun and the moon and asks meals from them threatening to touch them in case of refusal and thus to desecrate
their holy character. It is the shadow of her basket that
causes the eclipse and so it is to remove this Mâng woman, this

importunate creditor, from the sun and the moon, that people are asked, to give offerings to the luminaries and alms in charity to Mángs and Dhers on this earth. This story explains why it is that Mángs go about for alms and why the words ધણ દીન છૂ મહેલ are uttered in our streets.

It was usual among the Parsees until a few years ago to say prayers on such occasions and to recite especially the Máh-bokhtár Nyáish in the praise of the moon during lunar eclipses. Mr. Gaspard Drouville said of the Zoroastrians in Persia in the early part of this century that (¹) " Ils adressent leurs prières au soleil, et les-jours d' eclipse sont pour eux jours de désola-tions et de deuil ; ils se posterent alors la face contre terre et ne se relevent qu'au retour des rayons de cet astre."

Extracts from the late Mr. Edward Tyrrell Leith's Manu-script Notes on the subject of—

"THE DOG IN MYTH AND CUSTOM."

(Continued from page 806.)

Liebrecht Zur Volks-kunde, p. 350.

The Bœotians had a custom to pass between a Dog cut in half, as a means of purification. Liebrecht sees here a puri-fying new birth brought about by a sacrifice He points out that Dogs were often employed as Purification-Sacrifices among the Greeks and Romans.

Ib. p. 349.

The cow, if she is desired to be fruitful, is led between the front and back parts of a cart after they have been separated.

Ib. p. 350.

Diodorus relates that an Egyptian King dreamt he could only be happy and reign long if he cut all the priests in two and passed with his retinues between the parts.

Liebrecht speaks of the custom of taking the hair of the dog that bites one.

Dog Sacrifice.

See Pictet, Vol. III., p. 252.

Achilles throws 2 dogs and 4 horses on the pyre of *Patroklos.*

Pictet. Vol. III., p. 252, p. 253. See Grimm., p 247, p. 254

Cæsar states that the Gauls burnt with the dead all he had loved and also animals.

The Russians immolated a *Dog,* a cock and a hen with the dead.

(¹) Voyages en Perse faites en 1813 Tome II. p 193.

Dog-Demon.

" O my friends, drive away the long-tongued *Dog* of a demon, who would approach the ever-victory-conferring sacrificial viands placed beside the exhilarating expressed juice, *i. e.*', Soma."

Sama Veda, Part 11-1-8.

" Of the nourishing sacrificial liquids (let no marrer of sacred rites hear even the sound). Drive away therefore every DOG, as polluting the solemnity, in the manner the sons of Bhrigu beat off the Dog Makka.

Ib. Part 11-2-22.

Dog's Burial-Suicide.

In the middle ages in Germany suicides were subjected to a dishonourable burial called the *Dogs-burial*. The corpse was flung from the window or dragged from the spot where it lay with ropes by the common executioner, placed on a Knacker's cart and buried under the gallows or place of execution or where dead cattle were buried. The term " *Dogs-burial* " refers probably to the manner of Jezabel's death, who was flung from the window and devoured by dogs. This shews that exposure of the corpse was considered a dishonor by the Jews of that day.

The Lithuanians sacrificed horses, 2 hounds and a falcon with the dead.

Grimm. Ver brem, pp. 349–25(.

Black Animals.

The color black was with the Greeks, that of animals offered to the infernal deities or at funerals.

Pictet, Vol. III., p. 253.

To ward off evil spirits from a babe, in the Island of *Rügen*, a knife is placed in the bed, in order that it may cut off the head of the " *Saalhund*," the evil spirit.

Hecuba was transformed into a bitch.

Dog.

Prokis (the dew according to *Cox*, Vol. II., page 91) is deserted by Kephalos, her lover, who afterwards returns in disguise and wins her love again. When she discovers the deception she takes refuge in Crete and receives from Artemis a spear which never fails to hit its mark and a DOG which always seizes its prey. She gives both to Kephalos who, while she is in hiding, kills her with the magic spear.

Cox Mythology of the Aryan Nation, Vol. 1., p. 459.

In Baldin's dream, in the *Elder-Edda* we read—

Cox. Vol. II.,
p. 94.

" Then uprose Odin, the all-Creator
And flung the saddle on Sleipnir's back,
And downwards rode he to Nebelheim
Where a *Dog* met him from the lofty mansion of **Hel.**
Spotted with blood on his front and chest
Loudly he bayed at the father of song :
But on rode Odin, the earth made moaning
When he reached the lofty mansion of Hel."

Dog in Avestha.

Havelacque
L'Avesta
Zoraostre et le
Mazdeisme,
.337.

Whether the respect which the *Mazdeans* professed **for** the dog was a special motive, or was a recollection of **ancient** occurrences of ancient beliefs of which the true **meaning** may have been forgotten, is what we cannot tell : should **we** simply view the cause of it in the gratitude which the **dog** so justly inspired for its good services in a society, where the country life, the cultivation of the earth, the breeding of cattle played so considerable a part ? Perhaps both are correct.

Dog-Angel, Spirit of Ancestor.

The first twin pair roast a sheep and they dropped three handfuls of the meat into the fire and said, "this is the share of the fire." One piece of the rest they tossed to the sky, and said, "this is the share of the Angels " A bird, the *vulture*, advanced and carried some of it away from before them, as a Dog ate the first meat.

Dog-faced Men.

Pliny His.
Nal VII.,
11 14-22.

According to *Megasthenes*, on a mountain called *Nulo*, there live men *whose feet are turned backward*, and who have eight toes on each foot ; while on many of the mountains there lives a race of men having *heads like dogs*, who are clothed with the skins of wild beasts, whose speech is barking, and who, being armed with claws, live by hunting and fowling.

Hist.Générale
des Voyages
(Prevost) La.
Haye, Vol.
IX., pp.
271 272.

Carpini (1246) in his ' Voyage to Tartary' tells of a nation on the shores of the Northern ocean who had the hoofs of an ox and the face of a Dog, and of another race dwelling near the desert which were formed like dogs.

THE JOURNAL

OF THE

ANTHROPOLOGICAL SOCIETY

OF

BOMBAY.

ORDINARY GENERAL MEETING, held on Wednesday, the 27th June, 1894.

MR. H. W. BARROW, *Vice-President*, in the Chair.

The Minutes of the previous Meeting were read and confirmed.

The election of the following new members was announced :—

Mr. G. Lawrence Gomme, President of the Folklore Society, London, 1, Beverley Villas, Barns Common, London, S. W. ; and Mr. C. C. James, Drainage Engineer, Municipality, Bombay.

The following donations were acknowledged and thanks voted to the donors :—

To the Library.

From the Anthropological Institute of Great Britain and Ireland, Journal Vol. XXIII., No. 4.

From the Royal Asiatic Society, Ceylon Branch, Journals Vol. XII., No. 43 ; and Vol. XIII., No. 44.

From Wien Mittheilungen der Anthropologischen Gesellschaft in Wien, Band XXIV., Heft II.

From Berlin, Zeitschrift der Gesellcshaft Fur Erdkunde, Band XXIX., 1894, No. 1.

From Berlin, Zeitscrift Fur Ethnologie, 1894, Hefte 1.

From Berlin, Verhaudlungender Gesellschaft Fur Erdkunde, Band XXI., 1894, Nos. 4 and 5.

49

From Netherlands Indie, Bijdragen.tot-de-Faal, land, en Volken Kunde for 1894.

From Paris, Melusine, Tome VII., Nos. 2 and 3.

The following paper was then read :—

On some BEHARI CUSTOMS AND PRACTICES.

By Mr. SARAT CHANDRA MITRA, Corresponding Member of the Anthropological Society of Bombay.

IN Behar, the wife's elder sister does not appear before and talk to her younger sister's husband. Of course, this custom holds good of the higher classes of Beharis. The younger sister's husband is called বহিন আমাই, and wife's elder sister is looked upon more in the light of a mother-in-law than in that of a sister-in-law. The wife's elder sister also, in her turn, looks upon the younger sister's husband more in the light of a son-in-law than in that of a brother-in-law, and, consequently, treats him as such. This Behari custom is quite the reverse of that prevailing among the Bengalis. In Bengal, the wife's elder sister not only appears before her younger sister's husband, but talks to him and cracks jokes at his expense. The brother-in-law, in his turn, can only flirt and crack jokes at the expense of his wife's younger sisters only, and not with her elder sister.

The Beharis consider it consistent with propriety and decorum to flirt and crack jokes with their মামী or mother's brother's wife, and, on the other hand, think it improper to crack jokes with those ladies who stand to them in the relation of grand-mother, that is to say, with their father's and mother's mothers and aunts (paternal and maternal and otherwise). In Bengal, however, the মামা or mother's brother's wife is looked upon more in the light of a mother than anybody else ; and to crack jokes with her, in Bengal, would not only be considered as highly improper, but would also be considered as a sign of the want of good breeding. A Bengali, on the other hand, can crack jokes to his heart's content with those ladies who stand to him in the relationship of grand-mother. In Bengal, a grandson's cracking jokes with a grand-mother means that he can say to her that he can marry her, call her his wife and indulge in free and unrestrained talk with her;

whereas she can call him her husband, can say that she can
marry him and indulge in that sort of language.   On the other
hand, a father's sister (पिसी), mother's sister (मासी), mother's
brother's wife (मामी) are looked upon in the light of a mother,
and the tie of relationship with them is hedged in with such
sanctity as cannot be violated even by talking freely with her.
The Beharis, in this respect, differ from the Bengalis in not
looking upon the mother's brother's wife as a mother, in
cracking jokes with her and calling her names.   The Bengalis,
resident in Behar, look upon this Behari custom as repugnant
to their notions of propriety.

In Behar, to beat one with an earthen pot (हंड़ीसे मारना),
or the mere threat to do it is considered as highly insulting.
This method of retaliation is always resorted to by womenfolk
in Behar.   If the हंड़ी or earthen vessel be कैले or one blackened with soot, then the insult is all the more keen and cutting.
Lately I saw an instance of this curious practice.   Our Hin-
dostani cook at Chupra, lately had occasion to fall out with an
Âhirini आहिरिनी or milk-woman who supplies milk to our
household, and, in the course of altercation, gave her a blow ;
whereupon the milk-woman poured forth the vial of her wrath
by threatening that she would beat him with a hândî or earthen
vessel (हंड़ीसे मारब).   My wife also tells me that she also saw
an instance in her father's place at Bankipore.   Once, she tells
me, a Behari Brâhman cook beat a Behari झाड़ or maid-servant
for some reason or other, who retaliated the assault by striking
him with a blackened hândî or earthen vessel which was lying
in the court-yard of the house, and which she picked up for
that purpose.

There is a curious way of greeting prevalent among the
lower classes of Behari women.   Whenever a low-class Behari
woman meets another of her sex after a long time, or after
long separation, they greet each other by clasping each other
with their arms round the neck, and beginning to weep.*   Greet-

---

* This way of greeting is adopted even in pastimes by little children. There
is a kind of game called *Churnik Mauniya*, in which several girls construct
houses of dust and prepare cakes of clay to present to others whom, for the time
being, they consider their relatives. They take these to another girl's house of
dust for the purpose of presenting them to her. *The girl to whose house a girl*

ings after long separation are always expressive of joy and pleasure at seeing each other after a long time ; but it is difficult to
make out what these Behari women mean by giving full vent
to their long-pent-up griefs and shedding tears on such a
joyous occasion. Perhaps they act up to the principle enun-
ciated by the myriad-minded Bard of Avon in the following
lines :—

> " Give sorrow words ; for the grief that does not speak.
> Whispers the o'er-fraught heart and bids it break."

Of course, such an absurd custom does not prevail in Bengal.
Bengali women never weep, like their Behari sisters, on such
joyous occasions as meeting after long separation. In Bengal,
if a death takes place in a family, and the friends and relatives
of the deceased come on a visit of condolence, the practice is
for the bereaved members, especially the female ones, of the
family to weep or give expression to loud lamentations, for the
departed one. But it is considered an ill-omen to weep by
way of greeting on such joyous occasions as meeting after long
separation or after a lapse of long time. In Chupra, I have
frequently come across such instances of greetings. Hearing
loud wailings in the street, I have often sent out servants to
enquire what was the matter, and they used to come and
laughingly say that the women had been weeping because they
had met after a long time. It is only lately that I came across
instances of this method of greeting. On the occasion of the
Rámanavami festival, a fair is held at Tháway—the country-
seat of H. H. the Maharaja Bahadur of Hutwa—where there is
a temple dedicated to the Goddess Bhaváni. In fact, it is considered as a पीठस्थान (*Pithasthán*) or a place where one of the
dismembered limbs of Satl—the spouse of Siva—fell, after her
corpse had been whirled round by her husband with his *trisúla*
or trident. Now this place being but a few miles from Hutwa,
I went thither to see the fair. While perambulating through
the grounds—in and among the various booths that had been
erected by the many tradespeople who had come thither in
hopes of driving a roaring trade—I heard loud wailings in one

or two places, and I, at first, thought that some mishap had
occurred to somebody. But, subsequently, I found out that it
was the weeping of women who had met each other at the fair,
and were thus greeting in this fashion.

While on the subject of greetings, I may mention here—
though it would be somewhat out of place in a paper dealing
with the customs and practices of the Beharis--that there is a
curious way of greeting in vogue among the Bhootias—a hill-
tribe inhabiting the higher altitudes of the Himalayas, in and
about Darjeeling. When one Bhootia salutes another, he
pushes his own tongue out of the mouth and then pulls or
scratches the ear of the other. The other Bhootia, also, recipro-
cates the greeting by lolling out the tongue and pulling or
scratching the ears of his acquaintance. An European lady,
who had sojourned in those parts and among the hill-peoples
inhabiting those tracts, for a long time, thus writes about the
Bhootia greeting : *

"Presently Fanchyng—a young Bhootia woman, the wife of
one of my servants, who had accompanied us on this expedition—
uttered a short, sharp cry, and, springing to her feet, exclaimed, 'Oh ! Mem Sahib, look !' and was off like an arrow.
Her quick and eager eyes had descried her brother's (who had
been missing from our camp) form, standing amongst the
little knot of men who were assembled round the watch-fire.
I did not see the *greeting,* but no doubt *it was attended with
great pulling of the ears and lolling of the tongue,* and other
odd demonstrations of welcome and delight, as the manner of
these people (the Bhootias) is." Again : "Many of the
peasantry, also, had by this time collected together to see us,
and as they recognised old acquaintances amongst the members of our camp, *an exchange of salutations took place, the form
being to push out the tongue, genuflect, and scratch the ear*—a
ceremony we frequently saw performed during our stay in this
singular country."

The lower classes of men in Behar, such as the Kurmis,
Kandus, Kahárs, who mostly follow the profession of palankin-
bearers, &c., salute each other, when meeting in the streets,

---

* "*The Indian Alps and How We Crossed Them.*" By a Lady Pioneer.
London : Longmans, Green, & Co. 1876. Pages 438 and 526.

&c., by saying " *Ram, Ram.*" Rama, King Dasarath's son, is a more popular deity among the Beharis than among the Bengalis. The belief that anything expressive of the name of the deity tends to the salvation of a man from sin is the origin of the salutation " *Ram, Ram*" among the lower classes of Behari men when accosting each other in the streets. Similar salutations expressive of the name of God or the Creator are to be found among other races of men all over the world. The expression " Ram, Ram" is, on the other hand, expressive of disgust among the Bengalis.

The Hanumân or Entellus Monkey (*Semnopithecus entellus*) is held very sacred by the Beharis, and is often worshipped by them as a deity under the name of Mahâbîrji. There are images of the Mahâbîrji to be seen almost in every temple, which are regularly worshipped. The Hindus of Chupra were lately very much exercised in mind over the attitude of the " city fathers" of that town, who proposed to acquire for pub-lic purposes a piece of land containing a Neem tree having an image of the Hanumân or Mahâbirji engraved thereon, and to lop off some of the branches thereof. The Hindus of that town entered an indignant protest against such high-handed proceedings on the part of the local Municipality, and carried the matter up to the Commissioner of the Patna Division, who stayed proceedings pending an amicable settlement of the whole affair. There are troops of the Entellus Monkey to be seen in Hutwa, which often devastate the orchards in its neighbourhood. But, as it is held sacred, there is a standing order of the local authorities not to molest or otherwise mal-treat these monkeys, even should they be guilty of dire offence-In the time of the late Manager of the Hutwa Raj, gram used to be daily given to the Hanumâns infesting Hutwa and its neighbourhood. Large earthen troughs were placed in the ground under the large Peepul tree close to the *math*, and large quantities of gram used to be soaked in water contained therein, which were doled out to these monkeys in the evening. Strangely enough, the monkeys gathered in large troops in their feeding-ground just at the prescribed time.* But this

---

* On Mount Jakko near Simla lives an old Fakir surrounded by all the monkeys of the neighbourhood. At his beck and call, his simian companions

humane arrangement has been discontinued since sometime past. So sacred is the Hanumân held in Hutwa that none dare strike, let alone kill, one of these monkeys, for fear of being visited with condign punishment. On one occasion, a Hanumân had been killed in a village near Hutwa, as it had become rabid and bitten a child severely. Enquiries were made, and it was found out that the monkey had been killed by the villagers. They were severely taken to task for this offence. In the Upper Provinces of Northern India, too, this monkey is held sacred, for there is a temple dedicated to the Monkey-god at Benares, and there are troops of sacred monkeys at Muttra, to kill one of whom is considered an inexpiable sin. In Bengal, neither the Hanumân nor the common Macaque monkey is considered sacred.

The origin of this idea of sanctity†attached in Behar to the Hanumân or Entellus Monkey is that a mythical animal of that species is said to have accompanied Râma in his expedition to Ceylon against the demon-king Râvana, to have bridged up

---

assemble about him *Vide* Marchioness of Dufferin's " *Our Viceroyal Life in India*," Vol. I , p 136.

† That this monkey is, also, sometimes killed for sacrificial purposes there—by showing that it is not held sacred, will appear from the following account of an unconscious survival of Spring Human-Sacrifice existing in a remote part of the Gorakhpur District of the North Western Provinces :—

"On the Western precincts of the town of Gopálpur, in the district of Gorakhpur, there is a small hamlet inhabited by the tribe of potters who manufacture tiles only, unlike their brethren of the town who manufacture earthenware vessels. The inhabitants of the village, I am writing of, live mainly on the produce of the soil which they cultivate with care, and the manufacture of tiles brings them money sufficient to pay the annual land-rent. They are considered, therefore, first-rate cultivators rather than potters. Ten years before I had often occasion to visit the village. being in possession of some land in the same village, and the potters being connected with my family as debtors. Then I saw that the potters—men and boys—used to hunt a monkey (apparently the Hanumân, for it is very common in Sâran and the adjoining district of Gorakhpur—the common Macaque monkey being very scarce) in the month of Mágh. the commencement of spring, and crucify it on the margin of village lands. They said that their doing so over-awed the monkeys in general, who damaged the fields and kept the demons and evil spirits off the field who, they said. destroyed the young plants. Be what it may, this is apparently an unconscious survival of spring human sacrifice. My father, who permanently lives in Gopálpur, tells me that the practice has not, even now, totally died out in spite of the Brahmanical prejudice against it, as Brahmans regard monkeys in general as the incarnation of Hanumân. *Vide North Indian Notes and Queries* for December 1893. Note No. 317.

the narrow strip of sea intervening between ·that island and
the mainland of Hindustan, and to have otherwise rendered
that hero yeomen's services.

In Saran, the lower classes of the people believe that looseness of the bowels is produced by one of the intestines getting
dislodged from its usual position within the abdominal cavity.
If a person is having too many evacuations of the bowels,
the people superstitiously say that his नाड़ उखाड़ गया है, that is,
his intestines have got out of position. So the only remedy
they adopt in such cases is to send for the local quack who
rubs the abdominal region vigorously and is thus believed to
set the intestines in order.

In Behar, the lower classes of women affect a peculiar kind
of brass collar-like ornaments called पेंड़ी (Peyñri) which they
wear on their legs. It is heavy, nearly one foot in breath, and
serrated all round the edges. It cannot be put on the legs
except with the aid of the blacksmith, who fits the ornament—
rather instrument of torture—on to the legs of the woman
with his hammer, while she lies stretched upon the ground
writhing with pain. Such is the partiality of Behari women for
these ornaments that they would rather undergo the torture
of putting them on than forego the pleasure of indulging in
this vanity. Curiously enough, the heavier this ornament is
the more beautiful is the wearer thereof considered. The same
is the case with thick bell-metal bangles worn in Behar by the
Âhiriuis or women of the Âhir class (the milkman caste of
Behar). These bell-metal bangles are worn sometimes on one
hand and sometimes on both, and reach up to the elbow-joint of
the wearer. The greater the number of the bangles, the more
beautiful is the wearer considered. This reminds one of the
ornaments of the native chieftainesses of the interior of Africa,
described by Stanley in his *Boy Travellers on the Congo*. These
ebony-skinned beauties wear round their necks enormous coils
of brass wire or heavy hoops of iron, and the heavier the coils
or hoops are the more are the personal charms of the woman
enhanced. Strange case of fashion in deformity.

In Behar, persons suffering from some painful or incurable
malady, often take a vow that, in case they recover from their
illness, they will visit some sacred shrine, not travelling by

foot, but crawling on their chest, and offer *puja* to the deity presiding over that fane. I have seen instances of this vow occasionally in Chupra. Lately I came across one or two persons, in the Fair at Tháway, crawling on the breast and going to the temple of the goddess Bhawání there. The method of proceeding is as follows : the person takes a bit of stick in his right hand, and then, kneeling down, stretches himself at full length on the ground. Then stretching forth his right hand, draws a line on the ground with the stick in his hand, and then gets up and advances a little and places the great toe of his right foot on the line drawn in the ground and, then kneeling down, again stretches himself at full length on the ground, and, in the manner aforesaid, again draws a line with the stick in his right hand and again gets up and proceeds in aforesaid manner till he arrives at the temple. In this way, the persons performing the vows, travel over great distances from their homes to the shrine. After arrival, he offers up *puja* to the goddess and his vow is thus performed. I have heard that, in Bengal, also, this form of vow is in vogue. Trustworthy persons have informed me that persons go in the aforesaid manner to the temple of the god Táraknáth at Tára-keshwar in the Hugbly district and perform their *puja* there.

Another popular form of vow performed in Behar on recovery from illness is महावीरजीके भ्र जा चढ़ाना or erecting a flag-staff in honor of the monkey-god Hanumán or Mahábírjí. First of all *puja* is offered to the monkey-god, then a tall bamboo-pole surmounted with a streamer of red cloth is planted in the ground, and, last scene of all, some Bráhmans are fed. I saw an instance of this ceremony in Chupra. The *taid* or native mohurrir of a Bengali pleader of the Chupra Bar had an attack of cholera, but recovered from that fell disease. After his recovery, he performel this ceremony by way of thanks-giving to the Great Healer of all human ills and sorrows.

On MARRIAGE CEREMONIES *among the* KAPOLA BANIAS.

BY Mr. TRIBHOWUNDAS MANGALDAS NATHUBHAI.

THE ceremonies are various and numerous. Some of these ceremonies are prescribed by the Shastras and some are based on custom. In regard to the ceremonies based on custom it should be observed that ceremonies differ as whims or caprices differ. Those prescribed by the Shastras are unalterable, as the Shastras are the Revelation of the Divine word, but those, based on custom, are capricious. They differ with times and circumstances. But it should be observed in favour of these ceremonies, that in performing the ceremonies, there is a secret underlying, that *the symbolism of to-day has been the belief of yesterday.* Ceremonies in old times were observed with a political and religious view. But at present they have lost their political significance, though it is alleged that ceremonial actions, done with an unbiased and pure mind, turn out good results, and it is said t hat some have originated, from experience of old ladies (which is termed Doshi Shastras). The religious signification of the ceremonies enjoined by the Shastras has been preserved, which is that performing the ceremonies means abiding by God's will and commandments and ask his favour in the way prescribed by the Shastras in any thing we do, as the proverb says, " man proposes and God disposes."

Thus various ceremonies are observed, some as enjoined by the Shastras and others based upon custom. The list of all the ceremonies is as follows :—

    *(1) Vridhi Shrádba or Benediction ceremony.

    *(2) Lagan Lakhvoo or fixing the marriage day.

    *(3) Adará Shesh or ablution ceremony.

    (4) Gotraj Worship.

    (5) Panch Kan Viná or sorting five different kinds of grain.

    *(6) Khát Pujan consisting of—

        (1) Arghya Sampádan.

        (2) Punhyá Váchan.

        (3) Mandap Ropan. (Pillar erecting.)

    (7) Chák Vadháv (welcoming the wheel-tyre).

(8) Lâdka Lâdu.

(9) Pithi anointing ceremony.

(10) Ukardi Notarvi. (Inviting dogs, &c., or bringing clay as some say.)

•(11) Grih Shânti. (Propitiation of the Planets.)

(12) Hathe Vâlo Vâtvo. (Powdering or grinding by hands.)

(13) Lâdi Dodi.

(14) Varnu. (Present of clothes, ornaments to a bride, &c.)

(15) Kalvo. (Present to a bridegroom of clothes, &c.)

(16) Procession and arrival at bride's house.

(17) Ponkhnoo. (Welcome of the bridegroom.)

*(18) Madhu Park Archan. (Entertainment of the bridegroom by Madhu Park.)

(19) Cheda chedi Bandhan. (Tying the ends of garments of both the bride and bridegroom)

•(20) Hasta Melâp. (Joining the hands.)

*(21) Kanyâ Dân. (Giving the bride.)

*(22) Swasti Vâchan. (Blessing giving.)

(23) Removal into Mâhiru.

(24) Removal to Chori.

•(25) Lajâ Homa.

*(26) Mangal Ferâ.

(27) Kshetrapâla (Hindrance removing).

*(28) Saptapadi.

*(29) Kansâr Bhakshen.

(30) Blessing, given by the ladies.

*(31) Matrukâ worship.

(32) Aki Beki. (Odd and even game.)

(33) Uvatâr consisting of clothes giving, &c.

(34) Gorav feast. (Grand feast to the bridegrooms' party.)

(35) Bowing to some goddess.

In the list of all the ceremonies given those that are marked by an asterisk are enjoined by the Shastras with the particular object thereof, numbering 14, while the rest are based on custom, the true origin whereof cannot be traced out except the belief prevalent in traditional times termed " Doshi shastsras."

It is a rule that the bridegroom should come to marry at the bride's house, though they may be situated in distant localities or in distant countries. If the bride and bridegroom reside in distant quarters or in different countries, then for the sake of convenience they have to come near each other. In that case the bridegroom's party is to remove from his residence near the bride's locality. This shews the general respect for the tender sex, which is also seen in wooing which begins from them.

Then follows the description of those ceremonies :—

The first ceremony performed at the commencement of every auspicious ceremony is the Vridhhi Shradha. This ceremony is described in the naming ceremony. Then follow other ceremonies.

The second ceremony that is performed in a marriage is called गृहमुहूर्त (Grith Muhurat) or नम नखतूं Lagan Lakhvoo (fixing the marriage day). The ceremony is performed by the family astrologer. The character of the ceremony is that the family astrologer, provided with all the requisite materials for worship, after taking his seat, scatters a quantity of a red powder called Gulál on a wooden seat called Pàtlà, which is placed where the ceremony is to be performed. After doing this, he invokes the god Ganpati, notes down on a piece of paper some points concerning the marriage, and then fixes the day on which the marriage should be performed, that day being considered as the fittest one for performing these ceremonies. This he writes on a piece of paper, which is called either the " लमपत्रिका " or " लमपड़ी " (Lagan Padi*). After the astrologer finishes writing the family priest, who is present there, makes the auspicious marks of " Kankoo," called " Chandlas," on the foreheads of the persons present and rice stuck over those marks. Then the astrologer reads aloud what he has noted down in the Padi. This being over, four of the nearest female relations of the bride's party, of

* It should be noted that the Astrologer writes two Lagan Padi, one of which is given at the bridegroom's house as an intimation to him of a certain day being fixed for the marriage ceremonies. The other Lagan Padi is given at the bridegroom's house on the marriage day, which he brings with him when he comes to marry, and the first thing he does is that he gives it over to his mother in law. These Lagan Padis serve as records of a marriage celebrated.

whom her mother should necessarily be one, come and worship one after another the god Ganpati, with kankoo and rice. After the Ganpati Pujan is over, the astrologer, who has written the Lagan Padi, marking the forehead of the bride's mother with a patch of kankoo, makes a packet of it after having a rupee, turmeric, betel-nuts and rice placed in it, fastens it over by a string called नाडु (Nadu) and places it in the skirt of her saree (silk garment). Then are distributed the coriander seeds mixed with treacle. The priest as well as the astrologer are given a present which consists of 1 seer and a quarter of wheat, one cocoanut, 5 betel nuts, 5 turmeric pieces, and one rupee. This present is called an Akhyana.

The ceremony being over, all those present are bade goodbye by giving cocoanuts to each one and one rupee alms वांभणा) (Dakshina) to Kandolia Brahmins jointly, the caste men of the officiating priest.

The character of the Lagan Padi is of the following sort:—

I.—In the beginning are written some Sanskrit verses invoking the god Ganpati for the welfare of one's daughter whose marriage is to be solemnized.

II.—Then are noted down the names of the bride, of the bridegroom, and of their parents.

III.—Then follows the description of the caste, religion, the date (तिथि) "Tithi," days (वार) "Var," the mention also of the Lunar Mansion (नक्षत्र) (Nakshatra) and the conjunction of planets (योग) "yoga," and marked in a square the situation of the planets.

The second ceremony that follows in order is called (आगराशेष)' Adara Shesh, which is performed in the morning of the next day. In that ceremony a bride is bathed and decorated.

The ceremony is as follows:—

An auspicious mark of wheat called Sathia (स्त) with a betel-nut and a pice over it is made on the place intended for the bride to bathe. Then the bride takes her seat on a wooden stool called (बाजोठ) " Bajot " placed on that mark called Sathia (सार्थिया). Then the paternal aunt of the bride comes near the bride and patches her forehead, hands, and feet, with kankoo, mixed with rice. Then the bride is given seven leaves of betel, seven betel-nuts, seven turmeric pieces, one

rupee and one cocoanut.* Then four out of the by-standing
ladies of the bride's party pour a few drops of oil through
mango leaves† on the hair of the bride, four times each and
then anoint her with a yellow fragrant powder called " Pithi "
(पीती). Afterwards milk is poured on the bride's head through
Durbha (दर्भ) grass. This being over, the aunt again comes
forward and makes a kankoo mark on the bride's forehead
and takes back all those things previously given her, and
these things are delivered over to the family priest. Then
follows the ablution ceremony, *i.e.*, the bride is given a bath.
After she bathes, the installation of the gods Ganpati and
Gotraj (गोत्रज) follows. The materials for their worship
being—

1. Fragrant white powder called अबील (Abil).
2. Red powder called गुलाल (Gulál).
3. Red lead called सेंदूर (Sindur).
4. Camphor.
5. Fragrant incense (अगरबत्ती) (Agarbati).
6. Lamp of ghee.
7. Flowers.
8. Leaves of betel.
9. Betel-nuts.
10. Cocoanuts.
11. Clarified butter.
12. Treacle.
13. Sugar.
14. Rectified sugar.
15. Six annas and a half in coppers.
16. Quarter of a rupee for " Adarashesh " (one four-anna
piece).
17. Wheat, quarter of a seer of treacle, quarter of a seer
of ghee, one rupee.
18. Lápsi, *i.e.*, wheat flour, ghee and treacle cooked
together, for Gotraj.

---

* This is called a *posh*, because they are given in the cavity of the hands.
† The mango leaves are considered sacred among the Hindus by the following
authority :—

आम्र जम्बूरसूकासन्ववोधाम्बरधारिणाम् ।
पल्लवाः पञ्च पञ्चानामभिषंकार्यमुत्तमाः ॥

19. Mixture of rice flour, turmeric and water called "Khichi" (खीची).

The family priest then spreads a white piece of cloth on the Bajat and makes five (5) Sathias on it, one on each end of the Bajat and one in the middle of it with a pimpal leaf on each of these five Sathias. Gotraj* goddess is then installed on rice, arranged in a circle on a wooden seat (Bajat), while beside it Ganpati is placed on a pimpal leaf. The bride then takes her seat on another stool which is furnished with a rich cloth.

The priest then recites some Sanskrit verses and causes the bride to worship the god Ganpati. After this four of the ladies place small pads called वडी (Vadi) of that खीची (Khichi), near the installation of Gotraj. They make some forms of red kankoo called Ghavli (घवली), on the wall adjacent to the Bajat, and there Gotraj is worshipped as Ganpati is worshipped. The worship being over, the bride's aunt lets a handful of wheat slip four times from the bride's back, which wheat is collected by the priest, who also lets wheat slip from the bride's back three times. Then the aunt, as before, marks the bride's forehead with a chandla (patch of kankoo) and that wheat is given over to the bride's aunt on the marriage-day, when she again performs the same ceremony. The bride then herself makes a mark of kankoo on the priest's forehead who gives her blessings, reciting some verses. Afterwards the bride is given a quantity of treacle to eat. and she then, bowing to the Gotraj deity, brings the ceremony to a close.

Then follows the ceremony called पंचकणविणा (Panchkan Vina), i.e., the ladies while singing, sort five different kinds of grain.

The origin of this ceremony is the general belief that these grains represent the various materials out of which sweets, &c., are prepared for marriage feast.

---

* Gotraj.—This word means literally a deity of a family. A cocoanut is used to represent this goddess. It is a custom that a cocoanut decorated and reddened with kankoo, representing this deity, is changed when a new child is born. Here it should be observed that Gotraj does not change but the cocoanut merely is substituted by another at the time of a son's marriage and at the pregnancy ceremony.

These five kinds of grain are :—

One seer and a quarter of pulse called अडद Adad.

.. ,, चणा Chanâ (gram).

गहूं Gahun (wheat).

चोळा Cholâ.

,, ,, मग Mug.

Then is performed the auspicious ceremony of erecting a pandal called मंडपमुहूर्त Mandap Muhurat, or, in other words, Khat Pujan.

खानपूजन (*Khat Pujan.*)

It consists of the following materials of worship :—

12 Cocoanuts. One small wooden pillar.

2 Fruits called मिंढोल Mindhol.

One bundle of fragrant powder called पीठीपडो Pithi Pado and red Kankoo.

30 Small white or red grains called चनोठी chanothi.

30 Cories. 10 Seers of betel-nuts.

Dried fruits, such as almonds, etc.

Murdàsing मरडसिंग five seers in weight, half a seer of red hair-tying string called नाडू (Nadu).

Treacle.

Clarified butter.

Sugar.

3 seers of turmeric.

Leaves of the mango tree.

Leaves of the shamdi tree.

Plantains.

Pieces of sugar-cane.

Wheat.

Pomegranates.

Before the ceremony of Khat Pujan is performed the first that takes place is called अर्घ्यसंपादन. Then follows the पुण्याहवाचन ceremony and then the ceremony of Khat Pujan follows. The Arghya Sampadan and Punhya Vachan (Blessing giving) are given in connection with the Grih Shanti ceremony.

The ceremony of Khat Pujan is performed at a small pit dug for erecting the pandal. When that pit is worshipped four lady-members as well as four male members of the family step there and take that wooden pillar,* which is reckoned as auspicious, and go round that pit four times, and at the fourth turn they fix the pillar underneath the ground. Afterwards the ladies and gentlemen disperse with cocoanuts, and the worshipping of that pillar by the parents follows. A'ong with that pillar's worship are worshipped also the ten guardian deities ददादिक्पाल † Dash Digpalas, marked as they are on ten heaps of rice with one betel-nut on each of them. Round that pillar four cocoanuts are placed before them. Then the priest dips the ends of a cocoanut into water and blesses the bride's parents by sprinkling water over them. The cocoanut is then placed in the skirt of the saree of the bride's mother, after which molasses is distributed and the party disperses. Here the mandap murhat or Khat Pujan ends. Then follows the ceremony of the चाक्रवधावु (Chak Vadhav), i.e., the welcome of the चाक (chûk) wheel-tyre.‡

All the ladies of the bride's party in a procession, preceded by the beating of drums and bands, go to the gate of the compound to perform this ceremony. There a female potter is present with a wheel tyre and four earthen pots. Four ladies throw kankoo drops with rice on the tyre and four circular pots and make a kankoo mark also on the forehead of that potteress. She gives over those pots to the ladies, receiving in return an Akhyana or a present consisting of rice, &c. The ladies then retrace their steps, each of the four having one pot in her hand.

This being over, they go to the bridegroom's house with sweets called Ladka Ladu and Posh in a plate and two rupees.

The bridegroom takes his seat on a Bajat, with his face to the east when his mother-in-law makes a kankoo patch on his forehead, hands and feet, and gives over the posh to him.

* The reason why four members come is that the shastras have prescribed four pillars to be erected, as these pillars represent the four deities नंदनी, नलिनी, मैना, उमा and which are the residing goddesses in the four directions. But this rule has been superseded and the custom is to erect only one pillar.

† The ten guardian deities are :—
इन्द्र, अग्नि, यम, नंऋति, वरुण, वायु, सोम, ईशान, ब्रह्मा, विष्णु (अनन्त).

‡ The original custom was to go to the potter's house, but here as all are not situated in one locality the female potter comes at the house and thereat they welcome the wheel-tyre and earthen pots are received.

His mother receives the plate, worships it, takes out sweet balls from it, and places two rupees in the plate, hands it over again to the bride's party with rupees four distributing cocoa-nuts to all the ladies there.

Then the bride's party returns home and the Pithi (पीठी) applying ceremony to the bride is performed. The articles required for this ceremony are :

Dhupel oil.

Fragrant yellow powder called पीठी.

Four mango-leaves.

Sweetmeats called Dahitras.

Cuminum. जीरं

Salt.

Mustard.

Cotton.

Four spiced cakes, called Pâpad.

Matches.

Round sweets.

An Iron Ring.

The ceremony proceeds as follows:—

A wooden seat is placed where the ceremony is to be performed. The bride is required to stand upon it, holding in her hands the Posh* which is given to her by her paternal aunt. Afterwards oil is poured on her head through mango leaves and पीठी (yellow powder) applied to her body by four ladies. Then all the things above mentioned, from Dahitras downwards, except the iron ring, the bride places in the *saree* of the by-standing four ladies, and they throw these things in a basket beside her. Having performed this, the ladies with a lamp called Juman Diva (जुमणदिवा) go to the square at the end of a street or at the end of a compound ; they carry with them a pot full of water, one sweet ball, one betel-nut, one pice, kankoo and rice. There at the square they dig a little pit and bury those things carried, and return home covering that pit with clay.† This ceremony is

---

* Posh consists of 7 betel leaves, 7 betel-nuts, 7 turmeric pieces, one rupee and a coco nut.

† Some say that the origin of this ceremony is that women go to bring clay for the sacrifice in the Grih Shanti ceremony.

called उकरडी नोतरवी (Ukardi Notarvi). Some say that this means inviting the dogs, &c., who frequently live upon the rubbish at the street to feast at the marriage. The iron ring which is mentioned above is then fastened round the bride's wrist, in order that she may not be influenced by an evil eye, and the maternal uncle of the bride gives her two rupees and asks her to come down from that stool.

Grih Shanti महशान्ति—Propitiation of the Planets.

In this ceremony many ceremonies take place; some are performed in the house and some in the compound of the house. The first ceremony that takes place is called the installation of Ranadevi (Surya's wife). In this ceremony two pots of water are kept, and upon them are placed cocoanuts. These cocoanuts are decorated and covered by silk-cloth. Then these are worshipped and a female personage dances there, and as if she were the goddess inspired she utters responses to any questions that may be asked. This ceremony, it should be observed, is performed by the Kapola Banias, but my family forms an exception to it.* This being over, the मातृका Matrukas are installed. The मातृका (Matrukas) are sixteen in number and there are seven मातृकां (Matrikas). Their names are—

गौरी पद्मा शची मेधा सावित्री विजया जया ।
देवसेना स्वधा स्वाहा मातरो लोकमातर: ॥
धृति: पुष्टिस्तथा तुष्टि आत्मदेवी तथा च ।
गणेशोनाधिकर्यस्तु वृद्धौ पूज्यास्तु षोडश ॥

The above sixteen are elderly goddesses, and they are installed to avoid obstacles on these auspicious occasions. Together with these the seven inferior goddesses are also invoked, their names being

ब्राह्मी, माहेश्वरी, कौमारी, वैष्णवी,
वाराही, इन्द्राणी, चामुण्डा.

Brahmi, Maheshwari, Kaumari, Vaishnavi, Varahi, Indrani, Chamunda. These are called घृतमातृका. †

---

* This ceremony also forms a part of the pregnancy ceremony.
† घृतमानृका Grut Matrukas, i. e., deities which are marked by ghee and kankoo.

These goddesses are installed on one of the walls of the house, as is shewn in the annexed diagram and are worshipped by the father.

Here these points are marked with Kankoo.

. . . .
. . . .

Then there are placed six earthen pots, on each side of the Matrika, three placed one above the other. Then, in the above two on each side are placed grain, and they are covered over by silk pieces of cloth and are fastened crosswise by a string called नाडा (Nada) and the lamps of ghee are placed over them; afterwards the father comes into the compound and begins with Grih Shânti (महशान्ति) ceremony. It proceeds as follows :—
A square of the red earth is made in the mandap. There two wooden stools called Bajat are placed in the east of that square. On one of these the respective positions of the nine planets are marked in rice. Then first begins the worship of Ganpati. A golden image of the god is placed in a copper dish and is worshipped. Then a pot full of water is worshipped, which worship is called वरुणपूजन (Varun Pujan), i.e, worship of the Water Deity. Then the water-pot is placed on the north-east of that stool on which the positions of the planets are marked. Then follows the worship of the planets. This being over, the next ceremony that follows is अर्घसंपादन *Arghya sampadan or अर्घपूजा (Arghya Puja), i.e., worship of the deserved persons by sprinkling water over them. On an auspicious occasion any one of the six persons is said to be worthy of worship. These are :—

आचार्य, ऋत्विग्, वैशाद्यो, राजा, स्नातक.

---

* See Photograph No. 2.

the preceptor, the officiating priest, the parents-in-law, the king and holy man. The ceremony is of the following sort :— Two earthen crucibles or कांडीयां (Kodyan) are taken, and in one of them are placed eight things, *viz.* :—

आपः क्षीरं कुशाग्राणि दध्यक्षततिऽास्तथा ।
यवाः सिद्धार्थकाः स्नाने अर्घोष्टागः प्रकीर्तितः ॥

i.e., are placed water, milk दर्भ, (Durbha) grass, curdled milk, rice, seasamum seeds, barley seeds, white sarshav seeds, &c. Then the other is placed above the first and both are fastened by a string called नाडा (Nada) and this joined one is worshipped. Afterwards the father holds these fastened pots into his hands, and his wife stands behind him having a jug full of water called (Padya) पाद्य in her hands. Then the Brahmins recite some verses and are worshipped by water out of that pot. Then the preceptor blesses the parents and the ceremony of कंकणबंधन (Kaukan Bandhan) follows, in which the string called Nâda is tied round the right wrist of the father. Afterwards the mother worships the preceptor. Then she is tied also with that Nâda on the left hand. Afterwards the pot of water which was placed in the north-east of the planets is taken and given to the father. The mother stands behind him touching his shoulders with her fingers, and the hands of both are reddened with kankoo. The father holds that pot on his right shoulder. The pot is again worshipped, and wheat, and 5 sorts of leaves called पञ्च पल्लवा : and clay, &c.,* are placed in it. Then follows the ceremony of पुण्याहवाचनं† (Punyah Vâchan) a blessing-giving, in which the father stands holding that pot in his palm and the mother stands beside him with a cocoanut in her hand. In this ceremony the priest recites blessings to them.

Then the bride is sent forth from the house and she worships the god Ganpati, placing wheat before the installed god, which wheat she brings from the place the goddesses are

---

* This pot contains 5 kinds of leaves (5 kinds of leaves are given before), 5 sorts of mineral (कनकं कुलिशं नीलं पद्मरागं च मौक्तिकं gold, emeralds, rubies, diamonds and sapphires, pearls), seven sorts of clay, are—Clay from the stable of a horse, an elephant, from the confluence of a river, from the palace courtyard, from the place cows are kept, from the root of the trees, &c.

† See Photograph No. 3.

marked. Mindhol* (मींढोळ) is tied on her wrist. Then an oblation of cocoanut, ghee, barley seeds, &c., called Ahuti, -is given to the sacrificial fire and the ceremony called in general महशान्ति (Grih Shanti) comes to a close.

Then follows the ceremony of हाये वाळो वाटवो (Hathe Valo Vatvo) in which are required sweet balls, Dahitras, &c. These things are placed on a triangular slab of stone. Afterwards two members of the bride's party, one male and the other a female, sit facing each other and keep the slab between them. They then grind or powder those things. It should be noted that these two persons cannot be the parents or who are to perform the Kanyâ Dân Ceremony. They are given some money for powdering those things.

This being over, the ceremony that follows is called Ladi Dodi (लाडीडोडी). The meaning of the expression is that half as much more than the number of sweet balls given above in Ladka Ladu are being taken from the bridegroom's house to the bride's house. There the bride is made to sit as was the bridegroom in the ceremony of Ladka Ladu, and she is given that plate containing sweet balls, rupees, &c. Afterwards cocoanuts are distributed to the ladies present.

Along with this, or some time after, the ceremony of वरणु (Varnu), i.e., present is performed. In this ceremony the bridegroom's party, having cholis, bodices and sarees, come to give these things to the bride to be worn in the marriage ceremony. (It is a custom that until these things are not given her, she cannot decorate nor prepare herself for marriage.)

Similarly in the case of the bridegroom, he is given by the bride's party a turban, a silk Digogi, an under-garment, four sweet balls, Dahitras, &c. These things are what is called Kalvo (कलवो). (He also cannot prepare for marriage until he is given these things as the wife could not till she receives Varnu.)

Then both the bride and the bridegroom being given these things, they prepare for marriage by putting on, one thing, at least, if not all, out of the things given to them.

---

* Mindhol is used as it is called Madan Fal, i. e. (the fruit of love).

The preparations on the part of the bridegroom being over, he, in a grand procession, leaves his house for the bride's on horseback, having in his hands the Lagan Padi and Posh, and in some cases his sister is seated behind him.

At the entrance of the mandap at the bride's house he dismounts his horse and is welcomed by the bride's mother. This welcoming ceremony is called Ponkhanoo. The following things are required in it :—

Two earthen crucibles fastened together into one called संपुट (Samput).
Small balls of wheat flour called Indipindi.
Yoke, धुसर (Dhusru).
Kankoo.   Pestle, मुसळ (Musal).
Rice.   One long spinning needle.
Jug full of water called कलश (Kalash).

The ceremony follows :—

The bridegroom, just as he alights from his horse, is made to stand on a Bajat placed at the door. The bride's mother welcomes him by marking a Chandla on his forehead. He in return gives over the Posh and the Lagan Padi to his mother-in-law, and then he is welcomed by his mother-in-law who turns that yoke, &c., four times round his neck. (It is also a custom to touch the bridegroom's nose.)

This being over, the bridegroom is brought to the marriage pandal, where two stools are placed—one in the east and the other in the west. On the stool in the west, Darbha grass called विष्टर * is placed, and takes his seat on it facing to the east. On two stools facing to the north, the bride's parents also take their seats. Then the मंगळाष्टक (auspicious stanzas) are repeated.

The officiating priest repeats verses here. The verses are :—

श्रीमत्यङ्गजविष्टरो हरिहरौ वायुर्महेन्द्रानिल-
श्चन्द्रो भास्करवित्तपालवरुणाः प्रेताधिपादिग्रहाः ।
प्रद्युम्नो नलकूबरो सुरगजर्धितामाणिः कौस्तुभः
स्वामी शक्तिधरश्च लांगलधरः कुर्युः सदा मंगलम् ॥

That is, O you gods, deities, may you ever try to do well

---

* विष्टर (Vishtar) means twenty-five blades of Darbha grass placed side by side.

(to this pair, &c.). Then the bride is brought by her maternal uncle and is seated on the other stool to the east. Then the bride's parents wash the feet of the bridegroom as well as of the bride and colour them with kunkoo. The bride and bridegroom are separated by a sacred cloth called अन्तर्पट (Autarpat), held between them. Then the ceremony of मधुपर्क (Madhu Parka) is performed, in which the bridegroom is worshipped. The मधुपर्क ceremony is as follows :—

THE MADHU PARKA CEREMONY.

This ceremony is performed after the bridegroom comes to the bride's house and sits in the mandap. The things requisite are :—

> Honey.
> Curdled Milk.
> Ghee.

All these mixed in a vessel of bell-metal are called मधुपर्क (Madhu Parka). These kept ready, the bridegroom is seated with his face to the east, and the bride's father sits in the south, having his face towards the north. The bride's father vows to receive the bridegroom with Madhu Parka, saying " I hereby with this Madhu Parka, entertain the bridegroom, come to marry my daughter." Then the god Ganpati is invoked to avoid hindrances. The bride's father folding a cavity of his hands asks the bridegroom to be worshipped. The bridegroom consenting, the ceremony follows, in which the bridegroom sips twice that mixture, at every time the priest reciting some mantras.

Then the वरमाला (Varmala *). i. e., an auspicious garland of strings, is put on the neck of the bride. Then the end of the outer garment of the bridegroom is fastened to the end of the bride's garments, which is called छेडाछेडी बंधन (Cheda Chedi Bandhan). Then the right hand of the bridegroom is joined to the right hand of the bride, which ceremony is called हस्तमेलाप (Hast Melap) (joining the hands). Then the ceremony of Kanya Dana is performed. The (Sankalpa vow) for giving a daughter is made by the bride's father, as follows :— To-day I give this my daughter to this bridegroom for his wel-

---

* (Varmala—A cotton thread string, measuring three arms.)

fare in this birth, as well as for the continuation of mine and his species, and to benefit our ancestors. So vowing with water having rice and kusha grass dipped in it, he gives one betel-nut and a betel-leaf wrapped with string to the bridegroom, saying इमां कन्यां प्रतिगृह्यताम्, *i. e.*, accept this daughter whom I give you to-day to be your wife, and the bridegroom says प्रतिगृण्हामि " I accept her." The betel-nut and leaf are called मदनफल (Madan Fala). They are given with the belief that perpetual love may exist between them. Afterwards prayers are offered to god, and the Brahmins present there recite blessing verses for the married couple, which is called स्वस्तिवाचन (Swasti Vachan). This ceremony of कन्यादान (Kanyá Dàn) being over, the pair is taken to a Mahiru (a well-furnished place in the house). Afterwards the pair is removed to the place where a चोरी (Chori) is erected, *i. e*, 36 earthen pots are arranged, nine on each side, supported underneath by seats and having a small crucible over them—earthen pots which were brought from the potter's are placed one above the other in the four corners.

In the interior of this Chori the pair is seated side by side. Then the pair goes round this Chori four times. For three times the bride is on the right side and on the fourth she is on the left.

Then the लाजाहोम sacrifice is performed, in which first the hands of the pair are reddened with kankoo, and then the bride's brother gives in the right hand of each of the pair barley and sesamum seeds. He gives this four times, and all the four times these are thrown into the fire, the verses recited at the time are, सूर्याय स्वाहा, इदं सूर्याय, सोमाय स्वाहा इदं सोमाय, प्रजापतये स्वाहा इदं प्रजापतये, अग्नये स्वाहा इदं अग्नये. That is, four oblations mixed with ghee, and those seeds are offered to the four different deities—Sun, Moon, procreating deities, and the Fire. Then the bride and bridegroom again go round, which going round is called मगलफेरा (Maugal Ferra, auspicious turnings). The bride in the first three precedes her husband, while in the fourth the husband precedes. Then before this auspicious

---

Note.—In the ceremony of Kanyá Dàn the bridegroom is given one silver ring, one tooth-pick, one ear-pick, and one silver elephant along with the things that are given as dowry.

turning ceremony is over, the क्षेत्रपालनिवारण (removing the hindrance of Kshetra Pála) is performed. The object is that Kshetra Pála (one of the servants of Siva) prevents marriage ; till the pair goes round three times, no hindrance takes place, but on the fourth turn this क्षेत्रपाल (Kshetra Pála) prevents. Consequently he is worshipped as follows :—The husband touches the क्षेत्रपाल with the big toe of his right foot, and the bride's brother on the fourth turn holds-up the big toe of the bridegroom's foot. This is supposed Kshetra Pála hindrances. Then the bride's brother is given as much as he asks, and the hindrance is supposed to cease.

Then follows the सप्तपदी (Sapta Padi) ceremony. In this ceremony seven heaps of rice are made, and the bride rubs out all those heaps by her feet, as well as the bridegroom touches those heaps with his right foot. This is called Sapta Padi. The object is, that demons, &c., prevent the bridegroom to carry this bride, and this rubbing out indicates that he has brought his wife, baffling the attempts and efforts of those devils residing in all the seven continents of this universe. It should be noted here that the marriage covenant is held binding after ceremony of mangal ferra is over.

Then comes the bride's mother taking Kansar (कंसार) mixed with sugar and ghee in a dish. The bridegroom then gives that Kansar to his wife to eat, who vows therefrom never to dine before her husband. The object of this ceremony is that the bridegroom says, I infuse my life, soul, blood and every-thing into your body, that we may be called from this time to be one both in mind and body. This being over, four of the family ladies come there—two of the bride's party, and two of the bridegroom's party. Each comes one by one. They welcome the married couple by the wheat saying as follows: The first lady blesses the bride to be in सौभाग्य (Saubhagya), i e., never widowed like शिवपार्वती. The second blesses the couple to be like that of Krishna and Rukmini. The third gives the simile of Surya and Rannade (his wife). The fourth that of Indra and Sachi. This being over, the bridegroom gives seeds given in his hand to the bride and the bride scatters them on the head of her husband, saying शतंजीव (Shatam Jiv), i.e., may you live a hundred years.

This brings to a close the चतुर्थाकर्म (Chaturtha Karm) cere-- mony.

Afterwards the pair leave the marriage pandal and enter the house, where they both together worship the goddesses, divine mother Matrukas. Afterwards they there play एकी बेकी, Aki Beki (a play of odd and even), in which are required silver ring which was given to the bridegroom in the Kanyá Dán ceremony, 7 Korees, 7 pices, 7 betel-nuts. In this ceremony all are collected and the bride and bridegroom play there. If the bride wins, the popular belief is she will domineer over her husband, and if otherwise, the bridegroom will keep his wife in entire sway. Then the married pair is given blessings, and both the husband and the wife, rather the bridegroom and the bride, leave for the bridegroom's house. Then is performed (उवतर) Uvatar (ending ceremony).

This ceremony is performed generally on the day after the marriage, or some two or three days after the marriage ; in case the day be not auspicious or there may be some inconvenience. In this ceremony the clothes are given to the bridegroom's relations. Before marriage the bride's father asks the bridegroom's father to send him a list of his relations, those only who may be entitled to take clothes (पहेरामणी) ("Paharamni," as it is called). On the day fixed for the Uvatar, those relatives come and take clothes according to their degree of relation.

On that day a grand feast called Gorav (गोरव) is held at the bride's house. In that feast the bride dines with the nearest of her husband's relations who give her as much as they like. This gift is called पीठीड्रव्य. Then after all finish dining, the bride and bridegroom are brought together and are seated on two stools. There, first the god Ganpati is worshipped. The worship being over, the bride's mother comes there and gives to the pair Posh, and marks the foreheads of both with kankoo. Then she gives to each of the pair a dress called Paharamni. The dress of the bridegroom consists of shawl, turban, &c., while that of the bride consists of saree, bodice, cholies, &c. The pair being given their dress, clothes are distributed to the other relatives. The clothes being distributed, the pair leave the seats and go into the house where the divine mothers were marked. There the mothers are worshipped. After the worship again the pair plays the game of odd and even. Then the bride's brother breaks in pieces seven spiced cakes on the back of the bridegroom. Afterwards the pair welcomes the mandap by sprinkling kankoo drops over it. This is called "Mandavo Ochhadvo." Then the pair is made to touch the carriage wheel, though the original was to drag it, but actual dragging is not performed, it is only touched. Then a vessel of bell-metal containing kansar (uncooked) and one silk cloth in it is placed in the lap of the bride, and the lamp called Juman Diva is given in her hands and then good-bye is said to her as well as to her husband. This brings to a close the marriage ceremonies.

The closing ceremony is to bow down to goddesses Samundri and Mahaluxmi and to worship the goddess Gotraj. The days fixed for going to the goddess are Tuesday, Thursday and Sunday, as they are considered favourable.

ORDINARY GENERAL MEETING held on Wednesday, the 26th September 1894.

Mr. KHARSETJI RUSTAMJI CAMA, *Vice-President*, in the Chair.

The Minutes of the previous Meeting were read and confirmed.

The election of the following new member was announced :—

Veterinary-Surgeon Dhunjishaw Navrozji Patel, G.B.V.C., Kalbadevi, Bombay.

The following donation was announced and thanks voted to the donors :—

To the Library.

From the Superintendent, Government Press, Madras—Administration Report of the Madras Government Museum for the year 1893.

From the Authors—A Note on the Tract of Country south of the river Son, in the Mirzapur District, N.-W. P., by Messrs. W. Crooke and G. R. Dampier, I.C.S.

From Berlin—Zeitschrift Fur Ethnology Heft IV.

From Nederlandsch—Indie—Bydragen Tot de Taal-land-en Volkenkunde.

The Honorary Secretary drew attention of the members present to the paper on " Some Rude Stone Implements from Back Bay, Middle Colaba," written at his request by Mr. Fred. Swynnerton and published in the Journal of the Society, No. 4, Vol. III. The Honorary Secretary said that the paper when read and published was received with some doubts, Mr. Swynnerton's views being considered mere assumptions. A copy of the paper, with the collection of the implements, was sent to Mr. Boyd Dawkins, Professor of Anthropology and Geology, at the Owen's College, Manchester, who confirmed the author's views. Along with the flints, flakes and implements a fossil tooth was found, whose nature could not then be ascertained. Mr. Swynnerton wrote : " To estimate the comparative age of the flints might seem ridiculous, and the question is rendered more difficult by a fossil tooth I find close to one of the more perfect flakes. This is, I believe, the first fossil belonging to a mammal found at Bombay, and it is, therefore, unique. I have not yet ascertained to what kind of animal the tooth belonged, but it bears on it evident marks of having been in earth for some time, and possibly may have come out of the indurated mud I have before mentioned as occurring here and there on the shore. The tooth is undoubtedly stone, and the mud on it is also fossilized. One of the flints has also some semi-fossilized mud upon it, and might have come out of the same stratum as the tooth. It would be interesting to know whether the worked stones have been chipped on the shores when the latter was pretty much as we now see it, or whether they have been in the alluvial matter forming part of the shore and have only comparatively recently been washed out by the sea. Do the flints belong to the same period as the fossil tooth ? and have they come out of the same stratum? The tooth, I may say, was found on one of the higher portions of the shore, about half way between high and low water, where flints are numerous." With regard to this subject, Professor Dawkins says : " The tooth which I have registered is very interesting. It is the 2nd upper true molar of Hipparian, and of the Pluocene type." The Honorary Secretary observed in conclusion that those of the members who were interested in pre-historic studies had a vast field yet unexplored in their close vicinity waiting for further researches.

The following paper was then read :—

" CERTAIN SOCIAL QUESTIONS CONNECTED WITH MARRIAGE and INHERITANCE among the HINDUS."

By MR. TRIBHUWANDAS MUNGALDAS NATHUBHAI.

MARRIAGE.

Introduction.

The Hindu mind has firmly grounded its belief in the theory of Karma or actions. It is held that our actions produce results, good or bad, according as they are meritorious or otherwise (in conformity with the Divine will). Not only do these actions affect our present birth, but they unfailingly affect our future birth. It is the desire of all beings to have a regeneration desirable to them, and the general tendency of mankind is to long for a better one. In order to secure this aim, no agency is held so powerful as our actions. This theory, in short, may be sketched as follows : —

Actions are divided into three kinds: the Kriyamána (those done in the present life; the Sanchita (or collected) and Prárabdha (or done before, i.e., in the past births).

The first class called Kriyamána (क्रियमाण) consists of actions a man does in his present tenure of life. The second called Sanchita (संचित) consists of those actions done that are stored together, and which, in accordance to their development, produce effects. The third class called Prárabdha which, in popular phraseology, is ranked synonymous with " Fortune," consists of those developed ones, out of the Sanchit class, and which are consequently ready to produce effect in our present existence, which may be accounted to be a result of the actions of our past life.

But a question may arise, why all our actions do not produce equivalent effects in our present birth, and what necessity there exists for our regeneration, which as has been regarded is the result of our Prárabdha actions. An answer to this question would lead to the theory of regeneration. The simple and short answer that can be given (for fear of too much dilation) is that the object of regeneration is to perfect our soul in all its entirety. Just as a plant, until it is developed and perfect, will not give us desired fruit, so this soul, which is environed in our human tabernacle, cannot give its desired fruit of salvation, until it is developed in all its entirety; consequently a human body is obliged to be subject to regeneration, if it is not able to be perfect within one existence, and regeneration follows the actions. As noted above the Sanchit actions are, " a collection of actions done in various preceding generations," while Prárabdha consists of all those that have been developed to bring forth results, out of those stored actions. All the actions done by a man in his present birth are not capable in a majority of cases to produce instantaneous and immediate results. Some affect immediately, and some take time to affect. Out of those that are thus stored, some that are developed, precede the imperfect ones, and the chain of generation goes on, till the true essence or Tatva is attained and then our soul becomes free or attains absolution. Thus, our actions bring forth results according as they are good or bad. To have a better life both present and future our Hindu Shastrakars have regulated our conduct by prescribing some sacraments. These sacraments, as prescribed by the Hindu Theology, are sixteen, but all Hindus are not eligible for all of them. The Hindus are not one class. The four main divisions of a Hindu society are the Brahamins, Kshastriyas, Vayshyas, and Sudras. These communities are in a descendant degree, and each class following is ranked inferior to the one preceding it. But very little religious distinction is preserved between the first three orders, and they are designated by the common appellation of a Dwij.* A Dwij has to undergo all these sixteen sacraments for securing his aim. It should be observed here, that all these 16 are allowed for a male Dwij. A Dwij woman is

---

* A Dwij means literally twice-born, i.e., once while he is born, and secondly, he is said to be born when he puts on the sacred thread. This second birth of his, qualifies him for the performance of religious rites by repeating the Mantras of the Vedas; while regarding those that are not Dwij, i.e., who have not put on the sacred thread, ceremonies are performed, not by the repetition of Vedic Mantras but by the Mantras of Smriti

restricted from some of these. In the case of a Sudra the eligible rites are only ten. The sixteen sacraments are—

गर्भाधान...	...	...	Conception.
पुंसवन ...	...	...	Male-bearing.
सीमंत ...	...	...	Pregnancy.
जातकर्म	...	...	Birth ceremony.
नामकर्म	...	...	Naming ceremony.
निःक्रमण	...	...	Taking the child out of doors.
अन्नप्राशन	...	...	Feeding with rice, &c.
चुडाकर्म	...	...	Shaving.
उपनयन	...	...	Thread girdling.
केशान्त ...	...	...	Cutting of the hair.
चतुर्वेदाध्ययन	...	...	Studying four Vedas, Rig, Yajus, Sam, and Atharva, each forming a separate sacrament.
समावर्तन	...	...	Returing from the preceptor's house.
विवाह ...	...	...	Marriage.

The sixteen sacraments which are prescribed to attain the desired ultimatum mark the different stages of a Hindu life. ·

The Hindu life is divided into four stages. These four stages are : Brahmcharya (Studentship) ; Grihastha (house-holder) ; Van Prastha (Retirement) ; and Sanyas (Asceticism). Now the first extends from the boy's wearing the sacred thread to the time he studies ; the second stage after his return from his preceptor's house till he becomes infirm and unable to work ; the third is the time of old age ; and the fourth is the last stage.

The second stage is unlimited in its extent. It extends to a longer period than all other divisions. It is the most important of all stages, socially, politically, and religiously. It begins with marriage, and ends when he is past the serving age. It is in this age that he tries to utilize his earthly existence to its best advantage ; herein it is that his interests become one with the society at large ; herein he gets progeny which is indispensably necessary for a man to have his burden alleviated

and comforts secured in after years, as well as to perform his
obsequies for the repose of his soul; consequently, as it is
quite manifest that marriage plays not an insignificant part in
the history of human life, the theory thereof is summarily
sketched as follows :—

    (1)   The origin of marriage.

    (2)   Age of marriage.

    (3)   Parties elligible for marriage.

    (4)   Time when marriages should be performed.

    (5)   Persons authorised to give a girl in marriage.

    (6)   Different kinds of marriages.

    (7)   Relation of marriage to inheritance.

    (8)   Advantages and responsibilities of marriage.

    (9)   Description of ceremonies performed.

   (10)   Account of expenditure for marriage and other
         ceremonies.

(1) THE ORIGIN OF MARRIAGE.

In every society there is an innate desire for the continuation and preservation of the society. To satisfy this desire
the institution of marriage has been organized. This institution, then, has no other object than the regulation of sexual
unions, which aim at the satisfaction of the sexual appetites
which are an impulse or a " charm which impels both man
and beast to provide as far as concerns them for the preservation of their species." The Hindu view of marriage is " to
pay off ancestral debt" by having a continual line of male
succession, whose duty it is to give periodical offerings
(श्राद्धपिंड) to the deceased that he may thereby get repose in
his next birth, and, as a passing remark at may be observed here
that on this account that a father leaves all his property to his
sons as a compensation for the offerings he expects from him,
in his after-life and for the burden of maintaining a family
thrown upon him.   –

(2) AGE OF MARRIAGE.

The age of marriage is not explicitly stated by Manu. He
lays down that one should marry after he returns from his
preceptor's house after studying the Vedas, that is, he should
be generally married when he is of age. But no definite time
is fixed for the marriage of a daughter. The only prohibition

53

that is laid down is that, she should not be married before she is six. For the first six years a girl is under the possession of three deities, Fire, Sun and Moon, each of whom possesses the girl in succession for two years. After she is past six years, from six to eight she is called a Gauri and from eight to the age of twelve she is called a Kanyâ and at that age she becomes fit for the Kanyâ Dân ceremony. After twelve she comes to puberty and is called a स्त्री (woman). In the Vayshyas and Kshatryas, a girl is generally married when she comes of age. She is married after she has undergone all the sacraments prescribed for her and becomes fit for the last sacrament, viz., विवाह. Manu, in his well-known work of Smriti, defines the differences between the ages of the bride and bridegroom as follows :—

त्रिंशद्वर्षोद्वहेत्कन्यां हृद्यां द्वादशवार्षिकीम् ।
त्र्यष्टवर्षोऽष्टवर्षां वा धर्मं सीदति सत्वरः ॥

This means that —

"a person who has reached the age of 30 is allowed to marry a girl of twelve, while one of 24 years a girl of eight." Though this rule is not strictly observed, yet it is in conformity with modern observations that when there is such a difference of age, a male child is sure to be born which is the chief object Hindus desire to achieve by marrying. This view is also supported in a book called the Lady's Guide (by an American author) wherein the author shews :—

If a father is younger than the mother	100 girls :	90·6 boys.
A father and mother equal in age	„ :	90 „
Do. is older than the mother by 6 years ...	„ :	100·4 „
Do. do. do from 6 to 9 years	„ :	124·7 „
Do. do. do. from 9 to 12 years... ...	„ :	143·7 „
Do do. do. from 18 and more	„ :	200 „

(3) PARTIES ELLIGIBLE FOR MARRIAGE.

The selection of persons to marry is restricted by two rules :—

(a) That persons should not marry who are सपिण्ड or सगोत्र* (i.e., related to each other within seven degrees where the common ancestor is a male or in the same family).

(b) That they must marry inside the same caste.

1.—The ultimatum, as stated before, that a Dwij attains by marriage is to have a line of succession for the repose of his soul in his next birth, which repose solely depends on his being offered periodical offerings (पिण्ड) by his son after his death. Now, the persons related to a common ancestor within five degrees through the mother's side and within seven degrees from the father's side, are not eligible for such offerings, and hence they should not intermarry.

Thus, Manu says:—

असपिंडा च या मातुरसगोत्रा च या पितु: ।
सा प्रशस्ता द्विजातीनां दारकर्मणि मैथुने ॥

i.e., a person called द्विज i.e., Brahmins, Kshatryas, and Vayshyas should marry that girl who is not of the same family (गोत्र) as father's, and who is not related to the mother within five degrees.

II.—That they must marry inside the same caste. The validity of this restriction cannot be ascertained from a religious point of view. The system of mixed marriages, i.e., marriage between persons of different castes was not obsolete, even in the days of Manu. For he says that—

पाणिग्रहणसंस्कर: सवर्णासुपदिश्यते ।
असवर्णोस्वयं ज्ञेयो विधिरुद्वाहकर्मणि ॥

---

* The word गोत्र in Hindu Shastras is a very noteworthy one गांव literally means a family. Originally all persons called Dwij are supposed to have descended from the eight Rishis—Vishwamitra, Gauttam, Agastya, Jamdagnya, Bhrigu, Vasishtha, Kashiapa and Atri. And the group of the descendants of any one of these is called सगोत्र (of the same family). But the number of Gotras mentioned in the Shastras, though virtually they should be eight, is yet fixed to be forty-nine, and it is understood that persons having the same Rishi for their common ancestor should not intermarry.

This means, that persons should marry girls of the same caste, but when marriage is solemnized with girls of different caste, it should be celebrated by different ceremonies. This evidently implies that though marriages in the same caste are preferable, yet negatively, he says, that mixed marriages are also allowable. However, in the course of generations, so many difficulties arose that the rule which was originally an optional one, has been rendered compulsory. For, when mixed marriages were allowed, then the nation which was one whole, branched off into innumerable different communities, and the gulf so much widened that it was regarded a sacrilege, if one would drink or eat with the other. Also difficulties began to be felt in guiding succession, and the rule was made a compulsory one.

Saying so far of the general rules restricting parties to be married, the qualifications that are noted and are necessary to be observed in the case of bride and bridegroom should be mentioned :—

Manu, in his code, says, that one should not marry her who has any defect in the organs, but should marry her whose gait of walking is like that of an elephant, or a swan, who speaks measured words, and who is ever healthy.

The responsibilities imposed upon a father in choosing a husband for his daughter are not less heavy. Manu says not only that a man should marry his daughter inside the same caste, but he should give her to one who is born of a rich family, who is virtuous, and who is educated.

(4) TIME WHEN MARRIAGES SHOULD BE PERFORMED.

The Hindu year based on the changes of the moon is divided into twelve months, but all these twelve months are not selected for marriage. The only selected ones are those in which the ... Venus does not set. The selected months are, Magh, ...ishakh and Jaishtha. These are the months most ... marriage, and in them the planet Venus does ... The reason why Venus is considered necessary ... pposed to be the planet influencing love affairs, ... ly a belief has been held that when she is in rise, corresponding is the rise in love between the pair. But the months named above are not the only ones in which marriage is solemnized. There are other months, viz., Margashirsha, in which marriage can neither be said to be good nor bad. In the remaining months, the Shastras prohibit marriage celebration. But though these months are mentioned, there is a difference of opinion in the selection of months Some say that Jaishtha is not a favourable time for marriage, when the bridegroom and the bride are the eldest children. At the same time, some writers, Narada, &c., declare all months favourable, without an exception. So far, saying of months, it should be said that the Hindu Shastras have been also precise in appointing certain dates and days favourable to marriage. These days and dates are not selected for once and ever, but every time their ascertainment depends upon the planetary positions and constellations. Apart from this it should be said that a marriage is ranked favourable when in the case of the bride, the planet Jupiter is powerful, i.e., he may be in that position in the solar system, wherefrom he most effectually produces his good effects, and for the bridegroom, the luminary Sun should be in an efficacious position.

The positions then should be known in the figure here. The numerical figures denote the divisions into which the system is divided. It can be seen from the above, that when the planet Jupiter occupies the houses numbered 2, 5, 7, 9 or 11, he is considered powerful, while in the case of the bridegroom the Sun is considered auspicious when occupying numbers 3, 5, 7.

Thus the Hindu mind is much influenced by the astrological points as noting the positions of planets, &c. This is observed with the idea, that happy coincidences of times and places produce inevitably good results. Though primary consideration is given to Jupiter and the Sun, yet other planets are not left unconsidered, but the consideration is not very significant.

(5) PERSONS AUTHORISED TO GIVE A GIRL IN MARRIAGE.

It should be observed here that the persons authorised to

give a bride in marriage or to perform the **Kanyâ Dán** ceremony, are पिता पितामही भ्राता पितृकुस्थायेतुश्यादिमोतृकुस्यां मातामहः मातुलादे॰, &c., *i.e.*, the ceremony should be performed by the father. But if he be dead, the grandfather or the brother or some one of the paternal uncles; in default of all of these, the maternal grandfather, but if he be not living, the maternal uncle; and if none be living, then recourse must be had to the mother : and, if the mother be deceased, then the girl herself is authorized to perform the celebrating ceremonies.

(6) DIFFERENT FORMS OF MARRIAGES.

The sacred institution of marriage has been classified into eight kinds; and the classification follows the line of difference in the ceremonies performed in each. The chief object to which these eight tend, is to bring forth general happiness in this as well as in the next birth. These eight forms are—

> ब्राझो दैवस्तथार्षश्च प्राजापत्यस्तथा सुर: ।
> गान्धर्षो राक्षसंश्वैव पैशाचश्चाटमो धमः ॥

These 8 are—Brâhma, Daiva, Ârsha, Prajapatya, Âsura, Gândharva, Râkshas, and Paishâch.

(1) ब्राझ Brâhma is defined as—

> अच्छाय चार्चयित्वा च श्रुतिशील्खते स्वयम् ।
> आहूय दानं कन्याया ब्राझो धमः प्रकीर्तितः ॥

i.e., a father, after inviting a person who is learned and good-natured, gives him his daughter with honours, then the rite is called ब्राझ (Brâhma. In it the bride should be dressed in gay attire, and should be given a dowry along with.

(2) यज्ञ तु वितते सम्यगृत्विजे कर्मे कुर्वते ।
> अलंकृतसुतादानं दैवं धर्मं प्रचक्षते ॥

That rite in which a daughter is married to the officiating priest when the sacrifice is going on, is called दैव (Daiva)—

(3) एकं गोमिथुनं द्वे वा वरादादाय धर्मतः ।
> कन्याप्रदानं विधिवदार्षो धर्मः स उच्यते ॥

That rite in which a daughter is given, receiving from the bridegroom one or a pair of cows "*for their mutual use*" in religious observances, is called आर्ष (Àrsha).

(4) सह नौ चरेतां धर्ममिति वानुभाष्य च ।
कन्याप्रदानमभ्यर्च्ये प्राजापत्यो विधि: स्मृत:

That sort of performance when the father *actually* uttering the words, 'May you both together perform all duties, secular as well as religious," gives his daughter, is called a प्राजापत्य (Prajapatya). This form differs from the Bráhma in so far as no dowry is given along with the daughter. Nor is any qualification necessarily required in the bridegroom.

(5) ज्ञातिभ्यो द्रविणं दत्वा कन्यायै चैव शक्ति: ।
कन्याप्रदानं स्वाच्छन्द्यादासुरो धर्म उच्यते ॥

आसुर (Asura) is that rite in which a husband voluntarily takes a wife after giving as much wealth as he could afford to the kinsmen, and even to the damsel herself, as well as to her father.

(6) इच्छयान्योन्यसंयोग: कन्यायाश्च वरस्य च ।
गान्धर्वस्तु स विज्ञेयो मैथुने वामसंभव: ॥

गान्धर्व (Gándharva) which solely rests on mutual love, is that rite in which both the parties engage themselves out of their own accord and will.

(7) हत्वा छित्वा च भित्वा च क्रोशन्तीं रुदतीं गृहात् ।
प्रसह्य कन्याहरणं राक्षसो विधिरुच्यते ॥

राक्षस (Rákshas) is a name given to that engagement in which a person after slaughtering or torturing the damsel's relatives, takes her off *forcibly.*

(8) सुप्तां मत्तां प्रमत्तां वा रहो यत्रोपगच्छति ।
स पापिष्ठो विवाहानां पैशाच्श्चाष्टमो भमः ॥

Uniting with a girl when she is out of her senses, either through sleepiness or intoxication, is the last and the basest of all called पैशाच (Paishách).

No other part of Hindu law is so fruitful of controversy, as the Law of Inheritance. The reason for this anomalous

character of the Hindu law, as at present construed, cannot be
other than a complete break with antiquity, and in some cases
a direct antagonism to the old rules. It has been a task of
difficulty to reconcile these inconsistencies. If any expedient
is found out the remedy appears to be worse than the disease.
The principle, that underlies inheritance, is based on the
spiritual benefits to be conferred on the deceased proprietor,
and this belief is held to be universally true. According to the
old writers, descendants up to three degrees are entitled to
give periodical offerings. Consequently, actuated by the
motives of male succession, in order to be alleviated from the
burdens of this world, and also to get repose in the next world,
by the offerings paid by the surviving males, the Hindus enter
into a married life, but this marriage institution among the
Hindus is a very complicated affair. They have no one form of
rite, but their institution is divided into eight kinds, as noted
above.

All of these eight forms were neither practised nor originated
at one and the same time, but they show the different stages of
the social growth.

Mr. Mayne, in his treatise on Hindu Law and Usage, says
that all but the two, the Brahma and the Asura, are now
obsolete. (Sec. 80.) And again, in the same section, he says
that "the Brahma is the only legal form at present." This
assertion implies that marriage performed according to any
other rites is not valid, and the children of such other marriages are held illegitimate, and hence debarred from inheritance.
This interpretation may lead us to infer that marriage and son-
ship (inheritance) are co-related with each other. In old
times the marriage tie being loose, men wanted to have a son
in any way, somehow or other. This accounts for the different
sorts of sons as described in our Shastras. The list as given
numbers twelve sorts of sons.—They are Aurusa or legitimate
Patrika, Putra, Khestraja, Gudhaja, Kanina, Sahodha, Paunar-
bhava, Nishada or Parasava, Dattaka, Kritaka, Appaviddha,
Swayamdattaka.

¡. All of these twelve sons were recognised as legal, and
as the property of the father, but gradually as the society
grew advanced in ideas, and lawgivers turned their minds to

codify the laws moral, social, and political, looseness in the marriage tie disappeared, and the sacred institution of marriage came to be guided by strict rules and regulations. In these days when all of the twelve kinds of sons are not recognised, and only two of them are held legitimate, the naturally born and adopted ones, let us consider these forms and examine the propriety of the approved ones and the reason of the disapproved ones. It should be noted, that out of the eight kinds abovenamed, only the Brahma, Daiva, and Arsha and Prajapatya are approved ones, and the Asura, Gandharva, Rakshas and Paisách are disapproved ones. While the forms that are in vogue are only the Brahma and the Asura ones.

As for the Rakshas and the Paisach forms, which are disapproved, and which deserve to be condemned, nothing can be said in favour of them, for they are other names of *seduction and rape* in limited forms. Being of such a detestable character, they deserve to be condemned and disapproved.

Regarding the Gandharva, this form has been along with them also disapproved. When we refer to Manu he says:— आविग वैश्ययो राक्षसपैशाच्यर्जनात गान्धर्वासुर्यो &c.. *i.e.*, for Kehastryas and Vayshyas, Gandharva rite is allowed. The validity of this form has been also recognised by the Bengal Su lder Court when celebrated among the Kehastryas in the year 1817, but in other presidencies this form of marriage is invalidated in conformity with Mayne. Mayne says: "Its definition implies nothing more than *fornication*." How far this view can be said to be correct will be manifest when we shall define what Gandharva rite is. The Gandharva form of marriage is that rite, in which the parties engage, out of their own accord and will. From the above the form seems to be an engagement contracted by mutual will and love. Fornication, on the other hand, implies the sense of *lewdness* or *adultery*. To reconcile these two meanings is difficult and questionable. For if we observe the traditional examples of the renowned Draupadi, Sita and other ladies of note, the marriage performed in their case was the Swayamwar System or what can be called the self-selection system, while that in the case of Shankuntala, which was also by self-selection, is known to have been a Gandharva marriage. It might be alleged that such an interpretation as fornication might have made the form obsolete, or the very nature of the Swayamwar System, which was by open selection from among a number of candidates, assembled for the occasion in public, was not calculated to be much in vogue. The mortification of rejection in public might have no great inducement, and the number of young men, anxious to try their chance, might have in course of time dwindled. The system might have thus fallen into desuetude. The formal mode of Swayamwar System being not practised, the form might have been rendered obsolete and obsoleteness might have caused its disapproval and the disapproval affected inheritance rendering issue born of such a rite illegitimate. But if we examine this disapproval by the second criterion, viz., of caste rules, no such castal restriction can be found as prohibiting that rite to be performed.

If, on the other hand, the rite is followed, and the form approved or any other form in its place recognised to make such marriages as are performed at an advanced age, with a different law of succession, it will remove many of the inconsistencies and injuries a Hindu family at present suffers from, owing to one uniform system of celebrating their nuptial rites, and which can be said to have caused these inconsistencies. It will be a greater preventive to infant-marriages than such expedients found out as the Age of Consent Bill et hoc genus omne.

Next come the Prajapatya and the Daiva forms in which a daughter has been given to Brahmins because when the Brahminical influence was at its highest, people always were actuated by the motives of sanctity to give their daughters to Brahmins who were regarded as religious, and their power was regarded as equal to that of the gods, nay, even greater.

But now-a-days as the function of the Brahmins has been merely the performance of religious ceremonies, they are not held so powerful, and hence they might be accounted as rendered obsolete.

Then follows the Asura form which can be termed marriage by purchase. This form refers to the times when wives were scarcely obtainable by fair means, and when it was desirable to have wives from other sections of the caste to have a son, they were taken by giving an equivalent in return. This form is disapproved, inasmuch as the father actually makes a sale of his daughter by receiving an equivalent amounting to thousands of rupees, which receipt is forbidden entirely by Manu in his Smriti (Bk. III., sec. 5, chap. IX., verses 98-100).

Then follows the Arsha form which is an approved form and which is a survival of the one preceding it. In it no actual price is taken for the daughter, but only a nominal value in the shape of a cow or two is taken, which is slight, and is immediately returned to the bridegroom.

Last in order comes the Brahma form. The form is an approved one, and there is nothing even in its character rendering it objectionable. Here the connection is made permanent, and the authority which a father enjoyed passes over into the hands of the husband permanently.

But a question arises, do the Hindus celebrate their nuptial rites according to any of the forms as they are defined and approved? The answer to this question would be in the negative. Nowhere is performed the Arsha rite which is approved. Similarly, if we shall see the Brahma form, it is not practised as it is defined, but in a modified mode. The form as defined is that in which a daughter is given to one learned in the Vedas with some presents. The first condition is nowhere observed.

The Asura form is not also consistently observed. It plays a great part in determining the question of woman's property or what is called *Stridhan*. The word *Stridhan* is defined by Manu in his work (chap. 9) as follows :—

" What was given before the nuptial fire, what was presented in the bridal procession, and what was received from her brother, father or mother, and what was given in love by her husband, are denominated the six-fold property of a woman." Now, when a woman dies childless, the right to the succession of her property greatly depends upon the particular form she was married in ; for, when the form celebrated is Brâhma, or be any one of the four unblamed ones, then her property goes to her husband ; but if the form be Asura, then in case she has no issue surviving her, it goes to her father (Mayukh, chap. IV., sec. X.). Under such authorities, the father, alleging that he has received an equivalent from the bridegroom's party and that the rite was an Asura rite, and evidencing that fact from his ledgers and account-books, claims his daughter's property from her husband. The court taking cognizance of this kind of ledger-evidence, at once decides in favor of the father, rendering bare injustice to the husband. If closely examined, the father will be found unjustly holding his claim over his daughter's property. For, if we review with attention the inconsistent line of conduct the father had adopted during his daughter's lifetime, we will find that it is only a private* understanding for the time between the parties. When a father receives money from his daughter's husband, it naturally follows that he has no scruples in accepting trivial things, as water, tea, &c., at his daughter's house, but he refuses to accept them, arguing that he is forbidden to take anything of his daughter's. Forgetting his inconsistent conduct in his daughter's lifetime, at her death he claims of her property and he receives it at the cost of his son-in-law. But granting that he has celebrated the Asura rite, has there been any public avowal of his receiving the equivalent? The officiating priest neither knows of the form performed as Asura nor has there been made any reference in Lagan Padi, nor in the caste records where every such marriage is registered, nor in the invitation cards. To remedy these defects, if the aforesaid points be noted, that will prove a sure test, and would prevent injustice being rendered to the poor husband. Not only so, but it would some day or other put a stop to such a detestable practice in future, as it will be a constant reminder to the father of his receiving money when he dines or drinks at his son-in-law's, and at the same time people will cease performing such a rite, owing to the feeling of shame at their receiving the equivalent being registered in the caste records.

The ultimate view a father has in getting his children married and exercising a control over the marriage of his issues, is that stated above, that he expects from his children a fulfilment of the expectation of receiving periodical offerings for the repose of his soul after his death. In return for these expectations he recompenses them by entailing all his property to them. Thus, inheritance, as could be seen, has two main objects :—" It is given to compensate the sons for the offerings he gives to his dead father to secure him repose, and to maintain the issue of the marriage which was with the said view contracted by his father."

In these forms of marriage, it is stated that the bride's father selects the bridegroom who accepts the bride. But the observations of our common life experience will show that marriage is solemnized when the bridegroom's father accepts or approves of the bride, and the son marries her thus approved. In good many cases it generally happens that the betrothal takes place some years before a marriage is celebrated, and in that case the bridegroom is a minor. The match thus contracted is a mere game of chance and depends on favourable circumstances in future to prove a suitable one.

Nevertheless, granting that the match proves suitable, yet very often it so happens that dissensions take place between his wife and his mother, and the more so when there is a step-mother. The dissensions rise high, and when found irreconcilable, the father, holding his son responsible for his wife's actions, packs him out of doors with not a jot for his maintenance. The father forgets the responsibilities that were on him for the selection of the bride and devolves them on his son who had no vote nor voice in his engagement. The son being given nothing for his maintenance, and finding it hard to maintain himself, and the issue, takes recourse to the Court to ask for a partition of his father's property. But the Court instead of removing his difficulties rather increases them. In very few cases where there is nothing by way of self-acquisition, the Court accordingly awards him his share out of his father's property considering it ancestral, and sometimes the son's demand is dismissed, holding the property as self-acquired, and in some instances it so happens that the Court asks the son to wait till the amount of both the kinds of ancestral and self-acquired properties is determined. The determination causes expense and litigation. Many times it so happens that persons die out of anxiety before a due decision is arrived at. This expense and litigation are all owing to the modern constructions put upon the Hindu Law by the European lawyers. If close investigation be made of the family system among the Hindus, it will be manifest that *corpɔrate* property is the rule in the East, in contravention to the *individual* property in the West. In early day the family lived upon land, and consequently there was no scope for separate acquisitions. In those days property was held only as ancestral and not as both ancestral and self-acquired, as it has been done at present (Mayne, p. 245). But as civilization advanced, and the advance of the commerce therewith gave an impetus to men to follow various kinds of industry to* derive wealth, the wealth so derived from separate acquisitions brought into existence the second kind now designated as self-acquired property. The view of self-acquisition, although it has been referred to by Manu, has not been confirmed by other law-writers, Yagnawalkya and Brihaspati, who maintain that self-acquired property is at the cost of the family.

From the above it will be seen that a father cannot in any way have separate acquisitions, and so to avoid the expense and litigation above mentioned, it would be preferable if one of the forms only, the ancestral property, be taken as the standard and the other form be discarded. This will be more clear when we shall note what the Mitâkshará lays down :

In secs. 27 and 28 the writer says: that *Property is by birth,* and further he holds that they who are born, who are yet unbegotten, and who are still in the womb, require the means of maintenance, and hence he cannot dispose of his property as he likes, but is subject to the control of his sons and others. Property should be held ancestral only, *i.e.,* descended from ancestors, which one person enjoys during his life-time, after whose death it goes to his son on condition that he fulfils his obligations.

This division of property, into self-acquired and ancestral, has not only been instrumental in causing expense and litigation, but it slackens the tie of filial affections also.

The above theory of inheritance, based as it is on the offerings to the deceased for his repose in the next world, as laid down (3 Dig. 298), will be rendered clearer when the theory of excluding certain persons is examined. The prin_ ciple that underlies exclusion is that "one who is unable or unwilling to perform the necessary sacrifices is incapable of inheriting." Mayne quotes from Brihaspati that "a son who neglects the duty of redeeming his father is like a cow which neither affords milk nor becomes pregnant." He has no claim to the paternal estate, &c. It will be seen from the above princple that those who are defective in limb or sense, such as idiots, eunuchs, dumb or deaf, lunatics, are excluded from claiming their father's estate, though they are entitled to be maintained. Those who have been degraded from castes, *i.e.*, out-castes, are also recognised as incapable of inheriting, the reason of which is plainly "their inability to perform their sacrificial rites for the redemption of the soul of the deceased."

Hindu Society has never been at any one time regulated by any one code of regulations. The continual transformation, the large number of communities, and the vast area of land occupied by the Hindus with scarce any inter-communication have all contributed to the existence of several sorts of customs held binding in their respective localities. The want of any faithful record of the times has perhaps in some measure been made up by the fact that the several stages of the social growth are all visible in the customs that prevail all over the land Under these circumstances legislation would be out of the question, and the customs that are held to have the binding force of laws continue to be inconsistent and irreconcilable. The texts of old even are frequently arrayed on either side, the authors having recorded the customs and laws, each of his own community or district. When therefore all the texts are read together, they present equally authoritative and equally irreconcilable dictums. Under this category unhappily the subject of the testamentary power of a Hindu falls.

The origin and growth of the testamentary power among the Hindus has been a problem of great controversy, and consequently difficult of solution. The mention of such a word as *will* is nowhere found either in the Dharma Shastras or in the early law-writers. In early times, and even at present, as has been said before, the family property of a Hindu was looked upon as corporate, *i. e.*, the earnings of all the individual members went to the general property of the family, and

the father or the eldest member of the family was looked upon
or regarded as the Manager. In those days to claim such a
power as that of a devisor would seem something like a con-
tradiction to old rules. Still if a glance be cast at the times
when the Brahmanical influence was at its highest, such a
tendency would be observed in pious gifts or charities as they
were awarded to Brahmins to whom sanctity was attributed in
those days, and the gifts were held irrevocable. But by-and-
by as the natives came in contact with the early English settlers, who were mostly merchants, they got an instinct to follow
their mode of devising, and the power which was first confined
to religious gifts only under certain circumstances, *e. g.*, when
there is no issue, &c., afterwards extended to the devising of
property for purposes other than religious gifts, and without
restrictions.

But the influence of the English lawyers has gone even
farther. They have upset the very foundations upon which
that power was based. They have not only upheld the doctrine
of the father's right to devise, but have also put a different
interpretation upon the kind of property, rendering the property bequeathed a self-acquired, since the bequest so held
resembles a gift.

The origin and growth being so far described, the object
which the lawyers had in their minds while recognising the
power of the father to dispose of his property as he likes can be
no other than to give a free scope to the father, who is in case
the property be ancestral, quite incompetent to do so. But how
far this expedient accomplishes its desired object and how far its
acceptance has caused inconsistencies rather than remedying
them, has been a matter of consideration. To understand these
inconsistencies it is essentially necessary to analyse the existing
system of the Hindu families.

Among the Hindus the family in early times, as well as in
these days, has been very rarely a divided one. It is, on the
other hand, a joint family. The son, whether he is a minor or of
age, is exclusively under the parental control, and has to act up
to the commands of his father. All his separate earnings he is
to hand over to his father to be amalgamated with the general
stock of the family property, on a clear understanding that the

whole stock will be invested in himself after the demise of his father. The family is thus manifestly a joint one, and the present interpretation of WILLS proves not less a stumbling block to the whole status of the family in which filial affections and due reverential feelings are at present observed.

But apart from that a question arises—to what extent and what kind of property can be disposed of ? Mayne defines this extent in the following words :—" Whatever property is so completely under the testator's power that he may give it away during his life-time, he may also devise by will. Hence a man may bequeath his separate or self-acquired property (§ 380).

But property self-acquired as such does not exist in the sense which might entitle the father to absolute ownership. For, in a joint family where the sons coming of age, work with the father and have an income in common with him, it would be difficult to mark out the property forming the self-acquisition of either the father or the son. And again where the minor sons are married by their parents from motives both arthly an l s piritual it is but just that they should be entitled to a portion of the property, hitherto held by the father alone. Unlike an English father the Hindu father does not feel that he has discharged his duty to his children by giving them an education, fitting them for the world, but always anxiously discharges what to him is a duty, and gets his son married as soon as possible to ensure the regular performance of his obsequies and such other ceremonies. It is natural, then, that in anticipation by way of what is known as marriage settlement in other countries, the son should have been given the right to go shares with his father in his property, when yet a minor, incapable of adding to the property by his own exertions. Thus having due regard to the fact that a Hindu is religious above all, even in the most worldly of his actions, we find it, that he is not vested with anything like absolute dominion over property especially after he marries and has sons. Even in natural justice it would be due to the minor son who is *nolens volens* encumbered with married life in order to satisfy the religious neccessities of his father that he should receive a share of the family property by way of a marriage settlement.

As it has been already noted, the recognition of self-acquisition would not be consistent with the religious basis on which the fabric of social life is built with the Hindus. Perhaps separate property can be held justifiable in a case like the following:—When a father has not mixed the earnings of his son with his, nor has he thrown over him the burden of marriage, nor asked him to meet certain demands and obligations on his behalf; then and then only can a father be rightly said to have absolute power to dispose of his property as he likes. If these conditions are not observed, the present division of properties into ancestral and self-acquired is not in keeping with Hindu traditions.

So much full of anomalies is this subject of wills that it can be only settled when the ancestral and no other form is allowed to exist. Even the early law-writers justify this fact that there cannot be any other form of property than the ancestral, and the property being so held the interests of a father to enjoy that property are only *inter vivos*. But granting, on the other hand, the existence of separate property, it is questionable whether a member of an *undivided* family as the Hindu family, can bequeath his own shares in the joint property as he likes. At the same time separate acquisitions can hardly be said to be in existence. For when the earnings of the son are mixed up with those of his father, modern opinion has declared the nature of that joint property as ancestral. The European lawyers, at present, to do them full justice, have tried to determine the amount of each of the properties, but it is to be regretted that they fail, as they do not take into account some of the facts which are likely to escape their notice, for even if the amount of the earnings may be determined ; can they delineate the moral obligations which a son has *qua son* fulfilled on his father's behalf, and for which he stands in expectation of some compensation ? And again, the father's intention in bequest by will, can be only to keep the joint property intact and to ensure the maintenance of the succeeding generations from whom he expects offerings after his death up to three degrees. In cases where he so expresses his intentions and when he has no grand-children existing at the time, the Court holds a different view and sets aside the condition, confirming the will, as in the

Tagore case where the conditions of the will were set aside and the will was confirmed. The conditions being set aside, it is a fact that the object of the donor can hardly be said to have been preserved ;

Whereas the Court is bound to give effect to the intentions of the testator and to devise the best means to carry them out. Had the will been set aside *in toto*, the property would have descended according to the rules of Hindu Law, thus forming an ancestral trust, at any rate for three generations to come, an ample provision being thus made for their main tenance.

Having grown wiser, the testator makes a will, devising the property to his male issue, according to the rules of Hindu Law, with special care, to style it ancestral, by way of provision for his succeeding generations, for fear the son should be the full and absolute owner of the property, and the accumulations, at the cost of his grand-children in the hands of an English Court But still the subtlety of an English lawyer might argue the testator, out of his intentions. For he might say, the very fact that there is a will, goes to make the property self-acquired, and it devolves unencumbered to the son, with no proviso for his grandson. But such a view is inconsistent both with the intentions of the testator and those of the Court. For the testator who wished to give away certain portion of his property by will and secure the rest for the benefit of his sons and grand sons in the hands of his son, by making a formal will, is clearly frustrated by the Court, while the Court desiring to bestow on the testator the power to dispose of his property just as he wants it, is equally frustrated in its generous object by this mode of reasoning adopted.

Again supposing the grand-children are living, they would be clearly entitled to the benefits of the property if there was an actual trust created. But what should be the effect, when a testator, *ex abundanti cautela*, bequeaths his property as *ancestral* to his son and his issue according to the rules of Hindu Law ? The grand-children who have no other bequests in the will, are certainly within their rights in claiming a share in the property admittedly ancestral in the hands of their grand father. Would they be denied this right and the

property held self-acquired *because* it is given by will **as**
ancestral ?

Or would it be humanely maintained that it is self-
acquired so far as the sons go and ancestral so far as the
otherwise unprovided grand-children go? Granting, though it
is not possible, for the purposes of argument, that the property
is held self-acquired in both the cases, the donor will have still
a means left to secure his objects, and avoid the clutches of
the law. In his life-time he will enter into an agreement
with his son admitting that certain property is *ancestral* in his
hands.

Accumulations being, of course, an outcome of the *corpus*
follow its nature and are under the equal control of the father and
the sons. The father, being conscious of the fact that all control
over the accumulations is given up by the agreement, likes to
retain to himself, in the very terms of the agreement, the
right to spend the property as he likes. The sons having been
made to share the property, devised to them with the grand-son
by force of the *ancestral* nature of the property, this restriction
on their part is counterbalanced by the fact that the father
undertakes to spend sums only *reasonable in amount* and such
as he has hitherto been in the habit of making, giving his sons
the right to interfere with his mode of life, in case it should
have the effect of depriving them of their respective shares in
the joint family property.

In case he has no grand son at the date of the agreement, he
carefully confirms in his will the ancestral character of the
property and also by implication the accumulation, held by him
and thus secures his aims both of providing for his grand
children born subsequently, and of ensuring the validity of the
agreement, in spite of the bequest by will of the property.
There at least we may hope the poor testator will be given the
privilege of having his intentions acted up to, *viz.*, to devise
property in separate shares, greater or smaller, to his sons, to
avoid the difficulties of a partition suit, after his death, to be
queath a portion to his friends and in charity, and also to secure
provision for his grand-children. Should he be frustrated even
now the poor testator will have to cry out, " Save me from my
friends;" these Courts which are anxious to carry out my inten-

tions, and yet frustrate me, and are themselves frustrated. For they hinder him in doing what it is their intention to allow him to do, *i.e.*, to dispose of the property just as he likes, and unconsciously they come in his way when effecting what he has most at heart and what he is most anxious about for his religious welfare after death.

It will be difficult to rectify these inconsistencies as shown above, and unless the whole Hindu mind and life is changed, such a testamentary power of a Hindu can never be recognised, and in order to effect such a change, it would be necessary at present to restrict the operations of the will only to a certain extent, and under certain restrictions better calculated, to carry out the intentions of the donor and his responsibilities to provide for minor sons encumbered with marriage and certain other obligations in his behalf, whom he had not prepared for independent livelihood by devoting their time to the joint family. These conditions being definitely stated, those who wish to devise their property, will try to act up to these conditions from the very beginning and the difficulties that now beset them, in making a will, will be removed.

At present it is admitted that if a father's property is mixed with the grandfather's, so as to be incapable of being separated, it forms a part of the ancestral property. In the same way, it follows that if a son's property is mixed with his father's, it also becomes in its turn ancestral, because, on examination, we will find that the reasons for considering that property as ancestral in the latter case, are at least just the same, if not stronger, than in the former case.

In the first instance a father receives a certain property from the grandfather, as his son, and as such he is expected to perform certain obligations. If he does not perform these obligations, still as he has got the property in his possession and his right there being none to dispute, he enjoys it to his satisfaction, but being not fully satisfied with the enjoyment of that property alone, he further encroaches upon the property of his son, and unites it with his own. The son allows him to mix his earnings on the clear understanding that he will get his and his father's property together, after his father's death. On this understanding, they work together. The father not being content with appropriating his son's property with his own, asks him to help him in all his social and other business matters, on his behalf; he further asks him to marry a wife of his own choice, and expects not only him but also his children to perform his obsequies. The son agrees to do all these functions out of filial love and affection. It may well be remarked here that marriage is the chief thing among the Hindus, that makes the father and son more strongly united with each other. The time for marriage is generally the age when the son is able to understand his duties towards his father and himself and consequently a clear understanding between the father and the son must be made at that time to constitute a self-acquired property.

The time for dissensions is generally when a step-mother enters the field, and the more so when she has children. Then quarrels ensue between the mother and the wife, and so marriage, which was originally the cause of unity, proves in the end, the cause of dissensions and questions of inheritance crop up. Now whatever be the cause, when the father has in some shape or another, united his son's property with his own or even taken up his time for his interests, whether in trade or otherwise whereby he is prevented from laying by his own separate earnings, does it not stand to reason that the father's property should not be treated as self-acquired but should be ranked as ancestral?

The disadvantages of having two sorts of properties in the hands of a Hindu father, are again made clear by instances very common in life. The father quietly disposes of the ancestral property, when managing the joint family, and meets all his expenses therefrom, and at the end, shows a clear debit on the ancestral side, leaving all the assets in the self-acquired column. This is sheer injustice, but still in conformity with the views that prevail. The son, therefore, foresees the danger, and gets up a timely partition suit, which is inconsistent with the joint family basis of Hindu life, although at present allowed by custom.

The doctrine of two sets of property, side by side, is thus calculated to work mischief, and to judge from the effects produced by it, would be untenable on principles of Hindoo life;

whereas, in case the property is held ancestral alone, the sons will have every inducement to be filial, and will be duly re-compensed for their conduct, without any fears of disinheritance, unless they act otherwise and renounce all claims to the property in the hands of their father. On the other hand, when there are two properties or where there is self-acquired property alone, there will be an inducement to the son also, to keep apart his earnings from his father, and thus withhold what might be a great assistance to a poor father. This recognition of the doctrine of the self-acquisition of properties will be found injurious also to the interests of the deaf, dumb, &c., as well as to widows and other female members of the family, inasmuch as though entitled to maintenance they are deprived of their right, the manager being made the sole owner of the property.

All these difficulties are further aggravated by the appointment of unconnected persons as executors to a Hindu will. From the above remarks it is clear, how impracticable it is for one, to give effect to either the spirit of the bequest or even to the intentions of a testator.

It is necessary to have persons who have sympathy for the beneficiaries and who woud give full effect to the intentions of the testator, appointed as executors. The bequests to women and others not favoured by the Hindu Law ought to be carefully watched and given effect to. I will not here trouble you with all the qualifications necessary in an executor of a Hindu will, although it cannot be denied that executors may be a great help or hindrance to the carrying out of the will, according as they are suitable or not.

ORDINARY GENERAL MEETING held on Wednesday, the 31st October 1894.

Mr. KHURSETJI RUSTOMJI CAMA, *Vice-President*, presided.

The Minutes of the previous Meeting were read and confirmed.

The following donations were acknowledged and thanks voted
to the donors :—

To the Library.

From the Asiatic Society of Bengal, Calcutta, Journal Vol.
LXIII., Part 1, No. 3, 1894.

The following paper was then read :—

"*On the* ORIGIN *and* ACCOUNT *of the* KAPOLA BANIA CASTE."

BY MR. TRIBHOWANDAS MANGALDAS NATHUBHAI.

BEFORE venturing to give the origin and a summary account
of the Kapola Banias, as a preliminary, it is necessary to take
a bird's-eye view of the origin of the Indian castes, as at
present existing.

The problem of the origin of the Indian castes being full of
complexity, a definite and unanimous conclusion can hardly be
arrived at. Various critical researches have been attempted
to unveil the overhanging mystery ; but in the words of Lord
Bacon, it might be said that "the voice of the plenty affirms
rather a want than a correct investigation." Mythology an
tradition have not been wanting in propounding to us various
theories, explaining the formation of the Indian castes, in one
way or another, but all seem equally authoritative.

India is, truly speaking, the land of mystery. It has been
a land of mystery from its earliest ages to the present hour.
It stands beyond comparison in its mystic character to all the
other countries of the world. The ancient empires of the
world, Assyria, Babylon, Macedonia, &c , had not their histo-
ries lying in utter obscurity, but they are printed in books
from their being preserved in tablets or rocks. But the case
with India is quite the contrary. It is to be regretted, that
when the rudest nations are seldom destitute of some of their
chronological annals, the Hindus who have reached to a
high pitch of civilization and refinement, have not a single
work approaching to the character of a history proper·
Nevertheless, some fragmentary works have been traditted
down to us, from which a glimpse of some of the annals of India

can be obtained, without an accurate regard to the chronological order.

As can be seen from these fragmentary works, the history of India can be roughly divided into the following periods :—

(1) The Vedic Period.
(2) The Epic Period.
(3) The Budhha Period.
(4) The Smriti Period.
(5) The Puranic Peirod or later period marking the advent of the various Puranas. .

The Hindus are divided into four original castes—the Brahmins, the Kshatryas, the Vayshyas, and the Sudras, and each of these times has its theory peculiar to it regarding the origin of the caste—

(1) The Vedic Period is marked by the promulgation of the Vedas, which are the earliest sources of information on Hindu society. The chronological limits of this period have been marked by Dr. Max Müller between 1200 and 1000 B.C. In those times the following theory was held :—In the Purush Sukta, a hymn on the primeval male, it is said that,

Purush or Brahma is this whole universe, and is to be. He is Lord of Immortality, &c. The gods offered up this Purush in sacrifice, from which were erected four castes :—

यत्पुरुषं व्यदधुः कतिधा व्यकल्पयन् ।
मुखं किमस्य कौ बाहू कउ ऊरु पादावुच्येते ॥
ब्राह्मणो ऽस्य मुखमासीद्बाहू राजन्यः कृतः ।
ऊरु तदस्य यद्वैश्यः पद्भ्यां शूद्रो अजायत ॥

This means that the Brahmins were created from the mouth, the Rajanyas or Kshatryas from the arms, the Vayshyas from the thighs, and the last Sudras from the feet of that Purush. This allegorical statement may be supposed to imply that the classes might have arisen from the different avocations the people might have followed, referring to the different organs mentioned.

(2) But in the Epic times this allegorical statement of the Vedas has been rendered more literal. The Ramayana and the Mahabharata which distinguish the Epic period of India, have both special theories embodied in them for the formation of castes.

The Ramayana teaches us, that the four castes were the offspring of a woman named Manu, the wife of Kashyapa, a son of Brahma, and they or their issue having followed different professions, might have been classified as at present. The Mahabharata asserts that originally there was no distinction of classes, the existing distinction having arisen out of differences of character and occupation.

(3) Then comes in order the Budha Period, approximated between 600—200 B. C. This period is marked by its important reaction against the caste system, and the theory held in this period cannot, as a natural consequence, be literally conformable to either the Vedas or the Ramayana, but it came nearer to the Mahabharata. Badhha found the system of Indian caste then existing in such a vigorous operation, that though at first he recognized the primary doctrines of the castes and their powers and functions as laid down in the Vedas, yet, later on, he inculcated, that originally there was no distinction of castes, and the existing classes are divided according to their varying professions and rank.

(4) Then we arrive at the Smriti period. This period is marked by the various kinds of productions based on the Vedas, not the original texts, but recollections of them, as some parts had perished. Of these the best known and the commonly received as Law, among the Hindus, in their matters both secular and religious, is Manu's Smriti, written by Manu who flourished, as Sir William Jones mentions in his translation of Manu Smriti, in the 2nd century before Christ. Manu explains the formation of the castes as follows :—

Though he speaks of the formation of the different classes from the mouth, the arms, thighs and feet of the Godhead (I. 3), he does not consistently hold to this theory : He speaks in (I. 32) of Brahma becoming half male and half female, and

as creating Viràj in that female; of Viràj forming Manu; of
Manu were created ten Prajapatis; and of these ten Prajapatis, seven other Manus and Devas, and Maharshis and various
other creatures, apes, fishes, beasts, birds, and *Men*.

Coming finally to times marked by the advent of the
various Puranas, in none of them we find the slightest relaxa-
tion of the caste system, though in some of them we meet with
such passages, giving intimations and assertions worthy of
notice.

The Vishnu Puran describes the formation of castes as
follows :—

When Brahma, meditating on truth, became desirous to
create this world, creatures in whom goodness prevailed sprang
from his mouth; others in whom passion predominated sprang
from his breast. Those in whom passion and darkness prevailed sprang from his thighs, and others from the feet. All
these constituted the system of the four castes, Brahmins,
Kshatryas, Vayshyas, and Sudras.

In the remaining Puranas, however, we find a rigid adherence to the original texts of the Vedás.

From what has been said above, the origin and progress of
the caste-system in India is of course difficult to trace with
anything approaching certainty. Nevertheless, it should be
observed here, that these theories have all been at one in
inculcating the same duties for the four orders to be performed
in all times in all ages.

Manu, in his chapter on the Creation of Man, says :—

"For the sake of preserving the universe, the Being,
supremely glorious, allotted separate duties to separate classes
(which can be naturally performed from the specified organs,
viz., mouth, arm, thigh, and foot). To Brahmins, he has
assigned the duties of reading and teaching the Veda, of
sacrificing, of assisting others to sacrifice, of giving alms and
of receiving gifts. To defend the people, to give the alms,
to sacrifice, to shun the allurements of sexual gratification,
are in a few words the duties of a Kshatrya. To keep herds
of cattle, to bestow largesses, to sacrifice, to read the Scriptures, to carry on trade, to lend at interest, are the duties of
a Vayshya. One principal duty the Supreme Being allots to

Sudras, is to serve the before-mentioned classes, without depreciating their worth." This is the typical teaching on the subject, and is generally received at the present time.

As the Vayshyas are assigned the duty of keeping flocks and herds, carrying on trade, lending at interest, cultivating soil, &c., they can be conveniently divided into the following classes :—Merchants, who are generally called Banias, Herds-men, Cultivators, &c. Banias then are a particular species of the Vayshyas who carry on trade, and lend at interest.

1. The Kapola section of the Bania caste consists of a population of about 5,000 persons in Bombay.

2. There are many sub-sections of Bania Caste as exhi-bited in Appendix A (numbering 84).

3. The Kapola section is divided into two endogamous divisions, from outside of which persons cannot marry. They are the Delwadias and the Gogharees. The Delwadias and the Gogharees are named from their respective localities ; the Delwadia, from Delwada, a town near Jaffrabad, in the south of Kattyawad, and the Gogharees from Ghogha, a small village near Bhownugger.

The Delwadias in ancient days were at one with the Gogharee section, but from some reason or another intermar-riage with them ceased to be performed, and a distinction has been kept between them, that the Gogharees are not allowed to touch the dead bodies of Delwadias. To resume this practice of taking a daughter from the Delwadia section, the Gogharees began to offer large sums to the father of the bride of the Delwadia section, which equivalent the father was con-strained to accept owing to his straitened circumstances, and gradually intermingled with each other. Still. whenever a daughter of the Delwadia section is given in the Gogharee section, she becomes a Gogharee. On the other hand, when a daughter of the Gogharee section is taken, the receiver with his descendants ceases to be a Delwadia, and is looked upon as a Gogharee. Whereupon the Delwadia section dwindled into a minority, while the other one grew to a majority.

4. They follow the ordinary rules of marriage, viz., that persons must marry within the same caste and they must not

be सपिण्ड *i.e.*, they must not be within the seven degrees of a common ancestor. They allow a man to marry two sisters.

5. It should be noted herewith that though no restriction, either on religious or social differences, is based in intermarriage, yet in some countries a very slight restriction is based on geographical position, and the restriction consists merely in the payment of a nominal sum of fine, in default of which their Lahana* is stopped in their native town. This prohibition is not done by the caste, but by the particular inhabitants of that country for their own benefit, and is observed to a very limited extent in these modern and enlightened days.

The Kapolas are divided into many sub-divisions according to their special vocations. The whole of the Kapola section comprises eighteen Gotras. By the word Gotra is meant a group of the descendants of any one of the Rishis.

From the above, as we see, the Kapolas, descended from the eighteen original ancestors or Rishis or belonging to 18 Gotras, comprise various divisions which form their surname. These are again divided into many sub-divisions, and each sub-division was named or designated by the special vocation it pursued, or from its first forefather or otherwise. The tabular list given in Appendix B, numbering 50, will give a clear knowledge of all these divisions with their sub-divisions, and an explanation as to why they are designated at present by the special name.

Traditional Origin of the Kapola Caste.

6. The name Kapola is given to this section of the Bania

[NOTE.—Originally all the Dwijis are said to have descended from eight Rishis. Vishwamitra, Gauttam, Agastya, Jamdagnaye, Bhrigu, Vasishtha, Kashiapa and Atri, but their number is now estimated at forty-nine by the Hindu Dharm Shastras. Out of these forty-nine, the Kapola Banias comprise eighteen. The descendants of any one of these is said to belong to that Gotra. The characteristic of the Gotra is that Hindu Shastras prohibit Dwijis to marry who are or who belong to the same Gotra, *i.e.*, who are the descendants of the same Rishi. All the three classes, the Brahmins, the Kshatryas, and the Vayshyas, were called Dwijis, as they all wore the sacred thread, but the Banias do not wear it at present; this restriction is not observed in their case.]

* Lahana is the present given to all the caste-members in town on occasions such as marriage, &c., by the party performing the marriage.

caste, for when they got this appellation their Kapolas or cheeks were beautified by the earrings they had put on.   •

In the Skanda Purana a very interesting mythology is recorded tracing the origin of the Kapola caste.

Once upon a time, in the primeval age, designated as the Satyuga or the golden age, the sage Kanva was practising his austerities in the forest called in those days *"Papapnod"* (destroyer or dispeller of sins). The situation of this forest has been at present fixed near Than and Lakhtar in the south of Guzerat. Sage Kanva practised severe austerities, but a human being unless he be supernatural cannot escape the laws of nature. On a winter morning, early at dawn, the sage went to take an ablution in the river in the neighbourhood, and when he came out his body was found by a fowler quivering and trembling by the frosty cold of the season. The fowler thereupon collected some fuel and kindled a fire that the sage may have relief from his trembling agonies. The sage seeing the unexpected kindness in fowler blessed him to be one of the universal sovereign or a *Chakravarti Raja.* It so happened that one of the solar kings of Ayodhya, who was a pious and benign sovereign, was asking the favour of gods and sages to have him a son, for the barrenness was and has been regarded a curse by the Hindoos. The fowler thus blessed was born of that king and was named Mandhata. Whereupon the fowler, now born a king, in consequence of his original ruthlessness and cruelty, began to torment his people and harass them in every possible way, for the original tendencies and feelings of a man seldom miss him even in his second life. The subjects being disgusted at the despotism of the king Mandhata, went to the sages to ask for the redress of their grievances. The sages instructed the complaining subjects to go and take recourse to the sage Kanva in the forest of Papapnod. The subjects being answered in that way went to the sage and complained to him of all their grievances and asked for his protection. The sage Kanva whereupon sent his disciple Galav with them, with a message to t ɔ king to behave in a kingly manner and not to be tyrannical. The king *was so much impressed with the message* that he at once agreed to act up to the message. But he made up is mind to see the sage and set out from Ayodhya for the residence of Kanva. Kanva received the king hospitably, when the latter expressed his intention to be an ascetic rather than a king. The sage remonstrated with him so strongly that it was finally settled that Mandhata was to live just near the residence of Kanva. But being blessed with a benedic tion to be a universal sovereign, it was necessary that he should remain a king, and that there must be people inhabiting a certain tract which he must govern. For this the sage asked the divine favour, and was ordered that he should send out his pupils in search of the citizens and the city will be erected for the sage's favourite. Consequently, Galav, the most favoured of the sage's pupils, was sent out and he found some 54,000 men in the tract lying at the foot of the mount Girnar, in Sorath. He persuaded these men to accompany him and brought them to the city. Out of this number 18,000 were Brahmins, and 36,000 were Banias. The city was erected in a convenient and ornamental style, and these newly brought men were assigned quarters in it for their residence. Galav, in jest, gave to some of the Banias, numbering 6,000, the name of Kapola, the rest he named Sorathias, as having come from Sorath, and Brahmins he named Kundalias, who are now known by the name of Kandolia, from Kundals or earrings which both had worn and their cheeks or Kapolas were beautified by them. The Brahmins are now known by the name of Kandolias, and they are the officiating priests of the Kapolas and the Sorathias.

In the above story, it has been said that these Kapolas inhabited the tract of the Papapnod, but this name is changed in all the four ages, Satyuga, Treta, Dvapâr, and Kali. The following verse gives the names of each age :—

स्थापितं कण्वाल्यं नाम त्रेतायां कलुषापहम् ।
द्वापरे कपिलं कलौ स्थानकम्डोलकं स्मृतम् ॥

i.e., In the golden age, when the sage Kanva erected the city for Mandhata it was called after his name Kanvalaya, in the Tretá age it was named Kalushapaha (expeller of sins). In the Dvapâr age it was named Kampil, who was a king and had been there to expiate the sin of a Brahmicide. In the

Nevertheless, Polygamy is practised only in very few cases, and it is looked upon with great disfavour. Polyandry is not at all known to the caste.

11. They perform their marriage ceremonies according to the usual rite of Brahma which is a prevalent form throughout the whole of India, though in some cases an equivalent is received for the bride in which case the rite is called Asura. Notwithstanding, the ceremonies are performed according to the Brahma form. Various ceremonies are performed in solemnizing a nuptial rite, an account whereof is given on page 372. The binding ceremony is of the Mangal Fera, when the married pair goes round the chori fourth time.

12 & 13. Neither are widows remarried nor is divorce allowed.

Inheritance.

14. Being Hindus they follow the Hindu law, though to a great extent their cases are guided by custom, and custom sometimes overrules the maxims of law laid down. As a rule, in former times the eldest son used to take charge of the property of his father and divide it equally among his brothers if there be any. The youngest son was allowed to choose his share first. At present all the sons take charge of the property and divide it equally.

There is no rule in the caste code which would justify the son to demand a partition during his father's lifetime otherwise than for causes defined by law. Though at present on the authority of certain cases wherein the father willingly shared his property with his sons, the court has justified the claims of a son for partition.

They do not consider that property bequeathed by a will to the heirs resembles a gift to the legatee alone, as their mode of life requires that the whole family, especially the female members and others, such as deaf, dumb, who are only allowed maintenance, as well as the minors, ought to be maintained from the family property, which generally consists of—

(1) The property coming from the ancestor.

(2) The son's income going to the original stock.

(3) The provision for the regular performance of the obsequies of the ancestors up to three degrees.

(4)   The provision for the maintenance of the minors females and destitute members of the family.

When it is stated in the will, that the family is to be maintained out of the property, or the property is designated ancestral, and to go to the sons, according to the rules of Hindoo Law, they consider such property as ancestral, and not in the slightest degree resembling a gift given by will, as it would be a real hardship on the whole family and especially on the female or other destitute members of the family who really deserve their sympathy and support.

The father is not justified to encumber the ancestral property with debt even on his self-acquired property, and whenever so done and the property is a joint one, the son is perfectly justified in asking for a partition as stated on page 32B.

The Kapola Banias can adopt, and adoption follows in conformity with the rules of the Hindu Law. It should be observed here that some of the sections of the Bania caste do not adopt, and adoption with them is not in vogue. In adopting a son, no regular religious ceremonies are performed. Both the adopted and the naturally born are equally entitled to inherit.

The management of the family property rests with the eldest male member.

Religion.

15.   They describe themselves to be Vaishnavites in a majority of cases, though they equally revere both Shiva and Vishnu.

16.   Besides these deities of common worship they specially revere minor deities and goddesses which are given in the Appendix **B** attached. But in addition to these, they have special goddesses—Samudri,* the goddess in Than (their original habitation) and also a temple of Samudri, in each city where they reside, for both of which they give a specified sum of money for their management. These sums are given as specified in the account on marriage and pregnancy ceremonies. There are special days to go to bow down to the goddess : they are Tuesday, Thursday and Sunday, though other days are not disregarded.

---

* The shrine of Samudri is at Sundri, a village under Dhangadhra, 20 miles north of Than.

17. In all the ceremonies, both nuptial and funeral ceremonies, are instructed by the officiating priests who are called
Kandolia Brahmins, and Brahmins of other caste are not
employed for ceremonial purposes. These Brahmins are
received on equality by others of the same class.

Disposal of the Dead.

18. Both cremation and burying are in vogue among
them, burying for children under eighteen months and for the
rest burning. However when a woman dies with a child
in the womb, her stomach is dissected at the burning place
by one of the relations, and if the child be a female, it is
burnt along with the mother, but if a male it is buried
separately.

When a person is reported to be dying, he is shaved and
bathed and is then wreathed in flowers and basil seed, and
water is put in the mouth by the nearest relations stating that he
will do a particular charity after him. When he breathes his
last, the eldest son purifying himself by bathing performs the
obsequies, offering one rice-ball, to secure him repose. Afterwards the corpse is placed on a bier and carried to the cemetery
by the nearest relations. When the corpse is taken out of the
house, its feet are in front and the head in the rear. It is
preceded on its way to the burning ground by a person having
fire especially kindled at home, for burning the corpse, which
fire is carried by the youngest male member of the family.
The same position is kept till the cemetery is within sight,
whence after allowing the body to rest for a few minutes, the
position is reversed, the head in the front and feet in the rear.
Entering the burial ground, the corpse is placed on a pile
prepared for burning.

When the corpse is placed on the pile, with the rice-ball
placed on his right side, certain prayers are offered to the Fire
Deity, fire is applied to the right toe. The corpse, it
should be observed, is placed on the pile with the head to the
north. When it is wholly consumed, the bones are collected
and reserved to be carried to some nearest river or sea, and
the son-in-law gets a cow milked at the spot for washing them
with the milk. Then the ashes and bones are carried either to

the adjoining river or sea. The relations then return home bathing themselves in the nearest water-reservoir. Some preserve the bones to be carried to Benares to be thrown into the Ganges or to some other sacred place.

19. For the first thirteen days offerings are given. For the first three days, on the roof of the house, two crucibles filled with milk and water are placed with the object that the deceased may quench his thirst and allay his hunger on his way to Heaven, the journey being supposed a long one allegorically.

On the third day, or even earlier, the Uthamana ceremony is performed, in which the outsiders and relations, who have come to sympathize for the bereaved persons, are taken to a neighbouring tank or well, where they cleanse their mouth and hands. The priest there recites the particular positions the planets had occupied when the man had died, and then all go to bow down to a deity, where a lamp of ghee having 360 wicks is placed, with the attributed object that the deceased may not grovel in utter darkness on his way to Heaven, but may have it lighted, for 360 days of the lunar year, the time the journey is supposed to take. Bowing to the deity, all return home, when the chief mourner is given a turban by his father-in-law and all others return to their homes.

When the Uthamana ceremony is over the mourners don't sit on the verandah to receive the sympathizers as they did on the first two days at the house of the deceased. For the observing of Uthamana, the third day, from the death of a man, is the prescribed day, but if that day be either Tuesday, Wednesday, or Sunday, it is done earlier.

Every month, for a year, the day on which the person died is observed, after which every year succeeding the anniversary day is observed.

The Shradhha ceremony is performed every year in the second half of the lunar month of Bhadrapada, corresponding to the month of October.

On the anniversary day eight rice-balls are offered, three for each of the ancestors, both paternal and maternal, and one is offered for persons born of illicit connection, and it is kept separate and one for persons dying an unnatural death. In the Shradhha ceremony nine balls are offered, four for each of the ancestors, maternal and paternal, and two for others as in the Anniversary. In Anniversary as well as the Shradhha, the ball which is kept separate while the other balls are given to the crows is buried at the close of the ceremonies and the caste men who buries is obliged to bathe. When the Shradhha ceremony is finally brought to a close, eatables are thrown to the crows, after which Brahmins and other relations are feasted.

Internal Structure.

2). The Internal Structure of the caste is extremely complicated and can be best studied in the attached list. The caste is divided into two endogamous sub-divisions each of which is again divided into a number of various sub-divisions. The names of these are curious, some are local or territorial, while a few from the forefather or original founder of the section. The rule of exogamy restricts males from accepting a bride outside their divisions and intermarriage in the endogamous divisions is allowed, though it is restricted within seven degrees.

Occupation.

21. The Kapola Banias in a majority of cases have not transgressed the duties that have been prescribed to them by the great law-giver Manu. They are chiefly merchants, traders, landlords carrying on transactions in lending, &c., though some are servants or tillers of the soil.

Food.

26. The Kapolas live on simple vegetable food and milk, and abstain themselves from wine, flesh, &c.

Social Status.

27. In point of social standing they rank with the highest known caste of the Vayshyas. Brahmins may not hesitate to take water from their hands though they would not eat of their hands. The castes with which they eat is their own Bunia caste, and they do not take any cooked food of the other castes lower than them. They eat of the Brahmins only, a caste higher than them.

Jurisdiction of the Caste.

28. The caste has been delegated with powers in deciding certain questions, which questions as stated in Borrodaile's Caste Rules are as follows:—

Betrothal, Pallâ, Marriage, Widow Re-marriage, Maintenance, Inheritance, After-death ceremonies, Partition, Excommunication from Castes, Caste Observances, Adoption, and Miscellaneous questions.

Betrothal takes place before marriage, and is held irrevocable unless the parties engaged are labouring under severe bodily defects, and that even after consulting the caste.

Palla or dowry is the amount fixed at Rs. 400, which the bridegroom's father pays for the provision of the bride, and which amount is deposited either with the bride's father or with a third person.

Marriage is described on page 372. Various ceremonies are performed : some are prescribed by the Shastras, while the rest are observed following the traditional custom, some of which are peculiar to each family.

Widow re-marriage is not allowed.

Maintenance.—The deaf, dumb and others destitute of organs, bodily and mental, are excluded from inheritance, though they are entitled to be maintained.

Inheritance treated in para. 14, pages 428 and 402-417.

After-death ceremonies, in paras. 18 and 19.

The ceremonies are performed according to the Shastras.

Partition.—It has been described in para. 14. It will be more clear from the following text of Metakshara that a son, grandson, great-grandson, in the absence of their respective fathers, can demand a partition and division of ancestral property whether moveable or immoveable at any time.

Female members of the dividing family, such as mothers, daughters, widows are entitled to maintenance; daughters until marriage; mothers, widows, &c., till death, but they cannot demand partition.

When brothers participate in the property, a sum of money or its equivalent in money-value is set apart for maintenance and nuptial ceremonies of the female members.

When the family is rich, a share equal to a son's share is

set apart for female members, and its income is applied for their maintenance.

When a partition has been made during the lifetime of the father among his sons, the widow takes a qualified interest in her husband's share. The *corpus* of the fund is shared in by the sons and their surviving heirs after her funeral expenses have been deducted.

When the widow's maintenance has been sufficiently provided for by any other way, it is a question whether she would also get a share for maintenance.

Excommunication from castes, treated in para. 8.

Caste observances.—The Kapola Banias worship the goddess Samudri. The general festival in commemoration of the goddess is held on the 6th day of the 2nd half of Bhadrapad and on the 8th day of the 1st halves of Ashwin and Chaitra oblations are offered to the goddess.

They give caste-feasts on every occasion, both auspicious and otherwise, according to their might

The priests, both family and caste, are given specified sums as shewn in the attached account list. Whenever a caste-feast is given, presents are sometimes given to the castemen, which are called Lahana.

Adoption treated in para. 14.

Miscellaneous questions, like the dues of the priest, widow's right, &c.—For the dues of the priest, if a person migrates from one country to another, the priest of the new habitation receives the dues and such others. A widow cannot sell or dispose of her husband's property unless the heirs are consulted, if there be any survivor; in default of the survivors, she can dispose of her moveable property but not immoveable property, otherwise than for causes of her maintenance, and if the distant heir object to her disposing, and promise to maintain her, she cannot dispose the immoveable property.

All the decisions generally are given according to the sense of the majority in consultation with the caste Shett or headman.

Charitable Endowments of the Castes.

29. The Kapola Banias have originated a fund for the poor and the helpless of the Kapola Banias, which fund was started under the auspices of the late Sir Munguldas Nathubhai

Kt.,C.S.I., and is known as the Sir Munguldas Nathubai Kapola Nirashrit Fund, which amounts to Rs. 60,000.

Sources of Information.

30. It should be observed here that besides the Purana
which describe the origin of various castes, there are some
accounts preserved with bards, or who are called Barots of each
caste, from whom some information regarding the caste in
detail can be had, and the actual state of things existing at
present can be obtained from the intelligent people of the caste.

Caste Funds.

31. The caste has a fund also, the object of which is to
defray the general expenses of the caste. The caste-men are
required to give dues contributing to the fund. An account
thereof follows on page 24.

They have also a fund for buying the caste oart.

Caste Priest.

32. The caste has a priest whose duty is to assemble the
caste-men when there is a general meeting of the caste. He
has also to go to invite all the caste-members whenever there
is a grand caste-feast, after taking permission from the Shett.
He has always to collect caste dues from the caste-men, as
specified in the attached account, and to do such other duties
affecting the whole caste.

Family Priest.

33. There is a family priest, special for every family, who
directs the performance of all the ceremonies. The caste priest,
as well as the family priest, are both Kundolia Brahmins.

Pedigree.

34. The families preserve their pedigrees with great care,
and the genealogical trees contain names of the members in the
successive generations, in some cases dating as early as Samvat
725, corresponding to 669 A.D. (some of these are given in the
Appendix).

Ceremonies.

35. Besides marriage and death-ceremonies there are many
other ceremonies which the Hindus have to undergo, a list

58

whereof is given on page 394. Formerly the Vedic Mantras were recited at the performance of the ceremonies of Banyas, as they used to wear the sacred thread, but at present these ceremonies are performed according to the Mantras of Smriti, as they have ceased to put on the sacred thread long since. Each of these ceremonies constitutes many minor ceremonies. Some of these are regulated by Shastras, which are alike for all the Hindus, while others are by custom, in which case there may be a difference in observance.

Appendix A.

NO.	NAMES.	POPULATION IN BOMBAY.
1	Kapola Banyas	3,000
2 {	1. Mohod Dasha Mandalia	200
	2. Mohod Dasha Ghoghva	475
	3. Mohod Dasha and Visha Adarja ...	700
	4. Mohod Dasha Mandalia Surti ...	100
	5. Mohod Dasha Mandalia Nagora ...	200
	6. Mohod Visha Adarja Surti .	100
	7. Mohod Visha Ghoghva	50
	8. Mohod Visha Adarja Ahmedabadi	50
	9. Mohod Visha Adarja Khambati ...	220
3 {	1. Shrimali Dasha Khambati... ...	100
	2. Shrimali Dasha Ghoghari	175
	3. Shrimali Dasha Kapadvanji ...	200
	4. Shrimali Dasha Talabda	50
4 {	1. Nagar Bania Visha...	400
	2. Nagar Dasha Surti	75
	3. Nagar Dasha	60
5 {	1. Porvada Dasha Surti	300
	2. Porvada Dasha	400
	3. Porvada Visha	100
	4. Porvada Ghoghari	200
6	Harshola Visha	100
7 {	1. Jharola Dasha	200
	2. Jharola Visha Gujarati	65
8	Mevada Dasha	40
9 {	1. Deshavala Dasha Ahmedabadi ...	175
	2. Deshavala Dasha	100
	3. Deshavala Visha	400
10	Khadaita and Visha	100
11	Gurjar	175
12	Lad	1,400
13	Sorathia Visha	100
14 {	1. Vanspada Dasha	75
	2. Vanspada Visha	100
15 {	1 Dindu Nagori	65
	2. Dindu Surti	100

Appendix A—(*continued*).

Besides those mentioned in the above list, there are other Bania sections inhabiting the Presidency. The list of the Bania caste consists of 84 sections (from "Vastu Vrand Dipika," by Poet Dayárám), of which some are given above and the rest follow—

1. Achhuti.	36. Khandera.
2. Andorâ.	37. Kakadi.
3. Atsolâ	38. Lothia.
4. Anantvala.	39. Madhukára.
5. Akhata.	40. Marhera.
6. Adhia.	41. Mephada.
7. Babara.	42. Matia.
8. Bagdu.	43. Nanaval.
9. Barbhanâ.	44. Nidhuda.
10. Bajdâ.	45. Nagora.
11. Bathodâ.	46. Osveala.
12. Bardhama.	47. Panchajati.
13. Batera.	48. Padmavata.
14. Bhabhu.	49. Runakuda.
15. Bhajiutha.	50. Rasira.
16. Bhadia.	51. Rate.
17. Chandora.	52. Sura.
18. Chicha.	53. Sudhaval.
19. Chitarvala.	54. Surtivala.
20. Chitroda.	55. Sonara.
21. Chorval.	56. Sikle.
22. Dasora.	57. Singoda.
23. Golválá.	58. Sarvaka.
24. Goongdá.	59. Sâchora.
25. Gajuda.	60. Shri Shrimalî
26. Jayalval.	61. Tatel.
27. Jinda.	62. Tirsorâ.
28. Kukarval.	63. Utanimá.
29. Kallival.	64. Vedlav.
30. Khadáyaká.	65. Vaida.
31. Koruva.	66. Vadakhadakipala.
32. Kartavala.	67. Vapera.
33. Kathroti.	68. Valmika.
34. Kapojara.	69. Zodi.
35. Kadmadhu.	

Appendix A—(*continued*).

The names of the Bania castes from "Gnyáti Nibandh," by Poet Dalpatrám Dúyábhai.

1.	Agarvál.	33.	Jayilvál.
2.	Anervál.	34.	Jemá.
3.	Andorú.	35.	Kapola.
4.	Átbarji.	36.	Kadhervál.
5.	Árchitvál.	37.	Karberá.
6.	Bativará.	38.	Kákaliyá.
7.	Baruri.	39.	Kújotivál.
8.	Báyis.	40.	Kortávál.
9.	Bágriyá.	41.	Kambovál.
10.	Bábarvál-Bábar.	42.	Khadáyatá.
11.	Búmanvál.	43.	Khátarvál.
12.	Bálmivál.	44.	Khichi.
13.	Búhor.	45.	Khandevál.
14.	Bednorá.	46.	Lád.
15.	Bhágervál.	47.	Ládisúká.
16.	Bhárijá.	48.	Lingúyit.
17.	Bhoongarvál.	49.	Múnatvál.
18.	Bhoongdá.	50.	Medtávál.
19.	Chitrodá.	51.	Múd.
20.	Chehetrávál.	52.	Mevúdú.
21.	Dindu.	53.	Mihiriyá.
22.	Dindoriá.	54.	Mangorá.
23.	Disbávál.	55.	Mandáhool.
24.	Dasúrú.	56.	Mohod.
25.	Doyilvál.	57.	Mándaliyá.
26.	Gasorá.	58.	Medorá.
27.	Goojarvál.	59.	Naphák.
28.	Goyalvál.	60.	Narsinhpará.
29.	Harsorá.	61.	Núgar.
30.	Jambu.	62.	Nágadrá.
31.	Jharola.	63.	Nághorá.
32.	Jiranvál.	64.	Orvál.

Appendix A—(*continued*).

The names of the Bania castes from "Guyáti Nibandh," by
Poet Dalpatrám Dáyábhai—*contd.*

65.	Osvál.	75.	Sárviyá.
66.	Padmorá.	76.	Sohárvál.
67.	Palevál.	77.	Sáchorá.
68.	Pushkarvál.	78.	Shri Shrimáli.
69.	Panchamvál—Pánchá.	79.	Shrimáli.
70.	Stabi.	80.	Terotá.
71.	Soorarvál.	81.	Tiporá.
72.	Sirkerá.	82.	Thákarvál.
73.	Soni.	83.	Váyadá.
74.	Sojatvál.	84.	Zaliyárá.

No.	Divisions.	Sub-divisions.	Gotra.	Special deity.	Explanation of the Designation.
1	Sanghavi		Chandlás ...		They went on a pilgrimage to Kashi together.
2	Chitalia		Chandlás ...		From the village of Chital in Kattyawar.
3	Jangla		Parasar ...		From the unusual mode of their living as affected by the outsiders.
4	Mathuriá		......		Because they went to Mathurá as pilgrims.
5	Bhuvá		......		They went on pilgrimage to Mathura.
6	Mehtá		......		
		1 Jagdharia ...	......		They in old times administered states.
		2 Damralia ...	......		Inhabitants of Damrala village near Shihore.
		3 Bhalaria ...	......		Inhabitants of Bhalar village near Talaga.
		4 Khunta ...	......		Contentious people.
		5 Jaugla ...	Chandlás ...		They went out of their homes and returned affected with English manners.
		6 Masitia ...	......		Living near musjid.
		7 Mathuria ...	Chandlás		Their forefathers went on a pilgrimage to Mathura.
		8 Jangharia ...	......		Inhabitants of Jangbar village near Shihor.
		9 Vaspara ...	......		,, ,, Vaspara.

Appendix B—(continued.)

No.	Divisions	Sub-Divisions	Gotra.	Special deity.	Explanations of the Designation.
		10 Valia ...	......		Dealers in tobacco.
		11 Busa ...	.. ..		Easy-going.
		12 Bhuva ...	Chandlás ...		They gave corn and supported persons in famine.
		13 Dhanani ...	Gautam ...		They lived in Dharam, a village near Tunagad.
		14 Khalpada...	......		Sellers in papar.
		15 Pepdi ...	Gautam ...		Inhabitants of Pepdi village.
		16 Patel ...	......		Tillers of soil
		17 Botani ...	......		Inhabitants of Botad city.
		18 Shahukar	Gargas		Money Lenders.
		19 Vanká	......		Obstinate.
		20 Rashmiá	Parasar		
		21 Hukani	Vasishtha		Descendants of Haká Mehtá.
		? Karvat	Bhardwáj		From their faithlessness.
7	Parekh	......di	......	Ambas	Agents in cattle.
		2 Thika	Hárita	Do.	Agents in pottery.
		8 Pila	Kaushik	Do.	From the yellow colour of their body.

No.	Name	Sub-divisions	Deity (Do.)	Gotra	Remarks (Banking and Shroffing.)
8	Modi	4 Amath		Vasishtha	Banking and Shroffing.
		...5 Ratan Parekh		Harita	Proprietors or landlords.
		Desai		......	Inhabitants of Kundlá.
		2 Kundalia		......	Grass-dealers.
		3 Khad Modi		......	Inhabitants of Dholká.
9	Dholakia	......		Gautam	Inhabitants of Shihor near Palitana.
10	Shihorá	......	Khodiar	Parasar	Cloth-merchant.
11	Doshi	......	Kankai	Parasar	Grocers.
12	Gandhi	Mehta Gandhi, Nagara Gandhi.		Parasar	
13	Babaria	......		Parasar	Inhabitants of Dhár.
14	Sukhadia	......		Kashyapa	Confectioners.
15	Kanakia	......	Kankai	Do.	Corn-dealers.
16	Vora	1 Sheth		Do.	
		2 Mapara		Do.	
		3 Lotiá		Do.	
17	Bhutá Shethiá	......		......	Headmen.
18	Bhagat	......		......	Corn-measurers.
19	Dandia	......		......	Iron-sellers.
20	Kotharia	......		Harita	From their practice of devotional service.
21	Desai	......		......	From their contending with other persons.
22	Muni	......		......	Store-keeper.
23	Gotala	......		Gargas	Land lords.
24	Nayani	......		......	They preserve reticence when taking meals.
25	Barbhaya	......		Gargas	Irregular in their habits.
26	Shethia	......		Gautam	Descendants of Naya, the fore-father.
					They were 12 brothers.
					Headmen.

59

An account of money spent among the Kapola Banias at the time of Betrothal, Marriage, and Pregnancy ceremonies :—

In this caste the caste-men of the officiating family priest (who are called Kandolia Brahmins), the officiating family priest, the Kapola caste as a body, the caste priest, the caste deities the Samudri and Than Kandol, and the parties (bride and bride-groom) are given as below :—

(1) *The Caste-men of the officiating Priest or* the Caste of the Kandolia Brahmins AS A WHOLE.

Rs. a. p.

(a) 1 8 0 At the time of *Betrothal.*

    Rs. a. p.

    1 8 0 General alms called Bhursi Dakshina.

        Rs. a. p.

        1 0 0 From the bride-groom's party.

        0 8 0 From the bride's party.

(h) 44 4 0 *In Marriage.*

    Rs. a. p.

    2 0 0 At the time when the marriage day is settled or in general when the Lagan Padi is written—

        Rs. a. p.

        1 0 0 From the bride-groom's party.

        1 0 0 From the bride's party.

    5 8 0 When the Mandap pillar is erected—

        Rs. a. p.

        3 8 0 A due of the Kandola caste as a whole—

            Rs. a. p.

            1 12 0 From the bride-groom's party.

            1 12 0 From the bride's party.

        2 0 0 Miscellaneous alms or Dakshina called Bhursi Dakshina—

            Rs. a. p.

            1 0 0 From the bride-groom's party.

            1 0 0 From the bride's party.

            ———————

            5 8 0

Rs. a. p.
17 0 0 When the Grih Shanti Ceremony is
performed—

Rs. a. p.
13 0 0 For the worshipping materials—

Rs. a. p.
6 8 0 From the bride-groom's
party.

6 8 0 From the bride's party.

2 0 0 Bhursi Dakshina—

Rs. a. p.
1 0 0 From the bride-groom's
party.

1 0 0 From the bride's party.

2 0 0 Dakshina when the presents
called MOSALU are given to
the bride and bride-groom
by their maternal uncle—

Rs. a. p.
1 0 0 From the bride-
groom's party.

1 0 0 From the bride's
party.

5 4 0 From the time the Kanyá Dân
▲ ceremony is performed till the
close of the nuptial rite—

Rs. a. p.
2 2 0 From the bride-groom's
party.

3 2 0 From the bride's party.

6 0 0 Rechba or miscellaneous alms—

Rs. a. p.
2 0 0 From the bride's party.

4 0 0 From the bride-groom's
party.

0 8 0 Cocoanuts at the time of entering
the Chori—

Rs. a. p.
0 4 0 From the bride-groom.

0 4 0 From the bride's party.

Rs. a. p.

1 8 0   When the Chori is loosened—

  Rs. a. p.

  1 0 0   From the bride-groom's party·

  0 8 0   From the bride's party.

0 6 0   For Betel-nuts—

  Rs. a. p.

  0 4 0   From the bride-groom's party for betel-nuts, in weight 5 seers.

  0 2 0   From the bride's party for betel-nuts weighing 2¼ seers.

1 10 0   At the time the play of *Aki Beki* or odd and even is played—

  Rs. a. p.

  0 13 0   From the bride-groom's party.

  0 13 0   From the bride's party.

1 0 0   From the bride-groom's party, when the bride-groom is welcomed by the mother.

1 8 0   Dakshina when the ending ceremony is performed—

  Rs. a. p.

  1 0 0   From the bride-groom's party.

  0 8 0   From the bride's party.

  1 0 0   Dakshina when the pair goes to bow down to Mahaluxmi—

  ———— From the bride-groom's party.

  44 4 0

Rs. a. p.

(c) 1 11 6   In pregnancy ceremony—

  Rs. a. p.

  1 0 0   Dakshina given.

  0 8 0   Dakshina while Mosalu is given.

  0 3 6   Dues of the caste as a whole.

  ————

  1 11 6

THE FAMILY PRIEST RECEIVES—

From the bride's party.				From the bride-groom's party.			
Rs.	a.	p.		Rs.	a.	p.	
1	0	0	At Betrothal—	1	0	0	
Rs.	a.	p.					At Betrothal—
1	0	0	Akhyana.	Rs.	a.	p.	
24	1	0	At Marriage—	1	0	0	Akhyana at the time the Lagan Padi is received at his house.
Rs.	a.	p.					
1	0	0	Akhyana at the time the Lagan Padi is written.	Rs.	a.	p.	
				1	0	0	Akhyana.
							At Marriage—
1	4	0	Adara Shesh Ceremony.	Rs.	a.	p.	
				1	4	0	Adrastesh Ceremony.
Rs.	a.	p.		Rs.	a.	p.	
1	0	0	Akhyana.	1	0	0	Akhyana.
0	2	0	Gotraj Puja.	0	2	0	Gotraj Puja.
0	2	0	Ganpati Puja.	0	2	0	Ganpati. Puja.
1	4	0		1	4	0	
Rs.	a.	p.		Rs.	a.	p.	
1	0	0	Akhyana at the time when a pot is placed while removing to another place for the performance of marriage.	1	0	0	Akhyana when the water-pot is placed in the marriage Pendal.
1	0	0	Akhyana when the Mandap is erected.	1	0	0	Akhyana for erecting the Mandap.
3	10	0	Mabi Installation.	3	10	0	M a h i (Goddess) Installation—
Rs.	a.	p.		Rs.	a.	p.	
1	0	0	For seven Matrikás.	1	0	0	For seven Matrikás. (Goddesses.)
1	10	0	Nandi Shradha.	1	10	0	Nandi Shradhba (Benediction Ceremony.)
1	0	0	Akhyana.	1	0	0	Akhyana.
3	10	0		3	10	0	

Rs. a. p.

1 0 0 Akhyana when a Mindhol is tied to her wrist.

1 0 0 Akhyana in the Grih Shanti Ceremony.

1 0 0 Dakshina when Mosalu or presents are given.

0 4 0 At the time of Varuna Pujain Grih Shanti.

1 0 0 Akhyana when the Kanyá Dân Ceremony is performed.

1 0 0 Akhyana when the Chori is erected.

1 0 0 Akhyana when the closing ceremony is performed.

1 0 0 Akhyana when a wheel is dragged or carriage worshipped.

0 13 0 When *Aki Beki* is played.

8 2 0 For Randel Goddess.

——— ——

24 1 0 Total.

2 4 0 In Pregnancy—

1 0 0 Akhyana for determining the auspicious day.

1 4 0 Panch Masi—

Rs. a. p.

1 0 0 Akhyana when Mindhol is tied.

1 0 0 Akhyana for Grih Shanti.

0 4 0 Varun Pujan at Grih Shanti.

1 0 0 Dakshina in *Mosala.*

1 0 0 Akhyana at Kanyá Dân Ceremony.

9 0 0 Gora's Dapu (due)—

7 8 0 Dapu(due).

1 8 0 Digogee.

——— ——

9 0 0

1 0 0 Akhyana for Chori.

1 0 0 Akhyana when the b r i d e-g r o o m is welcomed.

1 0 0 Akhyana at the Uvatar (ending ceremony).

1 0 0 Akhyana when the chariot wheel is worshipped.

2 7 0 At the time of *Aki Beki.*

2 4 0 Akhyana in the Mandavatar ceremony.

1 0 0 Dakshina while going to bow down to Mahaluxmi.

8 2 0 For Randel Goddess—

Rs. a. p.
1 0 0 Akhyana.
0 4 0 Worship.
_____
1 4 0
_____
2 4 0
_____
27 5 0 Total Sum.
At the Pregnancy Cere-
mony—

1 0 0 Akhyana for ascer-
taining the day.
1 4 0 Panch Masi—

1 0 0 Akhyana.
0 4 0 Worship.
_____
1 4 0
_____
2 4 0 Total.

Rs. a. p.
0 2 0 In the water-pot.
0 10 0 For Mudrapan
(Dakshina in coins).
2 8 0 To be placed on the
two pots.
3 8 0 Alms to 14 Brah-
mins.
0 6 0 Ending ceremony
of the Goddess or
disposal of the Goddess.
1 0 0 Akhyana.
_____
8 2 0 Total Sum.

8 2 0 For the Randel
Goddess.
Items as above.

1 4 0 Dakshina while
welcoming the wife.
1 0 0 Akhyana at that
time.
1 0 0 Akhyana for the
ceremony.
_____
11 6 0 Total.

DUES OF THE PRIEST OF THE KAPOLA CASTE.

0 2 0 In the betrothal ceremony.
0 4 0 In the marriage ceremony.
0 1 0 In the pregnancy ceremony.
4 0 0 For inviting the castes to a general feast.
2 0 0 Alms for 4 persons.
0 1 0 When a general distribution among caste-men is
made both on auspicious occasions or otherwise *for each.*

DUES OF THE KAPOLA CASTE.

In betrothal—

Rs. a. p.
2 8 0 From the bride-groom's party.
1 4 0 From the bride's party.
_____
3 12 0

Out of this—

Rs. a. p.
| 2 | 4 | 0 | Kapola caste retains and |
| 1 | 8 | 0 | Due of the Samudri Goddess. |

3 12 0

13 8 0 *In Marriage*—

Rs. a. p.
| 4 | 8 | 0 | From the bride's party. |
| 9 | 0 | 0 | From the bride-groom's party. |

13 8 0

Out of this—

Rs. a. p.
| 10 | 8 | 0 | Kapola caste General Fund. |
| 3 | 0 | 0 | Dues of the Samudri Goddess. |

13 8 0

Rs. a. p.
1 4 0 *In pregnancy*—

Rs. a. p.
| 1 | 4 | 0 | From the bride-groom's party, which sum is due of the Than Goddess. |

17 0 0 DUES OF THE CASTE AT EVERY GRAND CASTE-DINNER WHETHER ON AUSPICIOUS OR INAUSPICIOUS OCCASIONS.

12 0 0 At marriage occasion—

Rs. a. p.
| 10 | 0 | 0 | For the Caste-fund. |
| 2 | 0 | 0 | For Samudri Goddess. |

12 0 0

12 0 0 For the death anniversary items as above.

5 0 0 At death time for the Caste-fund, till the fifteenth day.

602 0 0 At the time of betrothal the bride is given by the bride-groom's party.

Rs. a. p.
| 401 | 0 | 0 | For Pallâ. |
| 201 | 0 | 0 | For Ornaments. |

602 0 0 Total.

THINGS GIVEN TO THE DAUGHTER AND SON-IN-LAW IN MARRIAGE BY THE BRIDE'S FATHER.

TO THE DAUGHTER.

For saree.

For a chuda of ivory coated with gold.

For armlets, &c.

For silver ornaments of the leg.

For nose-ring.

For ear-ring.

The above things are given to the daughter in *Kanyá Dán* Ceremony :—

Things given in Chori Ceremony.

For silver ornaments.

For a dish, pot, &c., of brass.

Things given in Uratar or Ending Ceremony.

For a wooden seat called *Bajat.*

For a saree, boddice, petticoat, &c., &c.

TO THE SON-IN-LAW.

In Kanyá Dán Ceremony.

For a waist, a cow, a bed, &c.

In *chori.*

For a turban, a shawl and a gold neck-lace.

These are the least sums required to be *spent.*

On North Indian Folk-Lore *about* Thieves *and* Robbers.

By Mr. Sarat Chandra Mitra, Corresponding Member of the Anthropological Society of Bombay.

Every profession, not excepting even that of the light-fingered gentry, has its gods and goddesses to whom the persons following it pay their homage for success. The vegetable-sellers of Behar have their gods. The Kúhárs (कहार), and the palankeen-bearers and the Málláhs (मलाह) or the boatmen of Behar also worship particular deities, who, they believe, watch over their welfare and safety. Indian thieves and robbers and the rest of the marauding fraternity have also particular goddesses whom they worship, in the belief that success or otherwise in their pilfering expeditions depends on the favours or frowns of those female deities. To this end, they take care to propitiate the said goddesses by offering up *pujah* in the shape of sweets, cereals, and, sometimes, animal sacrifices too, before they start on their expeditions. Curiously enough, a female deity is invariably found to be the tutelary patroness of the Indian robbers and thieves. She is known in various parts of Northern India as *Devi* (देवी) or the goddess Káli in her various incarnations and under various names. In Bengal, the thieves and robbers are supposed to enjoy the special protection of the goddess Káli. In the North-Western Provinces and the Punjab, she is worshipped by the light-fingered gentry under the name of the Devi or Mátá—an incarnation of the Bengali goddess Káli. The Thugs, who had raised the profession of robbery by throttling and strangulation, into a semi-religious cult, also worshipped the Devî or Mátá, whom they invariably worshipped before starting on their marauding expeditions, and from whom they drew omens portending the success or otherwise of their undertaking. Before starting they also worshipped the sacred mattock with which the trenches for burying their victims' corpses were dug, with the offering of some *goor* or country molasses. This consecrated *goor* they always took *with them* on their expeditions. The Thugs were a very *superstitious* people—for verily conscience doth make cowards of *such* men—and believed in various portents. The hare the jackal and various other beasts and birds played an important part in their superstition. If they saw a hare cross their path, or a jackal to their right or their left when about to start, they accordingly drew the inference whether their expedition would be crowned with success or not. Colonel Sleeman, well known as the Superintendent of the Operations for the Suppression of Thuggy and Dacoity in India, has given detailed information of the various rites practised by the Thugs, and of their superstitions, in his work entitled "*Rama-seeana, or The Secret Language of the Thugs.*" The curious enquirer may also find additional information on the subject and gain peeps into the inner mysteries of a Thug's daily life in a work of fiction entitled "*The Confessions of a Thug,*" by that well-known Anglo-Indian novelist, Colonel Meadows Taylor.

In Bengal the thieves and robbers are believed to enjoy the special protection of the goddess Kâlî. Before the British rule was established on a firm footing in Bengal, dacoity and robbery were very much rife in that part of the country. Before the dacoits started on their expeditions, they used to offer up *pujah* to that goddess to ensure their success, and, after returning from a foray, used to make her an offering of part of the booty by way of thanksgiving. It is said that, in those days, the temple of the goddess Kâlî at Kâlîghât, south of Calcutta, and the temple of the goddess Chitreswari (চিত্রেশ্বরী),—an incarnation of Kâlî—at Chitpore in the northern suburbs of Calcutta, were much resorted to by dacoits and robbers who used to worship their patron-deity there.

The shrine of the deity Târaknâth—an incarnation of Siva—at Târakeshwar in the Hughly District, has, from time immemorial, been regarded as a very important place of pilgrimage by the Hindus of Bengal. At the present time, a branch line of the East Indian Railway has been opened from the Sheorá-phuli Station of that Railway to Târakeshwar, which conveys the pilgrims safely to that shrine. But in those pre-railway days, when the *Pax Britannica* had not been established firmly, almost all the pilgrims to that shrine had to travel thither on

foot or by bullock-carts. These pilgrims, in many cases, used
to take with them rich and costly articles for offerings to the
lord Tàraknàth. These excited the cupidity of the marauding
fraternity; and a colony of dacoits had accordingly established
itself near a village named Singur—now a station on the
Tàrakeshwar Branch Railway—which was situated close to the
highway which led to the shrine of Tàrakeshwar. These freebooters ostensibly used to lead the lives of peaceful agriculturists by day-time, but, during the night, used to sally forth
from their homes, armed with *lathis*, and prowl about the highway and rob the belated travellers of their belongings, and
often murdered some of them in order to get at their valuables. A place named केकालार माठ (the *matam* of Kaikàla, a
village in that neighbourhood) was the scene of many of these
atrocities; and in those days the very mention of the name of
that place was enough to send a thrill of horror through the
hearts of the pilgrims and wayfarers. Now, under the *aegis*
of British rule, so efficient is the surveillance exercised by the
Police that wayfarers and pilgrims travel, by night, through
that tract of the country, as safely as if they had been in their
very homes. Now these dacoits are said to have enjoyed the
protection of a goddess Kàli, whose temple is situated in the
aforesaid village of Singur and exists there to this day. The
dacoits used to worship here before starting on their plundering expeditions, and, after returning therefrom, used to
make valuable offerings out of the rich booty secured. This
goddess was, and is still known as, डाकात कालो, or the goddess
Kàli of the dacoits, and enjoys the notoriety of having been
the favorite deity of those marauders of Singur.

It is said that "there is honor even among thieves," and
the dacoits of Bengal were not wanting in this respect.
Before they committed dacoity in a person's house, they used
to send an anonymous letter to the good man thereof, informing
him of their intention to do so. One night they would gather
together in armed bands, and, with lighted torches, invade the
house.* After reaching there, they used to indulge in sword-

* The following is another account of their mode of attack:—"Their mode
of dacoity was also unlike what is followed now by their successors. They
would not suddenly attack an unwary or unprepared householder. First

prayed that they might be successful throughout the year in their various plundering expeditions. At the present time the ceremony is a novel and pleasing sight. The men and women are all dressed in their gorgeous holiday attire, and having made their offerings they gather together in lots and sing, dance and make merry generally for a couple of days, when they leave for their homes after a dip in the well-known Gaggar, a stream which appears to be sacred to the hill-people."

In Bengal, it is popularly believed. that thieves elude detection and capture in many cases, because the goddess Kāli has granted them the boon of protection from all danger (चोरेदेर उपर कालीर बर आछे). Thieves almost always commit thefts during the dark half of the moon(कृष्णपक्ष), the worship of the goddess Kāli always taking place on the 15th day of the waning period of the moon. There is a popular superstition amongst the Bengalis that if a male child be born on the अमावस्या day, or the 15th day of the dark half of the moon, the child will become a thief, as that day is consecrated to Kāli, the goddess of thieves and robbers.

Bengali and Behari burglars (सिंधेल चोर) are said to get their iron-hooks (सिंधकाठी)—instruments with which they make holes in the walls of buildings for the purpose of effecting their entrance therein, and which are the prototypes of the "Jemmy" of European burglars—manufactured in the following way: A burglar secretly goes to an ironsmith's (लोहार of Behar and कामार of Bengal) shop during the night, and there deposits a piece of iron, and some pice by way of wages. In the morning, the ironsmith, finding the iron and the pice, comes to know that they had been left there by some thief with a view to have the same turned into a "Jemmy." The ironsmith manufactures it accordingly, and, during the night, deposits it at the exact spot where it had been left by the thief. The thief comes thither secretly during the night and takes it away. Hence is the origin of the Bengali saying चोर कामारे याखा नाइ or चोरे कामारे साक्षात नाइ (there is no interview between a thief and a blacksmith). This saying is often cited when speaking of a person who gains his object or performs a certain act without having a personal interview with the person who has the power to grant that object, or to whom he is in duty bound to perform that act. Committing burglary is, in Bengal, called सिंधकाठा, and in Behar, सेन मारना. Hence it is popularly believed that thieves and burglars never commit thefts in ironsmiths' houses, out of gratitude to the latter. It is another instance of " honor among thieves."

Thieves play an important part in the " proverbial philosophy " of the Bengali people. When one person of bad character is likened to another of the same description, they are said to be चोरे चोरे मासतूत भाई, or thieves are cousins (mother's sister's sons) to one another. When one person defrauds another of his ill-gotten gains, the former is said to practise चोरेर उपर वाटपाड़ी or fraud on a thief. चोर पाल्ले बुद्धि वा.ड़े, or "shutting the stable-door after the steed is stolen," is applied to persons who become wise after the event. Thieves, when caught red-handed, are often thrashed within an inch of their very lives. Hence चोरेर मार, or " beating administered to thieves" is proverbial and synonymous with severe thrashing. If a person is severely thrashed, it is said of him ताके चोरेर मारे मरेछ or that he has been thrashed like a thief. A child possessed of mischievous habits is often dubbed with the pet sobriquet of डाकात or dacoit. If a person seeks for an opportunity of doing a certain act and gets it at last, it is said of him चोर्वाय भाङन वड़ा, or a thief seeks for a broken fencing. A thief may elude detection for some time, but he is sure to be caught one day. This has given rise to the popular saying चर पांच दिन माधेर एक दिन, or a thief may escape scot-free for five days but the good man of the house will catch him one day. Thieves are always artful dodgers, and, in allusion to their artfulness, the Bengalis say चोर दिया वड दिया यदेना पड़े धरा, or that the profession of stealing is a paying one so long as the thief is not caught. A person who steals trifles is spoken of as being a छिचके चोर. If sound advice is given to a person, but he does not act up to it, the proverb चोराना ज्ञान धर्मेर कादेवा (preach gospel unto a devil and he will not hear you) is applied to him. A thief cannot be detected except with the assistance of a a thief."* A servant or any other menial, who is notorious for his thievish propensities, is often spoken of as being a चोर सदोर, or " chief among thieves " or "arch-thief." If a person without making any attempt at concealment, deprives another of a thing or otherwise defrauds him, the former is said to commit दिने डाकाती, or " robbery by broad day-light." A Bengali bridegroom is often likened to a thief बरना चोर, because the former has to put up patiently with all sorts of liberties which the female members of the bride's family take with him on the day of his marriage, just as a thief, when caught patiently suffers the maltreatment which he receives at the hands of his captors. Or this saying may refer to the form of marriage by capture prevailing in primitive communities, whereby a person has to steal or carry away by force a woman before he can marry her. The saying चोरके बल चुरी करते गृहस्थके बले सावधान हते is often applied to a person who blows hot and cold in the same breath, that is to say, who tells a person to do a certain act with respect to another person, and, at the same time, tells the latter to beware of the former.

---

*The truth of the Bengali proverb was strikingly illustrated by the following paragraph which lately went the round of the newspapers.—" The maxim— " Set a thief to catch a thief " has lately been followed by the Lahore Police who have employed a Pathan,— an ex-rifle thief to boot—to trace the perpetrators of the theft of carbines from the Boys' High School. It is not perhaps generally known that released convicts are systematically employed by the police to do detective work, and particularly to recognise and identify old offenders."—The Amrita Bazar Patrika, Saturday, May 19, 1894

ORDINARY GENERAL MEETING, held on Wednesday, the 29th August 1894.

MR. KHARSETJI RUSTOMJI CAMA, Vice-President, took the Chair.

The minutes of the previous Meeting were read and confirmed.

The election of the following new Member was announced :—

Mr. R. A. Lamb, I.C.S., Acting Collector, Alibag, Kolaba District.

matter to the Rev. L. W. Pritchatt Shaw, the Railway Chaplain, who takes a great interest in such subjects, we decided to open some of the graves, and the following are a few rough notes on the discoveries we made, in which the graves are numbered in the order in which they were opened out.

The first group of graves dealt with was on the right side of the railway at 322½ miles, and is situated in Kanarapalayam village of the Mettupalaiyam Taluk in the Coimbatore District. The graves are spread over the ground at intervals of about 80 feet roughly in lines, and extending over two or three fields. One line of them runs at a right-angle to the railway about N. and S. and the circles of stones being very distinct we decided to make a start with them, and the following is the result :—

Grave No. 1.—Circle of stones about 14 feet in diameter. This was an ordinary grave dug out of the hard soil and containing a large egg-shaped jar placed obliquely with many small shallow bowls around it. At about two feet from the surface we found a large bowl inverted and much broken, which was placed as a cover to the larger jar, but all the pottery was so much broken that only a general idea of it could be gathered.

Grave No. 2.—Walking north from the last grave occurred a circle of stones 25 feet in diameter. We dug down here about three feet when we reached a rough masonry wall sloping outwards, and digging further a sort of passage was exposed with a large slab of stone sloping outwards on the one side and the rough wall just mentioned, with smaller stone slabs below, on the other, a rough paving about 1'6" broad being at the bottom. Nothing was found in this passage, but continuing the excavation we discovered a stone-chamber alongside, the large slab mentioned being one side of it, and at the end two smaller chambers, not so deep, lined with stone, such as are found in all these tombs and which were evidently entrances to them. The main chamber was very neatly constructed of single slabs of stone for the sides, ends and floor, and it measured inside, at the bottom, 8 feet by 4 feet *3 inches,* and at the top, 6 feet 6 inches by 2 feet 10 inches, *the depth being 6 feet.* It may be mentioned that the slabs of which this chamber is constructed are of a kind of stone

the passage itself. The object of the passage is not clear, but it may have been a sort of false tomb to put off people wishing to rifle the grave, which was evidently that of a chief or great man of the community.

In this grave were found some human bones, probably portions of only one skeleton, with the head placed towards the east, and besides some ordinary pottery, a very elegant jar with four legs, much like an old Greek amphora, and a ring of smooth red pottery which was evidently a stand for a round-bottomed vessel. These articles, which are in the possession of the Rev. Mr. Shaw, are shown in the photograph which I sent to the Society some time ago. They are particularly noticeable for the good quality of the ware and their fine, smooth, almost shining surface. It is not unreasonable to suppose that these things were brought from a distance, from some community more advanced in the art of pottery, and it is curious that several clumsy imitations of the tall vase were found in other graves, as though the local potters had tried to copy it, but not only did they fail with the shape but the material was inferior, so that the copies could not stand the pressure, and were in all cases considerably broken. Portions of two of these are shown in the photograph. It is interesting that in the amphora, as it may be called, was found a handful of grain which looked like paddy, but unfortunately it fell to powder directly it was touched.

Grave No. 3. 244 feet East of No. 2. The mound was 34 feet in diameter, but there was no chamber and only a few small pots were discovered. This seems to have been a group of small ordinary graves dug out of the moorum and then filled in with soil.

Grave No. 4. Merely a circle of stones but nothing was found.

Grave No. 5. There was no circle of stones here, but only a mound under which was a large stone covering a large coffin jar much broken, similar to the one shown in the photograph.

Grave No. 6. Circle of stones 24 feet in diameter, but in this only a large number of small lota-shaped earthen vessels were come across. As the vessels usually found in the graves are bowls for food, it is likely that the tenant of this grave was a noted wine-bibber, and therefore that these vessels, filled with liquor, were the last attentions paid to their friend, the defunct, by his boon companions. In this grave was also the spear head, in good preservation, shown in the photograph and which was forwarded to the Society. There was no stone-chamber and no burial urn.

There were about a dozen more graves in this group, but it was not thought worth while to explore further here, so our attention was directed to another large group of graves on high ground to the left of he Railway line, about mileage 322¼, situated within the same village limits.

Grave No. 7. Circle of stones 12 feet in diameter. Slightly below the original surface of the ground was a large slab of stone 6½ feet long, 3½ feet broad, and 14 inches thick, under which was the fine burial urn which is now in the Society's Museum and which is shown in the photograph. In the urn were a few bones.

Grave No. 8. Circle of stones 27 feet in diameter. A little way below the surface was a stone-chamber 8 feet 2 inches long and 4 feet 10 inches broad on the floor and 6 feet 3 inches long and 3 feet broad at the top, with a depth of 6 feet 6 inches. At one end was a small chamber 3 feet 3 inches square, with a rough hole between the two chambers 1 foot 9 inches square. The direction of the large chamber was between North and South and in the North-west corner were three swords and also the head of an axe, which is now in the Society's collection. Besides these metal relics were human and animal bones; of the latter, the lower jaw and teeth of a large carnivorous animal, probably a leopard. These have been sent to the Society. The peculiarity of this chamber was that it seemed to have never had any covering slabs over it, but apparently was filled in like an ordinary grave.

Grave No. 9. Circle of stones 27 feet in diameter in which was a small stone-chamber which contained no pottery or other articles.

Grave No. 10. Small very shallow chamber with nothing in it.

any more. Opposite this spot and just over the railway to
the east of the line, on a knoll in rather a commanding pos
the ground is stewed with round stones such as would be
with mud for building. The mud has entirely been w
away and there are no indications of walls about the place
this from its position and appearance I conclude to be th
of the village whose grave-yards we have been exploring.

A third group of graves was pointed out to us near the vi
of Kodidhasinur, which is about 2½ miles north-we
Karuimadai Station on the Madras Railway and about a
west of the line at 336½ miles. Here the mounds are far l
and more conspicuous than those dealt with hitherto, and i
over they are enclosed in circles of large slabs of stone or
upright in the ground instead of circles of mere boulde
no great size. Here only three graves were opened.

Grave No. 11. This was one of the most conspicuous
the mounds and stood quite isolated. The mound was
4 feet high and over 30 feet in diameter. Going down i
2 feet was a slab of stone 9 feet long and 8 feet broad and
18 inches thick. Under this was a round stone, a pi
quartz, 3 inches in diameter and about 2 inches thick, and
this was found the thick iron wand, shown in the foregr
of the photograph, in seven pieces, and which has been se
the Society. Beneath these were three stone-chambers o
same shape and about the same dimensions as those opened
where, but nothing was found in them. Of these chambe
were placed east and west and one north and south. Th
there is little to distinguish the round stone spoken of fro
thousands strewed about the fields, yet there is something
it which seems to indicate that it had a useful purpose. It
have been a weight or it may have been a stone for a sling, i
position, put away under such a heavy slab, shows that it
a thing to be taken care of. The wand also is a pe
implement, the use of which it is difficult to understand.
ordinary swords found in these tombs are thin plates of i
broader but not so long as the modern *tulwar*, wherea
wand was about 4 feet 6 inches long and about 3 inches
and 1 inch thick, so that it could not have been used as a cu

instrument, yet that it was used in the hand is evidenced by the fact that it had a handle with a knob forged at one end.

Grave No. 12. Another stone-chamber of the same pattern and dimensions. In this was a skull, apparently in fair preservation, but on being handled it crumbled to pieces. Near the skull were several iron beads, which had certainly been worn as a necklace. These beads were forwarded to the Society, and are formed of small strips of iron coiled up like a volute spring.

Grave No. 13. The peculiarity of this grave was that though it had a mound and circle of stones, it was absolutely empty.

At about 325¼ miles, beyond Karaimadai on the Madras Railway, to the west of the line, two or three graves were opened out, the contents of which were of no importance, except that a broken earthenware coffin or sarcophagus was come across, which was about 4 feet long, 2 feet wide, and 15 inches high, but it was in so many fragments that it could not be removed. This was similar to the coffins found at Pallavaram, and a sketch of one of which is given in the Records of the Government of Madras, No. 2102, Public, dated October 7th, 1886. The pottery found in the graves so far spoken of is all of the red and black variety, mostly with a high polish, which has been turned up elsewhere and is fully described in the reports to the Madras Government by the Superintendent of the Madras Archæological Survey. It is of various shapes and sizes, but mostly bowls for food, and it is all remarkably thin and well burnt. Specimens of many of the shapes have been sent to the Society and are shown in the photograph, but the heart-shaped vessel is out of the common and it was found in grave No. 2.

In another group of graves about a mile east of Mangalam Station on the Madras Railway, at 278½ miles, and in the limits of the village of Camampatty, Tuluq Palladum, District Coimbatore, where excavations were carried on, some rough stone-chambers were found of the same design as those already referred to, but smaller and altogether more roughly made. There are no mounds or circles of stones, and the only indication of the

over that part of the Presidency, and hundreds of them
opened out every year by the wadars for the slabs of
which are used for building purposes and particulary for c
troughs near wells in the villages. The wadars can gi
very coherent account of what they find in the graves, tl
they speak of many things like swords and armour, which
take no care of but throw away. One man referred
substance like paper or parchment which he had seen in
graves ; this may have been the mummified remains c
bodies, but the account was too vague to found any conjec
upon. In one of these Mangalam grave chambers, I noti
space partitioned off on one side by a slab of stone about
inches wide, like a ship's bunk, and in this the skeleton
found. The pots were ranged along the other side of th
in regular order, and all supported on small pottery st
Coming east about a mile from the Mangalam group of gr
and on the same side of the Railway, there is a collecti
graves covering several acres. They have mostly been op
but many still remain untouched; the place is, however, i
overgrown with jungle, and investigation would be troubles
Again, coming East and opposite 276½ miles on the M
Railway, and on the same side of the line, occurs an exte
area covered with slag, which is evidently the site of an an
ironworks belonging to the people whose graves have been
scribed. The native tradition is that there was a mud fort
the remains of which are visible to this day. Many of the
in this neighbourhood have deposits of rich iron ore in t
and within sight from this place is the well-known hill
Salem which is said to be composed almost entirely of
magnetic iron ore. The pottery found in the Mang
graves is in many cases different in shape from that found
the Kuraimadai graves, being principally in the form of
chatties, more or less compressed and with narrow mo
Tall food bowls also occur, but a special peculiarity is
each article was supported on a small earthen stand and ha
earthen cover, but though so much care was taken to clea:
mouths of the vessels, nothing but clay was found inside tl

Another peculiarity of the Mangalam pottery is that i
not of the red and black type, thin, and highly gl

but the ware is coarser and is of a light reddy brown colour with a wavy ornament, as though, when the pigment with which it is covered was soft, a comb, such as painters now use for graining, had been passed over it with a wavy motion. This kind of pottery is very common and much finer specimens of it than those found at Mangalam have been unearthed elsewhere.

Perhaps the most important find in these Mangalam graves was a simple copper or bronze bracelet formed of a piece of thick wire and two chatty covers with scratchings upon them which may be the letters of an alphabet or merely the private marks of the potter who made them or of the owner. In the one cover the marks are deeply cut and on the other one these figures are merely scratched on the surface as though it had been done by a child. It is perhaps idle to attempt to discover what these signs mean, whether letters of an alphabet or merely private marks; they are probably only the latter and they may be very primitive representations of a man or a woman and an animal, probably a cow.

The bracelet with the two marked covers with a selection of the Mangalam pottery, I had the pleasure to present to the Society and I trust they will be found worthy of a place in its valuable collection.

The legends relating to these graves are probably of little value in determining their age and indicating the race to whom they belong, but a few notes taken down of the statements made by the people now living in the neighbourhood may be worth recording. The graves are called Pandywar Kohd meaning Pandyan houses. The inhabitants of the country round Karaimadai are said to be descendants of refuges from some part of Mysore bordering on Canara whence they were driven by Hyder Ali, but they have continued the tradition, and in their way can give a very lucid account of the events of those old times. They say that the chambers opened out are not graves but were the dwellings of the people, who were a race of pygmies and this is proved by the fact that many of the covering slabs of the chambers are blackened with smoke, but none of those lately opened showed any traces of this. They say

people of the settlement all retired to rest and one of them, who
outside, put the flat stones over the entrances to the dwellings
and then himself hid away in a tree, where he slept and was
ready next morning to pull away the stones and let the people
out.   At last for their sins an earthquake or some other
great convulsion of nature occurred and entombed the people
in their dwelling houses, hence the bones now found in the
graves.   The people at Mangalam have the same story only
they add to it that the great sin of the people was that they
tied up the heads of "cholum" in their fields so that the birds
could not get food and died, and that the catastrophe which
overwhelmed them was a rain of burning brimstone from Heaven.
The size of the teeth and bones shows that the people were by
no means small and one jaw which was found was that of a very
big individual, it was larger than the jaw of any European with
which it was compared.   Unfortunately the bone was very
much perished and crumbled to pieces, but the teeth belonging
to it were forwarded to the Society.

Near where the Nilghiri Railway crosses the Bhowani river,
at the foot of the Nilghiri hills, there are said to be the ruins
of a large Pandyan settlement which is called to this day
Munuthumangalam,—village of three hundred virgins, and the
story related about it is this:—A giant named Pukka Surun
lived on the droog or mountain, now called by his name, which
stands on the southside of the Bhowani valley, and is a conspicuous feature of the landscape in looking south from Coonoor,
and he exacted from the villagers a virgin and two cart-loads
of cooked raggi daily.   These were supplied till they had given
up the three hundred virgins, when they could give no more
and the giant in his anger destroyed the village.   Besides
the daily tribute already mentioned, once a year a human
being, a male buffalo and a he-goat had to be sent as an offering
to the giant.   One day when the time came for this sacrifice, the
victim, when leading the buffalo and the goat towards the
mountain was met by the Pandyan king's brother, named Bhima,
who stopped the man and asked where he was going.   The
man told Bhima his mission, who replied that he was tired of
his life and he would become the sacrifice in his stead.   Bhima
went on and met the giant and fought with him and

overcame him. He then slaughtered the goat and the buffalo and feasted and returned to the village and told the people what he had done, but they, fearing that the giant was not really dead, but would in time return and punish them all the more severely, deserted the country and never returned. Tirumal Naik is said to have been the greatest king of the Pandyaus.

Ordinary General Meeting, held on Wednesday, the 28th November 1894.

Mr. Kharsetji Rustamji Cama, *vice-President*, took the Chair.

The Minutes of the previous Meeting were read and confirmed.

The following donation was announced and thanks voted to the donor : —

To the Library.

From Berlin—Verhandlungen der Gesellschaft pur Erdkunde zu Berlin Band XXI., 1894, No. 8.

The following paper was then read :—

The Dhangurs *and the* Dhávars *of* Máhábleshwar.

By Shams-ul Olma Jivanji Jamshedji Modi, B. A.

The correspondence which began on the 11th of December 1891, between the Government of Bombay and our Society on the subject of Mr. H. H. Risley's letter to the Government of Bengal, submitting a scheme for the continuation of ethnographical researches in the Lower Provinces of that Presidency and for their extension to other parts of India, has ended with a letter from the Government of Bombay, dated 31st August 1894, thanking the Society " for undertaking to circulate the ethno-

likely to deal intelligently with the subject." As a Parsee I interested in this scheme to some extent, and that especi in the case of a careful and scientific inquiry into the subj of the sixth question which says "state the popular traditi if any exists, as to the origin of the caste, naming the comu ancestor, if any; the part of the country from which caste is supposed to have come and the approximate time of emigration, as marked by the reign of any king, or the occ rence of any historical event, together with the number generations supposed to have intervened." A studious, care and scientific inquiry into the subject of this most import question may throw some light upon the subject of so emigrations of the Parsees or the ancient Persians, earlier later than that emigration well-known in history as that fore by the religious persecutions of the Arabs in the middle the seventh century. For example, according to Firdou Kanoaj, so often mentioned in the Sháh-námeh, passed by vir of an Indian king's last testament into the hands of the P sian King Beharám Gour, who must have sent a number of P sians to rule over the country. Again, Wilford in his Asia Researches (IX.) says "there is hardly any doubt that the k of Oodeypoor and the Mahrattas are descended from them (Persian princes) and their followers." Then Mr. Willi Hunter in his narrative of a journey from Agra to Oojein 1790 (vide Researches VI., p. 8) says, " The Raja of Oodeyp is looked on as the head of all Rajput tribes and has the title Ráná by way of pre-eminence. His family is also regarded high respect by the Musulmans themselves, in consequence a curious tradition relating to his genealogy. He is said to descended in the female line from the celebrated Anushirw who was king of Persia." Careful enquiries into the traditio of the origins of different tribes as suggested by Mr. Risley sixth question may throw some light upon curious traditio like those mentioned by Wilford, and hence upon the emigr tions of the ancient Persians other than those of t seventh century.

Being thus interested to some extent in the elabor scheme put forth by Mr. Risley, during a short visit Mahableshwar at the time of the last Diwali holidays, I spe several hours in collecting some information on the subject of the questions which the Government of Bombay has asked our society to circulate. The subject of my paper is the Dhangurs and the Dhávars, two of the four tribes living at Máhábleshwar. I do not pretend to present this paper as the result of any continued observations during a long residence. It is merely the outcome of a systematic inquiry based on the excellent questions framed by Mr. Risley. As the author of the questions asks us to name the sources of·our information, I will do so at the beginning.

I collected my information about the Dhangurs from the following persons :—

1. A Dhangur named Ithoo, son of Rúmá, son of Chiloo, aged about thirty, living in the village of Bhirváda, a little below the Babington Point.

2. Dháu, son of Raghoo, son of Patsoo, son of Vagoo, son of Baboo, son of Maloo, aged about 65, a Patel of one of the villages of Sindola, living in one of the few huts on the road leading to the Blue Valley.

3. Raghoo, son of Baboo, son of Ranoo, son of Javjee, aged about 60, living in a hut below the Bombay Point on the left hand side of the road of the Fitzgerald Ghaut leading to Mahád. Though the information is collected from questions put to individual members of a village, it is, in fact, in most cases, the information supplied by the whole village, because when I went to a village with my pen and note-book, I was surrounded by a large number of the inhabitants who, at times, modified and corrected the answers if not properly given.

1. * The name of the caste is Dhangur ધંગર. 2. The sub-divisions of the caste are ઘેબા Dhebá, અખ્ખાડ Akhád ખરઘા Barghái, ઘોઇફોડા Dhoinfoda, કતોર Katore, હીરવા Hirwá, જાનકોર Jánkore, ઘઇગુંદા Dhaigundá, શીંદા Shindá, ખૂતેકર Khootekar, ગોરા Gorá. These names are said to be the આર A′r names of the different sub-divisions. Members of these different sub-divisions intermarry, but they do not marry among themselves, e.g., a Dhebá can marry with a woman

of the Akhád, Barghálh or Dhoinfodá sub-division and *vice
versá* but not with a Dhebú woman.

4. The children of brothers and sisters may intermarry, as
the sister is generally married with a man of another Ár
name, *e.g.*, a Dheba man can marry his son with the daughter
of his sister who is married with an Akbád. Children of two
brothers cannot marry as they belong to the same Ár or sub-
division. Children of two sisters may intermarry if the two
sisters are married in separate sub-divisions. A Dhangur
may marry two sisters.

5. A Dhangur cannot marry a woman who is not a
Dhangur. Social status, geographical position and differences
or changes of occupation are no bar to intermarriages. The
difference of social position is no bar at all, as one of the Patels
said ગરીબાચા આમ હાય નાહ઼ી ધરાના તા કોણ ધરેલ? *i.e.*, Who is
to catch hold of the hand of the poor if not we ?

6. This tribe has come to Máhábleshwar a long time
before the advent of the British power here, a long time before
Sivajee Máháráj. They have come here from Satara.

7. The habit of the caste is wandering, but they do not
wander, out of the limit of Jávli táluká. As they live on the
products of their cattle, they generally wander in search of
pasture. Their emigrations are in most cases irregular, but
all Dhangurs are generally expected to return to their villages
in પોષ માસ *i.e.*, the month of Posh. The village of મેડા
Medá in the Satárá district was formerly their head-quarters.

Their huts are made of thatched roofs. Light and air are
admitted only from the front doors which are very low. In
the front are the cattle and their requisites. Next to that is
generally the fire place and the furthest from the door is the
place for sleeping. It is so dark at the furthest end, that even
at midday we are required to have a lamp to have an inspection, but they say that their eyes are habituated to see
things even in that darkness. The huts are more long than
broad. Being very poorly clothed and fed they are obliged
to build such huts to keep off the cold of the winter and the
rains,

8. They do not admit outsiders into their caste.

case of the first marriage but a મૂરત *moorut*. In this ceremony both are as usual besmeared with કંકુ ચોખે, and made to sit opposite each other; a little water is given in the hands of both and then the head of one is made to strike with that of another. This ceremony with a small customary feast to the castemen ·completes the *moorut* form of re-marriage. In the case of re-marriage the Brahmin or in his absence any elderly experienced man utters ઉલટી રીતે *i.e.*, the order of the words of prayer is inverted.

13. Wives are divorced or deserted for adultery. In that case they cannot re-marry even by *moorut* ceremony. The sin is sometimes expiated by giving a feast to the caste when the adultery is committed with one of her own caste, *i.e.*, a Dhangur, but never when committed with one of another caste.

14. On the death of a person, the sons have a right to his property. In case he has no sons the brothers have a right of inheritance. In any case the wife has a claim of maintenance as long as she continues a widow.

15. The Dhangurs are Hindu by religion but they seem to have their own village deities. Five deities are known among them. 1. મસોબા Masobá, 2. જોલ્લા Jollá, 3. બેહેરી Beheri, 4. જનની Janni, known as ગોઠાનેરી જની *i.e.*, Janni of Gothánerá, and 5. another જની known as the થલ્લની જની *i.e.*, the Janni of Thal. Of these five deities, Masobá and Beheri are male deities and the rest are female. Sunday is the favourite day for the worship of Masobá and Beheri the male deities and Tuesday for that of Jollá and the two Jannis. Cocoanuts, flowers, and fruits are the things usually used as offerings. These deities have neither temples nor images of their own. Natural rocks jutting out from the sides of hills or from a level surface of the ground form the *sanctum sanctorum* of these deities. I was led to see one of these. It is situated about a quarter of a mile on the left hand side of the road that leads us from the Sindhola to the Blue Valley and about half a mile from the village huts. A walk of about ten minutes, on a very rough footpath from the road, brings us to the *sanctum sanctorum* of the Janni of Gothánerá. It is a piece of natural *rock built* over with a small superstructure of stone with a *stone* stand in its neighbourhood for holding lamps. On the

flowing water. The potter also says (प्रार्थना) prayers playing on drums and bells.

21. They say that they are called Dhangars, because they carry on the profession of herdsmen and prepare milk preparations. That was their former and is their present occupation. Very few are agriculturists. What little they cultivate they do for their own use. If any Dhangor follows the profession of a Bhangi (sweeper), shoe-maker or barber, they outcaste him.

26. They drink wine. If a woman drinks wine they form a very low opinion of her morality. They eat fish and mutton of male goats or sheep, but not of female ones.

27. They do not eat food cooked by castes other than those of Hindus. They smoke bidders offered by others, if they are not once smoked.

THE DHÁVADS OF MÁHÁBLESHWAR.

Sources of Information.

1. Shaik Lál, son of Beg Mahomed, son of Noor Mahomed son of Ismáil, son of Sháh Jehán, son of Pirozeshaw, son of Fateh Áhmed, son of Báwá Ján. He is an intelligent man of 88 years, and the Patel of Dhávad-vadi, i.e., the Dhávad quarters of Máhábleshwar or Malcolm Peth. He is popularly known as Laloo Patel.

2. Majuk, son of Husan, son of Fatoo, son of Ali, son of Beheroo, son of Chán, son of Hasan, son of Bávájee, Patel of the Dhávar village of Nak-khinda, aged about 100.

3. Dhanoo, son of Báboo, son of Ibráim, son of Ali, son of Beheroo, son of Tánoo, aged about 60, the Patel of the village of Ranjanwadi, situated about half a mile on the left of the Cassum Sajun Road, which leads from the Satara Road to the Panchgani Road.

4. Abdul, an inhabitant of the village of Maloore, about three-fourths of a mile from Shin Shin Ghal or the Robber's cave, and about five miles south-east of Máhábleshwar.

5. Patel Hoosain, son of Chandoo, son of Rahiman, son of Ismáil, son of Beheroo, about 75 years of age, living in the

received from his ancestors, the Dhávars had come to Mahableshwar and the adjoining places with one Chandar Rav. More
who was a Sirdar of the Court of Bijapore. That their long
stay with the Hindoos had made their habits and customs
more Hindoo than Mahomedan.

The Bombay Gazeteer in its excellent description of Mahableshwar says nothing about their origin. Most of them say
that it was simply their profession of iron-smelters that brought
them to Mahableshwar from Satara and from Khandesh.
They came there in search of new forests for the preparation
of coal. An old Dhávar of Máchutar attributed their emigration to the time as old as that of Bhoj rájá.

7. Their habit is mostly settled. Their Head-quarters is
Malcolm Peth where there are about 700 Dhávars. Formerly
when their occupation was that of iron-smelters they wandered
from place to place in search of new forests for the preparation of coal. Their huts generally are as dark as those
of the Dhangars but not so long or deep, as they have
no cattle to keep. They are generally square in form.

8. They admit outsiders into their caste on their turning
Mahomedans according to the rules dictated by the Kazi.

9. They have infant marriages.

10. Polygamy is permitted among them, but polyandry
prohibited.

11. The Kazi performs the usual Mahomedan ceremony of
marriage mixed with some Hindoo customs. The bride and the
bridegroom are made to sit opposite each other with a piece
of cloth between them. The Kazi says the Mahomedan prayer
and shows the marrying couple a looking glass. Lastly he
throws rice over them and then the assembled friends and
relations do the same.

12. Widows may re-marry, but not with deceased husbands' brothers. In first marriages, the bridegrooms generally
go to the mosque before the marriage ceremony but not in
the case of widow marriages.

13. Divorce is allowed on paying the wife the ऄॖॎ(money,
i.e., the money fixed by the Kazi at the time of the marriage

The cradle songs of all nations whether educated or uneducated are the simplest expressions of parental affections expressed in the most simple language. Again, they generally begin with some words invoking sleep. Compare with the above simple words of a Dhávar mother the following words of an educated French mother. Both begin with a call to sleep, and both promise some good thing to the child in return for its quietly going to sleep.

> " Fais do do Henry petit fils,
> Fais do do, tu auras
> Le bon coco.

For twelve days after birth, the mother keeps the child by her side. It is on the twelfth day that she places it in a cradle. The following is the cradle song that is generally sung then and afterwards. It enumerates one after another the nine months of pregnancy.

એક મહીના લાગે ખીખી કાતીમા ગરવાર
ળા ઘલાઈ નખી રમુખ તેરા નામ
દોન મહીના લાગે ખીખી કાતીમા ગરવાર
ળા ઘલાઈ નખી રમુખ તેરા નામ
તીન મહીના લાગે ખીખી કાતીમા ગરવાર
ળા ઘલાળી નખી રમુખ તેરા નામ
ચાર મહીના લાગે ખીખી કાતીમા ગરવાર
ળા ઘલાહી નખી રમુખ તેરા નામ
પાંચ મહીના લાગે ખીખી કાતીમા ગરવાર
ળા ઘખાહી નખી રમુખ તેરા નામ
૭ મહીના લાગે ખીખી કાતીમા ગરવાર
ળા ઘખાહી નખી રમુખ તેરા નામ
સાતવા મહીના લાગે ખીખી કાતીમા ગરવાર
ળા ઘખાહી નખી રમુખ તેરા નામ
આયવા મહીના લાગે ખીખી કાતીમા ગરવાર
ળા ઘખાહી નખી રમુખ તેરા નામ
નવ મહીના લાગે ખીખી કાતીમા ગરવાર
ળા ઘખાહી નખી રમુખ તેરા નામ

The following are other nursery rhymes :—

નાના નાની આખ
આંગરા તીપખા ખાખ
દાદા દાદી આખ
અસખા ખિદખા ખાખ.

welfare of the soul; and so rigid is the adherence to the performance of the same that the observance thereof proves a superlative method of instructing how the belief in life after death is material and all-important among the Hindus. Their reasoning on this subject, when analysed, will be found to be very clear and explicit. Life and death, they argue, are the work of nature or its ag nt, the God Himself, but an observance of the rites enjoine l which secures them better lives lies in the power of man. Man, consequently, should not be found wanting to perform the prescribed ceremonies, inasmuch as it ensures a better birth after death.

The ceremonies that are prescribed for the attainment of the end aforesaid are not a few but many. A Hindu life, if we properly observe, is nothing but a life of ceremonies. As has been described in the previous lectures, there are various sacraments that are performed by the Hindus during their life-time as well as at or after death.

Death is one of the Sauskaras or sacraments. Various ceremonies, extending to not a day or two, but to thirteen days, and thereafter every month for the first year, and after that twice every year, called Shradh's one on the Anniversary day of a man's death, and the other on corresponding day of the dark half of the month of Bhadrapad called Máhálaya " Shrádh," are performed for the repose or benefit of the soul of the deceased, an account whereof is as follows :—

When the disease of a high caste Hindu is pronounced or in course of time proved to be past all hopes of cure, he is removed from the bed he may be lying in to a low bed, and is made to give away charities of various kinds, *e.g.*, giving alms to Brahmins or feeding the poor, or giving away cows, to them, &c.

Regarding the character of these charities, Dharma Sindhu lays down that, when a man is dying, he should give the foll owing charities :—

तिलादान, कृष्णेनु, पापधेनु, मोक्षधेनु, वैतरणीदान, &c., &c., &c.

The theory of reward and punishment after death, as well as *a belief in life* after death, so much predominates in the Hindu minds that the fact can never be better illustrated than by observing the reason of giving charities. As an illustration, one or two interesting passages are repeated while a cow is offered to Brahmins:—

ऐहिका मुष्मिकं बब समजन्मार्जितं क्षणम् ।
तस्यवै बुद्धिमावानु गामेकां इश्तो मम ॥
मोक्षं देहि हृषीकेष मोक्षं देहि जनार्दन ।
मोक्षहेतुप्रशानेन मुकुन्दः पीयतां मम ॥

&c.,   &c.,   &c.,   &c.

Thus, generally, though the Dharma Sindhu lays down to give four cows in order that a man may be free from his debts, his sins, that he may get salvation, and go to Heaven, yet very often only one cow is given, and the giving of the cow is called the Vaitarni Dan. Vaitarni is a river of blood supposed to exist between the mortal and the immortal regions. A belief is held that the cow so given by a man at his death-bed aids the man in crossing this river by catching her tail.

With the giving of the cow eight kinds of grains are given. They are, wheat, rice, tila, chana, mug, udad, bajri, and juvar. From the time a man is on death-bed, various names of deities and gods are repeated, as well as prayers are offered to them that they may aid him in securing his aim. The usually repeated verses are those of the Bhagwat Gita or of Punya Sukta and of Mrityunjaya.

When he is at the point of death, he is purified by a bath, and is dressed in clean and neat attire. Then he is laid on a place spread with cow-dung and the waters of the holy river Gauges is poured into his mouth by his son or heir or other near relations, saying that he will do a certain charity after him or observe fast on the eleventh day of each half of a month till a year or so or will abstain from certain kind of food, such as milk, for a certain period, &c. A lamp of ghee is kept burning where he is lying, and one ball of sweets is given to each of the Brahmins. With the water of the Ganges are placed in the mouth curdled milk and five minerals. It is also customary that the ground where the man lies is scratched by a knife.

When he breathes his last, his obsequies begin. These

and it is also of importance to note the qualification of a person entitled to perform these obsequies.

The Hindu Shastras qualify the undermentioned persons to perform the obsequies :—

The legitimate son of the deceased is the best of all the others qualified. But if there be more than one legitimate sons, the eldest of them is qualified. If there are more than two, the eldest and the youngest are qualified, but not the middle ones. But if either of these be not existing or be abroad or be defiled by sin or any incurable disease, the middle ones can perform the obsequies. In default of the legitimate sons, if the grandsons of the deceased are existing, they perform the ceremonies. But if a man has no male issue, and if he adopts one, then the adopted son can perform the obsequies. In default of all of these, the nearest kinsmen, according to the Hindu Shastras, can perform them.

It is on these qualifications of performing the obsequies that the right of inheritance is chiefly based. Family members having incurable disease and being, as stated above, disqualified for these obsequies are entitled to no separate inheritance but to maintenance only. That family member who is best qualified for the performance of these obsequies is also in the same degree qualified for inheritance. It is for this reason, *i.e.*, for securing inheritance for the person performing obsequies, that mother, wife, daughters and such near and ‚dear relations are equally exempted from inheritance. Although these obsequies are considered so very important, yet to beget a son or to get him married is considered still more important, as it ensures the continuance of the performance of the cere- monies till three generations. In a year when a performer of obsequies gets himself or his son or any of his family member married, or if his wife has advanced five months in pregnancy, he is not required to perform obsequies during that very year only, as it may be supposed that any of his abovementioned acts is quite sufficient to please his ancestors more than his performing obsequies. When such is the importance attached to having a son for performing obsequies, can it be for a moment supposed that a Hindu would even dream to bequeath his property as a gift to his sons

or heirs and expect no obsequies performed by them in
return, nor can a son be recognized as a Hindu *if he refuses to
perform* the obsequies.

So far treating of the persons qualified to perform the
obsequies, including Anniversary and other Shradhas, it should
be here observed that the obsequies can be performed by one
who has been invested with the sacred thread, and if the
ceremony of the investiture be not performed, *e. g.*, in the
case of the Vayshyas, who don't wear the sacred thread at
present, they are obliged to put it on for the time while
performing the obsequies.

When a person breathes his last, the performer of the
ceremony purifies himself and begins the ceremonies. The
first ceremony that takes place is of षट्पिण्ड Shatpindi,
i.e., offerings of six rice-balls. These balls are named
पाव, खेचर, सायक, भूत, सांतिक, निमित्त from the different
positions and conditions which a body undergoes from
the time it perishes till it is consumed by fire. After the
performance of this ceremony, the corpse is placed on a
bier, consisting of two bamboo sticks, placed parallel
to each other and joined by small sticks, and carried to the
burning ground. Only the sons can carry the corpse,
but if there be not more than one, the nearest relations
help in carrying it to the cemetery. The performer of
the obsequies must carry the corpse out of the house on his
right shoulder, on which shoulder he is not allowed to
carry other corpses, till his parents are living, and when the
parents are deceased, he can use any either the right or left for
others. On the way to the burning-ground, the corpse is
preceded by the youngest son or the youngest member of the
family carrying fire, specially kindled at home for consuming
it. This fire is generally carried in an earthen pot, but if
the deceased be a man in well-to-do circumstances, a copper pot
is used for an earthen one. At each of the ends of the bier
a cocoanut is hung, which cocoanuts are broken asunder when
the cemetery is within sight.

Mode of carrying the corpse.

is of a Brahmin or of any of the Dvij class, it mu
taken out of the western gate of the city; but if it bo
Sudra, it must be taken out of the southern gate. W
carrying the corpse out of the house, the foot are in the f
and head in the rear, when the cemetery may be almost wi
reach, that position should be reversed. The carrier of the
must precede the corpse, and no one should be allowe
intercept the corpse and the fire. Taking the corpse to
cemetery, it is placed down and preparations are :
for constructing a pyre of about a foot more in le
than the corpse to burn it. Huge logs of wood are coll
and heaped together, and a pyre in the form of a parallelo
is prepared. The corpse afterwards is given an ablution
is placed on the pyre. Then the officiating priests re
some verses invoking the Fire deity. As an illustratio
says, "May the God Fire with his flaming mouth con
this corpse, etc." Then the nearest relation who sets fire t
corpse goes round the pyre three times, with a lighted b
of charcoal in his hands, and his back towards the pyre, as
as the sacred thread, sifted from the right to the left. On
fourth turn, kneeling on the left knee, he sets fire to the co
from its right too. All the while the attendant priest rej
verses in honour of fire :—

" Salutation to you, O God Fire. Thou wert lighted by
May he, therefore, be re-produced from thee that he
receive eternal bliss."

Then other relations and by-standers set the pyre to flan
When the corpse is almost consumed, ghee is offered b
fire. Then after a while, when it is found totally consumed
ashes and bones are collected, and the son-in-law of the dec
milks a cow on the collected remains which are thrown
some sacred river, or into the sea. In some case the bones
preserved to be thrown into the sacred river Ganges.

The bones, as said above, are collected. This is called
Asthi Sanchaya ceremony. It is performed as follows :—

On the very day the corpse is burnt, or on the second, th
fourth, fifth, seventh or the ninth day, the bones of
deceased are collected. Though the abovementioned are
days laid down by the Dharm Sindhu, yet very often b

are collected on the very day or on the next day the corpse is consumed. However, this practice differs among the different communities. The Kapola Banias and others of the same rank in Hindu Society, as theirs, collect the bones on the very day. While in Southern India, the corpse is left in the cemetery burning on the day the man dies and on the next day, the relations go there and dispose of the ashes and the bones.

How the bones are preserved.

The bones after they are washed in the milk under the process abovenamed are collected, and tied up in a piece of silken cloth and the bundle so made is suspended to the bough of a tree in the burning-ground.

Then, on a convenient day these bones are taken down from the tree, and are sent with some one of the relations to Benares or some such other sacred place to be disposed of.

Formerly there being no Railway they were taken on foot and even now some resort to that mode of conveyance for fear of being polluted by the touch of the lower castes. If they are taken in Railway some gentlemen reserve a whole compartment for them.

Disposing the corpse and its remains on that day, and clearing the burning spot, the relations purify by ablution and give a handful of water to the deceased where he is burnt saying :—

"May this be acceptable to thee." Several verses of this character are also advised by the Shastras to be repeated, like the following :—"Foolish is he, who seeks permanence in the human state, unsolid like the stem of a plantain-tree, and transient like the waves of the sea." When a body formed of five elements, air, water, earth, light, and ether, to receive the reward of works done in its former birth, reverts to its fine original elements, what room is there for regret ? Not only so, but the Shastras totally lay down against the crying and mourning for the bereavement.

But this philosophical teaching effects not in the least, and the conduct of the mourners on that occasion explicitly shews how great the feeling of self-love works in the minds of persons, who are deluded by the mirage like happiness of

sooner or later, but all this reasoning is in vain. It is
business of wise men, therefore, to retrench the evils of life
the reasoning of philosophy, while it is the business of unw
to multiply them by adhering to a practice not sanctioned
the Shastras. Indeed, the Hindu Shastras give one of th
typical teachings on this subject, but it is pitiable that it is
least paid attention to in this respect.

After purifying by bathing the mourners return to th
own houses, though the nearest relations, first go to the ho
of the deceased, there console the bereaved and then return
their residence. Among some, it is the practice to ob
nim-trees and sip water before they enter their house; wh
some touch fire with the belief that the fire is the purifier
dispeller of all defilements.

The notion of defilement exists strongly among
Hindus. The relations of the deceased are restricted fr
enjoyments for a certain period of time, which period is
the same for all the classes of the Hindu Society;
Vayshyas for sixteen days, the Khastryas for twe
days, the Brahmins for ten days. Till those days, th
are not allowed to touch the holy things in the house
do the other persons keep intercourse or communication w
them.

For the first three days, or till the Uthamana ceremony
performed, on the roof of the house of the deceased, water
milk are placed, with the attributed object that the decea
may quench his thirst and allay his hunger, on his way
Heaven, the journey to Heaven being supposed a long
allegorically.

On the third day or even earlier, the Uthamana ceremo
is held, in which the relations of the deceased as well as o
siders come to the house of the deceased, to condole with
bereaved persons. They are taken thence to a neighbouri
tank or well, where they cleanse their mouth and hands. T
priest there recites the particular positions the plan
had occupied when the man had died and gives blessing
them. Afterwards they all go to bow down to a de
where a lamp of ghee having three hundred and th
wicks is placed, with the attributed object that the decea

may not grovel in darkness on his way to Heaven, extending till three hundred and sixty days of one lunar year, till which time the journey may endure.

Bowing to the deity, all return home.

This ceremony of Uthamana is performed generally on the third day from the death of a person, but if the third day be either Tuesday, Wednesday or Sunday, it is done earlier.

On the twelfth day the chief mourner is given a turban by his father-in-law, and he is since that time allowed to go out, till which he does not go out of the house, with the whole of his dress.

Having described so far, the various ceremonies that are performed from the time the person is about to die till his corpse is burnt, and some other minor attendant ceremonies, we shall now describe the Shradhha ceremonies.

Of all the ceremonies connected with the Hindu religion, the Shradhha is the most important and the most expensive of all the ceremonies. This Shradhha or obsequies ceremony takes place from the 2nd day of a man's death. Its main features are the feeding of large number of Brahmins and his castemen, and in the presentation of offerings to the spirit of the person recently deceased and his ancestors. I shall now give the particulars of these ceremonies as taught in the scriptures. The word Shradhha in Hindu Theology is so much significant that a proper sense of it cannot be adequately expressed by a single word. The word seems to bear some relation with the word Shradhha (श्रद्धा) meaning "FAITH" and the ceremony of श्राद्ध (Shradhha) can be said to imply ceremonies performed through faith. The faith in the Shradhha consists in giving such things to Brahmins as the deceased was using during his life in order that he may receive the same in his next life after death, and these ceremonies are observed with the uppermost idea of bettering the life of the deceased after his death. This Shradhha ceremony consists of the following features :—

(1) Sacrifice.
(2) Offerings of rice-balls.
(3) Feeding of relations and Brahmins.

There are four forms of Shradhha ceremonies, namely :—

Parvan, Akoddisht,

Nandi and Sapindikaran.

(1)   Parvan Shradhha is the name given to all those ceremonies that are performed on the anniversary, the ending day of every month, and various such ceremonies in which the offerings are made to the ancestors of three degrees, both maternal and paternal.

(2)   Akoddishta Shradhha is the ceremony in which to only one ancestor an offering is made. This category consists of all those ceremonies that are performed for thirteen days after one's death.

(3)   Nandi Shradhha is a rite performed at the commencement of any auspicious ceremonies of child- birth, marriage, pregnancy, &c., to propitiate the ancestor, and is at present known by the other name of Vridhi Shradhha.

(4)   Sapindikaran. When the rite is performed by offering a rice-ball with a handful of water, then it is regarded as Sapindikaran.

Thus, giving a brief exposition of the term I shall now indicate persons who are eligible for it.

During the first ten days, funeral offerings of rice-balls, together with libations of water and tila seeds, are offered as on the first day, augmenting, however, the number each time, so that ten balls and as many libations of water and tila be offered on the tenth day, and with this further difference that the address varies each time. In some cases mourning lasts only for three days. In some it lasts for one day only. In some for more than ten. In the first two cases ten balls must be offered either within three days or immediately after the mourning. During the first ten days a family Vyas is told to read and explain the Sanscrit verses from Garúd Purán which he does up to the tenth day.

The difference in the address consists in the mention of the part of the body that is supposed to be restored by the rice-balls. The first is for the head. The second is for the restoration of the ears. The third is for the restoration of eyes, nose, arms, breast, &c. In some other classes it is a practice that the pebble is worn round the neck of the performer of the ceremonies, and this pebble is recognised a type of the deceased. To this pebble they give offerings, but this practice is not observed among many. At the same time an oil lamp is left burning in the house for ten days. Though these ceremonies are ordained, yet generally offerings of ten balls are made on the tenth day, on which day the son goes to some water-reservoir and performs there these ceremonies. On the tenth day the Shradha ceremony called Dasha is performed in which are required the following things :—

> आंवळा.
> कंकोडी.
> Poppy seeds.
> Barley flower.
> 10 dates (ten in number)
> 10 pieces of cocoanuts (ten).
> 10 betel-nuts.
> 10 betel-leaves.
> Flowers.
> One Digogee and one undergarment, milk, ghee, curdled milk, sugar, a thread of cotton, cow-dung, &c.

At his house the son gives offerings of the cooked food and handfuls of water to the deceased and prays to the god Vishnu to assist the deceased in his aim of salvation. Then food is thrown to crows, &c., and Brahmins, relations and cows also are fed. This brings an end to the ceremony only of the 10th day. The ten days' ceremonies are, as observed, performed for the restoration of the body of the deceased and for the re-embodying of his soul.

On the tenth day early in the morning a barber is called, and all the near relatives who are qualified to mourn for ten or thirteen days get their heads and moustaches shaved and have their nails paired and clothes put on, and then remunerations are given to the barber. Then the eldest son, or who has performed the burning ceremonies, goes to a water-reservoir or a river, attended by a priest, to perform the ceremonies deceased after burning the corpse. The son going to this reservoir rubs clay, cow-dung, milk, curdled milk, ghee and Sarshad seeds, all mixed, on his body, and then he cleans himself by a bath. The rubbing is performed with the object that the performer of the ceremonies has now purified himself from pollution caused by mourning. Having bathed, he sips water, and facing towards the south he declares to perform the offering ceremonies of his father or his relative, as the case may be. Then rice-balls are offered, and are recited verses showing the embodying of the soul. The first ball is offered for the restoration of the head and water poured thereon, the rest are so offered with libation of water for the restoration of the complete body, over each such ball an offering of rice, betel, sugar, flowers, &c., are made. This brings to a close the ceremony of funeral offerings and then the son, attended by the priest, returns home purified and takes his food not containing salt, as is ordained by the Shastras. The second set of ceremonies begins from the eleventh day. The object of these ceremonies is to raise the shade of the deceased up to Heaven, which would otherwise roam among demons and evil-spirits. The first ceremony is called the Akadusha. The materials required for this ceremony are—

> Seven images of various metals, out of which, two of gold, two of silver, one of copper, one iron, and one lead.
>
> Two cocoanuts.
>
> Betel-nuts.
>
> Dates.
>
> Cocoanut-pieces.
>
> Sarshad seeds.
>
> Sugar.
>
> Honey.
>
> One bull and one cow for the ceremony called "बैल". If these cannot be had, they must be represented by two Mindhol fruits.
>
> Kankoo.
>
> Abil.
>
> Gulal.
>
> Camphor.

Saffron,
Sindoor (red-lead).
Nadoo.
Ghee.

Early in the morning on the eleventh day the son who has performed the ceremonies of the last day goes again to that water-reservoir to perform the ceremonies. Going there he bathes in the water, remembering all the sacred rivers, Ganges, Narbuda, &c. Bathing in the water he gives libations of water to the several holy rivers. Libations of tila seeds and barley grain are also offered to the several gods, deities, manes, &c. Then changing the wet clothes he takes his seat on a wooden seat placed on the ghât of that reservoir: There he worships the god Vishnu with all due devotional materials. The worship ends with a prayer to assist the dead as well as his survivors. Then, after worshipping Vishnu's image, the ceremonies of Shradhha commence.

In this ceremony, first the Vishwa Dewas are worshipped. Then forefathers of both sides, maternal and paternal, are again worshipped. Worshipping these, one's own feet are washed. Then sipping a little water and holding rice in one hand concealed by the other, the following address to Vishnu should be made :—

" O you god Vishnu, here I have these rice in my hand for performing the Shradhha ceremonies of the deceased, and may you raise his soul to Heaven from wherever it may be."

Thus addressing Vishnu, rice is thrown in four different directions, as in each direction the god Vishnu is supposed to exist in one form or the other and designated by different names. Then the rice-flour should be mixed with water. Then small balls should be made of that mixture. Then the offerings are made.

The offerings, as has been noted more than once, are given to attain Heaven, but are more effectual when performed at certain places. In the Aryan Theology the Aryans have regarded some places holy and sacred, and where the associations are more favourable for performing the ceremonies. The places are—

The holiness attributed to these places has its origin in belief that god has undergone various incarnations the propagation of religion and for the destruction of an ov growth of sin. In his different incarnations god lived those parts, and so the parts have been believed to be sac consequently before offerings are given, first it is rende necessary to suppose that place to be one of the above-m tioned, that attainment may be facilitated. Assuming place to be one of the aforesaid, first should be given offering of a great ball. These balls of rice-flour contain ri flour, milk, honey, ghee, tila seeds, sugar, curdled mi all mixed together. Then Durbha grass is placed as rop senting the God Vishnu and the ancestors and each offer is placed on a blade of Durbha grass. Now, on the elevo day and on all anniversaries, the number of balls is eig Three balls are offered for the paternal ancestors and th for the maternal one, and one for men dying by accide and one for persons born of illicit connections called f Vikraya,—is placed separate. Each time a ball is plac libations of water is also poured over it. Then these balls covered by a Digogou. A cotton thread is thrown rou them, and then flowers, such as Agustha and Bhangra, & sandal, &c., are scattered over these balls. The betel-n &c., are placed before them and recognise d as offerings. T taking water in the hands a prayer is offered to Vishnu t these offerings are given to the ancestors and to you, so may ever be for the welfare of us and our ancestors. the materials for this ceremony we have mentioned calves, one male and one female, which are required to h certain ceremonies performed upon them.

The calves, if actually brought or represented, are mar and the bull devoted to the god Siva, that the dece on whose behalf it is so devoted may be raised by their assist to Siva's heaven. This bull which is married is never yi but is let loose. Again, milk, cow-dung, &c., being products of calves are held holy things for performin sacrifice, and the aim of sacrifice is to propitiate the deit So these calves may be a means to secure the good-will : favour of the god. The ceremony is as follows:—

Before this ceremony of marrying the calves is performed, the first ceremony that is performed is to place five pots of water and to worship them. Then the Varun Pujan, that is, water-sprinkling ceremony to the Brahmins, is performed. Then the calves are decorated, with flowers and kankoo, &c. Then a prayer is offered to those calves :—

"O you lord of bullocks, may you raise our ancestors, both paternal as well as maternal, from the infernal abyss of hell to the glorius regions of Heaven." Afterwards they are married together, and then with a libation of water and tila seeds in the right hand and the tail of the calf in the left, the bull is offered to the deceased on whose behalf it is used. It should be observed that when a woman dies with her husband surviving her, then only a cow is to be used, but not both the bull and the calf. After offering it, Pindas or balls of rice are offered to all the spirits and gods and the ceremony is brought to a close ; closing these ceremonies the performer returns home and takes his food, feeding eleven Brahmins. If unable to do so one at least has to be fed. This brings to a close the eleventh day's ceremony.

Then follow the ceremonies of the twelfth day. On this day also the Shradhha is performed as on the eleventh day. In the ceremony, first the god Vishnu is worshipped and then the deceased is worshipped. Along with that worship reverence is shewn also to all the deceased ancestors. Then the sun and a lamp are worshipped. Then the Shradhha is performed, in which rice-balls are offered to the deceased and are worshipped as said before. Afterwards, on behalf of the deceased, presents are given to the Brahmins, called Armânu, which consist of wheat and ghee. In the Shradhha ceremony performed, balls are at first covered by a digogee ; then the balls, after they are worshipped, are again taken and elongated. Then a golden wire is thrust into that ball and a part thereof is taken, which part, with honey in it, is united with other balls given to the deceased, the other part united or mixed with the ball of the ancestors, and the third part with the forefather or great ancestors, so mixing the parts. On the twelth day a Shayya or

A golden image of the deceased is placed on the cot. Then a set of clothes of the deceased, a pot for water, and utensils for cooking food as well as the things which he was most fond of, are also placed on that cot. Then kankno patches made on each of the four legs of the cot, which must be a fine and a beautiful one. Regarding the cot it is said in the Dharm Sindhu that it must be made of teakwood. It must be wrapped by chips of ivory, the bed thereon must contain cotton of Akoda (   ) fine and soft pillows and cushions, with a sheet over it and fragrant with odoriferous substances. Then the Brahmin to whom this cot पलंग is to be given is worshipped.

Then worshipping the Brahmin, the cot should be given to him. The object of giving the cot is that the deceased may live secure in Heaven without a re-birth.

On the thirteenth day, the ceremonies are performed as follows :—

The first ceremony is of Vishnu Pujan (worshipping of Vishnu). Worshipping the god Vishnu, Latita Pujan is performed. In this ceremony in a plate one seer of rice is taken. This quantity of rice is divided into thirteen equal parts, on one of which a jug filled with water is placed. This jug represents the Latita. Then the jug is worshipped, and offered with clothes, rice, flowers, fruits, alms in money, 13 dried dates, 13 pieces of cocoanuts, 18 pices. This offering closes the Latita Pujan. Then the performer of the ceremonies, with the jug of water on his right shoulder, takes it out of the house, throws the water therefrom, and returns mourning. On his returning he purifies himself with a bath. Then a feast is given to Brahmins and relations. On this day, Lapsi is served in one plate. The quantity, therein, is divided into four parts, one of which is eaten by the crows, and the other is reserved for cows, the rest for the guests and the performer of the ceremonies.

The object of throwing eatables to crows is as follows :—

वयोसि वयसुतोसि वायसायसि नमोस्तु ते
सवमन्वकुलं पाप वाति नमतु वायसः

This represents a crow to be the personification of

Yama (god of death), and satisfying him amounts to satisfying the god of death.

The thirteenth day's ceremonies observed for the propitiation of the deceased, having been described, we shall now give the ceremonies that follow them.

It has been said in the Dharm Sindhu that from the 14th day of the deceased till one year, the ceremony of उत्क्रम श्राद्ध is performed.

> Milk.
> Gugal.
> Barley.
> Sesamum seeds.
> Barley flour.
> Flour of the Adad pulse.
> Seven kinds of grain (Rice, Mag, Adad, Juvar, Chana, Wheat, Tuvar.)
> One silken Digogee.
> Seven copper pots.
> Seven copper small plates.
> Cow-dung cakes.
> Two vessels of bell-metal.
> Seven small new Digogees (cotton).
>   &c.,   &c.,   &c.

Then for one year a lamp is kept burning in the house of the deceased, facing to the East or to the North, that the spirit of the deceased may easily traverse the path to Heaven.

Then sixteen ceremonies of Shradhha are performed for one year.

> Twelve, one every month on the date the person died.
> Traipakshi Shradhha after a month and a half.
> In the sixth month and the 11th month.

In the eleventh month the ceremony performed (the Varshi ceremony) is named the Nilohaha (Marriage of Nila). Nila means a cow and a bull. The reason of this observance is that the milk, curdled milk, &c., all the products of a cow, are held as propitiating god, and hence this ceremony is

In the commencement of the observance of this rite, the divine goddesses or Matrukas are installed, and the ceremony of Grih Shanti is performed. Then five jugs of water are installed. Then the Brahmins are worshipped; after that, certain gods, Indra and other Rudras are invoked. Then a cow and a bull are decked in ornaments, and prayers are offered to them for securing the deceased ancestors from hell. Then water-sprinkling ceremony on the tail of the calf follows. Sprinkling this water in honour of the deceased, &c., the balls are offered. Twenty-seven balls of rice are placed at the hoofs of the bull.

It is said that the offerings of rice-balls at the hoofs of the cow and bull secure a happy state in the next world for those on whose behalf such balls are offered.

In this ceremony twenty-seven balls are offered for those who have died lately on the paternal as well as on the maternal side, for those who have committed suicide, for those that have died by unnatural death, and so on.

Placing these offerings on blades of Kusha grass and sprinkling water, tila seeds and flowers, and throwing a silken digogee over the balls, the ceremony is brought to a close.

In the twelfth month the anniversary ceremony is held.

The anniversary Shradhha is observed on the date the person died. In it three rice-balls are offered to the father, grandfather and great-grandfather, and three are offered for the maternal father, grandfather, great-grandfather; besides these, two rice-balls, one called फश्र , which is offered for other relations born of illicit connection to one for those who died unnaturally.

In addition to this anniversary Shradhha, another called Mahalaya Shradhha is performed in every year in the month of Bhadrapod, corresponding to the month of the Solar year October. The number of the rice-balls offered in it is eleven.

So far we have noted the ceremonies that the relatives of the deceased have to perform from the time the deceased breathes his last down to the anniversary Shradhha; but different practices are observed in the case of women.

Regarding women, it should be observed that when a woman, *big with* a child, dies, though the ceremonies in connection with her death are just the same as are described for a male, yet when

things and when they have none it is useless to give
and so also with the Sanyasis.

Before concluding these pages, it should be noted
though the dead body is held sacred, yet a man who carr
and who is related to it, is considered defiled or unclean, f
body of an ordinary being does not contain all of the gra
deities which are supposed to be found in the body of king
are never considered unclean.   It is said that there are
guardian deities in a body. They are Moon, Fire, Sun,
Indra, Kubera, Varun (water-deity), and Yama (god of d
Now, in a king's body all these reside, and as these
determine cleanness or uncleanness, the king is said to be
while an ordinary man, in whom these deities do not re
regarded unclean.

The ceremonies and ways in which the corpses of as
are burnt are as well interesting and different.

When an ascetic dies, either his son or his disciple
first purify himself by ablution and shaving, and then shoul
form the ablution ceremony of the ascetic. Then his body
breast should be besmeared with sandal and other odorif
substances, and flowers, wreaths, and other garlands shoul
thrown round his neck. After performing these, his
should be carried to the cemetery, preceded by the noise of d
and bells. Then it should be placed in water or on the gr
Under the ground a pit should be dug as deep as his
length ; in that pit a smaller pit of a foot and a half
be dug, which should be besmeared with purificatory
stance. Then dipping the corpse in water by the F
Mantras it should be buried in that pit. Then the stick
the ascetic used should be broken, and its pieces shou
placed in his right hand. Then his head should be bro
a conch. Then salt and sand should be cast inside that
restore the level and to preserve the corpse from being to
by lower animals. Then the relations return home. I
should be observed that asceticism is not of one kind. It
four kinds : Kutichak is one who is clad in red garm
residing in forests, or in his own house, who has the
thread and who dines at his own house, and has three I
Bahudak is one who takes his meals prepared out of the

SD - #0013 - 211022 - C0 - 229/152/28 - PB - 9780282567798 - Gloss Lamination